ERP in Distribution

F. Barry Lawrence

Daniel F. Jennings

Brian E. Reynolds

THOMSON

SOUTH-WESTERN

Australia · Canada · Mexico · Singapore · Spain · United Kingdom · United States

THOMSON

SOUTH-WESTERN

ERP in Distribution

F. Barry Lawrence, Daniel F. Jennings, and Brian E. Reynolds

VP/Editorial Director:
Jack W. Calhoun

VP/Editor-in-Chief:
George Werthman

Senior Acquisitions Editor:
Charles E. McCormick, Jr.

Developmental Editor:
Taney H. Wilkins

Marketing Manager:
Larry Qualls

Production Editor:
Margaret M. Bril

Technology Project Editor:
Christine Wittmer

Media Editor:
Amy Wilson

Manufacturing Coordinator:
Diane Lohman

Production House:
Lachina Publishing Services

Printer:
Thomson/West
Eagan, Minnesota

Internal Designer:
Chris Miller

Cover Designer:
Chris Miller

Cover Images:
© Digital Vision

My sons Alex, Ryan, and Jarrod who are always there to bring joy when I get home.

Barry Lawrence

Kay, Courtney, Christopher, Jackson, Cole, and Jim for their support.

Daniel Jennings

To the many people I have been privileged to work with who have taught me so much about industrial distribution, and as always to my wife, Suzanne, for her continued love and support.

Brian Reynolds

Contents

Preface

Enterprise Resource Planning (ERP) systems have been praised as a panacea for solving the tremendous human, inventory, facility, and equipment management problems facing all firms today. ERP has also been panned as an impossible dream that, even if realized, will never deliver its promised benefits. It is neither. ERP is a tool designed to work together with other information management processes like e-Commerce, Customer Relationship Management, automation software, supplier and logistics tracking tools, a myriad of other software solutions, and the most significant generators and managers of information in any firm: people.

What does make ERP so significant is that without information automation and connectivity (the definition of ERP) within our firm, we have no chance of communicating effectively with our supply chain partners. Customer expectations are constantly increasing, and firms that are not using information connectivity to better understand their customers (protecting the top line, revenues) and decrease unnecessary costs (protecting the bottom line, profits) are experiencing the kind of margin pressure that will soon destroy many.

ERP is where the information automation/connectivity starts for most firms. This does not mean, however, that buying a large ERP system is the only way to go. As we demonstrate in this book, innovative firms have extended their legacy systems to near ERP status or have built ERP systems from combinations of back office accounting programs and bolt-ons, supporting any shortcomings with well-designed human processes. The essence of ERP is not the system. It is the process of connecting all information flows within the firm and using that connectivity together with analysis programs that both advise decision makers and make routine decisions for the firm.

The challenges associated with ERP are formidable but are becoming less so with each passing year. IT providers are making the systems more stable and more complete (able to meet all business needs across all business categories) and data and process standardization efforts are continuing to overcome connectivity issues. Perhaps most importantly, managers are developing experience and skills with ERP successes leading to environments that are better prepared for information automation, are more able to understand the benefits, and are more willing to accept change.

As with our previous work on information automation, "e-Distribution," this book represents the experiences and thoughts of many industry practitioners and a few academics. We want to thank the business partners of the Texas A&M University's Industrial Distribution Program without whose vision and support we could not have written this work. In particular we wish to thank IBM, Master

Halco, Prelude Systems Inc., PeopleSoft, Silvon, Selltis, Intuit Eclipse, and Dimasys for their continued support and desire to solve information connectivity issues.

There are more people to thank than can be included in this preface, but the efforts of our many business partners are thoroughly interwoven into this text. A special thanks goes to our good friend Bharani Nagarathnam whose wisdom and management skills in bringing these projects to their successful conclusion touches every part of this book. We also want to thank Charles McCormick, Taney Wilkins, and all the helpful and supportive people of South-Western Publishing Company for their hard work in making this book a reality.

About the Authors

F. Barry Lawrence

Dr. Barry Lawrence is the director of the Information Systems Consortium and holder of the prestigious 3M Fellows Award at Texas A&M University. As a faculty member of the Industrial Distribution Program and Thomas and Joan Read Center for Distribution Research and Education, he is involved in graduate, undergraduate, and professional continuing education teaching activities, funded research projects, journal publication, academic society meetings and publications, service, and industry contact. His teaching activities surround classes in logistics, Supply Chain Management, distribution information systems, and distribution strategy. He is a frequent speaker for distribution associations and private firms on topics ranging from logistics and inventory management to information systems for distribution channels (e-business). He has also served as an advisor to the Professional Association of Industrial Distribution (PAID), student chapter, since 1997.

Dr. Lawrence's research interests include ERP/e-business implementation and logistics (inventory and other asset management) redesign for distribution operations. He has worked on many large industry projects generating millions of dollars in funding for the university and its students. Some of his major initiatives include the Information Systems Consortium for Supply Chain Integration, the Supply Chain Information Systems Laboratory, and the Consortium for ERP Benchmarking and Standardization. These initiatives have enjoyed high visibility and enormous success in increasing the understanding of e-business and in forging significant strategic partnerships with more than 20 information technology and supply chain solution providers.

Dr. Lawrence holds a Ph.D. in Information and Operations Management from Texas A&M University, an M.B.A. from Southwest Texas State University, and a B.B.A. in Finance from the University of Texas at Austin. He has more than 10 years of industry experience in sales and distribution business.

Daniel F. Jennings

Dr. Jennings is a full professor at Texas A&M University and was formerly the Industrial Distribution Program Coordinator and Director of the Thomas and Joan

Read Center for Distribution Research and Education at Texas A&M University. He has held three endowed professorships in his academic career.

Jennings' corporate career includes engineering, corporate planning, and managerial positions with Armstrong World Industries, Kaiser Aluminum and Chemical Corporation, Olinkraft, Inc., Boise Cascade Corporation, and Certainteed Corporation in the United States, Canada, and South America. His industry experience involves manufacturing and distribution activities.

Dr. Jennings has served as a visiting professor at universities in Russia, France, Canada, Mexico, and Australia and has conducted executive development programs in the U.S., Canada, France, Mexico, and Italy. Dr. Jennings has performed consulting assignments for a variety of firms, labor unions, and governmental agencies in five areas: strategy formulation and implementation, value chain analysis, management development, organizational change, and human resource issues that are vital to a client's business. He also conducts economic loss analysis for a variety of organizations as well as participating in numerous workshops, programs, and seminars for industrial distributors, manufacturers, and trade associations.

Dr. Jennings has published over 130 articles in academic and practitioner journals and has authored 10 textbooks. His research has been described in both *The Wall Street Journal* and *The New York Times,* and he has received several best paper awards from the Academy of Management, New York University, Baylor University, Prentice-Hall Publishing, and McGraw-Hill Publishing. He also received the Outstanding Researcher Award while a faculty member at Baylor University. Dr. Jennings received a B.S. in Industrial Engineering (with honors) from the University of Tennessee, an M.B.A. in Finance from Northeast Louisiana University, and a Ph.D. in Strategic Management from Texas A&M University and is a Registered Professional Engineer.

Brian Reynolds

Brian Reynolds is the associate director of the Thomas and Joan Read Center for Distribution Research and Education, a part of the Texas Engineering Experiment Station. He holds a B.S. in Management from Pepperdine University and an M.B.A. from Texas A&M's Lowry Mays Graduate School of Business. Brian is affiliated with Texas A&M University's Industrial Distribution academic program.

He has more than 20 years of experience in the distribution industry, ranging from field sales and branch management to general sales management for a $75 million industrial distributor. He served as the director of the Quality Process and, following that, as director of marketing and integrated supply for a $200 million distributor. He was also the project team leader for selecting and implementing new distribution software and hardware, which went live on schedule and under budget.

Brian has designed and conducted training in field sales, sales management, branch operations, quality improvement, database marketing plans, statistical process control, and integrated supply. He has served in several volunteer capacities on industry trade association committees and task forces, including serving as a co-chair on a joint Industrial Distribution Association–Industrial Supply Manufacturers Association committee on Total Quality Process.

He has made presentations to the Industrial Distribution Association (IDA), the Industrial Supply Manufacturers Association (ISMA), the Institute for Supply Management (ISM), formerly NAPM, the International Quality & Productivity Center, the Institute for International Research, the National Association of Steel Pipe Distributors, and the Construction Equipment Manufacturers Association. He has also made numerous presentations, and conducted workshops, for industrial distributors and manufacturers.

Preparing for ERP

The Roots of Distribution Information Management

Distribution Perspective

Raymond Rumpf and Son had a nice little business. The firm sold fishing equipment and had found a niche market in the fly-fishing industry. The firm specialized in providing materials that fly fishermen used to make their own lures. Although a very profitable line, the fly-fishing materials were difficult to forecast and schedule. The firm had to modify animal pelts (hair was a popular material for making flies) and other materials after receiving them. This was a classic manufacturing process, with tanning and dyeing as the primary activities. As long as the business remained a sleepy little mom-and-pop operation, the schedules were run off simple spreadsheets or legal pads.

A young entrepreneur with family roots in distribution, Jared Kimmel, purchased the company in the late 1990s with an aggressive plan for the business to grow. Jared's growth plans meant the firm could no longer get by with the old tools. The firm had a small enterprise resources planning (ERP) system but it lacked the functions Jared needed for planning and scheduling. Jared was forced either to consider a new system, which would be difficult to purchase and adopt so soon after buying the firm, or to find a way to use the old system's tools more effectively. Jared struggled to decide whether the savings associated with ERP would have a quick enough turnaround to justify the expense.

Introduction

Distributors generate and manage a great deal more information than most organizations. The distributor has direct communication with the customer and the manufacturer, leading to large volumes of exchange, collection, and manipulation of information. Manufacturers have the same two-way relationship with their suppliers and distributor customers—but the number of customers and suppliers is typically lower and requires less information management. Generally, the distributor deals with hundreds of suppliers and thousands of customers. The manufacturer deals with even fewer suppliers and at best hundreds of distributors (see Figure 1.1). Since each customer and manufacturer contact point generates information, the distributor is in many ways the supply chain's information manager.

Retailers suffer the same problem, and for those distributors who serve retailers (sometimes called "two-step" distribution), the relationship is the same as that with their suppliers. Where the distributor serves thousands, the retailer may serve millions. The distributor often has the advantage of forming strategic alliances with its customers, which can lead to efficiencies in supply-chain information management not achievable with retail customers. This book focuses on distribution information management in general and the challenges faced in enterprise information management for the distribution function in particular. Two-step distributors and those that serve end users like utilities, contractors, original equipment manufacturers (OEMS), public institutions like schools and hospitals, MRO (maintenance, repair, and operations), and so on are typical environments for which we will address distribution information issues.

The level of potential information-sharing is one important measure of effective distribution information management. Distribution often interfaces with customers who can share information with their suppliers that will enhance the performance of the supply chain. Retail customers can be profiled or otherwise manipulated into sharing information but are not likely to be effective or willing to share information

fig. 1.1   *Manufacturer/Distributor Relationships*

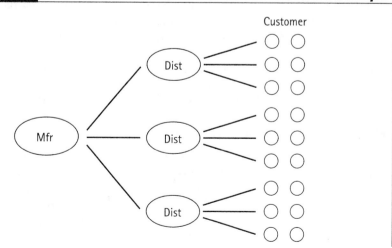

that can enhance supply-chain performance. Such customer ability to share information with the distributor even though limited in some channels, such as contractors, is a tremendous advantage to distribution over retail. Capitalizing on this advantage allows distribution to become a hero to the supply chain. The internal information-handling function of the distributor is critical to many essential distribution roles such as this one.

File Cabinets and the Black Hole of Information

Most distribution firms were born as specialized material handlers. When product was shipped from the manufacturer to the end-user, the most economic shipment size typically was larger than could be accepted efficiently by the customer. Supply chains needed a break-and-make-bulk intermediary with warehousing and material-handling capability closer to the customer. The break-bulk function reduced a manufacturer's shipment size to one the customer could use. The make-bulk function aggregated products from multiple manufacturers into a single order for the customer—sometimes called "one-stop shopping." Many distributors started as hardware stores or other stops along the limited logistical chains (such as train tracks or early highways) that evolved in focus from principally retail to distribution. Still other distributors got their start as purchasing/procurement agents for major corporations who needed a specialist to handle hard-to-procure parts. These agents would eventually form their own firms.

No matter their origin, distributors shared one common trait: the need to understand their customers. The friendly retail store owner had to identify with the local community, but a distributor not only had to understand personal and family relationships of their customers but also the structure of the customer's firm and the dependency of the customer's processes upon the distributor's delivery system. Keeping track of the customer's changing data profile and needs was daunting for distributors.

The first solution was the salesperson. Many came to believe that the key to great salesmanship was an organized mind that could store customer personal information (hobbies, names of the customer's children and partner, and so on), organizational needs (supplier product attributes, customer logistical needs, etc.), all the while keeping track of promised performance dates (when to make the next call, when a "hot" order was due in, and on and on). This glad-handing came naturally to the salesperson, who was more skilled in personal relationships than other customer value-adding-process staff. This walking database would determine the success or failure and distribution firms, who actively vied for the most-talented salespeople.

However talented these salespeople were, once information was collected the firm had to manage it in some way. The salesperson could only keep track of sales-related issues like customer preferences and could not keep up with what happened to most orders after they were placed—nor the impact of those orders on the organization or its suppliers. Tangible records of the relationship between individual customers and the firm fell into general files that could not be easily accessed: file cabinets stuffed with customer files.

The rapid advance of technology and increased capability of logistics systems (trucks, highways, rail, and material-handling equipment) led to more customers with greater technical needs than before. Talented salespeople were in short supply, so firms began to split up their duties to allow their best people to handle more customers. Financial records on customers were stored in file cabinets, and credit departments—not salespeople—determined whether the customer was "good for it," or a good credit risk that should be given the ability to charge purchases. (An important aspect of most distribution firms is their ability to finance small customers.) The process was more objective and less prone to error due to forgotten or unrecorded information.

Other sales force and sales management activities were absorbed as well. Manufacturers or even the distributors themselves began providing technical specialists (engineers or other specialists) to shadow the distributor's salesperson on sales calls involving highly engineered products. In addition, many business owners who had started as one of their firm's most important salespeople soon found themselves completely distracted by human-resource (HR) management. Owners who remained committed to the sales effort and regularly called on customers soon turned over human-resources issues—handling payroll, hiring, and complying with government regulations on employee management—to internal departments. Eventually these departments became ubiquitous in most firms. The information generated by HR specialists was stored in more trusty file cabinets and only accessed when necessary.

Soon the sales force split into two parts: one for the classic process of calling on customers at their locations (the "outside" sales force) and another for handling the day-to-day order-processing needs (the "inside" sales force). The inside sales force handled the volume business while the outside sales force took on more of a prospecting role. The two were inextricably linked, however, with the outside salesperson depending on the inside salesperson to maintain critical customer relationships, and the inside salesperson depending on the outside salesperson to generate the new opportunities without which the firm would slowly die.

The Distribution Operation: The Nexus of an Information Tidal Wave

Even with the split in the sales function and the addition of credit departments and other support functions, the problem of managing distribution information was getting unwieldy. The first issue surrounded the sheer volume of work; the second surrounded integration. The distribution operation was outgrowing the capability of human- and paper-based systems.

The volume-of-work problem had to do with the nature of distribution: Since distribution is essentially a function of tracking customer needs and then sourcing for those needs, the distribution process is information intense. The distribution process was critical to supply chain management (SCM) and, as new SCM theories were advanced, the classic distribution methodologies were challenged. For example, the

SCOR (supply chain operations reference) model was developed in the 1990s to describe the changing nature of supply chains from source-buy-sell to sell-source-buy and ship. This model followed SCM principles, which seek to eliminate redundancy in the supply chain by reducing redundant inventory and manufacturer/services.[1] The classic distribution model had distributors developing relationships with suppliers and holding product on the shelf for customer convenience (source-buy-sell). The classic distribution model went further, however, and the distributor became a marketing arm for the supplier. Distributors bought product, held it, and then attempted to sell it. This relationship was a considerable extension of the make-/break-bulk role and further put distributors at odds with emerging SCM principles.

The marketing role of the distributor became a significant value-add for their suppliers. The SCM movement, however, put further pressure on distributors to reduce inventory and other redundant processes within the supply chain. The SCM vision had the distributor utilizing more of the SCOR approach (sell-source-buy and ship). Such a process was even more information-dependent than classic distribution. Under the SCOR model, the distributor had to generate demand for products it might not have in stock. This business model required knowledge of when the product would be available and when it would be needed and an understanding of how the flows could be matched. If the distributor were to satisfy customers and key suppliers while practicing SCM, thereby lowering supply-chain costs, it would have to manipulate currently inaccessible information at a hitherto unimaginable level.

For manufacturers, the SCM model proved complex in that they need to know what the customer will want far enough in advance to develop production capability. For distributors, however, the problem is one of providing a time buffer for the manufacturer while simultaneously providing ready availability for the customer. This dual time factor is information–intensive, even more so with the advent of high-service requirements like just in time (JIT) delivery. Distributors are forced to track sourcing capability across hundreds of suppliers and respond to resource needs of thousands of customers. As servicing these customers and managing the supply network becomes more complex, the distribution function has been buried in—forced to efficiently manipulate massive amounts of information.

Problem: Integration of Information

The second problem came from integration of information. With multiple functional departments in the distribution firm accessing, modifying, and generating information, the firm could not hope to carry out intricate sales, marketing, and logistics activities unless all divisions operated off the same page. That page was a central database in which every division accessed, modified, and stored the output of its activities. The central database could not be maintained unless information entered into it was consistent, reliable, and accurate. That meant all data and interfaces (sales-order entry, invoicing, etc.) had to come only from consistently performing information tools that might be attached to the system. No variation is allowed in the exchange of data. This connected enterprise information system would come to be called enterprise resource planning (ERP). Many tools would have to be created and integrated to achieve the connectivity necessary for distributors to meet the supply chain's needs. Some of the first information technology applications developed for ERP systems affected the inside sales force, customer data-management programs, and inventory status reports.

Accounting software (spreadsheets, databases, and other more specialized programs) revolutionized the human-resources and financial functions in the 1970s and '80s. More-intense sales information like customer preferences and technical information were beyond the capability of such systems, however. In the early stages of e-business, the inside sales force got a great deal of attention partly because of the repetitive nature of ongoing relationships. The information handled by the inside sales force revolved around customer-service issues like fulfillment and logistics delivery needs.

This information had been well categorized and was stored for the quickest access possible by both the inside salesperson and the logistics arm of the distribution firm. The process was work intensive: The inside salesperson had to note delivery requirements either on logistics documents—sales orders or pick slips (a document directing warehouse personnel what to "pick" for the customer's order) or by directly telling the warehouse personnel of the customer's needs. This massive information exchange went on millions of times every day all over the world. By the late 1980s the environment for e-business to change the way we did business was ripe. But we are getting ahead of ourselves. The technology had been running a different course that would collide with distribution in the early 1990s.

Adding Functionality: Pre-Y2K Systems

Where the enterprise resource planning development started is debatable. Financial and human-resource systems were developed in the 1960s and '70s; one could also argue that statistical process-control systems began the process of automated business control. The answer depends on one's point of view. The 1970s saw the introduction of a new way to control a key issue that would propel the information automation process forward: manufacturing scheduling. Materials requirements planning (MRP)[2] was a new information system (IS) program used to schedule manufacturing processes to meet customer needs as laid out in a master production schedule (MPS). The MPS came from the individual product forecasts and was intended to ensure that customers got what they wanted in a timely fashion.

Soon it became apparent, however, that available capacity might not sufficient for the MPS . The MPS might call for more units to be produced in a period than the factory could handle. The simple solution was to reschedule parts of the production earlier or later. This required an understanding of customer requirements and capacity restrictions. Critical customers' production would have to be moved to earlier periods to avoid a stockout that could damage important relationships. Along came capacity requirements planning (CRP), which further enhanced MRP and allowed for complete and feasible scheduling of manufacturing lines. More issues lingered: Personnel needs, as well as either financing raw material acquisition or outsourcing of demand that could not be met with existing capacity were also important parts of the decision as was the need for a software application that took into account the entire firm.

Parallel with the MRP development arose a need for distribution planning that would coordinate with the MRP scheduling process. Distribution requirements planning (DRP) was developed to interface with MRP.[3] The MRP logic of putting demand into periods with identifiable capacity was extended to placing demand from branch operations into buckets for the regional distribution centers (RDCs) to serve, and then consolidating that demand into an MPS for manufacturing to serve. An RDC was, in effect, a superwarehouse that served branches in the same fashion as a branch served its customers. These branches were an inverse of the same subcomponent tree MRP used to schedule manufacturing needs (see Figure 1.1).

The MRP process looked like the roots of a tree as the subcomponents of end products were exploded through the bill of materials (BOM) for the manufacturing process and its suppliers to fulfill. The DRP process was the top of the tree, with the customer needs from different branches consolidated through the regional distribution centers to the master production schedule. Everything linked from customer demand all the way through the BOM down to the raw materials.

If the logistics side of the equation was nicely represented by the MRP/DRP relationship, then there must be a way to include financial and human-resource planning in the software application—or so many experts thought. MRP II, manufacturing resources planning, was created to connect all parts of the manufacturing firm under a single IS umbrella. MRP II was not to last long, however, as many firms (not just manufacturers) now looked to connect all parts of their business together. MRP II rapidly became ERP (enterprise resource planning) and applied to all firms. ERP embraced the concept of connecting all information within a firm (as did MRP II) but applied the principle to all firms. DRP and other fulfillment processes were encompassed in the effort to connect all processes, including many well-developed tools in finance and human resources.

Distributors went kicking and screaming (as did many manufacturers and retailers) into ERP, however. Connecting all processes in a firm is difficult enough when those processes are well understood, developed, and detailed—as they were in many manufacturing firms, which require a complete detailing of all processes. Distributors, by nature, had spent their existence giving customers whatever they needed and had developed unusual nonstandard processes that did not mesh well with ERP technology, which had been developed with manufacturers in mind.

The distribution community, along with many manufacturers and retailers, began adopting ERP faster than they ordinarily might have been willing to in the 1990s thanks to the threat of the Year 2000 (Y2K) bug. Y2K was a bug resident in virtually all programs, most of which had been written (programmed) with 1960s and '70s methodologies that entered dates in two digits (the last two) for each year. This meant that when internal calendars rolled over to January 1, 2000, computer programs would instead assume the date as January 1, 1900. The feared rollback of one hundred years would have unpredictable results, and it was assumed virtually all software would stop working. Early programmers assumed some other programming technology would come along to address the duplication before the year 2000.

As firms began to grasp the scope of the problem, many chose to adopt new ERP systems rather than trying to eliminate the Y2K bug from their legacy systems. These firms assumed they would need a new system eventually and did not see any reason to spend the same dollars to upgrade their legacy systems in the meantime.

table 1.1	Evolution of ERP[4]			
		Evolution of ERP		
1960s	**1970s**	**1980s**	**1990s**	**Y2K and Beyond**
Inventory management	Material requirements planning (MRP)	○ Manufacturing resource planning (MRP II) ○ Distribution requirements planning (DRP)	Enterprise resource planning (ERP)	Next generation integrated applications
○ Bill of materials (BOM) processor	○ Complex manufacturing operations ○ Process efficiency	○ Integration of departments ○ Supply/demand chain	○ Resource optimization (RO) ○ Supply chain management (SCM)	○ E-business ○ Customer relationship management (CRM) ○ Business intelligence
Planning the business	Tracking the business	Understanding the business	Improving the business	Predicting the business

The ERP movement gained momentum and soon expanded its scope to include customer relationship management software (discussed in detail in Chapter 13) and other forms of Business Intelligence (see Table 1.1).

The "Valley of Despair": Early ERP Applications in Distribution

As distributors and ERP providers struggled to understand how to automate distribution processes, the manufacturing community was having its own problems. Many distributors were slow to adopt ERP and they watched as manufacturers were shut down by ill-planned ERP systems. The shutdowns damaged not only the manufacturers but the distributors as well, when customer demand could not be met and distributor inventories gave out during the recovery period. Distributors questioned the wisdom of ERP, and many decided it was not right for their firms.

Some did take the plunge, however, and the results often confirmed their competitors' worst fears. The firm would "go live" (turn on the system and turn off its existing system) and immediately experience customer-service failures. Legacy systems at most firms had evolved over many years and were specifically designed to meet the firm's needs. The ERP system had likely not been completely programmed to capture those processes that were critical to important customer-service needs and so the firm's employees were forced to go offline to meet customer needs.

When offline, of course, the ERP system no longer knew what was going on and was, therefore, no longer fulfilling its mission of connecting the firm. Distribution personnel not only did not have a functioning ERP system but their legacy system was no longer available. The company in effect had moved back in time to before the legacy system existed and was no longer able to serve customers even at its former level. The firm's performance would decline for some time before efforts on the part of the firm's employees, the ERP provider, and consultants could improve the use of the new system. Consultants came to refer to this period of transition as the Valley of Despair.

What made the Valley of Despair particularly troubling was that its depth and length was firm dependent. The limited track record of ERP systems made it all but impossible to predict how badly or how long the firm's performance would decline. Project management techniques could be applied to reduce the impact but corporate culture would play a major role, and change management was not always up to the task of controlling employee and customer reactions to ERP implementation. For many firms, the automation of their information handling proved very painful indeed. Many came to refer to ERP as the "executive replacement program" due to the number of corporate executives who lost their jobs after adopting a new system.

Phasing It In

Many firms would essentially adopt the ERP system module by module. First those modules that matched up with the legacy system went live, while others awaited the implementation process to be finished. The result was a never-ending implementation, which could be construed as appropriate, since upgrades and maintenance of the system and processes that interface with it are an ongoing process. The problem arose when the resources associated with the initial implementation (consultants, internal teams, and ERP provider specialists) went their separate ways and an unprepared IT department had to take on the engagement of additional modules they were not trained to implement as an overload on their work schedule. This led to many companies underutilizing their systems—not getting what they paid for. Many executives would say of their ERP systems that they "bought a Ferrari and drove it like a Volkswagen."

The experience of one large firm, which we shall call MegaDist, is instructive. MegaDist purchased a well-known ERP system that could handle both distribution and manufacturing operations. The initial installation proved more costly than expected and, in order to meet its financial goals, MegaDist was forced to cut back on the project. The system was installed with the only remaining needs of additional value-add modules and training for MD's employees. As is often the case, MegaDist chose to cut back on these two areas. New modules were delayed and a group of team leaders were trained and expected to pass that training onto others rather than having professionals from the ERP provider team do it as had been originally planned.

The training did not go well. Invariably, MegaDist employees did not understand the complexities of the software and the team leaders did not have sufficient teaching experience to see the learning problems. Many problems were too complicated for the team leaders. When the team leaders went to the ERP provider for assistance, either the problem was not properly explained, or the response was poorly understood, which lead to insufficient explanations after the fact that did not always reach all users. The result was an undertrained workforce that immediately began entering errors into the system.

The modules that had been delayed became a problem as well. Many of the promises made for system performance were based on using these modules. For instance, MRP had been carried out differently at every MD manufacturing plant. Some used spreadsheets, others used small standalone products, and some just did the scheduling by hand following MRP logic they had learned from APICS (an industry society formerly known by its full name, the American Production and Inventory Control Society) or other organizational training programs. The ERP package selected was not optimal for distribution operations; nevertheless distribution had been forced to adopt it and was now struggling with it. Manufacturing had played a pivotal role in MegaDist's selection of the package. Decision makers were manufacturing oriented and insisted on a package that could integrate DRP and MRP. The irony was that MD's ERP system had been deemed inferior when distribution began implementation and so manufacturing decided not to take its scheduling onto the system. The principal features that had served as the selection criterion were therefore not activated.

This nonactivation of MRP led to slow, unintelligible messages from distribution to manufacturing. The decision was then made that manufacturing should operate in a vendor managed inventory (VMI) mode for distribution. Manufacturing would identify distribution inventory levels and decide when and how much to replenish distribution inventories. This gave MegaDist's manufacturing division a longer time window in which to plan its production schedule. End-customer demand management was now managed by the group farthest from MD's customers and not connected to the system. Since manufacturing performance measurement was based on machine utilization and worker-hours, performance metrics propelled manufacturing to make large production runs so that MD could avoid the shutdowns associated with machine changeovers.

The larger production sizes increased distribution inventories and frequently placed the inventory in the wrong products. The problem stemmed from manufacturing's lack of customer knowledge, performance metrics, and nonutilization of MRP. The part of MegaDist least qualified for managing inventory was not connected to the ERP information flow and was handling demand management for MD's most essential products.

When MegaDist managed to start coming out of the Valley of Despair, it started studying the problems and decided to turn on more modules. MRP topped the list. Plant managers, however, were opposed to the change due to compensation (metrics) and control reasons. If the accounting metrics showed a decrease in manufacturing efficiency, MegaDist's plant manager and department would be affected financially (smaller bonuses). Worse, if the DRP messaging caused the MRP schedules to change over machines too often (as was expected due to the smaller nature of customer orders compared with production run sizes), the loss in capacity caused by increased machine setups might cause stockouts that would adversely affect sales. Manufacturing feared stockouts would get blamed on poor resource management rather than MRP scheduling problems.

ERP Can Go Live

In spite of all the horror stories, many firms successfully pushed on and got their ERP systems working. ERP providers, meanwhile, continued to improve the systems and their implementation. The information automation movement that started in the early twentieth century with the invention of the computer was now moving to an enterprise (connected) level. Firms that had delayed adoption had saved themselves costs in the short term but by the early 2000s were faced with systems that could not support their growing information needs. ERP adoption was about to move into a broader marketplace.

Riding the Wave: Information Automation

The first great automation revolution occurred in the early twentieth century. Called the Industrial Revolution, it consisted of using the assembly line to simplify tasks and then automating as many processes on the assembly line as possible. The division of labor interfaced well with automation since workers could remain stationary and machines could be used to move products. The processes were extended to distribution warehouses and even office environments, where documents might pass from desk to desk via chutes and tubes or from company to company via fax.

This continual process was redirected by significant shifts in strategic thinking. Technology-inspired waves emanated worldwide and changed the global business landscape. First came just in time (JIT), a planning system designed to prevent wasted resources—whether excess inventory, damaged or scrapped goods, or facilities to store other waste (inventory and the like). JIT started in Japan but did not catch on in the United States, mostly due to a lack of perceived need and the difficulty many firms experienced introducing it in the late 1970s and early 1980s. JIT required quality products, and scrap could shut down a JIT line. The total quality management (TQM) movement first influenced U.S. business decisions, then to be followed by JIT.

A JIT factory trapped in a non-JIT supply chain was useless to the end-user, however. Supply chain management (SCM) came next and mandated that all members of the supply chain share information to make the process of serving the end-user more efficient. Companies teamed together in strategic alliances that would enable their supply chain to function much like a single firm. The amount of information exchange inside and outside the firms necessary to achieve this objective was so overwhelming that information technology was invoked to deliver SCM goals. The Valley of Despair that overtook MegaDist, with manufacturing not integrated with the information chain, is the perfect example of what can go wrong. The manufacturing division of MegaDist was impeding the success of the entire supply chain by working offline. Augment this example to the supply chain in which companies are operating on disparate systems that do not allow information sharing and the problem becomes even more acute.

E-business systems promised to solve this problem by connecting manufacturing and distribution systems across corporate boundaries. Information was not automated, and even when it was, the formatting and collection systems for data were not compatible. The only solution was complete information automation, which could also go hand-in-hand with process automation since any changes in product status brought about by movement through manufacturing, logistics, or distribution operations could be tracked, and status updates recorded, in real time. This second automation revolution will last as long or longer than the first and could add exponential value to world economic systems.

Conclusion

The information automation movement starts inside a firm's four walls. Until we can communicate seamlessly inside the firm, we cannot hope to do so with external parties like customers and suppliers. Firms that do not get a handle on their internal information flows will find themselves unable to keep up with the rapid advances in e-business. As supply chain partnerships advance, these companies will find themselves locked out of important relationships when unable to participate in information exchange.

The emphasis in this book is on the internal processes, only looking outward for connecting other firms to the ERP system. We discuss how to select an ERP system, implementation procedures, different modules and their value, and future directions as ERP evolves. Readers interested in expanding their knowledge of the supply chain and the role of IT systems in SCM are directed to the suggested readings in the References section at the end of this chapter.

The overarching purpose of the book is to guide a practitioner or IT specialist down the complex path of matching and automating processes onto the ERP system while maintaining a watch on customer needs and shifts in expectations. The book's development path is shown in Figure 1.2.

Part One lays the groundwork for understanding the purpose of ERP and how to establish a strategic direction as well as a tactical plan to approach system selection. The hierarchy starts with understanding information handling in a distribution context, moves to strategic issues, and finally takes the process down to the tactical level. Part Two looks at system selection broken out into its basic components of evaluating your processes, your organization's readiness for ERP, and investigating candidate systems.

Part Three begins with an examination of basic implementation issues like process automation on the system and the all-important database. Which modules to activate and the value they provide are examined and then the entire process is examined in light of the standardization challenge both from a data and process standpoint. The standardization issue is paramount to successfully implementing ERP. The next problem then becomes the change in processes and its impact on the corporate culture and its customers and suppliers.

Part Four looks at the powerful systems that can transform the company. Warehouse management systems (WMS), forecasting/replenishment, and human resources/ Financial modules are all examined. Finally, the entire system is tied together with performance metrics and evaluation systems like executive information systems (EIS). We end with an examination of what the ERP system can tell us and how that information should be evaluated.

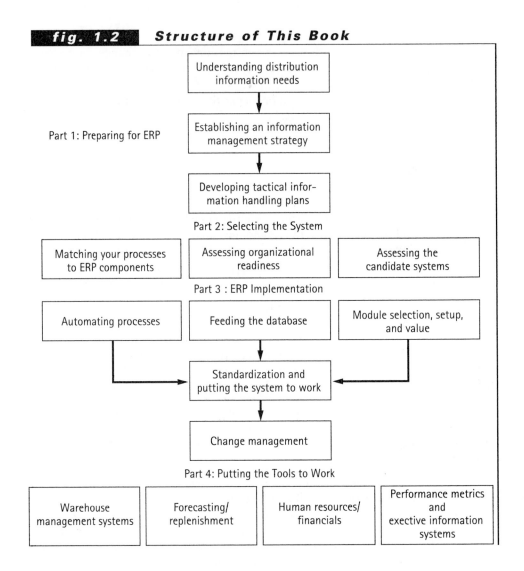

fig. 1.2   *Structure of This Book*

Part 1: Preparing for ERP

Understanding distribution information needs

Establishing an information management strategy

Developing tactical information handling plans

Part 2: Selecting the System

Matching your processes to ERP components

Assessing organizational readiness

Assessing the candidate systems

Part 3 : ERP Implementation

Automating processes

Feeding the database

Module selection, setup, and value

Standardization and putting the system to work

Change management

Part 4: Putting the Tools to Work

Warehouse management systems

Forecasting/ replenishment

Human resources/ financials

Performance metrics and exective information systems

Distribution Retrospective

Jared faced a common dilemma: When is the optimal time to upgrade information technology capability? Most firms face this problem at least yearly, if not more often. Jared must base his decision on the tradeoff between the costs of additional functionality versus the benefits associated with those capabilities. Jared's company also faced issues with cash flow to repay debt and ensure the ability to introduce new products as market conditions changed. Jared felt the existing system was an anchor that slowed the company down but feared the repercussions of overextending the business.

Jared decided to upgrade the existing tools and use the savings generated through better scheduling and planning to prepare for a more full-scale upgrade. The piecemeal approach would slow progress but had the advantage of protecting the company's financial position. Another benefit was the learning experience that came with tackling problems one at a time. Jared learned what functionality and data would be needed and how the various IT components interacted. This knowledge would prove invaluable when it came time to buy a new system. He would know what the new system needed and what implementation challenges the firm would face. Data collection would be understood and collection mechanisms already in place. Jared was unaware when he made the decision to take it one step at a time that the strategy would pay dividends well into the future.

Issues to Consider

1. Why is it important to consider the information-carrying capabilities of distributors?

2. Explain the differences in the "old way" of distribution versus the "new way."

3. Explain the role of "inside sales" and "outside sales" in the context of Distribution Information Management.

4. How is information technology a part of a series of supply chain initiatives today?

Case Study: Life Before ERP

Note to the reader: The following case is based on an actual distributor. The name of the firm has been changed for confidentiality reasons.

Davis Oilfield Supply specialized in fluid power equipment that operated under the harshest of conditions. A fluid power motor is essentially a pump that moves product through the use of hydraulic power. The firm also sold accessories to these power units like electrical motors, casings for protecting the equipment, and various nuts, bolts, gears, and so forth. The firm sold its products to oil companies for processing and otherwise moving oil and its byproducts. Although the firm had grown up supplying the energy industry, it had also created a thriving business with other manufacturing firms that had a need for fluid power solutions.

The firm had complex processes at work to serve its varied customer bases. The company could essentially be divided into three key functional areas. First came standard distribution sales where customers for their manufacturing lines purchased components. These customers had maintenance repair and operations (MRO) specialists who could handle installation and repair and would order from Davis as parts were needed for new manufacturing lines or as existing parts failed. The second set of customers was for repair. These customers would call Davis to get assistance with repairing motors that had failed either by sending the part back to Davis or by having a Davis technician come to their sites. The final customer base was customers that needed power units that were stronger or more specialized than those offered by Davis's suppliers. Some environments required additional protection for the motor or required a series of motors to increase the power output. Davis would build these units by fabricating cabinets to protect the motors, or skids (platforms) that carried an interconnected set of power units.

The technical sophistication associated with these applications led to a rich information environment with complicated processes to maintain. The sales force struggled with quoting. The operations division was challenged by inventory tracking and visibility problems. The manufacturing group had a hard time keeping track of the costs that went into their large power units. Repair also struggled with quoting since supplier information on product changes was often out of date or filed in multiple locations. Finally, accounting had great difficulty with invoices since inaccurate quoting and cost tracking led to missed costs that frequently could not be collected after the invoice was paid.

For a large distributor with an in-house information technology (IT) department, the solution might be an advanced (specialized) ERP system with bolt-ons for complex processes like quoting and warehouse management. The firm could not afford an IT department, however, and a large ERP system with expensive bolt-ons was out of the question. Even if it could afford such technology, the firm was aware that its processes were beyond the capability of virtually any bolt-on available at the time. The technology providers had not as yet captured the complexity associated with their products and processes (especially quoting).

The potential savings in lost costs, keying and rekeying errors, inaccurate quotes, and missed sales due to inventory problems were so large, however, that the firm felt it had to come up with better information-handling procedures. The company took each division and charged it with meeting its own information challenges. The ultimate goal was to eliminate errors that made their way into invoices, future quotes, and stockouts. To that end, the firm planned to measure the success of these programs based on invoice accuracy, quoting effectiveness, and customer service.

The sales force had several solutions for quoting new product sales in place. Some salespeople worked off forms issued by the firm that had to be rekeyed back into the system when submitted. This rekeying process introduced many errors into the system. In addition, the salespeople had a difficult time staying current with the latest changes in product. There was no easy way to access product information over the Internet or through a company extranet. This paper-based system reinforced the salespeople's isolation and sometimes forced them to "guess" or delay giving information to the customer.

Other salespeople were using self-designed spreadsheets or contact management software to manage their quotes. Most of these systems could not handle the complexity associated with their quotes so the salesperson would still have to carry out many tasks off the software and print out a document to be rekeyed into the system. Without compatibility between Davis's accounting system and the disparate sales force files, downloading was impossible.

The sales manager decided that a single spreadsheet, downloadable into the accounting system, was the best solution. He put a team together to capture all the methodologies the sales force used and come up with a single form that would allow them consistently to enter sales quotes into the accounting system. The contact management software already used by some of the salespeople seemed a logical choice but the compatibility with the accounting system would be difficult to program given the lack of IT skills in the firm. The sales manager decided to put together a task force consisting of himself, some sales associates, and data entry people from accounting. Their proposed solution was a common sales quoting form developed in spreadsheets.

Warehouse operations felt that a warehouse management system (WMS) was their best solution. The system would keep track of inventory movement through scanners and a terminal could be set up that would allow the sales force to check inventory in real time. The system would not be connected to sales, however, so reserving inventory for sales and repair would have to be entered on the WMS and separately recorded in sales or repair. The system was also costly and management was unsure whether the cost could be justified.

Manufacturing did not know what to do. They had been told that something called MRP could be used to plan their schedules but suspected that the made-to-order nature of their products would not work well with a "canned" MRP system. They also lacked the necessary bills of material (BOM) that described their products to drive an MRP system.

Repair was even more problematic. The suppliers stored information in different places (some on microfiche, others on the Internet, and some in both places). The difficulty in finding technical support information coupled with customer emergencies made repair a complex process. The repair shop looked to combine its various documents with the sales force's efforts to develop a standard set of quoting forms. Their progress was, therefore, tied to the sales efforts at standardization.

Davis realized there was no single system that could solve its problems. The firm was embarking on many efforts and hoped they could be tied together in the end. People would have to conduct double-checks at every information handoff—a waste of human resources. Timely updating of information would be essential. Even so, errors would be inevitable. As the management team pondered the possibilities, things looked bleak. The only bright spot was that the firm would come to understand itself better and be better prepared for new technology as it became available and affordable.

Case Challenges

1. Are things as bad as the case seems to predict? Assess the costs associated with continuing with the current business practices.

2. Assume the company should attack the problems one at a time. Where would you start? Would you suggest more advanced (expensive) solutions applied slowly rather than attacking all problems at the same time? Discuss the pros and cons of each approach.

3. Make the argument that understanding your firm is worth adopting temporary solutions like spreadsheets as suggested in the case. Explain the advantages of such an approach for each of the functional areas: sales, warehousing, manufacturing, repair, and accounting.

References

1. Supply Chain Council, Supply Chain Operations Reference Model, Overview of Score Version 5.0, http://www.supply-chain.org/slides/SCOR5.0OverviewBooklet.pdf.

2. Joseph Orlicky and George W. Plossl, *Orlicky's Material Requirements Planning,* 2nd ed. (New York: McGraw-Hill Trade, 1994).

3. David Frederick Ross, *Distribution Planning and Control,* Material Management and Logistics Series (Boca Raton, FL: Chapman & Hall, 1996).

4. Naeem Hashmi, "Mix It Up: The New ERP Data Warehouse Hybrid," http://www.intelligenterp.com/feature/hashmi.shtml.

2

Strategic Use of Distribution ERP Systems

Distribution Perspective

Planar Electronics was one of the largest electronics supply houses in the United States. The firm had grown through acquisition, as had the other giants in electronics, and found itself with multiple legacy systems in place in the 1990s. Suppliers were requiring real-time point of sale (POS) data to be sure they understood the market and could plan their capacity. Manufacturers' reps assisted Planar with technical support and also wanted POS data so that they could collect their commissions from suppliers. Meanwhile, customers were demanding inventory visibility. The firm's sales force was experiencing pressure to offer greater value-add through better, more timely technical information. Finally, the disparate systems caused missed sales when inventory could not be located. Inventory was growing rapidly in response but not achieving the desired fill rates and the operations group could not seem to get its hands around the problem.

Planar management knew that delivering the information its sales force and supply chain partners needed was essential, but the cost of such a large system would be extremely expensive. Planar was a publicly traded firm that could not afford to ignore the return on investment (ROI) for such a large investment. The company needed to do an analysis to convince its board of directors that the investment was a sound one. Given the size of the investment, however, management feared that "heads would roll" if the analysis was flawed and the ROI was not met. Worse yet, the analysis could be sound and the company still might not meet its objectives due to cultural resistance to the massive changes such a system would bring to every division—each would be forced to give up its cherished legacy processes. Upper management was nearly paralyzed from the internal debates going on, and the chief executive officer (CEO) knew that less-than-decisive action could bring down the wrath of powerful suppliers who might pull their lines and/or customers who might take their business to competitors who had already made the transition. All eyes were on the CEO and employee confidence was starting to crumble. What should the CEO do?

Introduction

The ERP difficulties of the 1990s stemmed from many of the same problems as the dot-com failures of early 2000. The dot-coms had not developed a strategy that took into account the true needs of the supply chain and properly addressed the technological shortcomings. Instead, many simply hoped the technology would develop fast enough to meet the supply chain's needs and that the technology providers understood all distribution channels even better than the channel members. The unrealistic expectations led to poor results for many firms.[1] The supply chain was more complex and less flexible than almost anyone imagined, and the technology did not develop in time to save the dot-coms. The dot-coms did not have a strategy to achieve their objectives in an adverse environment and did not have the metrics in place to tell their stakeholders when it was time to cut bait or develop a new strategy.

To be fair, the dot-coms never really stood a chance. Wall Street threw a fortune at them and locked them into a business model that could not succeed. Brick-and-mortar firms had the advantage of a proven successful business model and merely needed to properly assess the capability of technology (and its evolution) and match it with their customers' needs, supplier relationships, and corporate culture. This advantage meant those firms had a better chance of making the transition to successful use of e-business tools than did a firm with a new business model that few understood. The larger the firm, however, the more difficult this task becomes and, therefore, the more important strategic planning becomes. A small firm with financial constraints cannot buy as large a system and has a smaller management team with usually greater propensity to make instant decisions that will be accepted by the firm. A larger firm must have a well-thought-through strategy that can be "sold" to investors and employees. Failure to convince either set of stakeholders (not to mention customers) will mean a slim chance to meet objectives at best or an outright business disaster at worst.

The New Supply Chain Manager

The volume of information that comes through a distribution operation makes it a logical place for controlling the supply chain. Coordination of the supply chain is as important as information exchange. Research has shown that without a single party coordinating the flow of information, the impact of information exchange is greatly reduced.[2] Manufacturers and customers may wish to control more information but their position in the supply chain limits their access to the critical data from which they can coordinate supply chain activity. The unique position of the distributor in the supply chain has led some to argue that the distributor should be the supply chain manager whether it wants the job or not.

The complexity of the role has caused many distributors to fear the responsibility and other members of the supply chain to doubt the distributor's capability to carry out the task. Distributors often do not have and cannot afford the necessary technology to support supply chain information connections. Some customers have forced distributors to adopt the technology they utilize. When multiple customers insist on the distributor using multiple systems with differing communication standards, the distributor is often unable to do more than simply take the order, handle it manually, and then reenter it into the customer's preferred system (see Figure 2.1).

Some suppliers have resorted to more extensive use of direct customer communication by implementing websites and then relaying the transaction to the distributor

fig. 2.1 **Managing the Information Flows**

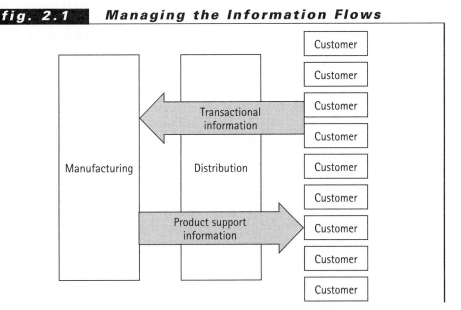

for delivery.[3] The method is commonly called "lead generation" and should not only provide better information but also tie the distributor more closely to the supplier through a mutually beneficial relationship.

These solutions have fallen short, however, as distributors have been forced to do inefficient work-arounds to meet customer demands like working offline from the supplier's site. The distributor may not be able to connect efficiently to each supplier site, especially if there are many suppliers with such sites or if the connection technology is too expensive. For example, a distributor may have different part numbers in its system than the supplier does for the same items. In such a case, the distributor may be unable to directly communicate with the supplier's website. The distributor will be forced to print the order, ship it through its system, and rekey confirmation and delivery information into the supplier's system.

In addition, suppliers often receive limited information not worth the relationship problems it creates with their distributor customers. In recent years, many suppliers and customers have learned that circumventing the distributor is not always the way to go. Some suppliers are looking to replace their distributors with more technologically advanced ones while others are seeking ways to assist their distribution network in the adoption and utilization of new technology. When the new systems first came about, however, the distribution channel itself looked primed for a complete overhaul with distributors as the big losers.

As e-commerce technology first became available, the doubts about the distributor's skills turned into a battle for control of the customer. Manufacturers sought direct channels either to capture more margin (get more profit by eliminating the distributor middleman) or to exert more control over their destiny.[4] Dot-coms tried to seize the customer relationship from distributors and retailers with little success.[5] Many distributors, meanwhile, sought to lock in customer relationships and reach for additional market share by rapidly automating their systems. Some made the transition, some failed, but at the close of the 1990s, most were still tangled up in the process of reinventing their firms. Ultimately, the dot-coms' technology failed and they ran out of money. The technology race slowed and focused on traditional channels as its base expanded to include all members of the supply chain instead of just outsourced partners like the dot-coms and application service providers (ASPs, discussed in Chapter 15).

It appeared as though the distributors would maintain their position for the present. Nevertheless, many were finding a rapidly increasing set of new expectations coming from both suppliers and customers. The heightened expectations were based on classic supply chain principles. Information handling, analysis, and delivery up and down the supply chain would be critical, and distribution would have to serve as an information analyst for both customers and suppliers.

Suppliers wanted POS information and improved distributor forecasting to soften the "bullwhip effect"[6] where information handling deteriorates as it passes back up the supply chain from end-customers through distributors to manufacturers. Forecast error caused by poor information exchange and coordination created a need for suppliers to adjust their production cycles when demand changed unexpectedly. The adjustments played havoc with the suppliers' factory planning process forcing adjustments in inventory, personnel, and other resources (see Figure 2.2). These adjustments

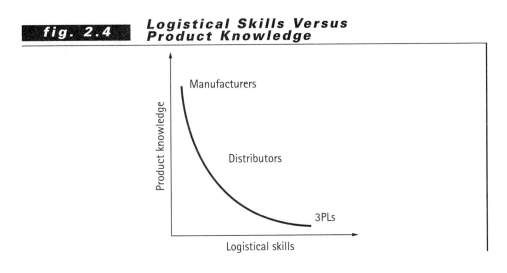

fig. 2.4   *Logistical Skills Versus Product Knowledge*

tionships that distributors have achieved. Many distributors remain wary and believe the day is coming when the big 3PLs will become a credible threat.

For the distributor to take over these roles—forecaster/capacity planner for manufacturers and inventory/procurement manager for customers—was not only logical but potentially synergistic. The "inside" knowledge about the customers' needs, both present and future, should increase the ability of the distributor to assist suppliers in planning. This would require the distributor to have real-time visibility into activity at every customer's location and to be able to analyze that data to create information that the supplier could use for more effective planning. The connection would be expensive and might require the use of many e-business tools. First and foremost, to connect the customer to the supplier and deliver analysis, the distributor needed a system that connected its own internal flows and could conduct just such an analysis. This internal system (commonly called ERP) would be essential to the distributor acting as the supply chain information manager.

Information Power and Use

Most members of the supply chain have a poor understanding of information power. Some understand that the benefits associated with reducing inventory and/or increasing sales are significant, but most do not know how to manipulate that information to achieve the purported results. This lack of results has caused many distributors to delay getting involved in information automation. After the dot-com bubble burst, this decision appeared wise, and many distributors counted themselves lucky for not having been ERP or e-business pioneers.

The reason for the dot-com collapse was not, however, that they had the wrong idea. In fact, Dell Computer and many other firms have proven just the opposite.[7] When applied correctly, information management is a devastating competitive weapon. Many experts agree that this is the future but would rather not be on the leading edge. One fishing distributor put it this way: "We know we cannot afford to be on the leading edge. Therefore, we tend to trail behind the leaders but always try to keep them in sight so we know what is around the corner and can evaluate it before it impacts our way of doing business."

The dot-coms and other technology providers both over- and undersold the value provided by new information management technologies. The confusion created in the early stages of ERP and e-business caused many business leaders to believe the IT claims were simply hype. The overselling came from inflated promises on what the technology could do and when it would be available. With what is commonly referred to as "vaporware," IT providers anxious to make a sale would discuss functionality that could add great value but had not been programmed or tested yet. Many of these vaporware solutions would never materialize when the provider could not make the program work. These failures led to a general distrust of IT providers when their customers felt they had been promised the moon.

The underselling came from a poor understanding of what could actually be accomplished with less-expensive, better-planned investments. In a mad rush to completely connect the company, a slower steady process of step-by-step full implementation that the firm could absorb at a feasible rate and cost got pushed aside in the rush to flaunt a shiny, new, complete ERP package.

This quick adoption strategy was driven by two factors. First, the Y2K (Year 2000) problem had many concerned, even terrified, that their business would be paralyzed by the bug embedded in all systems that could not adjust for the new millennium. The Y2K problem stemmed from the early programming efforts in the sixties and seventies where the year in the code was described with two digits (such as 75 instead of 1975). These older codes were still embedded in most software packages since most software had evolved (been built up) over time and lay on top of older coding. This meant that when the new millennium started, a system would think it had gone back in time to 1900 instead of forward to 2000.[8]

The unpredictable results of such a development caused near panic with some fearing basic services (utilities, water, and food supply) would break down and worldwide havoc would ensue.[9] The problem proved to be grossly overstated. Firms responded in two different ways. Some firms hired programmers to apply a fix or patch to their systems to cure the problem. Others decided to buy the new Y2K-compatible ERP systems. Those who chose the latter rushed their ERP development to meet the Y2K deadline and suffered the worst ERP problems.

The second reason to adopt ERP made more sense. These firms looked at the e-business movement and decided that a lack of internal connectivity would prevent firms from being competitive in the future. The assumption was correct but, as explained in Chapter 1, the cost of implementation was grossly underestimated and those firms also suffered from ERP problems.

The implementation problems were not the only issue, however. The technology limitations meant that programs needed to be well thought through and required, therefore, involvement from the key process owners in the business. These process owners included everyone from the sales force to management to accounting to dock workers. Most firms were unwilling to commit their most valuable human resources to such projects. The use of such key process owners raised the cost of the implementation to a breaking point for most firms. As a result:

❍ Systems were only partially implemented.

❍ Training was not emphasized.

❍ Failure was inevitable.

To achieve the savings or increases in sales possible under improved information management, expectations must be realistic and objectives and ultimate use of the information must be clear. The power of information management is mighty.

Using IM Power to Advantage

One of the greatest causes of excess inventory is forecast error. Inventory is one of the largest assets on most distribution firms' books. Forecasting is all about information management. The older or less complete/accurate your information is, the worse your forecasting becomes. Poor forecasting forces firms to carry larger inventories to prevent stockouts. The remaining stockouts are a direct result of the inability to forecast and to carry sufficient inventory to meet the forecasting problems (lack of resources).

Another major cause of inventory problems is supplier performance failures. While not necessarily a pure information play, the distributor who tracks and reports performance to its suppliers is more likely to get improved deliveries. In addition, better forecasting along with the sharing of those forecasts with suppliers can also lead to improved supplier lead times and fill rates. Even if supplier performance is not improved, tracking supplier deliveries allows for more accurate calculation of inventory needs, thereby reducing inventory or increasing customer service.

Customer service also improves with better information management. One strategy is to transfer inventory from slow-moving into better-selling/more-profitable products when forecasting or supplier lead times improve. Another is to improve customer visibility of the product in the supply chain so that customers can better plan their operations by anticipating when products will become available. A customer can then hold purchases of other products that go with the delayed item until the product gets there. The customer can reduce its inventory as a result by not carrying the other products while waiting for the critical one to arrive. If a certain product is delayed and the customers can see with some certainty when it will arrive, they can also better plan when to shut down their lines and start the new product run (a machine changeover).

Realizing Cost Savings

Many IT providers have documented the transactions cost savings.[10] Transaction costs are the costs of entering activity on the system. If the system is paper based, it takes longer to enter the activities, and the opportunities for error multiply every time someone touches the process. An automated system usually requires less handling and often has automatic entry tools (such as bar code scanners), which lead to a tremendous reduction in human effort and errors. The transaction cost savings are usually the most highly stressed advantages of information automation but have not always been captured in practice because firms find themselves using work-arounds when their implementation does not go well. These work-arounds generally defeat the purpose of automation by reentering human interaction into the system.

Customer profiling and market analysis become possible when the firm has a centralized database that is easily accessed and analysis programs that will develop reports useful to suppliers and customers. Some value reports would include:

1. Market analysis for a product category that suppliers could not create since they do not see their competitors' sales

2. New product introduction opportunities developed from missed sales, customer input to the sales force, analysis of quotes, etc.

3. Identification of customer process problems from product failure rates and order frequency

Financial performance improvement by speeding up the invoice process and increasing its accuracy is a major boon for most firms. Accounts receivable (A/R) is typically another of the distributor's largest assets and any reduction in days sales outstanding (DSO = A/R divided by average daily sales) can have a significant bottom-line impact. A reduction in invoice processing time of one day can take a day off DSO. Invoice accuracy also has a considerable impact: When errors are eliminated customer satisfaction increases and profitability is preserved. Many distributors report that the entire profitability of a sale can be eliminated when full costs are not captured due to late entry into the system or a general inability to keep track of costs.

Many other cost-saving opportunities exist: freight bill auditing, schedule sharing, technical information for sales efforts, real-time updates to government regulated documentation . . . the list is very long.

IT providers did not exaggerate when they stated the potential savings associated with ERP and other IT systems. Their mistake was in focusing on only a few and not considering whether some smaller initiatives targeted on the big dollars (inventory and DSO) should be better detailed, trained for, and rolled out first with specific steps and goals in mind. The focus instead was on transactional savings (well understood by IT providers), which could be achieved only with a completely connected system. In addition, the system rollout milestones tended to be focused on the implementation and often did not extend beyond the installation of the system.

Milestones must be established for more than just the system rollout. They must include expected savings and when those savings should occur. Failure to meet expectation (ROI) milestones should cause a pause in the implementation to assess what is going wrong and how the firm can get back on track. The metrics should be specific and timely so that the firm reacts before chaos sets in.

The projected use of the information should provide the milestones and establish who should be involved in each phase of the project. A major problem erupts when a process is put in place without significant involvement from the primary users of that process. Many firms installed sales supporting mechanisms without involving enough people from the sales force. The rollout would inevitably immediately run aground when salespeople (particularly those in remote locations) encountered a problem they could not solve while the customer was waiting. Or the system designers, in their hunger for more information about the customer, required the sales force or others to work harder after the new system was in place than they did before. Most people expect a new system to make their life easier, not harder, and will become disillusioned if the new system is seen as less efficient than the old one.

When designing what the process will do for the firm, the beneficiaries of the process should help define what its goals are and what information is to be gathered based on the planned analysis. The analysis must be defined up front and based on the desired outcome. Only after a complete planning based on the systems goals should the information collection function be considered.

The Strategy and Structure of the Information-Driven Distributor

Distribution is in transition from human databases on the sales side and inventory managers on the resource side to data-driven marketing efforts on the sales side and scientific capacity planners on the resource side. Making this transition will require more than just new technology—it will require a major cultural shift in the way distributors view themselves. To date, most distribution firms have operated in a loose, entrepreneurial manner with employees from the sales force to the warehouse making heroic efforts to meet customer needs with processes that are less than optimal.

The heroic efforts made everyone feel good but did not solve the fundamental process problems that drove the failures. Distributors were well designed to increase sales and could, up to a point, cover up customer service process problems, but profitability would ultimately have to suffer. Sales increased, but so did the problems, and margins began to narrow.

To meet the new challenges, the distributor's sales and operations would need new tools and an understanding of how to use them.

○ Outside sales would need remote access the information system.

○ Inside sales would need complete visibility and more powerful analysis tools.

   ○ *Inventory availability*

   ○ *Sales (transaction) profitability*

   ○ *Product technical support*

To access and properly use these new tools, the sales force would also need new skills. Technical and logistical customer support, for example, can be delivered only by a better-trained sales force that understands the tools. This training requires a commitment of funding from management and of time from the sales force, both of which can be scarce. The basic structure of a distributor's operation worked against taking salespeople away from their customers as the company's very survival depended on their remaining productive.

Glad-handing and keeping all customer information in the salesperson's personal files will not allow the system or the company to remain efficient. Many salespeople consider their customer information as their own (not the company's) and hold it as a trump card in negotiating salary or job security. The ERP or other system would need to routinely collect this information and hold it centrally. Many salespeople would view this as a threat and a loss or dilution of information they see as proprietary.

A strategy that does not match the firm's structure (personnel, culture, and support mechanisms) is doomed to failure.[11] To be successful, the distributor would have to consider how its structure must change or how to adapt the strategy to the new structure or both (see Figure 2.5). The sales force is one of the most powerful and significant forces in most distribution outfits. New processes must consider their needs and outlook.

The sales force has a tremendous impact on the success of any program but is especially invaluable with information-related ones since sales controls so much of the critical customer information. If the sales culture resists supporting improvement efforts due to past failures or the fear of a loss in income or power, the firm will have to either repackage the new initiative to make it seem worthwhile or answer the "What's in it for me?" question for the sales force.

The sales force has a long memory when it comes to new management initiatives that cause problems for the customer or the salespeople themselves. The problems encountered are exaggerated as they are repeated until it seems that any action that is not an absolute success is written off as dangerous to the company's well-being. Salespeople's opinions are taken very seriously by most management teams since salespeople have the ear of the customer on the one hand and are the spokespeople for customer to management on the other. If a significant number of salespeople (especially top producers) oppose a new program, it will most likely fail.

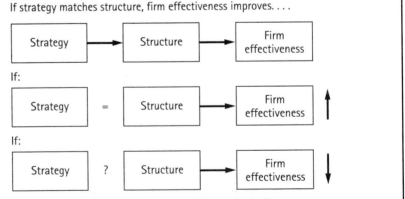

fig. 2.5 *Strategy Structure Match*

If strategy matches structure, firm effectiveness improves. . . .

If not, the firm's performance could actually decline.

One manufacturer was interested in extending its understanding of its sales to distributors. It adopted customer relationship management (CRM) software that was intended to track contacts and bids made by the sales force. The intention was to do a better job of predicting customer needs and evaluating the success of bids. If the bids were unsuccessful, the company might be able to identify a pattern explaining why. The company could then take action to counter that pattern by arraying resources (sales force education, additional technical support, new product designs, etc.) designed to secure more business. The intent was to make the sales force more successful—a win-win strategy.

The problem was that the sales force viewed the CRM system completely differently. They assumed since it was computer technology that at a minimum it should make the quoting process and customer contact management easier. At minimum they wanted it to be significantly easier to use than their existing systems (laptop organizers, date books, PDAs [personal digital assistants], etc.). A logical extension, many thought, would be for the system to offer them visibility of inventory and manufacturer technical information in real time so that they could better service their accounts.

However, the CRM system had been designed for the company to be able to track the sales force, not for the individual salesperson's convenience. The resulting system took a long time to update, add existing accounts to, and maintain in general. Some salespeople feared the system was designed to learn about their customers so that they could be replaced more easily. The net result was that most of the sales force resisted the system and it failed. In a few years, the company decided to try again with a new system. This time the sales force was to have no choice: Use the system or go elsewhere. Two years after the system's introduction, it was still doubtful it would work.

This time the problem was that the "What's in for me?" question had not been answered or had been answered in a negative fashion. The sales force saw the system as an additional burden, taking them away from selling (costing them money) or, worse yet, as an incursion on their job security. Nevertheless the company mandated that whoever did not use the system would have to leave. This negative environment was not a good start for a project as ambitious as this one. The sales force can resist without appearing obstructive. Narrow interpretation of what data should be entered as opposed all that was intended was one possible tactic. Or sales could delay entering quote information until the transaction were complete—eliminating the ability of the company to evaluate lost quotes, leaving prized customers off the list until caught, and then pleading it as a mistake. There was a way around almost every facet of the new system. Ultimately, it could not succeed without the sales force's buy-in.

The sales force issue was perhaps one reason that so many initiatives started in the warehouse rather than in the field. Still, to achieve automation for internal processes, warehouse operations, purchasing/planning, and transportation, decision making had to become more scientific. The new warehousing capabilities offered by internal connectivity (enterprise information management, or EIM) would require better-trained warehouse personnel at a minimum. In reality, to truly take advantage of the systems, warehouse, planning, and transportation managers would need to have greater analysis skills than ever before. This implied a better-educated and more technically trained workforce.

For most distribution warehouse operations, the workforce consisted primarily of low-paid pickers who pulled and shipped orders. The receiving clerks may have had better training—especially if the warehouse operated under ISO 9001, a popular quality-certification program that requires complete documentation of all distribution processes, or other well-documented sets of processes. Warehouse management generally worked their way up through the ranks, came over from sales, or came from outside the firm with some specialized training from APICS or some other organization. In short, the warehouse personnel were not well prepared to go with a new information technology that would rearrange their operations and require new processes to succeed.

Culture was an issue in the warehouse just as with the sales force. With the sales force, the cultural problem revolved around their perceived importance, which gave them leverage in resisting new programs. For the operations group, the cultural issues revolved around heroic deeds from the past. In most organizations, the operations division gets challenged on a regular basis to do the "impossible" for the good of the firm. One electrical manufacturer tells of a customer that suffered an outage from a hurricane that so strained its ability to serve its territory in Louisiana that it had to accelerate the schedule on a new plant by months. Since the large power unit produced by this manufacturer was critical to the plant's opening, the customer appealed to the supplier to accelerate its schedule.

The supplier in turn asked its suppliers to shorten lead times and provide alterations to the product that the manufacturer would typically handle in an attempt to shorten production time at the plant. Heroism was called for throughout the supply chain, and the typical rules of engagement and operational efficiency were thrown out. The company and its suppliers met the new schedule, the customer was delighted, and everyone celebrated. The problem became that operations at all these companies now held an IOU on their management and would remind them whenever a change in processes was to come that this great feat was pulled off by the old system.

This sort of heroism happens on a regular basis in most firms. In fact, the more disorganized a firm is, the more likely heroics will be needed as mistakes made elsewhere have to be covered by operations. Sales overpromising on customer deliveries or purchasing missing a need to buy are excellent examples of mistakes that will ultimately cause crises. The just in time (JIT) movement where customers are getting deliveries just before a product is needed has especially strained operations divisions and added to the need for heroics. These IOUs build up and eventually give operations the ability to "scare" management out of change for fear that the next time a crisis arises, the company will be paralyzed by its new systems. Disorganized processes are usually the basis for the heroic culture. Ironically, the disorganized processes the new technological systems are designed to replace can sabotage the new processes.

Many manufacturing firms started making the transition to better-trained personnel with their scheduling functions in the 1970s and 1980s. Organizations like APICS began offering certification to factory planners and inventory managers, which led to a more sophisticated operations division. Quality gurus like W. Edwards Deming[12] stressed the importance of doing things right the first time and reducing efforts on inspection and other heroic recovery methods. Distribution has been slower to adopt the investment in operations staffing that is critical to the success of new technology investments.

The information revolution continues to have a profound effect on distribution operations. Hourly wage earners continue to disappear as their jobs are automated away, like they have been in manufacturing over the past century. The automation will lead to a smaller, more highly trained workforce that produces greater throughput. Higher throughput will be supported with both information automation and physical automation (carousels, conveyers, etc.). To be effective with these tools, the workforce will have to be creative and adept at process design. The challenge will be greatest in channels where the product is more difficult to move or track with automation tools (physical or information) like building materials, pipe/valve/fittings, and the like.

Most distribution cultures are unprepared for these structural changes in both their processes and culture (sales or operations). For the most part, salespeople are too powerful and fiercely independent. Many will view information automation as a reduction in their worth and will resist implementation programs. To be successful with the sales force, compensation programs will have to be redesigned to match the new environment. For the operations group to be successful, warehouse, inventory, and transportation planners will have to be upgraded from their status as second-class citizens and be better compensated. Without a redefinition of their importance, top talent will not be attracted to these positions. Without this top talent, information automation and ROI on new systems will fail.

Justifying the ERP Investment

Perhaps the most difficult part of new system adoption is justifying the investment. Investors set high expectations for such investments and want detailed schedules for obtaining the ROI on projects. Most firms find this process difficult because assessing the value of process improvement implies an understanding of the process's current capability and then an assessment of the cost savings/sales improvement resulting from the new process. To quantify benefits, we must understand those benefits and capture them as they occur so that they can be properly attributed to their sources.

Quantifying the Benefits

Quantifying the benefits means using the goals and metrics established at the outset to guarantee the system gets credit for what it actually contributes. It also means using the goals and metrics to determine early on when goals are not being met so that corrections can be made. These corrections have been especially important to new IT projects since early failures will impact future portions of the implementation.

Calculating ROI first requires an understanding of what the company performance expectations are regarding invested funds. Many firms use a minimum internal rate of return (IRR) that they expect the firm to achieve. Others set a hurdle rate for new projects to be accepted. A typical IRR will be in the 15 to 30 percent range for many firms, but hurdle rates are frequently much higher due to the competition for limited funds and a wealth of potential projects that can be implemented.[13]

Once the ROI is understood, it can be applied to decisions on system capacity and measuring the cost/benefit relationship of each investment in functionality and the total influence of information technology. Total necessary system capacity depends on company size and the number of transactions involved (the two are usually related since larger firms will typically have more transactions than smaller ones and vice versa). The issue is largely about hardware, although the need for networking can lead to higher software and communications support costs for global and national, versus regional and local, operations. Functionality refers to the system's capability to automate some functions (purchasing or scheduling, for instance) or its ability to provide analysis that can be used for decisions (transportation, warehousing, and so on).

The system capacity can be considered a sunk cost, like the cost of the building for a new business. Functionality, on the other hand, is the skills the system now holds and, much like the offerings a company makes to its customers, it becomes the cost justification for the entire system. Each additional functional program should add value (reduced cost or increased sales) and be used in cost justifying the entire system. If a functional program does not add sufficient value, it should not be added to the system.

Before assuming an ERP system is nothing more than the sum of its parts, however, we must consider the synergy resulting from connecting our processes. Interconnecting all processes in the firm increases the accuracy of information fed to any single program and the timeliness of its availability. So the system can be evaluated by its subcomponents but should also be considered in the aggregate.

ERP systems can cost from a few thousand to several million dollars with the principal differentiators being functionality and capacity. The decision on how much functionality is necessary frequently depends on the company's size. Smaller firms frequently cannot afford large systems. Larger firms require more functionality since their processes are less flexible and more prone to error if not exactly defined.

The decision to adopt an ERP system is often driven by the cost of disparate systems. Multiple databases with work-intensive, error-prone hand-offs tasks can drive up cost as much as customer service failures can from not properly controlling operations—but a single database with the ERP system has its own high costs. Firms struggle with finding the right advisors who understand their businesses.

Consultants and other solution providers are often hired but the additional cost tends to make justifying the system even more difficult, especially when the consultants have to be brought up to speed on processes the company does not understand well enough itself. In addition to consultants, the ERP provider has its set of recommendations and restrictions. Finally, the remaining dot-coms and application service providers (ASPs) have offered to host ERP systems for customers who can then access the system only as they need it and not go to the expense of buying and maintaining their own systems. These options have left many confused as to which direction to go with their IT decisions.

Whatever the solution, the most widely shared opinion has been that a common system and database is essential. Many firms have struggled with pulling these systems together and still wonder whether a single database is worth giving up the

| fig. 2.6 | *Step-by-Step ERP* |

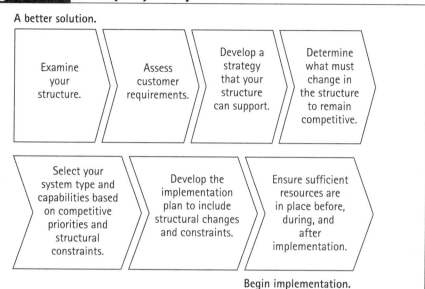

functionality of their individual standalone solutions. The cost mounts up as they try to standardize to a single system and functionality is lost. The payback requires the firm to capitalize on the synergy created by the connectivity while improving or at least not losing the capability of the legacy systems.

The process is greatly facilitated if the firm understands its processes well and can assess its needs and evaluate the options. A step-by-step methodology that first assesses the firm's capability and then its customers' requirements should guide the firm through the selection and implementation process. The next steps are to process-map the firm and develop an understanding of its structural constraints (cultural and otherwise). The final steps are to develop an implementation plan and ensure sure that resources are in place to successfully complete the plan (see Figure 2.6).

Conclusion

The ERP decision is highly strategic in nature and requires considerable self-examination and planning based on the firm's capabilities and culture. Unlike many decisions to add capacity, information technology affects people personally and professionally, is very sensitive to failure to meet planned objectives and timetables, and requires buy-in from all affected parties. The strategy and structure of the firm must be addressed and the implementation plan must consider human and technological constraints.

ERP and e-business suffered harsh setbacks in the 1990s, but the potential benefits will continue to push the movement forward. The distributors' position in the supply chain indicates they will play a key role in the information automation of the supply chain. The internal connectivity of distributors must go forward.

Distribution Retrospective

The Planar CEO found out that developing an information strategy is more difficult than he might have imagined. He decided that management confusion would be the quickest path to failure. He assembled his team and they discussed what the system should be expected to do division by division and what the benefits would be. The discussion became quite heated, with the VP of Operations claiming his group could not achieve proposed benefits with any system if the sales force did not do their part. Incensed, the VP of Sales pointed out that the future of the firm, not to mention the ability to pay for this system, rode on his team's shoulders and if the system did not support them properly or otherwise interfered with their ability to carry out their work, the entire firm could be at risk.

Everyone now turned to the Chief Information Officer (CIO) and asked him what the impact on the sales force would be. The CIO shifted uncomfortably and mumbled something about asking the IT providers and that he needed consultant support. The CEO stood up and said, "We will go forward and we will not give our company away to consultants and IT providers. I want task forces assembled with the best from our operations group and sales. Consultant and IT provider support is to be minimal and only in an educational or advisory role. All reports will detail how our processes work and how they would work better after automation. The benefits are to be recorded and timetables for implementation set up. I want this completed before a single IT program is evaluated. This management team will provide our task forces with whatever support they need."

The VP of Sales immediately protested bringing his best people out of the field where they were needed the most. The VP of Operations said that pulling his best off the job would affect customer service. The CIO said that the company and his people would not understand the technology without a lot of hand holding.

The Chief Financial Officer (CFO) had remained silent until now. She said, "This is not optional. The Board of Directors told us they would not wait for us to become *obsolete. They also will not tolerate a failed implementation. Our jobs are on the line; this must succeed."*

The CEO then challenged his colleagues, "I need a strategy for the board but before we can develop one, we need to understand how our company operates and we need resources that are capable of responding to the strategy. Put your teams together and put them to work."

Issues to Consider

1. Why is the coordination of the supply chain as important as information exchange?

2. Explain the concept of information power.

3. Should the sales function be changed if a distributor is to be information driven?

4. How might a distributor determine the feasibility of an information technology system?

Case Study: ROI and Justifying the ERP System

Note to the reader: The following case is based on an actual distributor. The name of the firm has been changed for confidentiality reasons.

Jackson Electrical Supply was a large distributor with operations in the United States and Central and South America. The company had been acquiring global distribution operations and, as a result, it now had multiple ERP and other legacy systems in place. The company was trying to achieve complete connectivity in a global environment. Many within the firm, including investors, were very disappointed that the investment they had made in a large, well-known ERP system had not paid off and years after its introduction was still not fully implemented. The new systems the firm kept inheriting were further complicating the effort to achieve a complete implementation.

A great deal of debate surrounded the failure of the system to deliver on its promise, but some believed it was the lack connectivity that resulted in multiple handoffs causing the lack of efficiency. When the system was first adopted, the centralization of data had revolved around the U.S. operations, all of which were taken onto the system at once. Before the implementation was complete, however, the firm acquired its first foreign acquisition.

The new acquisition was in Brazil, and the problems with integrating the logistics operations and understanding the new market took precedence over integrating the new operation into the ERP system. The Brazilian operation was concerned about the ability of the system to handle its customer relationships, local currency, human resources issues, and a host of other things. Mostly the Brazilians were concerned about overloading their people with having to learn how to do things the "Jackson" way and integrating systems with the new firm at the same time. The Brazilian workforce was not as well trained on modern distribution methodologies as the Jackson people were, and Jackson did not have Portuguese-speaking specialists to help them. For the time being, the firms decided to get to know each other better.

The connectivity issue got put on the back burner again when Mexican operations were added a couple of years later. The U.S. operations had taken its "eye off the ball" as well since the lack of connectivity globally made it difficult to achieve its objectives at home. Many thought the emphasis on ERP had died out and that firm had refocused its objectives on global growth. This may have been the case until the company missed its profitability goal for the second year in a row.

The ERP implementation and global acquisition excuses were not holding up this time. The Board of Directors wanted a detailed description of what had gone wrong. They especially wanted to know why the ERP investment had not panned out. The questions came during an economic downturn and resulted in a lot of finger pointing as various divisions tried to explain why they were not using the system as planned and not getting the savings or service improvements promised when the system was adopted.

Many blamed the system and claimed the company needed a new one. This was not an option for the current management team, however, since any attempt to throw out this size of an investment and start over would likely mean a lot of new faces in the corporate offices. The decision was made to make the system work globally.

The first issue was establishing connectivity within the system itself. This required networking capability and additional hardware that had to be justified. The firm did not have the network to connect its foreign operations to the United States. Management was going to have to ask for additional hardware (servers, etc.), software (networking packages), and charges from telecommunications networks for information exchange. In addition, they needed to ask for funds to convert the foreign locations. Some of these funds would go toward training and implementation and some would have to be allocated for licenses and additional ERP provider support. The CFO was fairly certain the board would approve training and implementation as well as license and networking expenses but was not comfortable explaining why they would need additional consultant and ERP-provider support. The board would likely go for the request since they, too, believed the lack of connectivity was the main culprit, but the CFO knew this was likely going to be the last straw if results were not achieved quickly.

The connectivity would also require the shutdown of other systems in the network, which essentially meant that new implementations would have to be planned for these divisions. A task force would have to be assembled consisting of people in those divisions and experts from divisions that had already completed the implementation. The divisional implementations would have to run concurrent with the networking rollout. Finally, the cultural bias against the system would have to be reversed by an analysis of ultimate benefits and tying those benefits to the "What's in it for me?" question for all users.

Management had their work cut out for them. They set up a schedule with milestones for accomplishments and called in the consultants, hardware providers, networking consultants, and ERP providers for advice and to establish the system framework and begin implementation planning. To be sure their implementation was a success and that the system got the credit it deserved (obtained its ROI), they put teams of internal experts together with the consultants to determine what would be accomplished and what the bottom-line impact would be division by division and for the company as a whole.

The board approved the CFO's proposal, but only after an admonishment that they wanted reports in a standardized format to be presented every quarter. Failure to meet planned objectives would have to be thoroughly explained and a plan on how the firm would get back on track also would be required.

Case Challenges

1. How did the firm get into this position? Was it poor decision making? Does the ERP system share some of the blame?

2. How should the firm go about proving that the ROI on the system will be achieved? What should they measure? Where will the savings/increased sales come from? How do they prove the results actually occurred and are attributable to the system?

3. How should they use the consultants and the ERP provider? What expectations should they place on these outsiders? How do they help the foreign operations to get online?

References

1. CNet News, Dot-com failure pace decelerates, http://news.com.com/2100-1017-941861.html?tag=prntfr (accessed on 09/23/02).

2. Funda Sahin,, "Value of Information Sharing and Physical Flow Coordination in Supply Chains: Vendor-Manufacturer Relationships" (PhD diss, Texas A&M University, May 2002).

3. F. Barry Lawrence, Gail Zank, Daniel Jennings, Gary Stading, Robert Vokurka, and Ramasubramanian Narayanan, "Alternative Channels for Distribution: E-Commerce Strategies for Industrial Manufacturers," *Production & Inventory Management Journal* 42, no. 3 (2001): 1–12.

4. Ibid.

5. Foresight, Electronic Commerce Task Force Report, http://www.thetwinstar.com/150301.pdf (accessed on 09/23/02); Order Management: Integrating Demand and the Supply Chain (Aberdeen white paper, 2001), http://www.oracle.com/applications/B2B/OrderManagement/Aberdeen_Overview.pdf (accessed on 09/23/02).

6. Hau L. Lee, V. Padmanabhan, and Whang Seungjin, The Bullwhip Effect in Supply Chains, *MIT Sloan Management Review* 38, no. 3 (Spring 1997).

7. Michael Dell and Catherine Fredman, *Direct from Dell: Strategies That Revolutionized an Industry* (New York: Harper Business, 1999).

8. Senate Special Committee on the Year 2000 Technology Problem, http://www.senate.gov/~y2k/faq.htm.

9. Ibid.

10. BCG Research Re-Evaluates Size, Growth and Importance of Business-To-Business E-Commerce, http://www.bcg.com/new_ideas/new_ideas_subpage5.asp (accessed on 09/23/02).

11. Daniel F. Jennings, Daniel Rajarathnam, and F. Barry Lawrence, n.d, "Strategy-Performance Relationships in Service Firms: A Test for Equifinality," *Journal of Managerial Issues* (forthcoming).

12. W. Edwards Deming, *Out of the Crisis,* MIT Center for Advanced Engineering Study, 22nd ed. (1994).

13. Eugene Brigham and Louis Capenski, *Financial Management: Theory and Practice,* 6th ed. (New York: The Dryden Press, 1991).

3

Information System Tactical Planning

Distribution Perspective

Jefferson Building Supplies is headquartered in Los Angeles, California, and has multiple branches in Southern California and Arizona. The company had recently decided to acquire an ERP system and wanted to begin implementation. As part of the ERP selection process, the company had laid out a strategic plan. In a nutshell, the plan called for Jefferson to become a totally information-integrated firm that tracked its customers' needs and the company's ability to serve those interests while increasing market share and profitability.

David Samson was head of the purchasing and planning group. David was to spearhead the return on investment (ROI) for the system with his group. The expectations for inventory reduction and improved customer service were particularly high. The president had informed David that the holding company was demanding the firm produce a solid ROI on the system. The president was unsure how to represent that number but did not want to wait and just hope everything would turn out all right. He had asked the ERP provider and their consultants for an estimate but the answer did not sound realistic. The consultants also said that the ROI would occur only if the company could execute the plan well. In addition, the numbers were very general and the president was concerned that they might not be representative of Jefferson's environment.

The president wanted David to do an analysis and give him an estimated savings based on the automated capabilities of the ERP system. He told David the study was to serve two purposes: First, it would act as a roadmap for David's group to meet their planned objectives. Second, the president would share the results with the consultants and the ERP provider so that everyone understood the mission and its goals (including the holding company). If the implementation began to fall short of planned objectives, he wanted it uncovered fast and corrections made before the schedule could slip. If the goals turned out to be unachievable, he wanted to be sure everyone was held responsible for their roles and that the holding company was notified immediately.

"I'm not going to kid you, David" the president said, "Everyone says the big savings will come in inventory reduction and transactional accuracy from eliminating all the keying and rekeying we do daily. That means your group is going to be one of the biggest contributors to the system's success. You know how we work around here. If sales increases are the only outcome of this implementation, we will have a heck of a time proving the ERP system was responsible. Inventory must decrease; your group must deliver."

David took a deep breath. He did not know how to design this implementation and had just been told that he was responsible for measuring and controlling its success in his area. His group also had the biggest expectation placed on them. He thought about his people and wondered whether they had the skills to pull this off. It did not seem fair for the president to make such a request of him. He was a purchasing expert, not an ERP specialist. He thought for a moment about getting his résumé in order but then it occurred to him that if he did succeed, he would be quite valuable to Jefferson and maybe even more so elsewhere. Where to begin and how to proceed?

Introduction

The introduction of an ERP system requires a completely connected information plan for the firm. Essentially, an ERP system is a single database surrounded by application programs that take data from the database and either conduct analysis or collect additional data for the firm. The connectivity comes from the centralization of all data, the attachment of all applications to the database and one another, and the use of applications in all aspects of the firm. The completeness of the information picture is where the enterprise resource planning system got its name.

The problems with ERP implementation were not so much driven by poor strategies but by poor tactical planning. Developing a mirror image of your firm on an information system is a highly tactical process. Each application captures a process or a group of processes that represent some part of the firm. Application planning requires that each process be thoroughly understood before matching it to the information-automated methodology. As the processes are detailed, the firm develops an understanding of how it conducts business.

This process examination offers some significant benefits. First, it allows the firm to plan the transition to the ERP environment. Second, the process detailing allows the company to improve outdated or less than efficient processes. A common comment about information automation is, "If you automate a broken process, you do stupid things really fast."

Process Mapping for Information Automation

A common method used for tactical planning is process mapping. A process map details an activity or series of activities the firm carries out to support its mission (see Figure 3.1, for example). Firms use process maps to identify which activities are carried out and how. Depending on the method used, the symbols in the process maps can mean different things. Each block, triangle, diamond, or other shape may indicate a physical action like the square in Figure 3.1 where delivery takes place (at the beginning) or a decision (like the diamond where the process questions whether the shipment was complete or not).

The different steps take us completely through all feasible outcomes for a process under all potential scenarios. A key requirement of a process mapping exercise is that it be complete with all activities identified and paths through the map reaching their logical end. Failure to do so could lead to missing critical components when the system is activated. This is where many implementations fall apart, when a critical process is not properly detailed and then introduced into the information system. After the system goes live, these overlooked activities/processes will surface and cause company personnel to go offline to meet customer needs. When the company begins to go offline, the failure of the system to meet its objectives begins.

The process maps can be used to establish which processes are actually in use, what the true mission of those processes is, and how the processes can be auto-

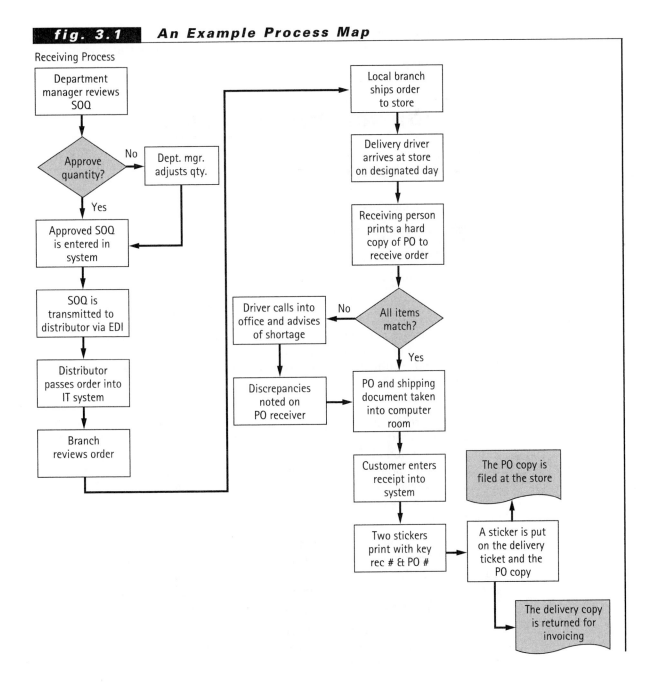

fig. 3.1 *An Example Process Map*

Receiving Process

mated. The first step is to figure out which processes make up the company. This self-discovery phase is not as obvious as it may seem.

One firm had considerable problems with offline activities. They formed a transactional accuracy team to find out why. The team was composed of management personnel from finance, operations, and sales. When they started the process mapping exercise, they found that their receiving process had 47 steps. The complexity of a process that had no direct interface with the customer was a real shock.

Suddenly, the difficulty employees were having working with the ERP system made a lot of sense. The firm decided that to make effective use of the system, it would have to go about simplifying these processes.

Distribution Process Drivers

After mapping processes, the next step is to determine the true mission of those processes. The following are some process drivers:

1. Critical customer service issues

2. Efficient asset management

3. Empowerment of employees

4. Easing the workload for employees

5. Inefficiency evolved and perpetuated from outdated processes

Customer service is frequently a key process driver. Distribution processes have grown over time in response to customer needs. Most distributors started out with one facility and eventually, as their customers grew and opened new locations or as they sought new markets, added new locations. Consider, for example, the firm depicted in Figure 3.2.

This firm started as a single operation in Chicago founded by a family. As business grew and some of its larger customers moved to other sites, the firm followed them. In time, the firm found itself with 12 branches mostly located in the Midwest. The logistics of a 12-branch operation were more complex than when the firm first started. The owners decided to consolidate shipping from their suppliers into the Chicago branch since it was the highest-volume branch with the most experienced management.

The decision to route all inbound materials through Chicago led to some financial and control benefits. The financial benefits were the ability to ship from suppliers at truckload rates (less expensive than less-than-truckload) as well as the larger buys getting supplier discounts. Other benefits were the ability to centralize purchasing and exercise greater control over inventory and other financial decisions.

The company was next sold to a group of investors with a vision to expand the firm nationwide. A professional management team was hired and the former owners retired. The management team then began a process of acquiring other firms in the same line of business with operations in different parts of the country. The acquisitions proved difficult to integrate into the firm since they had different cultures, customer relationships, information technology, supplier relationships, and so on. The firm had to take each acquisition and determine how to transition it to the firm's way of doing business. Inevitably key personnel left, often leaving behind poorly understood processes that customers depended on.

After a few years, the company had integrated many of its acquisitions but had many redundant processes and locations. The firm decided it was time to bring every-

fig. 3.2 *An Example Distribution Network*

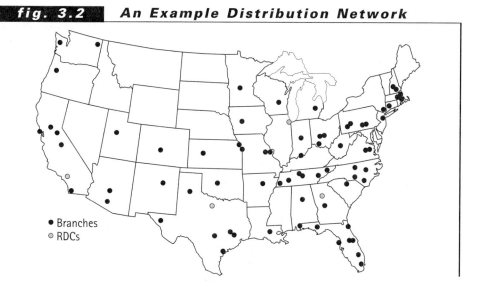

• Branches
◦ RDCs

thing under one umbrella. A facility network optimization study was run to determine which branches should be kept and which should be consolidated, and the firm decided to adopt an ERP system to consolidate and increase the efficiency of its information handling.

As the process mapping began, the firm faced several challenges. First, the more recently acquired branches were using processes for customer service that the rest of the firm did not. For example, the return goods process for the firm stated that a customer could return an item if it was a fast seller with no restocking fee for 30 days. The restocking fee was a charge for taking back an item and usually reflected the loss the firm would suffer from damage to the product or the fact that the product was not a stock item or was a slow mover that would increase the firm's inventory. The process employed for assessing the restocking fee was special orders, slow movers, or items returned after 30 days and before 90 days would be assessed a 15 percent restocking fee. Anything beyond 90 days, the firm refused to take back. The recent acquisitions used different policies and claimed they would lose key customers if they enforced the return policy. Return authorizations from the firm's suppliers were very specific and complex. If the firm did not have a consistent policy, then automating the information flow between the corporate offices, the branches in the field, and suppliers would be impossible.

Other differences included delivery lead-time promises from the branches to their customers, forms submitted for quotes, sales transactions forms, and many others. Designing an ERP solution that carried out these activities and collected information in a consistent fashion looked impossible without disappointing many customers. The firm would have to examine its relationships closely to determine how to make new information technology solutions work without seriously damaging customer relationships.

While the inconsistency hampered the ERP introduction, ERP planning might be good for the company. The firm's inconsistency in processes had led to lost profitability (consider the returns policy or lack thereof). Management hoped that eliminating inconsistencies might lead to higher profitability or better overall customer service. The process mapping exercise might lead a business process redesign (BPR) initiative that would make the firm more competitive.[1] Bottom-line, the firm had been in transition for so long that settling on one methodology at all sites seemed unimaginable, especially where customers were concerned.

Changing Processes to Suit Information Systems

Some processes are designed to achieve efficient asset management. The example firm had processes in place that attempted to optimize asset management but might have to be changed to suit the information system. A good example was the inventory planners' approach to international orders. The system would try to compute lead times based on averaging all orders. The planners, however, would order internationally when they had sufficient time to get the product in but would order from U.S. suppliers when delivery problems arose. The system had no way to differentiate between the two (international and domestic) and so its average lead-time calculation would be wrong for both local supply and international.

Human-based processes like purchasing/planning, warehouse management, and so forth were not visible to the customer but still had a definite impact on profitability. The firm had, therefore, more flexibility in dealing with these processes since the customers' perception of service was not at stake as long as the changes did not negatively impact performance. Changes could have a negative impact on profitability if the ERP system could not achieve the same levels of efficiency that the human-based processes did. In addition, the ERP system could suffer from decreased confidence on the part of inventory planners and other asset managers if they did not believe it could perform at least as well as their current processes did.

ERP systems are designed to deliver powerful solutions to asset management since they are based on best practices, as defined by some recognized organization like ISO 9000.[2] These organizations have developed stable procedures, which carry out routine asset management tasks that can be programmed. The main problem with such approaches is the variance, both real and employee-perceived, between company processes and the best practice methodology used by the system. Company experts will identify these gaps and may or may not be able to find ways to transition their processes to the ERP system procedures. Even with these difficulties, standardized procedures for process mapping can provide a nice overview or base template from which to begin.

Same Task, Multiple Processes

Many companies operate in an entrepreneurial fashion where employee decision making is concerned, especially when it comes to the management of far-flung operations. This approach is especially prevalent in businesses like our example Chicago firm, where acquisitions often are viewed as independent entities out of a fear that aggressive changes will lead to a loss in sales. No firm acquires another with the intent of destroying it. Therefore, until the firm understands the acquired firm and its customers, it will often empower the existing employees of the acquired firm to do whatever is necessary to keep customers happy.

The problem with this approach is that the company may have as many different processes for the same task as they have acquisitions. Standardization on one methodology per process is the only way to enable a powerful ERP system but will often strip employees of their power to make it happen for their customers. The result is often negative consequences for both customers and employees who feel the firm does not respect their skills or opinions. The problem escalates when malcontents share their concerns with customers.

For the example firm, the process matching required the firm to link the sales force to the branches, the branches to the RDCs (regional distribution centers), the RDCs to their suppliers, and then link all other functions that support customer needs in one consistent pattern. In addition to the linear relationship represented by material movement forward through the network to the customer, the firm had to consider the relationships among branches and between RDCs (transfers or multi-site customers, for instance). A key question should be answered before linking all these asset-managing activities in the information system: Is the physical network efficient or can it be improved before information automation?

Other reasons for how processes developed over the years are the easing of workloads for employees or just gradual evolution. While processes that ease the burden on employees make perfect sense, employees often resist the new methodologies out of a concern that the new system will increase or complicate their workload. This concern is usually rooted in customer service again since an overworked firm will have difficulty meeting customer needs. These processes have evolved over time and frequently are defended more out of a fear of the new system than from a true assessment of their worth. Sometimes the best solution is to simply address concerns by explaining how the new system's processes will function even better than the old ones. A more complicated problem arises, however, if the concern is not about customer service but that a gatekeeper is defending the process.

Gatekeepers

Gatekeepers are individuals usually in positions that carry power beyond their rank within the organization. Sometimes these individuals have a skill set that is hard to duplicate and/or is feared by others within the organization. Information technology skills are commonly used to become a gatekeeper. Others use their relationship with a powerful manager or access to critical information they have brought under their control over the years. Gatekeepers use the control of access to information or management to create a working environment in which they are perceived as indispensable and, therefore, can design their jobs to their satisfaction. Many gatekeepers are tyrants who may abuse their power to intimidate their co-workers and deflect inquiry into their actions.

Gatekeeping does not apply only to a single powerful individual. Most people have developed a process in their jobs that works well and will resist any attempt to change it. When multiplied across an entire firm and all its employees, these legacy processes become a formidable obstacle. The examples can run from something as simple as a warehouse employee who prefers to pick items without using a scanner to something as complex as a plant manager refusing to use the ERP system's material requirements planning program because he feels more comfortable with spreadsheets that others cannot see until he is ready.

Laying Out a Tactical Plan

The tactical plan should be in place before process mapping begins but may evolve as a give-and-take with environmental conditions uncovered by the study. In order to support the corporate strategy, the firm must connect its resources to build a tactical plan that supports the corporate strategy. For distribution firms, the components of their tactical plan include the facility network, the information network, and the sales and support personnel (see Figure 3.3). Within this network of resources, the firm builds a tactical plan that accesses resources according to a demand management plan.

The tactical pyramid is built off an inventory stratification strategy that is maintained by the information system. The system is responsible, together with inventory and other asset planners, for determining which assets will be available, in what amount, and where within the facility network. This array of resources across the facility network will determine ultimately which customer service levels the firm will maintain. The desired service levels are, therefore, the drivers of this physical network layout.

The next level is the location and capability of the facilities and allocation of customers to each facility and process. If the inventory plan calls for inventory to be

fig. 3.3   *Tactical Planning for the Information Automated Distribution Firm*

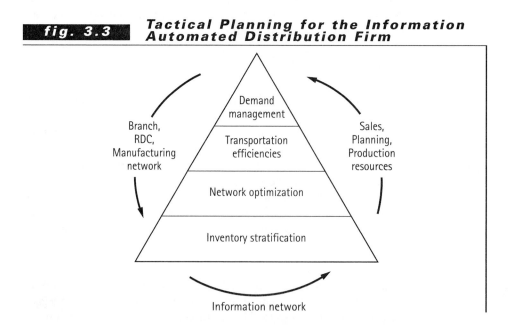

fig. 3.4 **Information Flows Across the Physical Network**

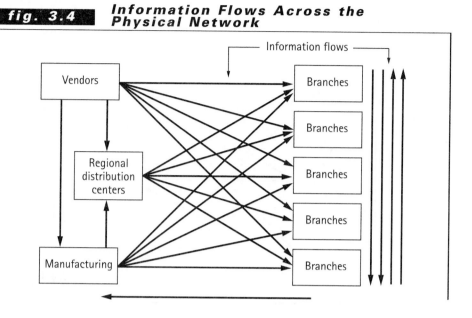

held and a customer to be served from a particular location, the location must exist and be capable of meeting the customer's needs. The transportation network further supports the facility network. The cost of the company fleet or common carriers is a significant contributor to how many facilities a firm will have and where they will be located. If the fleet cannot deliver in time to meet customer demand, the firm may be forced to locate closer to the customer. The combination of these resources (inventory, facilities, and transportation) to serve the customer is referred to as demand management.[3]

New information technology will give the firm the opportunity to exchange information more quickly and accurately, which leads to reduced inventory, which leads to a reduced need for facilities but may imply a need for more effective transportation planning. Depending on the ERP system's capabilities or the use of bolt-ons (added IT packages for ERP that specialize in a particular area like transportation), the firm may be able to create a great deal of value (reduced costs or increased sales) and may also wish to make considerable changes to its facility and inventory networks to capitalize on this value. These decisions should be envisioned in the tactical plan so that the information system is configured to carry out the appropriate activities. The relationship between the IT network and the physical network is depicted in Figure 3.4.

If the volume/quality of information exchanged is enhanced, the firm can reduce assets, which increases the ROI on all operations (see Figure 3.5). Demand management combines resources and trades them for better information management. This requires, however, that information management become scientific and well supported by the firm. In short, the physical network has been connected for most firms throughout their existence; their information flows must now do the same.

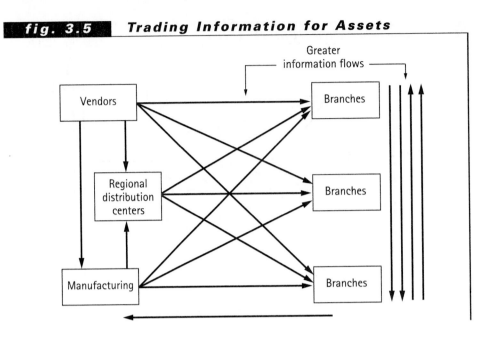

fig. 3.5   *Trading Information for Assets*

Automating Processes

Once the process mapping begins, the first step is to establish how the process works so that the firm can determine how to automate it. The current type of automation will have a major impact on how the planning should proceed. Any of the following forms of automation may be in use:

○ A legacy system—Legacy systems are computer systems cobbled together over the years by the firm. They typically include individual modules that may or may not be linked together. The most common characteristics of a legacy system are a lack of functionality (they are limited in what they can do), out-of-date information handling processes that make them difficult to connect to other processes, and their highly specialized processes that make them difficult to eliminate. The lack of functionality is a result of programming things in as needed rather than taking a broader view of the company's needs and buying the latest capability. The out-of-date information-handling processes come from obsolete programming techniques. Programming has come a long way over the past 20 years and many legacy systems simply have old, inefficiently coded processes. While these first two issues are good reasons to replace a legacy system, the last one (specialized functionality) is a problem. Most firms have developed core processes that are unique and have created information system support for those processes. The uniqueness of these processes makes switching to another system difficult if it does not support them.

○ Another ERP system—Some firms have already implemented an ERP system and want to switch. The opportunity to "do it right" after examining what went wrong with the first system is appealing but a lot of companies blame the previous system for their troubles rather than looking at what they should have done differently. One firm installed an ERP system that could not support its quoting system. This disconnect was proving expensive so the firm decided to switch to a system that could connect to its favored quoting bolt-on. The new ERP system, however, did not complement its logistics operations and was unable to track inventory and other transactions to the firm's satisfaction. The firm, at the time of this writing, was looking for another system. The fact that the company had automated its processes to ERP made switching easier, but its lack of planning was what had led to these expensive system changes.

○ Bolt-on—Bolt-ons are systems that handle a specific task and connect to the ERP system for data exchange and interactions with other functions. These programs are usually more sophisticated applications than found in typical ERP systems since they were developed for a specific purpose. The key issue with bolt-ons is their integration into the rest of the company's processes. If bolt-ons are in place when a new system adoption is underway, then, at a minimum, the firm should find a fairly well-designed process in place. The principal challenges will be either transitioning the process to one on the new system or integrating the bolt-on with the new system.

○ Spreadsheets—Spreadsheets are among the lowest forms of information automation. The use of spreadsheets has been quite popular in recent years since they are easy to understand and allow information ownership to stay with the local process owner. The use of spreadsheets implies some thought has been given to automation but not nearly as much as when some programming or some sort of bolt-on, legacy, or ERP system is in place.

○ Whiteboards—Whiteboards do not represent any form of automation. They simply demonstrate a desire to share information. Many manufacturing or transportation schedules are put up on whiteboards in firms. Other than the consistency of reporting, the process mapping and planning exercise is starting from scratch.

○ In someone's head—This, too, indicates no automation and, worse yet, a possible reluctance to share information. This information management environment is the most difficult to translate to automation.

In addition to type, the degree of automation is important. If a firm has automated some processes but not others, the automation of all processes can still be slow and may even become confused by existing automated processes that will have to be turned off (over the protests of process owners).

If the processes are all on a system and the firm is essentially only considering an upgrade, the firm may experience a fairly easy transition since much of its planning has already been developed in its initial automation effort. In addition to the planning advantages, the standardization of processes may already be completed, making connection to suppliers and customers much easier.

If the processes are on a competing system with different standards in place, the firm may need to do some data scrubbing, eliminating the inaccuracies or inconsistencies in stored data, and/or fundamental process redesign. Data scrubbing is necessary when number systems or other ways of identifying data were handled differently on the old system than on the new one. Many firms find themselves having to create translation tables to match up the old data with the new system. Data scrubbing is a somewhat routine task but, given the massive amounts of data many firms have, it can be quite time consuming.

The old system may not have supported some processes or may have others that will not be supported by the new system. If a process is to be used with the new system but was not supported by the old one, the process mapping exercise is starting from a nonautomated position. If the process was supported on the old system and not on the new one, the firm may have a problem unless that process can be migrated somehow to one supported by the new system.

A common phenomenon is for information handling to be on a combination system. Combination systems are some sort of linkage between human processes that operate offline and information technology like those named above (ERP, bolt-ons, spreadsheets, etc.). These systems are typically only loosely connected. This sort of environment will need a great deal of process replanning before adopting a more connected solution (see Figure 3.6).

After examining the automation status of the firm, the next step is to look at the individual processes to determine their flexibility for modification to a higher degree of automation. Flexibility is a function of how complex the process is and who controls the process. The "who controls" question depends on the interest they have in turning their processes over for automation and, if they choose to resist, how much power they have. Power can be real power associated with a position that is not easily overruled or other types of power that make the individual able to resist information automation effectively (like the gatekeepers discussed previously).

Process complexity makes mapping and automation difficult and increases the opportunities to incorrectly design the information system. If a process is extremely complex, the process mapping exercise must be very complete to avoid the loss of any critical functions. Process redesign can simplify such processes for the good of

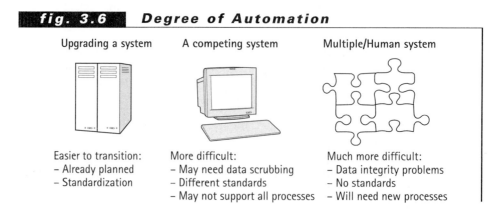

fig. 3.6   *Degree of Automation*

Upgrading a system	A competing system	Multiple/Human system
Easier to transition:	More difficult:	Much more difficult:
– Already planned	– May need data scrubbing	– Data integrity problems
– Standardization	– Different standards	– No standards
	– May not support all processes	– Will need new processes

the system and maybe the company itself but must be carefully thought through to avoid misalignment between the new system and the actual business process.

If the system cannot handle the complexity of the process, the issue becomes what effect not bringing on this process in its current form will have on other processes and overall system connectivity. If the system can handle the complexity after modification, the issue is how much modification will be required and what impact that modification will have on the process and/or the information system. If, for example, the ERP system does not calculate inventory status the same way the firm does, the cost and impact of modifying the system to the company's method is weighed against the impact of complete loss of the process or cost of modification of the process to the ERP system's method.

A good question to ask is, "What drives the process complexity and can it be made less so?" Process simplification enables automation. Complexity is usually driven by human involvement. If the involvement is principally customer driven, the process will be difficult to change. If it is internal, the process should be more flexible.

Process Mapping Distribution Functions

Distribution firms can be divided into several key functional areas, each with its own set of processes to map as well as processes that connect the functional areas to one another and with customers and suppliers. The major distribution functional areas are sales, financials, operations, and inventory control and replenishment.

The functional areas each offer opportunity for operational cost savings and/or sales increases. Sales automation, for instance, can reduce costs by enabling a higher sales productivity per salesperson. Even in a largely commissioned sales environment, a more effective sales force will establish longer-term relationships with customers. Increasing sales with existing customers saves the company a great deal of expense in advertising and other expenses associated with creating and building new relationships. Sales increases result when the sales force has more information available for customer relationship management and has more time to work with customers through automation of routine paper pushing. Sales can also be driven by the system itself when improved customer information handling reduces errors and increases access to product and inventory status for the customer. A fully connected system can bring great benefits through the sales force. A starting place for process mapping sales is the general sales process (see Figure 3.7).

For operations, real-time information allows for better control over picking, shipping, and receiving. The reduction in transaction costs from automation coupled with the reduced errors makes for considerable savings. Increased accuracy in orders picked leads to a higher level of customer satisfaction that will drive higher sales. Transportation has also benefited greatly as firms have worked to reduce private fleet costs and optimize fleet utilization through better planning of needs.

For the inventory control and replenishment functions, the opportunity to reduce costs is well documented.[4] The new ERP systems offer sophisticated forecasting and

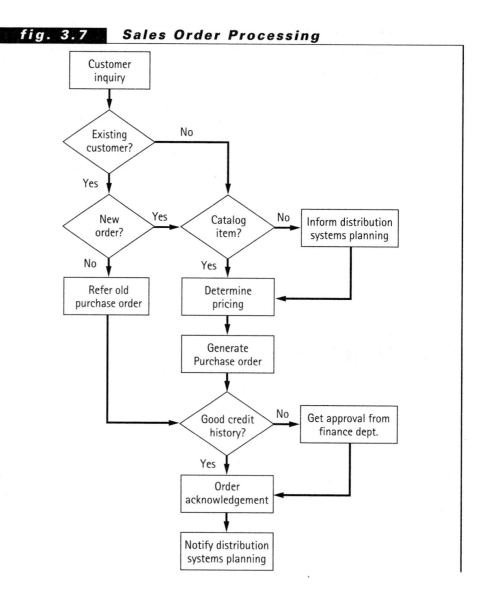

fig. 3.7 *Sales Order Processing*

inventory management procedures that can significantly reduce the need for inventory.[5] The distributor's inventory function is a major target for improvement in most supply chain management programs (see Figure 3.8).

Financials also offer opportunities. Most distributors have major opportunities to improve their profitability through reducing errors in invoicing, increasing the speed of invoice processing, and reducing cycle times for customer remittance through electronic funds transfer (EFT) or automated faxing of invoices. With automated faxing , an invoice is automatically faxed when the information system recognizes a sale. One firm that examined this option considered the savings to be the cost of postage and, more importantly, the time it took to deliver the invoice. The reduction in cycle time to get the invoice to the customer results in a reduction in days

| fig. 3.8 | *Distribution Operations* |

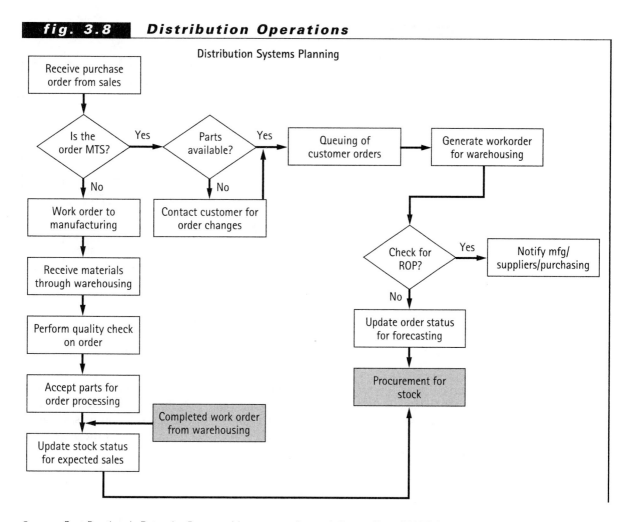

Distribution Systems Planning

Source: Best Practices in Enterprise Resource Management, Research Report, Texas A&M University, 2003.

sales outstanding (DSO), a measure of how much debt the company has with customers at any one time. Reducing DSO can have a major impact on bottom-line profitability. Process mapping credit demonstrates where such process improvements can be achieved (see Figure 3.9).

To match ERP functionality to distribution operations requires that the process maps be categorized along ERP capability areas. After the process mapping/matching activity, the planning for how the system will interconnect and how human processes will be redefined is critical. The first consideration is the appropriateness of the ERP processes. ERP systems are generally designed around best practices, but those processes may still not be appropriate. Best practice may have been built off distribution channels that do not match the adopting firm's business. Another problem to watch out for is when best practice is not be properly implemented on the system.

The human processes that will remain must be planned with the same intensity as the automated ones. If people are not consistent and reliable, they will fill the system

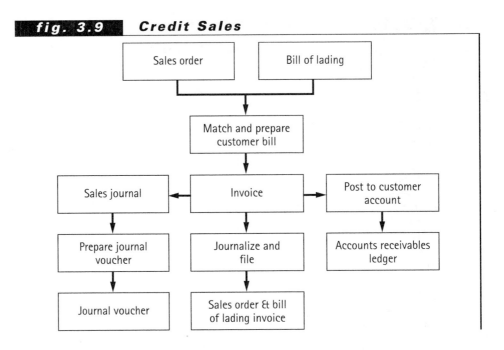

fig. 3.9   *Credit Sales*

with data-integrity problems. Data integrity describes whether the data in the system is, in fact, accurate. A lack of data integrity is the bane of interconnected systems. The best way to maintain data accuracy is to design solid processes that do not introduce error into the system. When connecting personnel to the system the firm must answer the following questions:

1. What are the human resources supposed to do?

2. Why?

3. How?

4. When?

5. What's in it for me?

6. What's in it for the company?

The first four questions should be addressed in training. The "What's in for me?" question needs to be addressed from either a productivity or compensation standpoint. Compensation may mean that the employees will be directly rewarded as they become more successful (as in a commissioned sales environment) or that they will be indirectly rewarded by making the firm more successful (profit sharing, retirement, or job security). Top management must throw its support behind effectively answering this question. Failure to address it is an admission to employees that the new system does not matter enough to demonstrate its value or that employees do not matter enough to ask for their assistance. Either message is negative and can help sink the system.

When to Modify Your Processes and When to Modify the System

A fundamental tactical decision comes when the firm has to decide whether to modify its processes or modify the ERP system. IT firms stress the importance of not modifying a system for a couple of reasons. First, system modifications exist only at the customer site that did the modification. That means that when the system gets upgraded, the improved system may not be able to interact with the modification. A second reason not to modify is that modifications may have unpredictable results when matched together with the rest of the system. If a modification changes and/or adds new data, the system may not interpret it correctly for other programs.

So when, if ever, do you modify the system, and when should you modify the process to match the system's way of doing things? If a process is a core process, you modify the system. If noncore, you modify the process. If the process is core but modifications to the process will either not hurt or may possibly improve it, you modify the process.

A final consideration is to examine the core/noncore strategy in light of technological changes. As technology progresses, which processes will become obsolete? As customer/supplier expectations change, which processes will become obsolete? Which new ones will appear? To modify or not to modify depends on taking a forward view of what will be needed in the future. If a process is going to have to undergo change in the near future, it may be best to act now. If the process is soon to be enabled by new technology, the best bet may be to handle it separately and position it for the anticipated capability.

Process Planning

Once the processes and their significance are understood, it is time to get down to actual implementation planning. The maps need to be examined to determine and eliminate redundant/unnecessary steps and determine where automation can have an impact. As part of the planning process, the firm must keep sight of strategic needs as process redesign goes forward. To do so the firm needs to setup metrics and milestones to measure progress on process changes (see Figure 3.10).

The proposed redesigned forecasting process in the figure will use mathematical models as the basis for forecasting. After running the models, the system will run error metrics to determine whether the forecast is running correctly. If the error metrics indicate that the forecast is working properly, the model next takes forecasts that are working correctly but can be improved by human input to work through a combination forecast with the planners. If the error metrics indicate a severe problem that is not explainable by simple forecast error, the firm needs to investigate the underlying processes to see whether the system is functioning properly.

First check for human error by seeing whether the sales figures intended for forecasting are, in fact, the data the system is being given (investigate the data extraction

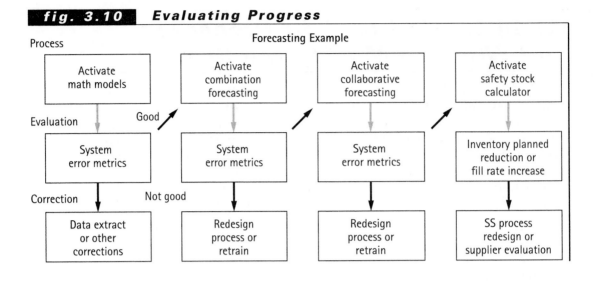

fig. 3.10   *Evaluating Progress*

process). After a successful mathematical forecast, the combination forecast is determined and tested with the same system-generated error metrics. If the combination forecast does not lead to improved forecasts, the problem may be the way the system is designed to interact with the planners (it may ask for the wrong information), or it could be a training problem. This is a good example of designing and preparing human processes to the same degree as the system plan and design.

The next step introduces customer information and will require more human interfaces. This step is handled in the same fashion as the combination forecasting since it represents a human/automation combined solution. Finally, the forecast is improved to the greatest degree possible and the result is translated into inventory reduction. The inventory reduction is a measurable savings that can be used for system ROI justification. If everything that can be done to improve forecasting is being done as envisioned in the initial strategic and tactical planning, yet planned savings are not being achieved, the firm will know immediately and be able to adjust its expectations. Waiting until the promised savings fail to materialize, only leads to disappointment and not knowing why the system seemingly failed to deliver.

Conclusion

Tactical planning gives us the ability to lay out how our processes will be automated and to determine what the projected savings will be. Failure to set realistic expectations and follow milestones that determine when an implementation is on track and when it is missing the mark has led many to both overestimate what their system would achieve and miss opportunities to meet or exceed objectives. The tactical planning process must be detailed and overlaid with customer expectations and corporate objectives. Process mapping matches the firm's functional activities with information technology, but interpretation of the maps and determining how to match them to technology requires the firm to consider its customer relationships, technological

and one in Arizona. The company was founded by four friends in 1983. Don Pallone was the CEO who also looked after human resources. Thomas Anderson was the CFO, a college buddy of Don's. They met Robert Harper, VP of sales, when they both worked for one of the major electronics distributors in the United States. Michael Peters, the youngest of the four, worked as a global logistics manager for a major consumer electronics manufacturer before joining Max.

Max Electronics' primary market was in California, Arizona, and parts of Nevada, but it had customers from as far away as Texas. Its product line included capacitors, circuit protection devices, inductors, resistors, potentiometers, connectors, surface mount components, relays, and switches. The company grew from a single office and warehouse in 1983 to seven branches in 2000. The total number of employees had grown to more than 60. The electronics market boom in the year 2000 helped sales grow more than 30% from 1999 to $32 million. The company was looking to expand its operations and maybe open another sales office in Nevada.

The company ran on a semi-ERP developed during the early 1990s by a small local software company. The system was basically an extension of an accounting package Max had first purchased in 1990. The software company was run by an energetic young professional who at that time was eager to add more functionality to his system and approached Max as a beta site at which to introduce new capabilities. Max agreed to help by adding the IT company's new modules such as inventory and warehouse management as they were introduced. The software was designed per Max Electronics' requirements. The arrangement worked well for a while.

The software company also sold the package to other small electronics distributors and expanded its business. In spite of this growth, however, the IT company was not able to keep going. The firm was overextended and could not keep pace with new competitors offering greater functionality. The firm had also struggled with making its software applicable to other distribution channels. Max hired two previous employees as consultants for software maintenance and troubleshooting. They visited on a biweekly basis for maintenance or when emergencies occurred. The software, however, was no longer being developed or upgraded and, as Max's needs and market grew, it was quickly becoming outdated.

Max had grown and needed more functionality in forecasting, inventory management, and quoting systems. Customers were requesting more visibility into inventory and order status. The online ordering system was not integrated with the inventory and warehousing system. Some suppliers needed POS information on their product line, which was difficult to gather and process.

The company executive team decided to upgrade Max's information technology system. The option of adding bolt-ons to the existing system was not even considered because of the system complexities, since no upgrades were available and the tech support for the existing system was weak. They wanted to understand the myths and realties behind mid-market ERP selection (50-million to half-billion-dollar firms roughly) and implementation, its hidden cost, and its return on investment. The year 2001 saw a dramatic slowdown in sales due to an economic recession, and the forecast for year 2002 didn't seem promising. The executive team thought this would be an ideal time to transition the company to a new system in order to meet the likely ramp-up in demand coming in the next few years. An ERP selection and implementation team was formed with Bob heading the team. The team comprised one experienced and one relatively new person from each of the departments. A couple of sales managers from various branch offices were included in the team. They decided to conduct a survey of mid-market ERP and evaluate three or four systems to make a decision.

Don decided to investigate the possibility hiring of a consultant to assist the team. He had heard John Newman make a presentation on process maps and their use in ERP system selection. Don came away with a new outlook on what Newman described as one of the most critical success factors in ERP implementation, matching business processes to ERP system functionalities. Newman's discussion on best-practice processes in the industry and how they were implemented in ERP systems shed some light on an area they might have overlooked. Don invited John in for a meeting in June of 2001 to discuss how Newman and his team could help in process mapping Max Electronics and assist in the ERP implementation. Don wanted to know whether the processes they were following were best practices or whether any improvements could be made to the existing processes. He also wondered whether the ERP system would, in fact, have best practices included and whether those practices would work for his firm.

He was also interested in being sure that all departments, processes, sales offices, and their fledgling Internet business would seamlessly integrate in their new ERP system. Don wanted to get the selection and implementation of ERP right the first time, as he had heard several horror stories of ERP failures. Don wanted the management team and employees made aware of the cost involved on this project and that everyone's commitment was required to make it a success. The project plan was put in place, and the project kicked off in September of 2001.

Newman started the project with several meetings with various departments and some visits to sales offices around the state. He divided their distribution business in to four core categories:

1. Sales order processing

2. Distribution system planning

3. Finance

4. Warehousing

Each category had subcategories and processes (see table 3.1) associated with it. Newman and his team started their process-mapping exercise with the sales order process. They process-mapped the quoting process, outside sales force's activities, inside sales force order management, discounts and credit structure, and order processing. There were some inconsistencies in these processes at different branches. Customer requests were accommodated and there was no companywide policy on discount and return privileges. These rules were flexible according to branch, customer account size, and salesperson requests.

The meeting reconvened after lunch. Mike was starting to see why this exercise was necessary. The firm had multiple ways to carry out tasks, and customers in dif-

table 3.1	*Process Map Categories*
Sales order processes	○ Order generation
	○ Order processing
	○ Order fulfillment
Distribution system planning	○ Inventory management
	○ Planning
	○ Purchasing
Finance	○ General ledger
	○ Accounts payable
	○ Accounts receivable
	○ Contracts & pricing
Warehousing	○ Inbound Processes
	○ Receiving
	○ Storage
	○ Outbound processes
	○ Pick ticket generation
	○ Order picking and packing
	○ Shipping

ferent locations were relying on these processes. The legacy system had either accommodated (through modifications) these needs or was not engaged and the processes operated offline. Newman demonstrated that these offline and otherwise variable approaches were not only expensive in terms of errors and the inventory those errors created but also prevented the firm from going with virtually any ERP system unless prohibitively expensive modifications were made. He pointed out that the ERP providers would resist excessive modification and were probably right to do so. He suggested that each process had to be evaluated to determine its mission and value to the firm.

Newman then opened the floor for discussion. The discussion started with Bob raising a question as to why different processes at different branches could not be accommodated with a new ERP system. His position was that the customer was more important than the system and that expecting the customer to accommodate Max did not make sense, especially in this economy. Newman, to Bob's surprise, agreed. He stated that expecting the customer to bear the burden was not reasonable. The configuration of the new system would have to address critical customer needs. He went on to point out, however, that the new system could meet the customer's needs more effectively in some cases than the old way.

Newman pointed out that the sales force, Bob's group, would have to sell customers on the new approach in such cases. Bob shifted uncomfortably at the idea of asking his sales force to "sell" customers on a new process rather than a new product. He did not know whether they could make the shift. Newman went on to say that in cases where the customer must have the old process, the system would have to be modified. Newman quickly said, however, that these cases would be fewer than most salespeople or others would believe. The management team would have to sell the company employees before the company could sell its customers that the change would be for the better.

Case Challenges

1. Do you think a technical representative from an ERP provider should take part in this exercise? If so, will it help the team to map the processes, aligning it to the best practices, or will it be biased toward processes programmed in the ERP?

2. What can be done to motivate customers to accept the changes proposed under a new ERP system? How soon should the company begin introducing the changes to customers?

3. What will happen after Newman's study? How will it aid in the selection of an ERP system?

References

1. Lynn Kubeck, *Techniques for Business Process Redesign* (New York: John Wiley & Sons, 1995).

2. Travis Anderegg, *ERP: A-Z Implementer's Guide For Success* (Greensboro, NC: Cibres Inc, 2000).

3. David Simchi-Levi, Philip Kaminsky, and Edith Simchi-Levi, *Designing and Managing the Supply Chain: Concepts, Strategies, and Cases* (New York: McGraw-Hill/Irwin, 1999).

4. Steven Nahmias, *Production and Operations Analysis* (New York: McGraw-Hill/Irwin, 2000).

5. F. Barry Lawrence, Daniel F. Jennings, and Brian E. Reynolds, *e-Distribution* (Mason, OH: South-Western Publishing, 2003).

Selecting the System

4

The Selection Process

Distribution Perspective

Mary Freeman was the recently appointed Chief Information Officer (CIO) for Anderson Steel, a steel service center. Steel service centers are distributors that specialize in metals distribution. The company had 10 branches in the southwestern United States and focused its efforts on heavy industrial customers who manufactured everything from train cars to large machinery. Its typical customer did a great deal of fabrication that meant buying steel and other metals in precut patterns that could be welded together as its products were assembled. Anderson Steel did cutting and slitting operations (cutting metal into customer desired lengths or slicing it into thinner rolls) for its customers, but its biggest business was in prefabricating metal panels or other metal forms through a laser or plasma cutting process. Truck and other vehicle manufacturers were among its largest customers.

Mary had been asked to examine the company's legacy system in light of some new strategic plans the firm had in mind. She asked different specialists from sales to operations and came away with the conclusion that the legacy system would have a difficult time handling the new processes. In particular, the firm was going to connect its customers' buying history to every transaction so that the inside sales associate could compare the discount structure with the customer's value to the firm before deciding whether to offer a discount. The legacy system could not make such a connection and it was clear that no one understood the system well enough to say for sure how to program the modification. When she then considered other extensions to the process that would match customers' requirements with what the operations division could actually accomplish, she soon realized the legacy system had to go.

Mary reported her findings to the CEO. The CEO told her to begin investigating new systems. Mary was worried that the company did not realize the seriousness of adopting a new system, especially one this large. Mary had been through an ERP implementation at her previous employer and had seen just what could go wrong.

As she started thinking about the team she would assemble, she hoped she would not regret taking on this assignment. She had participated in but not led the last ERP implementation she had seen. This time it was on her shoulders, and as CIO she would have nowhere to hide if this project went bad.

Introduction

Once the decision is made to move away from a legacy system, the firm is faced with an even more daunting challenge: the selection process. Most firms will not decide to make the financial and frequently courageous investment in an ERP system without some serious soul searching. It is not unusual to hear an executive say something like, "We have a computer system that is 10 to 15 years old; it does everything we want it to do because we have modified it to the nth degree. The problem is that all of those modifications over the years went undocumented by a series of programmers that passed through our company and moved on. We know we have to do something about it."

Statements like this are a good indication that enough organizational pain is being experienced with the legacy system to provide sufficient motivation to make a change. The dilemma facing most firms is deciding which ERP system will meet the company's needs today, enable it to gain capability for tomorrow, and not put the business in jeopardy during the process. Frequently the company will begin the search process by talking to firms in similar lines of trade and asking questions like, "What kind of computer system are you on?" "Do you like it?" "Does it do everything you want it to do?" This process is the "toe in the water" that usually helps the firm decide that either the existing system is not so bad (although the firm may be in denial) or it should perhaps go ahead and seriously consider the change.

Another reason for change may be that the company's legacy system simply cannot handle the load being placed on it. The system response times may have degraded to the point that users spend more time waiting for the system to respond than they do actually performing their jobs. Yet another reason could be system functionality. The legacy system simply may not be able to deliver the capabilities the organization requires. The net result in either case could be that users go offline to perform necessary tasks when the current system cannot. Performance problems can be solved to some degree by upgrading hardware. This is really just a temporary fix, however, since it is only a matter of time before the organization has to face the same problem again.

Some overriding reason motivates change, however. It may be the inability to meet some important customers' requirements, the acquisition of another firm, or a series of acquisitions that yield an array of dissimilar systems that cannot be integrated together. Whether it is a small firm with one location or a large multibillion-dollar distributor trying to integrate recent acquisitions, the challenge is the same and the risks are just as serious.

Few challenges are as difficult for an organization to face as selecting a new information system. A new ERP system offers the potential for unprecedented information accessibility and analysis, along with the opportunity to integrate the information management of each functional part of the business to allow the seamless flow of data. On the other hand, a poorly selected or implemented ERP system creates havoc within a firm. Many firms have suffered virtual paralysis after an implementation went awry.[1] Implementation must be planned and managed well and begins with the selection procedure.

The ERP selection and implementation process, for many firms, has been painful indeed. Most firms have heard the horror stories about how one company was simply put out of business because of its new computer system, or how many hundreds of thousands—or millions—of dollars were spent on systems that did not do what the company expected them to do.

The ERP system is rarely the culprit when it underperforms. The blame rests more on the selection and implementation process. Firms can expect a great deal of organizational pain, but the pain can be mitigated by a well-thought-through plan and a well-managed process. This is hardly the sort of business activity that should be delegated to an individual or group of individuals without the full cooperation, involvement, and support of top management.

Forming the Selection "Delta Team"

Once the executive management group has decided to move the organization from its legacy system to one with greater functionality and connectivity (ERP perhaps), a team must be formed that represents many of the principal departments in the company. This team is referred to in this book as the delta team. The name is not meant to imply a militaristic approach; the mathematical expression for change is

fig. 4.1 *Building the Selection Team*

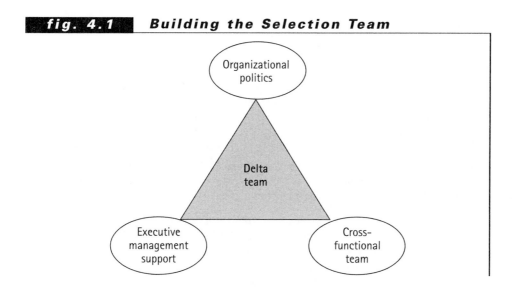

delta, making the name appropriate. The mission of the delta team should be clearly defined so that its activities and expectations are clear and its mission is fully supported by the company's executive management (see Figure 4.1).

The software selection team, no matter what it is called, should not underestimate the power of organizational politics. If one department believes that another "less-important" department is really the driving force behind the new ERP selection process, it may exert considerable effort to derail the process. For this reason, the delta team should be made up of as many different departments as is practical. This team should not be larger than around 10 to 14 people—any larger and it can become too unwieldy and difficult to manage. At a minimum, all functional departments should have considerable input in the selection process from start to finish.

Defining the Mission Statement of the Delta Team

The mission of the delta team should clearly spell out what its activities will be in achieving the company's clearly defined expected deliverables. The delta team's line of reporting should be directly to the executive team. The executive team is sometimes called a "steering committee" in reference to its guidance role, which also indicates its true purpose. The steering committee should act as friend and mentor to the selection team.

Frequently, however, the steering committee sees its role as the traditional command and control of the project. It prefers not to get involved in details like

❍ How will the software work?

❍ How will it support individual key functions?

○ How will the corporate culture adjust?

○ How does the new system support customers?

○ What changes will it require of employees?

The steering committee, instead, may push timetables to answer the inevitable "When will we see some results from this very expensive project?" "Are we still on schedule? Why not?" When combined with a resistant corporate culture, this type of leadership can make for a beleaguered selection team surrounded by critics and a lack of support from above. This may sound like heresy to those who trust that the management team will expect and enforce the meeting of objectives and timetables and prevent waste and/or slipping deadlines.

In routine, well-understood projects (setting up a new warehouse, bringing a new customer into the operations), the goals are to adhere to strict schedules and avoid cost overruns. The problem with ERP is that it is not routine and not well understood by the firm the first (or possibly the second and third) time it is undertaken. The IT firm may be quite capable and have considerable experience, but the introduction of a new ERP system is very personal and most strongly affects the adopting firm. Because every firm's culture is different, the IT provider will always be in a new environment that it cannot completely understand or follow. Much will be happening outside of the IT provider's knowledge that the selection team and steering committee will have to deal with before, during, and after implementation.

The firm is far better off if these issues are prepared for in advance, even as part of the initial system selection. The steering committee should view the ERP selection process as not just another project to be completed in a timely fashion but as a complete business reorganization with all that implies. It cannot drop responsibility on a small team (even a cross-functional one) and then sit back and act as judges of how well the team is performing. The steering committee must get involved in planning, strategizing, replanning, and restrategizing and be visible participants to the entire firm (see Figure 4.2). Failure to do this will cause many in the firm to ques-

fig. 4.2 **The Role of the Steering Committee**

Plan and strategize

Drive and guide change

Through the organizational culture and structure

Be seen assisting and working with team

Achieve desired results

Replan and restrategize

tion whether this effort is a serious reorganization or simply another test case that management is fascinated with today.

The mission of the project must also include financial and nonfinancial goals. This is very important to developing a clear understanding of why this project is important to the organization and what the expected benefits will be—answering the question, "What's in it for the company?" (See Chapter 3 for more details.) The establishment of these goals will provide guidance to all involved in the project regarding why this effort is being made. It will also create an articulated list of benefits that the entire organization should receive as a result of such a difficult endeavor.

Establishing the financial goals of the project will also provide a measure against which the total cost of the new system can be compared so that the financial benefits can be clearly understood. Many legacy systems required significant maintenance that may have required substantial internal IT resources. If the new system is expected to require fewer resources, those cost savings should be identified as one of the expected outcomes of the project. Many legacy systems require significant maintenance, which usually means that there may be an IT staff that is large and expensive as well as independent programming consultants hired periodically to complete specific tasks and then leave. Many firms have these IT consultants in-house on a continuous basis. Their cost, if it can be eliminated, should be added to any decreased load on the IT department.

Improved capabilities to deliver better customer service should also be identified. It may be impractical to quantify these expected outcomes,[2] but they need to be documented to the greatest extent possible because many people, especially salespeople, will see these benefits as further justification for the new system. The buy-in from the entire organization is critical, and few departments carry more influence than sales. The sales force thinks less about costs and more about customer service, so system justification based on improving customer relationships will be more likely

fig. 4.3 *Financial Justification*

to win their support. With the sales force on the firing line with customers and typically directly compensated by their sales productivity, this justification addresses the sales force's "What's in it for me?" question from Chapter 3 (see Figure 4.3).

Conducting Needs Analysis

A needs analysis of a change of this organizational impact should be carefully planned. A clear understanding of the current business processes is essential to making the appropriate system selection. One of the first tasks of the delta team should be to embark on a detailed analysis of the process and information flows within the company.

This activity should be done to identify the core business processes (see Chapter 3) in the organization and create process flow diagrams that depict the way the work is actually done. Documentation is a time-consuming activity that requires involvement from process owners to the point of nearly completing the maps themselves or at least reviewing the maps in several iterations until satisfied that nothing further can be added to make the map more complete.[3] Many distributors that are ISO 9000 certified may have done this already as part of the ISO work instruction documentation requirements.[4]

Another very important step in the needs analysis stage should be for the delta team to break into subteams and meet with each functional part of the company. A significant amount of time will need to be dedicated to this process since it is here that the needs of the users are identified and documented. Another valuable outcome of this level of user involvement is that the users see evidence that their needs are being considered as the selection process moves forward. One possible approach is to interview as many people in the company as is practical to find out what they like best about the current system, what they really dislike about it, and what they would like to be able to do with the system to make their jobs easier.

The benefits of this analysis will become evident when the new system is installed and turned on—the users will have a much higher level of commitment to its successful operation because they were involved in the selection process. In addition, the selection of features will also be greatly enhanced if understood in advance by the key users of those features. Users will have a difficult time understanding potential features if they have not been involved in the investigation of the need for improved functionality.

The delta team should develop a list of system capabilities during its departmental interviews. This list should represent the system features that each functional department must have in the new system or those capabilities from the legacy system that must be retained. The development of this list should not be confused with giving the users the freedom to decide which features of the legacy system they want to transfer to the new system; rather, it is an exercise in identifying the critical functions that the new system must be able to perform as well as or better than the legacy system. This list can be referred to as the "must-have" list (see Figure 4.4).

A second list should be developed that includes the system features or capabilities that would be nice to have. In other words, whatever the current system cannot do

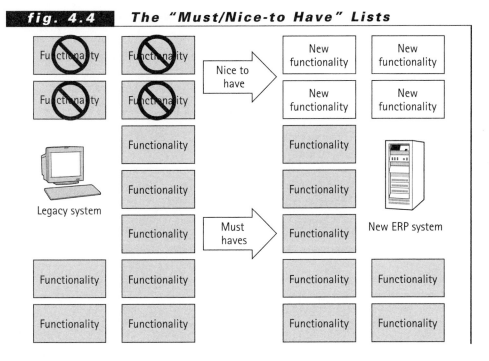

fig. 4.4   *The "Must/Nice-to Have" Lists*

that if made possible would make the users more productive. Far from an open-ended trip down fantasy lane, this is a clear opportunity to look for features that might not otherwise be considered. These features may not be part of the standard ERP system capability, but they could offer the opportunity to uncover needs that would be beneficial to other users.

The input from users should be included in the development of a questionnaire the delta team will use in its evaluation of the proposed solutions. The questionnaire should be used at every ERP system demonstration so that gaps between the system's capability and the identified needs of the users is documented. This documentation will have many beneficial uses as the process moves forward.

Creating Process Flow Models

The delta team should identify the core business processes to be documented. For distribution firms, this would typically include high-level processes such as the sales order process, warehouse operations, inventory management, financial activities such as accounts payable/receivable, cash applications, and purchasing, and so forth. After the core business processes are identified, each should be further analyzed at the next level of granularity. Within each of the core processes are a number of sub-processes that should also be process-mapped (see Figure 4.5).

Creating process flow diagrams can provide valuable insights into overly complex work processes and redundant activities. The identification of these complexities and redundancies offer the opportunity to eliminate them rather than build these

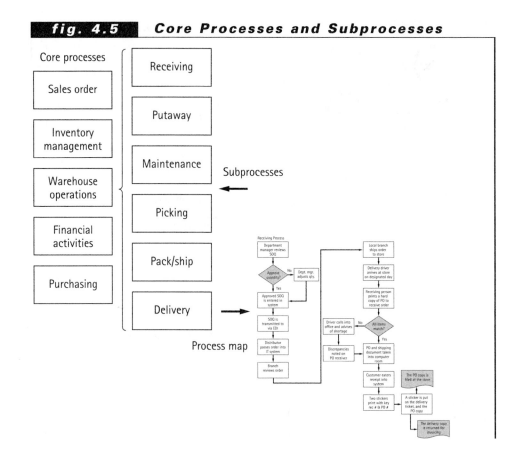

fig. 4.5 — **Core Processes and Subprocesses**

inefficiencies into the specification requirements for the new system. Each of the functional areas of the business should be studied to understand which aspects of information and process management are critical to the day-to-day functions of the organization.

Establishing System Selection Criteria

The delta team must use due diligence to establish the selection criteria for the ERP system. Due diligence refers to a thorough, well-documented analysis of all variables that are traditionally or should reasonably be investigated. One of the criteria could be that the new system be able to run on the distributor's existing hardware. While this will certainly reduce the complexity of the selection and implementation process, the distributor may miss the opportunity to optimize the new software by running it on newer hardware technology.

Certain base criteria must be identified that are the "table stakes" for any prospective solution to be considered. These may include the capability to conduct e-business, a specific database platform, a substantial existing installed base (current users), financial stability, a large installed base of firms in the same vertical channel, and so forth. Most of these criteria should fall into the category of deal breakers (eliminating the solution provider from consideration). Some table-stakes aspects include

❍ Financial strength—The financial strength of any potential ERP solution provider should be a major selection criterion. Given that the distributor is likely to have the ERP system in place for many years, it is in the adopting firm's best interest to be reasonably sure that its ERP provider be financially sound. Experiencing the organizational challenge of implementing an ERP system is not the kind of experience that most firms want to repeat too often, so choosing a well-established solution provider with a strong financial position is essential.

❍ Size of installed base—The number of other firms using the potential system and length of time the system has been used in the industry are key criteria. Longevity itself is not so much a crucial factor, but if a large number of firms has been using the system for a while, it may indicate that the potential ERP provider's software is be doing its job well or at least has eliminated many potential problems. In addition to a large number of users, it is also important to know how many of provider's current customers are in the same industry as the adopting firm. Having a large number of users in the same business for a fairly long time suggests that there will be a large population from which to pick when, and if, it comes time to make user-site visits.

❍ Active user's group—The presence of an active user's group may suggest that the ERP provider is sincerely interested in getting feedback from its current users, and it may even be that the user's group has some input into new features and other product enhancements. If possible, it is a good idea to attend a user's group meeting to observe the process and also to have the opportunity to meet a large number of current users at one time.

❍ Range of modules—This characteristic, although not as significant as those previously mentioned, is important because an ERP system with a wide range of modules offers the firm the opportunity to enhance its capability by adding modules that provide additional functionality. Each potential ERP provider will typically offer many different modules that the company may not be able, or even want, to buy and install during the early stages of implementation. It may be years before some of the features from the other modules are attractive enough for the firm to invest in them. Still, having the opportunity to expand, or scale, the ERP system's capability to meet the growing needs of the firm is an important attribute. As of the early 2000s, ERP system boundaries had not been established and many tasks formerly handled by bolt-ons like warehouse management systems (WMS), transportation modules, e-procurement, and the like were being added. This spreading out of ERP was leading many providers to acquire bolt-on firms in an effort to differentiate themselves from their competitors. Which systems they added were frequently driven by what their customer base valued. For instance, an ERP provider with customers that managed their own transportation fleets (like building materials distributors) might be more likely to add a transportation module. This channel-driven strategy furthered the need for an understanding of which systems similar businesses were using since

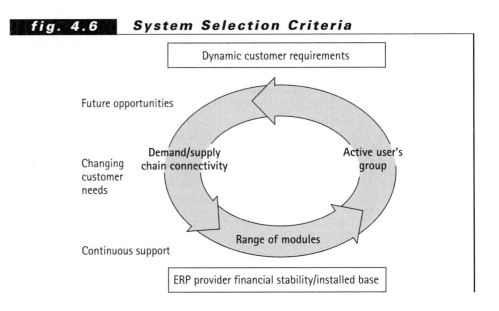

fig. 4.6 *System Selection Criteria*

Dynamic customer requirements

Future opportunities

Changing customer needs

Demand/supply chain connectivity

Active user's group

Range of modules

Continuous support

ERP provider financial stability/installed base

the potential functionality growth would more likely mirror the adopting firm's future needs.

❍ Demand/Supply chain connectivity—As manufacturers, distributors, and customers become more closely linked in the demand/supply chain, the issue of connectivity, or integration between systems, is increasingly important (see Figure 4.6).

The delta team should establish a selection hierarchy through which each potential solution should pass. At the beginning, there may be four, five, six, or more possible ERP solutions available to choose from. No firm could sufficiently scrutinize each of them before making a final decision, so there must be a process to reduce the number of possible solutions.

Assuming that there are multiple potential solutions to pick from, the delta team should establish a series of gates through which each solution must pass in order to proceed to the next level of consideration. For the final candidates, the first gate is the table stakes discussed previously. The next set of gates gets to the "nice-to-haves" and cost/ease of implementation issues.

Initial Product Demos

After the ERP solution provider has passed to the second level of evaluation, a series of product demos should be scheduled. These demos are typically done at the adopting firm and usually consist of a demonstration of the primary selling features of the system. "Selling features" is an important phrase because the solution provider's sales team most often conducts the ERP demos. This does not automatically imply that the sales team will mislead the firm, but it frequently means that the system's most attractive features will be prominently demonstrated. As the saying goes, "All software runs perfectly on an overhead projector."

At this point, the delta team should be armed with a detailed questionnaire. The questions should address specific required functionality. The team may hear answers like, "Yes, our system does that" or "We have a work-around for that." The last statement begs fuller explanation and demonstration in a real-world test of the system. The word "work-around" is always a red flag. The team should stop the presenter and ask for a clear explanation regarding any required functionality that is not sufficiently demonstrated.

At this level of evaluation all of the required functionality should be fully demonstrated. This requires patience, as it is reasonable to expect that an in-depth demonstration could take six to eight hours or more. This is an important and expensive investment, but time spent on understanding the proposed strengths and weaknesses is critical to the project's success.

Technical Support Resources

The ERP provider's technical support resources are an important element to be evaluated. There are two levels of technical support to examine. The first will be the on-site support available when the system goes live. This is obviously a critical time and the ERP provider should have sufficient experienced support people to be on the firm's premises for a reasonable length of time during the initial start-up. What constitutes a reasonable length of time will vary with the complexity of the organization. In large multibranch organizations, support people are likely to be needed full-time for at least the first week, maybe longer. In a single location distribution operation, a few days may be adequate. The number and complexity of software modifications will also be a factor because the modifications may not always work as first envisioned.

The second level of required technical support will be the ongoing needs of the users. As the users become more familiar with the new system, they will encounter certain features and functionality that may cause some difficulty. If and when this happens, the ERP provider will need to provide technical support. It is important that the prospective ERP solution company demonstrate that it has the technical support staff to handle the needs of the firm.

Channel-Specific Consultants

It may be advisable to consider using a consultant to help guide the selection process. Selecting the right consultant can be a critical decision to make toward the success of the project. It is usually wise to ask a consultant's references how they felt about the work performed. The other companies do not necessarily have to be in the same line of trade as you, but it is important that the consultant understand your business classification (distributor, manufacturer, retailer, etc.), vertical channel (electrical, building materials, food, pharmaceuticals, etc.), and customer base (MRO, raw materials, contractors, etc.). Consultants knowledgeable about your business should be able to ask your firm and the potential solution providers the right questions to find the best solution. An experienced consultant can also listen to the responses to your questions from the software companies to tell you when you should be concerned about an answer. Consultants can also help interpret the answers for you so that you really understand what the answers to your questions mean and what the impact should be on your decision.

The best consultant is particularly knowledgeable about the firm's particular line of trade or vertical industry channel. A considerable amount of time may be saved by using the consultant's knowledge regarding the most appropriate ERP system to begin considering, reducing the research necessary for selecting candidate systems. Industry trade associations or trade publications may also be good sources of information about ERP systems designed for your particular industry.[5]

As a pile-on, there are a growing number of companies that have developed software specifically written to assist in the ERP selection process. A quick search on the Internet will yield a host of applications written to provide assistance from selection, development of a request for proposal (RFP), to the implementation phase. Of course, selection of an ERP system is far too complex to allow a software package to do it for you. These utilities were written only to assist the firm in narrowing the field to a more manageable number from which to choose.

Creating a Test Database and Test Order Type

A database of vendors, products, customers, and the like should be developed for use in the evaluation process. This database should be a subset of the firm's actual products and customers so that it represents a legitimate sample.

Several different classes of orders should be created that represent all of the various combinations of order types that would need to be handled by the ERP system. Included in this should be orders that range from the simple to the highly complex. All possible scenarios should be considered in developing these test orders, including the following:

❍ Items that are purchased in one unit of measure but sold in other units of measure. For example, chain may be purchased in 500-pound drums but sold by the foot, or fittings may be purchased in bags of 100 but sold in any number.

❍ An order that includes items from stock along with items transferred from another company branch location or with several items that have to be purchased from another source.

❍ Special items or made-to-order products.

❍ Customer returns. The return-goods process should include standard off-the-shelf inventory items, items that were transferred from another branch, nonstock items that were ordered from a supplier, and so forth. All possible permutations of return-goods orders should be developed and tested in the new system.

Developing and testing the potential ERP systems with multiple order types is a critical part of the evaluation process. This testing is usually done at the solution provider's site.

Current User Site Visits

A critical element of the evaluation process is to visit other ERP customers that are currently using the system being evaluated. If the customer is in the same line of trade, selling the same kind and volume of products as your company, so much the better. The better this is planned, the more benefits it will yield. The adopting firm should ask for an unedited list of current users from which a few can be chosen for a site visit.

Once the sites to be visited are identified, the delta team should develop a questionnaire that will be completed by the visiting team. The questionnaire should address as many of the critical requirements as possible. The value of a preformulated questionnaire prevents the team from forgetting important questions. General questions that should be considered for inclusion on a site visit questionnaire include

1. Why was this particular ERP system chosen?

2. What other solutions were considered?

3. Why were they not selected?

4. Has the system's performance met or exceeded expectations, or has it not met expectations? (Get a specific answer to any unmet expectations.)

5. Did the ERP solution provider meet expectations during the start-up?

6. What is the quality of the ERP solution provider's technical support?

7. What were the biggest problems that occurred during implementation and how were they resolved?

8. If the firm had any custom modifications written, how well did the modifications function? If problems occurred, how quickly and how well were the problems addressed?

9. Did the ERP software company provide adequate training? How could it have been improved?

There are many other questions that can be asked and the adopting firm should spend a great deal of time developing and refining its list. Expect that the questionnaire will be revised quite a bit after the first site visit, which will result in a better set of questions for the next site visit. (See Exhibit 4.1 for a sample questionnaire.)

Another less tangible, but very important outcome of these visits is the discussions and informal conversations that will occur between the visiting team members and

exhibit 4.1 *Example Site Visit Questionnaire*

Concept2—2002 Vendor Reference Questions

Company

- Name of company, contact, and phone number?
- What is the nature of your business, products, type of industry, sales channels (B2B, B2C)?
- Do you do international sales and shipping?
- What size is your customer base?
- By what means do you receive sales orders (web, phone, email, mail, walk-in, etc)?

General

- How long have you been using the software? What was your former system?
- How many total users and concurrent users?
- What convinced you to choose it?
- What other business systems did you consider?
- Would you choose this vendor and business system again? Why?
- Are you satisfied or disappointed with the system? Specific problems?

Software

- What do you like about the software?
- What don't you like about the software?
- What version are you using?
- Does the software meet or exceed your expectations? Is there any aspect of your business that the software could not handle well? Any software bugs?
- Do you use most of the modules?
- Did you have any modifications done? If so, have there been any problems, and how has it affected your upgrades?
- Is the system (and the platform and operating system) easy to maintain?
- How well do new releases work?
- What is the quality of the documentation?
- Typical system response time, especially during order entry?
- How efficiently does the system handle the order entry and fulfillments/shipping process?
- What related 3rd party software do you use?
- Adequate data access/reporting, flexibility, simplicity, and performance?

System

- Briefly, what is the configuration of your computer environment (network, etc.)?
- How much IT support is required, overall and daily? What is the size of your IT staff?

Implementation

- How long was the implementation process?
- Did you do much re-engineering of the business?
- How well did the implementation process work?
- Did you encounter any problems during implementation, and if so, what was the biggest?
- How was the training? Is the system easy to learn?

Vendor

- What do you like about the vendor? Did they deliver as promised?

Source: *Prelude Systems Inc.*

the people being visited. It is during these offline discussions that a great deal of information will be shared. This might include how well satisfied the current users are with their decision to use the system in question, their satisfaction with the implementation, and how they view the ERP company's performance in the entire conversion process.

Other useful questions are, "If you had it to do over again, would you still choose this system?" "What would you do differently?" The questionnaire should include a page for comments that were made that may be important to the decision process. Another beneficial outcome of these visits is meaningful dialogue with established colleagues that can be contacted later for follow-up or to clarify issues that arise after the initial visit.

Making the Decision

At some point the process must lead to a decision. Assuming that the features and functionality of the proposed ERP systems have been diligently studied, all of the questions asked and answered appropriately, the site visits concluded, and all of the core user requirements satisfied, a final choice should be possible. No system will be perfect, and the firm probably has made certain concessions to some relatively minor deficiencies and is now ready to make the call on which system to select.

If there have been two very close contenders the choice will almost certainly disappoint some of the users—just a few individuals or an entire department. The executive group should make a concerted effort to fully explain why the choice was made and what the rationale was for making the decision. This may not completely diffuse all objections but may minimize any political fallout that might otherwise occur when "buyer's remorse" sets in. The implementation and go-live periods will doubtless carry their own problems, causing second-guessing of the selection team and resistance to continuing with what is viewed as a system preordained to fail rather than one still to be fully implemented. Executive support and involvement could make the difference at this time between a successful adoption and poor performance followed by a need to reinvent the system.

Conclusion

The selection process is one of the most difficult aspects of acquiring a new ERP system, but it is arguably the most important. All of the work that was done to document and understand the critical functions and needs of the organization, examining the alternative solutions in the system demonstrations, conducting exhaustive current user site visits, and the other steps discussed in this chapter will prepare the organization for the next step: implementation.

While the implementation process will be just as demanding as the selection process, it is safe to say that a poorly selected ERP system flawlessly implemented will still be a poor fit after the rigors of implementation are long forgotten. So the message is clear: Take your time, do the work, and choose wisely.

Distribution Retrospective

Mary and her team worked diligently. They queried people within the firm to learn about the critical processes and developed a wish list for new functionality. They especially examined the internal connectivity envisioned in the new corporate strategy. After fully examining the internal issues, the team looked at potential providers. An initial list was developed based on first using a software selection package, then calling companies in similar industries, and finally working with an IT consultant from their channel. The list was then compared in detail with their operations and a "short list" was developed.

The short-list firms were asked to hold meetings with the firm and given a test database from which to demonstrate their software's capability. The meetings were long and arduous as the team had to listen to the same responses to arguments they had been battling inside their firm for months. The list was further pared down from five providers to three based on some discussions of work-around solutions for critical processes that made the team uncomfortable with some providers' ability to fit in their environment. The short-list candidates were asked to provide references and the IT consultant was asked to find others that were using the same systems.

The team then developed a questionnaire to use on site visits to firms that agreed to discuss the candidate systems. After the visits, the questionnaires were evaluated, and follow-up with some of the references was conducted by phone to clarify points before final reports were written on each. The team then submitted the reports and their recommendations to the steering committee.

The steering committee noted that two systems had been close contenders and asked some pointed questions as to why one had been chosen over the other. The questions were answered, but one committee member (the VP of Sales) did not agree and shared his sentiments with others in the firm and with the runner-up ERP provider. The ERP provider saw a potential opportunity to overturn the team's

> recommendation and asked to be allowed to present its case to the steering committee. The other two short-listed firms followed suit and demanded the same. Mary's process was out of control, but events were out of her hands as the VP of Sales was insisting on the hearings. As Mary expected, the meetings only produced more arguments, and the CEO decided that the original decision should stand.
>
> Mary left the final decision meeting dejected and tired. She had won, in a manner of speaking, but she knew the confusion at the end would cause major implementation difficulties as rumors of the decision flew throughout the company. Mary would have to face a difficult implementation with no guarantee of success.

Issues to Consider

1. How should the steering committee interact with the delta team?

2. How should the delta team collect information from users?

3. What should the delta team use for initial selection criteria?

4. What are the benefits of site visits to current users of candidate systems?

Case Study: ERP Selection

Note to the reader: The following case is based on an actual distributor. The name and location of the firm has been changed for confidentiality reasons.

Bob Parker was an IT jack-of-all-trades. After years of travel as a salesperson for Industrial Products Inc. (III), a mid-sized fastener distributor, he came to the conclusion in 1995 that he'd had enough. When the company started investigating upgrading its information technology that year, he jumped at the chance to lead the project. When Bob had graduated with a degree in MIS (management information systems), he had sworn he would never return to IT. He liked dealing with people and found programming to be a tedious, time-consuming task. He did not like the isolation and found other programmers to be too introverted for his taste.

He had noticed recently, however, a shift in IT priorities away from programmers, which he now considered to be primarily highly skilled technicians, to business process owners in IT design. The shift was driven, he believed, by supply chain management and its fusion with new e-commerce technologies, and would only grow in complexity as IT systems became more sophisticated. There was a need for what he had heard called "domain experts," individuals with a working knowledge of programming and IT capabilities, but whose greatest strength was their understanding of business processes. With his background in sales and operations and a degree in MIS, Bob thought he fit the profile exactly. Bob joined the firm in 1982 as an inside salesperson straight out of college, moved to outside sales, became the store manager for III's counter sales in the home office (Detroit), and had eventually become the firm's first general manager.

A few investors, two of which were on the management team—Nancy Thompson, CEO, and Jack Foster, CFO—privately owned the company. III was being pummeled with new SCM programs like Integrated Supply and quality programs like ISO 9000. ISO 9000 was a European-driven program where participating firms were required to document their processes in detail and demonstrate that those processes were consistent (ISO documentation).[6] Many argued that a consistently poor-performing process was just as worthless as a well-designed but inconsistent process. One executive at a pipe/valve/fitting company told Bob that under ISO 9000 you could make a chocolate valve as long as you were consistent about it and documented the process. Bob understood the frustration others felt but, as a former programmer, he knew nothing could be programmed without consistency. He thought ISO 9000 had a place in his firm's approach to better IT systems.

III's largest customers agreed. The big automakers were experiencing considerable pressure from critics to become ISO certified or at least adopt some sort of certification process of their own.[7] Because the certification process for ISO was European-driven, and although the Big Three (Ford, GM, and Chrysler) did not agree with the ISO standards at the time, they did launch their own program called QS 9000, which was designed specifically for the automotive industry.[8] III was faced with a need to address ISO 9000 for some customers and QS 9000 for the automotive ones. They would have to begin a detailed process-mapping activity to meet each set of standards.

Meanwhile, the supply chain management movement was picking up steam. Integrated Supply (I/S), an SCM program where the supplier managed its inventory and complementary products at the customer's site, was becoming very popular.[9] The I/S movement required considerable logistical skill on the distributor's part since it had to manage its inventory in multiple customer locations and coordinate the same for other suppliers also.

In addition, the I/S movement was taking on serious IT characteristics, too. The automakers first tried to tie their suppliers to them through reverse auctions (where all quotes came through a site that ultimately resulted in auctioning off a business category) that were delivered through sites the suppliers were expected to connect to in one fashion or another.[10] The early reverse auctions met with considerable supplier resistance and also had the potential to interfere with SCM programs like Integrated Supply. The experience, however, led to an understanding of how to use the Internet in business transactions and set up IT infrastructure to introduce tools to connect suppliers and further automate vendor managed inventory (VMI) and I/S relationships through online ordering and inventory visibility.

Where these systems would lead or what functionality they would require, no one could say for sure. One thing was clear, however: If III did not have some capability to connect to these customer-driven initiatives, they would soon be unable to compete. Their large customers were not making participation optional; you got on board or you were left out. The quality programs (ISO 9001 and QS 9000), SCM programs (VMI and I/S), and IT initiatives were coming together to create a complex, integrated, information-based environment where the technologically challenged would not be able to play.

III's management was quite clear: They would not be an also-ran with these big customers. They had no intention of blindly jumping into disastrous IT investments as so many of their competitors had. They would instead meet the demands of customers as conservatively as possible. The problem was that the most conservative approaches all pointed to the inability of the legacy system to handle these new customer initiatives.

So Bob had his work cut out for him. He had to transition the firm into information connectivity, or ERP as it was popularly known. He had to determine what functionality the firm needed, match it to a candidate list of systems, and ultimately recommend a course of action. The firm had avoided ERP adoption for a long time, and many in the firm patted themselves on the back for not having suffered the same fate as many competitors and suppliers that had adopted ERP and suffered the well-publicized difficulties.

Bob knew that these failures had been driven by the combination of ERP systems that did not match distribution processes well and firms that did not commit to thoroughly understanding their own processes before trying to transition them to ERP. ERP providers had made great strides since the 1990s and the horror stories were no longer so common. Bob also felt that a firm that made a concerted effort at understanding itself through process mapping and a thorough program of matching those processes to ERP systems would be more likely to have a successful adoption.

Bob's first task was to meet with the steering committee. The steering committee was composed of Nancy, Jack, David Brown (the company's VP of Sales), Steve Clark (VP of Operations), and Bob himself. The discussion first revolved around the make-up of the selection team that Bob would lead. Bob wanted two people from each functional area: one top performer and one new employee. Bob felt the top performers would help ensure that critical, customer-supporting processes were well represented. He wanted the new employees for two reasons. First, he wanted someone who did not have sufficient knowledge about the firm's processes to find work-arounds for information failures. He felt this would ensure the system was able to support average employees. The second reason to choose new employees was to include people who would accept the new system more readily since they might not be tied to legacy processes. He knew debates would break out within the group with the new employees challenging the experienced ones over why the new technology would not work under varying conditions. He saw this as a healthy process that would force the experienced people to consider new ideas or further define processes that the new system could not support so that modifications or alternative systems would be considered before adoption.

Bob felt the composition of the selection team was critical to the process's success. He immediately met resistance, however, when David (VP of Sales) asked incredulously how the firm could spare one of its best salespeople for the task. Steve also protested pulling one of *his* best people off. He pointed out that his top people were not only important for their direct responsibilities but for training and leadership with others. Nancy listened with her head bowed. Jack decided not to comment about losing anyone in finance since he could see the pressure Bob was under and felt he should support whatever decision Nancy made. After some thought, Nancy asked Bob how he felt about going forward without the best, and Bob replied he did not want the job unless he had full support. This was his first request, and if it was not going to be supported, he feared the steering committee was not prepared for the necessary commitment to get the job done.

Bob did not like compromising before he even got started, but deep down he agreed that taking a top salesperson out of the field was too damaging to the firm. He said he would work around the sales force's schedule. He would have to have operations' and other functional departments' support, however. Nancy said he would get it and Jack nodded his agreement. Steve said nothing but did not look happy.

Nancy then said that all steering committee discussions were to be kept confidential. The steering committee would speak in unison and in support of the selection committee at all times. Everyone agreed. Bob glanced at Steve and wondered whether he would keep his word. He worried that the first thread that would unravel his project had been pulled.

Nancy next instructed Bob to develop a budget and timeline for the selection process. The steering committee would meet every two weeks until a provider was selected, after which it would coordinate with the ERP provider on an implementation plan. Bob sensed the budget and timeline could turn stressful if things did not proceed as planned, especially since he may have created an adversary on the steering committee in Steve. As Bob stood up, everyone wished him luck except Steve, who was preoccupied with his personal digital assistant. Bob sensed Steve did not want to make eye contact.

Bob decided to start by process-mapping and exploring the strategic intent behind the existing processes. He also planned to include process maps on the customers' new IT initiatives. The new customer connectivity processes were not necessarily required at present, but some would be soon. Some guesswork about what would be required was involved, and Bob's team would have to project what functionality would be needed. Bob also asked the steering committee to provide his group with a vision statement for the new system that would describe what the system was to achieve and what the firm would look like after the transition.

Suddenly, Bob realized that the process-mapping exercise was the beginning of the type of process documentation that ISO 9001 and QS 9000 required. He began to believe that maybe he should recommend certification first since customers would likely come to require it in the very near future. He felt the documentation would make the ERP selection and implementation process much easier and would also give customers time to identify their requirements. On the other hand, he dreaded going back and revising his timeline and suggesting such ambitious programs before completing his initial charge. What to do?

Case Challenges

1. How do the market forces affect III's need for a connected IT system? Is the sense of urgency to change justified?

2. What do you think of the steering committee's commitment to the project? Will Bob get the support he needs? Was it a mistake to back down on his request for a top salesperson on the team?

3. Is Bob's contemplating putting back the timeline to carry out certification a good idea? What will be the likely reaction of the steering committee?

References

1. Kyung-Kwon, Hong and Young-Gul, Kim, "The Critical Success Factors for ERP Implementation: An Organizational Fit Perspective, *Information & Management* 40, no. 1 (October 2002): 25–40

2. F. Barry Lawrence, Daniel F. Jennings, and Brian E. Reynolds, *e-Distribution* (Mason, OH: South-Western Publishing, 2003).

3. Robert Damelio, *The Basics of Process Mapping* (Shelton, CT: Productivity Inc., 1996).

4. International Standards Organization (ISO), Standards Catalogue, http://www.iso.ch/iso/en/CatalogueList Page.CatalogueList (accessed December 15, 2002).

5. Google Directory: http://directory.google.com/Top/Business/Transportation_and_Logistics/ (accessed October 10, 2003).

6. International Standards Organization (ISO), Standards Catalogue, http://www.iso.ch/iso/en/CatalogueList Page.CatalogueList (accessed December 15, 2002).

7. American Society for Quality, http://qs9000.asq.org/ (accessed December 15, 2002).

8. Rudolf Czekalla, *QS-9000 Documentation Development Tool for Quality Systems for Automotive-Parts Manufacturers,* (R C & Associates, Canada, 1999, http://rcglobal.com).

9. F. Barry Lawrence and Anoop Varma, "Integrated Supply: Supply Chain Management in Materials Management and Procurement," *Production & Inventory Management Journal* 40, no. 2 (1999), 1–5.

10. Covisint, Automotive Industry Marketplace, http://www.covisint.com/.

5

ERP Implementation

Distribution Perspective

Brian Roberts was the CEO of a mid-sized (50 million) food equipment distribution firm, Custom Food Products Inc. (CFPI). The firm supplied ovens, silverware, plates, and virtually anything else a restaurant or hotel would need to set up operations other than the food or furniture. Brian had commissioned a selection committee to find a new ERP system for the firm last year and they had now completed their work and were ready to present their choice. The company had been using another ERP system that was unable to connect to the quoting system used by the sales force. The quoting system had been specially developed for the food equipment distribution industry and was highly effective. The inability to connect the two systems, however, was causing considerable problems for CFPI.

CFPI's sales force would work with large restaurant chains and hotels in first building out their facility and then supplying them with tableware and other necessities after the restaurant opened. The initial installation was extremely important since it was a large transaction with many opportunities to make mistakes on the bid. Winning the quote was doubly important since failure to win cost CFPI not only the sale but possibly all follow-up business in daily necessities (plates or silverware) and in servicing the ovens and other equipment the customer installed as well.

The ERP system contained information that was crucial to the quoting process. Information on inventory status and customer pricing was also maintained in the ERP system. To access this information, a salesperson had to return to the office with notes from the customer and make out the quote at a desk with simultaneous access to the ERP and quoting systems. The process involved a lot of keying and rekeying, which led to errors in both systems. The quoting system sometimes had incorrect pricing entered into it or an incorrect quote (one that left out freight, for instance) that would not be corrected since invoicing occurred in the ERP system. Future salespeople under similar conditions would use these stored quotes, and the former mistakes would be inherited in future quotes.

The selected ERP system had the capability to connect with the quoting system. The problem going forward was to break the sales force of bad habits like working offline and to implement a connection that could be accessed wherever the salesperson happened to be. The implementation of this new system would be difficult from an operations perspective, but the company had implemented ERP before and was better prepared this time as far as internal operations were concerned. The interface to the sales force was new, however. Salespeople had been spared much of the pain of ERP implementation before since the system could not connect to their quoting system. The salesperson would merely pull the needed information from the ERP system and proceed as always with the quoting system. A staffperson at CFPI carried out entering the results from quoting into the ERP system.

Now the salesperson's work would interact with the system in real time. The connection meant nobody would be rereading and interpreting what the salesperson had done. The direct connection meant the salesperson had to know how to work with both systems and guarantee the input was accurate. Brian had worked with the rest of his company in ERP implementation and still considered it to be one of the most difficult tasks imaginable. Including the sales force was going to produce new challenges.

Introduction

Once the decision has been made and an ERP solution has been selected, it may seem that the most difficult stage of the process has been completed. In reality, the most critical and challenging stage is only just beginning. Implementing an ERP system will try the heart and soul of any organization, but it offers the potential to take the firm to new levels of information management. During the 1990s, many found that there were three aspects to virtually every ERP system implementation: first, it was more difficult than expected; second, it typically cost more than originally anticipated; and last, it took longer than envisioned.

A major problem with the three aspects was that they varied from firm to firm, making it difficult to estimate the cost at one particular company. Factors that led to the implementation being more difficult than anticipated included

O Critical processes that were more difficult to transition to the ERP system at one firm than at another (see the Distribution Retrospective for an example involving quoting systems).

O Employees at one firm might be better able to handle new technology than at another firm due to

   O *Higher-salaried workers.*

   O *An industry with high-technology products that have already necessitated training and other resources to be put in place.*

   O *A less change-resistant culture.*

O Fewer financial resources.

O Low-level IT infrastructure within the firm and with customers and suppliers.

ERP implementation could, for all of the foregoing reasons and more, cost more or take longer than originally anticipated as well. Recognizing that some or all three of these outcomes may occur will help minimize the impact when they do. Most of the pain associated with the installation of an ERP system is experienced because the new ERP system does not change just departments or divisions—it changes the entire organization.

Two of the principal reasons for ERP implementation breakdown are failure to diligently select the right system for the company (discussed in Chapter 4) and a poorly designed and executed implementation process. Inadequate and poorly thought out implementation is one of the most frequently cited reasons for ERP disasters.[1] While implementation is a critical step in the process, this stage has frequently been blamed for problems that really originated elsewhere. Obviously, if a poor selection is made, it will be virtually impossible for the net outcome to be positive, so the selection process is clearly the first critical step. Implementation is next and must be well thought through and thoroughly planned. Metrics for success and milestones for the implementation must be developed, and execution must be driven from the top down with an understanding that while things may not always go as planned, the firm must diligently stay the course.

Planning the implementation process should be given as much or more critical thinking than the system selection process. Since the ERP system will affect all functional areas of the firm, a well-planned implementation process will help to alleviate organizational disruption and user anxiety, but it cannot completely eliminate them. Management must anticipate the stress the transition will cause and alternate between the roles of a strict disciplinarian (for moving the project forward) and a compassionate listener (for employees struggling with the new methodology).

The attention of the delta team will now shift from the rigors of studying all of the potential ERP systems and making a selection to now implementing the plan to put the new system to work. After working through all of the steps involved in selecting the new system, the delta team is now more knowledgeable about its capabilities and challenges than anyone else in the organization. Their role will increase in importance as the implementation proceeds.

The selection team has developed a broad and deep level of knowledge regarding the distributor's business processes as well as in-depth understanding of the selected ERP system. It now knows more about the organization than any other group in the firm. Keeping this team functioning at its highest level would enable the company to tap into its expertise as problems with the new system arise.

A different, more subtle problem can arise with the veteran delta team. When team members do finally return to their regular jobs after having spent some heady times on the ERP project, they may begin to feel that they have outgrown their old jobs and begin looking for a challenge to replace the rush they felt while on the project. Organizations should be aware of this potential reaction and plan what to do if it occurs.

Another threat comes from consulting firms, or the ERP provider itself, poaching delta team members. A member of the selection team understands ERP, firm processes, the reasons for ERP selection, and the challenges faced in selection and implementation as well as their potential solutions. The selection/implementation team, especially those who served on both, are quite a valuable resource. They have developed new skills, no different from going back to school for an advanced degree or certification, except that their expertise is difficult to acquire in school. If the firm does not recognize and appropriately reward the team members, someone else undoubtedly will.

Many firms make their selection and work partially through the implementation only to be left with one or two individuals from the original team. The remaining ones are likely high-ranking members of the management team that could not better their situation outside of the firm. Although still valuable, the remaining team members may not have the hands-on technical expertise of a mid-level player. The company is left with no technically skilled members of the team and will be forced to go outside the firm and hire them at a higher cost than the people they lost. In many cases, the selection/implementation team will go to work for consulting firms and then have to be rehired by their original employer to solve the problems created by their exit—at a premium cost. One firm lost a key member of its team and was forced to rehire him at consulting rates that ran nearly a half-million dollars a year, far more than his original salary. It had never occurred to the firm that he might be worth a great deal more after the implementation. In fact, the implementation had caused so much stress in the firm that many were happy to see him go since they blamed the selection team for every misfortune that could be linked to the new system. Soon all members of the selection team left, and only then could the firm see its mistake: It had a new system and no clue as to how to properly use it.

Team Building and Deploying

The ERP solution provider will usually provide a recommended training plan for new users. Frequently, the ERP company will offer training at its location in a train-the-trainer type of instruction so that the students will then be able to go back to their organization and train the rest of the firm's personnel who will be using the new system. The train-the-trainer method can be very effective if the subsequent user-training plan is well thought out.

Problems arise, however, when the trainers are not effective teachers or their training is not sufficient. The trainers are frequently also responsible for other duties and can be hard to reach when problems occur. In addition, the trainer may not have any technical expertise. While being more of a process expert than an IT specialist is a good thing for training fellow non-IT types, it can be a problem when the trainers are the only ones others can access for more technical problems. A lack of coordination between the trainers and the IT specialists at the firm or the ERP provider can lead to excessive dependence on the trainers beyond their skill level.

The timing of the training is critical. Train too early and people may forget most of what they learned; train too late and the organization may not be ready when it comes time to start using the new system. The training schedule must be built around the implementation schedule—not what is most convenient for the firm's employees. This constraint can be especially difficult when training the sales force. Input from the sales force can make or break an ERP implementation and salespeople are generally the most difficult cluster to pull in for training.

The success of the early stages of the ERP adoption process will, to a large degree, depend on the quality of the training the users receive. The firm must develop job function–specific user manuals, written procedures, and flowcharts to support training and ongoing operations. The firm should use departmental champions to help plan and facilitate training. Trainers should be selected based on their communication skills and knowledge of the new system. Subject-matter experts should play a role in assisting the trainer. These subject-matter experts will play a critical role in bridging the gap between IT understanding and the real world.

Firms with multiple branch locations should develop a train-the-trainer plan that comprehensively covers functional and location issues. Each location in all likelihood will have at least one individual that management has recognized as a high-potential candidate that can take on these types of roles. It could be an inside salesperson, customer service representative, or someone with administrative responsibilities. These field trainers should begin indoctrination to the new system well in advance of the actual go-live date. If, during the selection stage, the company has identified a current user with multiple locations, the branch trainers should have the opportunity to meet with the current user trainers and learn from their experiences.

For those firms with only one location, trainers should be identified from each functional department within the company. These people will serve as an invaluable resource for their departmental co-workers when the system is turned on. Functional experts should match the system and the firm's structure in the same fashion as envisioned during the strategy/structure match planning from the system selection phase (see Chapter 4). There should experts in finance, operations, purchasing/planning, production, transportation, sales, marketing, and other key departments.

Developing a Project Management Process

At the outset of the implementation planning process, the organization should seriously consider using project management procedures. Many software packages have been developed to support project planning and scheduling. Regardless of size, the implementation of an ERP system will affect virtually every functional area of the firm. Due to the complex nature the implementation process, it is critical to map and document each step of the plan.

The plan begins with the goals and milestones for the entire project. Goals include such things as planned implementation dates, budgetary objectives, cost savings or increased sales to be achieved by system activation, and so on. The milestones are the major markers that indicate to what degree the project has been completed. Milestones are critical for resource planning. Cost planning for human resources is simply good management of the firm's financial resources, as some—consultants, programmers, and ERP specialists—are contracted out at considerable cost.

Internal human resources are, in many cases, even more valuable. Since they are already charged to the firm, internal experts often have their time wasted by ineffective planning. Failure to plan the use of internal resources correctly will result in escalating project costs that are hidden from view. Salespeople who have to spend more time struggling with the new system than working with customers may not hit the bottom line in the same fashion as an external consultant, but the loss of their time will have considerable impact on firm profitability. The same can be said for operations specialists, especially those skilled enough to be used on an ERP implementation. Frustration is the result of poor planning as important human resources are prevented from meeting corporate and personal goals. If the process continues to suffer from poor planning, the firm will experience more than just the loss of time; it could lose valuable people as well.

There are a number of robust project management software packages but they are no substitute for a skilled manager who will use the tool to its greatest effect. Project management tools will keep schedules, align resources, calculate critical timelines, and assist the manager in controlling what must occur, when, and with what supporting resources. Beyond the initial project scheduling, however, is the art of knowing when to adjust schedules, what resources can be moved to reduce timelines or overcome bottlenecks, how resources can be used to their greatest effect, how to lead team members, and what the probabilities are that certain tasks will be completed within the planned horizon.

Most of the project management software packages will include features such as Gantt charts and critical path schedules (see Figure 5.1) that will document the status of the overall project and all of the subtasks associated with each of the major steps. Also included in most is the ability to allocate specific resources to the project. These resources will include, but are not exclusive to, individuals in the company and

fig. 5.1   **A Gantt Chart**

Project steps:	Qtr 1			Qtr 2			Qtr 3			Qtr 4		
	Jan	Feb	Mar	Apr	May	Jun	Jul	Aug	Sep	Oct	Nov	Dec
Explore market need												
Develop concept for product												
Begin development cycle												
Develop GUI												
User interface test evaluation												
Alpha version release												
Quality assurance testing phase 1												
Fix outstanding problems from alpha												
Beta version release												
Quality assurance testing phase 2												
Fix outstanding problems from beta												
Design box and CD labels												
Begin advance advertising campaign												
FCS preparation												
Final quality assurance testing												
FCS release												
Production and packaging												

Source: Dimays Project Charter, Dimays Software, 2002

the time they will need to devote to the process. The software should also include the ability to assign the cost of human resources time and other financial requirements such as required training and the facilities and equipment to conduct in-house training. Costs associated with external consultants should also be capturable.

The use of a project management software package will also enable the delta team to provide the executive management group with regular reports on the status of the project. This capability is useful since the overall progress of the project may experience delays due to the inability, or unwillingness, of different functional departments to provide necessary information or assistance. If this occurs, it may be necessary for the executive group to exert influence or provide resources to enable cooperation.

As the implementation plan is developed, the team must establish reasonable timelines and expectations. A schedule that is too aggressive may look good on paper, but when implementation milestones begin to slip the overall plan will suffer. Failure to adhere to the plan will feed fears that the system was a bad decision. In addition to the need for early wins, the system implementation should be as smooth and seamless as possible to minimize stress on the organization and convince users that the selection was a good one. Establishing realistic expectations is key to this objective since unrealistic, unmet ones contribute to the fear of failure.

It is at this stage that some of the other current users visited during the selection process can be helpful. The delta team should contact as many of the current users of the selected ERP system to ask as many questions about their implementation experience as possible. If industry consultants were used in the selection process, they may also be a useful source of guidance concerning implementation plan development. Care should be exercised when involving consultants in the implementation process, however. Some consultants are very experienced at selection but less knowledgeable about implementation.

Data Scrubbing

Data integrity is one of the most significant challenges facing the successful implementation of a new ERP system. Data integrity refers to the need for any data introduced into the system to be accurate. Data incorrectly gathered means the system does not, in effect, know what's going on, a disastrous development for an information system. Data integrity problems are introduced to the ERP system by poorly designed processes (keying, rekeying, and offline activities in general). Most legacy systems have been in place for many years and many different people who may no longer be with the company have input data into the system.

The new system must have clean data to start with or it will be handicapped from the moment it goes live. If the data integrity problems are significant enough, they can destroy any hope of better performance from the new system since the legacy system probably had processes, coded and human, that controlled for data integrity problems to whatever degree possible. These processes will likely not be in place for the new system. The proper approach to data integrity problems does not involve design processes to get around them, but instead processes toprevent their occurrence in the first place.

fig. 5.2   **The Need for Data Scrubbing**

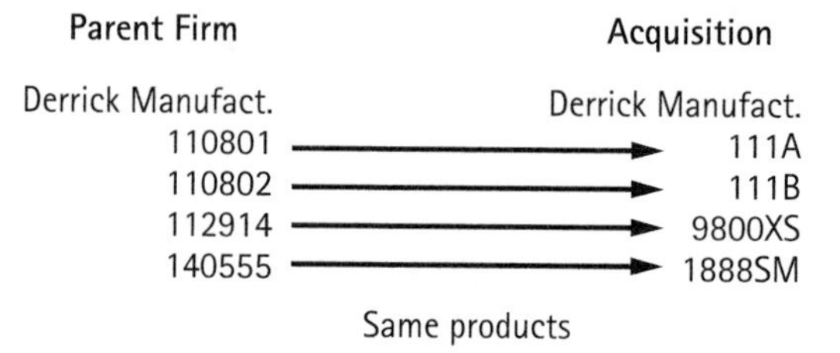

Parent Firm	Acquisition
Derrick Manufact.	Derrick Manufact.
110801 ⟶	111A
110802 ⟶	111B
112914 ⟶	9800XS
140555 ⟶	1888SM

Same products

ERP providers encourage users to stick to the system processes rather than building their own for precisely this reason. Data integrity comes from poorly designed processes whether incorrectly coded as modifications to the system or from human interfaces that have not been as well designed as those in the ERP system. Human interfaces are highly irregular and will introduce error in irregular and elusive patterns. A coded (automated) process that creates error will do so in an identifiable pattern but will input error at an alarming rate.

Before the new processes are activated, however, the data in the legacy system must be migrated over to the new system. Product descriptions from the legacy system, for instance, are usually inconsistent and will require a considerable amount of work to standardize. The product numbering method in the legacy system may differ from that planned for the new ERP system or there may already be data issues in the legacy system that will cause unpredictable problems when taken into the new ERP system. Figure 5.2 shows an example where an acquired operation is running on one ERP system and the new owner is on another. The numbering of products from the same manufacturer has different SKUs and data-scrubbing will have to be performed to match the acquired firm's products to the parent firm.

One firm was transitioning its operations from multiple legacy systems at differing sites into a single new ERP system for the entire firm. The transition was proceeding one system at a time, and each time a legacy system's data was introduced into the new ERP system the firm went through a data-scrubbing process. The rest of the firm's activities were put on hold since the data in the remaining legacy systems was difficult to access, IT specialists were stretched thin with the data-scrubbing process, and the information that could be accessed from the legacy systems was difficult to interpret and contained data integrity problems. The data-scrubbing process effectively shut down the rest of the firm's initiatives.

Implementing Modification Change Management Process

In the selection process considerable attention is paid to how well the native capability of the ERP system meets the distribution company's operational requirements. Once the ERP system is chosen, the gaps between the system's capability and the requirements of the users must be identified and processes put in place to deal with them. As the selection process unfolded, the chosen ERP system's shortcomings, relative to the requirements of the users, should have been well documented. This documentation should include a distinction between those shortcomings, or gaps, that are mission-critical functionality and those that are "nice to have." Mission-critical functionality includes those capabilities without which the firm could not meet some key operating requirements.

Mission-critical gaps must be closed. There are different methods frequently used to overcome gaps. The different approaches include the following:

1. One method is to study the process in question and determine whether the business process can be redesigned so that the standard functionality of the proposed system can be used. The objective in this approach is to meet the business needs of the users but change the way the work gets done so that no software modification is required. This approach is preferable because it requires no costly modification of the software. Another benefit of using the standard functionality is that time-consuming modification testing, which can delay the process, is not required. A third benefit is that as new revisions to the software are introduced, expensive modification recoding is not required, which enables the firm to take advantage of software updates without the added cost of modification coding. This alternative is obviously the most desirable, but should not be done at the expense of any capability that meets specific customer needs or in any way degrades the firm's ability to maintain some competitive advantage.

2. The second method is to avoid the easy trap of defining software modifications so that the new system works like the old one. This is easy to do because the old process was well understood by the users and would represent the least amount of change necessary. The firm should not pay to replicate poor business processes simply because they were well understood. In many cases, the new system was selected because its processes were best practice, and to modify to what the users feel most comfortable with would be to lose much of the envisioned value of the new system. If the new ERP system provides for 75 to 85% of the functionality required for any given process, then serious consideration should be given to adopting the new process.

3. The third method is to modify the system either through the use of bolt-ons that can carry out the mission-critical processes and interface with the new ERP system or by coding in modifications. Modifications have advantages and disadvantages. The disadvantages have been described earlier and include difficulty when new system revisions (upgrades) are introduced and potential problems introduced by poorly designed and tested programs. The principal advantage is significant, however. The modification, if properly designed and coded, will likely fit exactly with the company's needs and will not include many unnecessary processes that do not fit (as may be the case with a bolt-on).

Once the desired modifications have been identified and documented, the list needs to be scrutinized to ensure it represents all required modifications. There is a clear and important distinction between desired and required. The firm's executive group should be the final arbiter in determining all approved software modifications. The delta team should be held responsible for presenting the proposed modifications, or "mods," to the executive team for approval. Typically, each mod will be requested by one of the functional areas of the distribution firm. The requesting department should be required to defend the need for software mods to the executive team. The requesting department should be able to make a strong enough case to the executive group in order to justify the need for changes to the standard ERP software offering.

Conducting a Modification Testing and Approval Methodology

The firm needs a methodology for testing and approval of the software coding change. The acceptance process will likely become a part of the contract between the distributor and the ERP solution provider. The contract language should list each modification as subject to specific approval and acceptance criteria. Modifications frequently interfere with system performance or other processes that access the same resources (data, analysis programs). As such, the modifications may violate agreements between the ERP provider and the adopting firm. The ERP provider may not agree to support a system that has had damaging modifications added to it without proper approval.

Modification final acceptance will probably not occur on the date the system goes live. It is more likely that some time period will be specified after which acceptance will be deemed to have occurred if any problems with the mods have not been documented in writing and the ERP provider notified of the nonconformance.

Pretesting the System

A good method for improving the chances for smooth system activation would be to conduct a series of mock go-live sessions. These should be planned to replicate the actual operating environment, including real orders being entered, stock transfers from branches, purchase orders issued to suppliers, receiving of incoming orders, and the receivables and payables functions. Several of these mock go-lives should be performed so that any unexpected outcomes can be identified and addressed in a low-risk environment. The solution provider should be actively involved in this process so that it documents any problem that appears to be a software issue. This is also a good way to further refine the work process instructions that the distributor has developed for the new operating environment.

Pretesting the system should also include the development of required system-generated reports. Most firms have developed over many years highly specialized reports that provide critical information to the users. A thorough analysis of the users' current reports should be conducted to first eliminate the need to replicate unused reports and also to clearly define the information that the users really need. Most ERP systems have a number of standard reports available and these should be studied first to determine if they provide sufficient decision-making information. If the standard reports are not adequate then custom reports may need to be developed.

Some of the reports are ad hoc, or generated as needed, and some are reports that need to be produced at routine intervals. The process of reviewing all reports to determine which are needed and which are redundant or no longer relevant is important since this is a common waste of IT resources. Reports get requested and the system routinely generates them for users who may have stopped using them or decided they are no longer useful but did not take action to eliminate them from the system. Introducing such reports into the new system is a waste of IT resources. Any reports that the firm requires the ERP provider to introduce should be subject to the same scrutiny as the functional modifications.

One valuable outcome of the mock go-lives would be the test results of modifications to the software. These tests should provide evidence that the mods are functioning as intended. It is far better to find out in a test environment that a modification is not functioning as intended rather than find out in the heat of battle on the actual go-live date.

Activating ERP Processes

There are several important decisions to be made for the actual start-up of the new system. One choice is to make a complete cutover, which is establishing a date at which the old system will be turned off and the new system turned on. Another potential method would be to run the old system in parallel while bringing the new system online. Arguments can be made as to why one method is preferable over the other. A cutover offers a clean break from the old system to the new and essentially forces the users to adopt the new system because it is the only way to conduct business. Running the old system in parallel with the new one offers an increased sense of security because the users have a fallback solution if the new system causes too many problems.

Another option, for firms with multiple locations, is to bring one or more branches up at a time on the new system. This phase-in approach helps to isolate the disruption and reduce its scale so that when the inevitable problems are encountered they may be more manageable. Dealing with the problems at one or two branches is much easier than if the problems were spread throughout the entire enterprise. Encountering and dealing with start-up problems with a small number of locations usually means that the start-up at the next set of branches will be a little smoother because those problems will have been addressed at the first start-up branches and solutions will likely already be in place.

Establishing the War Room

In large, multilocation firms the establishment of a place where all of the delta team members can be at the time of the go-live date should be considered. This location, called the "war room" by some firms, should be set up so that each delta team member has a computer terminal or laptop (for problem solving or e-mail) and a cellular telephone so that any employee can easily reach a member of the team for assistance and information about the new system. The reason for keeping the selection/implementation team all in one place is to increase the possibility that one or more of the specialists can answer the user's question since each will likely have developed an area of expertise that will not be common to all. Putting the team in a single location is also helpful since the entire team will be exposed to problems the users encounter and can detect the difference between problems that constitute individual events and ones that are symptomatic of a more widespread problem.

In one example, a firm went live with a new ERP system and while most things seemed to be going well, the warehouse had an issue. The warehouse started getting the packing slips that were printed by the new system and found that the font size on the packing slip was too small to be easily read in normal warehouse light. The delta team received so many calls from branches that were experiencing the same problem that something had to be done right away. The fix was relatively simple: They increased the font size of the packing slip print process. This is a fairly benign example of the benefit of having the war room in place, but if there had not been one place for all of the user problems to be focused on, it may have taken quite a bit longer for the extent of the problem to be identified and corrected.

System Acceptance and Go-Live

At some point in time the new system will be turned on. Regardless of the method used in making the conversion, whether it is a complete cutover or a phased-in process, the organization should prepare itself for an unprecedented level of organizational turmoil. The best most organizations can hope for is minimal pain with little or no evidence visible to their customers. Recognizing that all of the functional areas of the company will be affected, the firm should determine which parts of the business are most critical and prepare for the various scenarios that may unfold.

Many firms rightly believe that anything that negatively affects the customer should be a major part of this process. The inability to ship product to the customer will generally get the most attention, followed by the ability to produce an invoice. Some firms will buy inventory ahead of the go-live date that may put them into an overstock situation for a short time specifically to cover the inability of the new system to replenish inventory in a timely fashion.

The sales department plays a critical role in the period immediately following the go-live date. Since it is closest to the customer, a process for collecting its feedback and quickly resolving customer problems must be in place. The sales force should be diligent in determining the impact of the new system on customers and be proactive in helping its operations and IT divisions find solutions that will protect the customer.

Conclusion

Implementation represents a critical major step in ERP adoption. This critical step is an exciting time and one that is fraught with peril and uncertainty. As in the selection process, the pain of implementation can be minimized with careful planning, foresight, and disciplined execution. Top management should expect there to be considerable disruption in the day-to-day routine of the company. The length of time for implementation is always longer than anyone expects, and haste will be rewarded with an increased chance of failure. Patience, vigilance, and unwavering support are required of top management to ensure that the pain is minimized and users have confidence that the newly implemented ERP system will improve their productivity, ease their workload, and increase customer satisfaction.

Distribution Retrospective

The new ERP system was an improvement since it allowed for interaction with the quoting system. The new implementation would require a well-designed implementation with special attention paid to the integration of the sales force. Brian decided that the sales force had to be trained early on and taken through a couple of mock go-lives. The processes surrounding the quoting system interface with the ERP system would have to be well planned and the sales force taken through it in a safe environment.

Brian directed the implementation team to design the process to be as seamless and automated as possible. He did not want to introduce the old way of doing things into the new interface. He especially wanted to make sure the new process did not take on any of the old process's flaws (keying and rekeying, data integrity problems). The implementation team was able to focus its attention on the sales force but it were dealing with an unusual situation in one respect: the addition of a bolt-on.

The team set to work training and preparing the sales force, and the sales force was instructed to look for any problems that would lead to customer disruptions. The team and the sales force would also have to deal with the data integrity problems in both systems so as to avoid introducing error into the new system. Brian was more comfortable than he had been with the last implementation but was concerned since this one got so close to the customer. The process would have to be handled carefully and thoroughly.

Issues to Consider

1. After selection, what role, if any, should the delta team play?

2. How should implementation be managed?

3. What are data integrity and data scrubbing and why are they important to the implementation process?

4. What is meant by the term *mission-critical functionality*?

Case Study: ERP Implementation

The following case study is based on a PeopleSoft implementation. The firm described and actions taken are real, but names have been changed for confidentiality.

Baron is a leading North American producer of electrical products. Formed in the 1950s, Baron manufactures protective equipment for sensitive controls and components for computers, test equipment, and industrial control equipment. Baron sells to North American electrical markets through a distributor network to original equipment manufacturers (OEMs) as well as to construction, plant maintenance, and repair industries.

Baron sales exceed $500 million annually. Baron believes it has the best design and manufacturing capabilities in the industry, capable of making anything from standard to modified to tailor-made products. The firm is ISO 9001 certified, the first North American manufacturer of its kind to achieve this certification. The firm's brand name is one of the most widely recognized in the industry.

Baron went through a typical selection process for choosing an ERP system. It began by evaluating a wide range of players, then narrowing the field to five for in-depth vendor demonstrations and evaluations. The main drivers for Baron's decision to implement an ERP system were to build a platform for growth and to achieve Y2K compliance. Baron required an ERP vendor that had an international presence, whose software ran on the IBM AS/400 platform, and that had the flexibility to allow changes to the software as business needs changed.

The evaluation process took four to six months, with Baron selecting the PeopleSoft World solution based on cost of implementation, flexibility, and international presence. At the time of selection, Baron was integrating with a new business partner and therefore wanted a strong ERP partner that could support both implementations. Another factor in the selection of PeopleSoft was its business partner relationships with other software firms, which could provide additional functionality to the ERP system.

Baron also placed a major emphasis on cost, especially the cost of implementation. The main justification for the implementation was to get off the mainframe system and achieve Y2K compliance. Baron's legacy systems had been heavily modified and were quickly becoming outdated. "Moving off of the mainframe system was a major cost reduction in the cost of ownership and the staff size needed to maintain the system," according to the Director of Application Architecture.

Project Team and End-User Training

Once the PeopleSoft system was selected, a team of 20 business users with firsthand knowledge of their process areas worked together to map the As-Is and To-Be processes. Baron contracted with a third party consulting firm for consulting expertise in what the PeopleSoft system could do. The implementation team consisted of 20 business users, seven to ten IT members, and consultants from the consulting firm. The process leaders, who created documentation and trained users in their departments, did training for end users internally. Training included play time on the system, before and after each shift, so that new users could try out the system and increase their knowledge and comfort with it. Baron went live with PeopleSoft in May of 1997.

The first area where Baron achieved benefits from the system was finance. Financial close time has decreased from seven days to 3.5 days. In the past, the financial close period was hectic. In addition to a faster close time, Baron achieved improved financial control. Finally, the improved financial control enabled by the system let Baron focus on cost savings. Baron increased its return on sales in 1998.

Baron also managed a 20 percent increase in productivity in its distribution area, achieved at the same time as a staff reduction of 17 percent (150 employees to 125). Baron was able to move more product with fewer staff. It also eliminated three positions in the administrative office (two in shipping and one in receiving). Overtime in the department was eliminated through increased productivity.

In the past, productivity improvements were difficult to measure. The large size of Baron's distribution center made it difficult to schedule and monitor picking and loading activities. With the new system, Baron was able to schedule and monitor individual employee order and line activity on an hourly basis. Tracking revealed process problems and hindrances that prevented some people from making their goals. For example, fulfillment of some orders required more walking, more steps, and more units to be carried in order for those workers to move the total poundage that others moved. Performance is now tracked on a daily basis. Employees point out ways to improve the process that, in turn, improves Baron's overall productivity.

Quality in logistics increased as well with the new system. Baron experienced a 30% decrease in mispicks through the use of bar coding, which improved accuracy because workers were no longer keying in numbers themselves. The system alerted workers to mismatches, so workers knew immediately if they had picked the wrong product. Finally, inventory accuracy increased from 97 percent to over 99 percent since the system was installed. The warehouse had paper-based systems that moved products. Now, the employees use scanners to read the bar coded product.

Baron manufactures a range of products, from standard to modified to fully customized products. Each of these required a different manufacturing process (build to stock, configure to order, make to order) and had different cycle times. With the new ERP system, Baron has been able to cut cycle times in half—or better—for all three manufacturing processes. For example, the cycle time for making standard products dropped 60%, and the cycle time for custom products was cut by more than half.

With legacy systems, Baron managers had limited access to timely, detailed information. Letting users choose the level of analysis made the information warehouse useful to executives and analysts alike. Even more important, translating queries into business terms means that business users could query the information warehouse directly. An example of the improved control Baron had was in the area of pricing adjustments (rebates) to customers. For instance, a salesperson could ask to give a pricing adjustment to a customer, justifying it on the basis of price competition in an area and the expectation of $100,000 in sales from the customer. The salesperson and the sales manager would monitor the anticipated increase in sales by directly accessing the data warehouse.

The ERP system also enabled Baron to track supplier performance. For example, Baron could spot underperforming suppliers through time-based data on suppliers. The system gave real-time control over supplier performance and, therefore, added credibility to the figures. Baron was moving toward complete supply chain management with the new system enabling the process.

Case Challenges

1. One of the principal reasons Baron chose to get the new ERP system was a desire to be Y2K compliant. Was this a good reason? Why or why not?

2. What sort of information was tracked or should be tracked to achieve the warehouse efficiencies described in the case?

3. How should the process of sharing information with suppliers have been set up? Should the company have planned it into the ERP implementation?

References

1. Kyung-Kwon Hong and Young-Gul Kim, "The Critical Success Factors for ERP Implementation: An Organizational Fit Perspective," *Information & Management* 40, no. 1 (October 2002): 25–40.

The ERP Components

Distribution Perspective

Mountain Lakes Power Transmission (MLPT) had implemented a new enterprise resource planning system last year and was now trying to make the investment pay. The firm was a $50 million supplier of power transmission equipment (bearings, belts, gears, etc.) to small and mid-sized manufacturers located principally in the Midwest. Their customers had recently started demanding higher levels of service—consignment inventories in particular—and were depending more and more on the MLPT inside sales force rather than meeting with outside salespeople who could monitor activities at the plants.

Customers were experimenting with just-in-time (JIT)–related programs like vendor managed inventory (VMI) and integrated supply (I/S). VMI was a program where the supplier (MLPT in this case) would manage the inventory at the customer's site and, in many cases, actually own the inventory as well. I/S was even more extreme, with MLPT owning the inventory and managing/owning inventory from other distribution channels (fluid power, electrical, general line, etc.) as well. MLPT had been scrambling so hard to meet these service demands that profit margins had suffered. Inventory at MLPT had grown to ensure it did not cause the customers' lines to shut down (heavy penalties could be assessed for failure) and the firm now had multiplied its inventory across all these VMI and I/S agreements. The result was a huge increase in inventory and a strain on all the firm's divisions as both sales and operations people jumped through hoops to ensure customers did not stock out.

Jay Brown was the president of MLPT and was convinced the firm would not be able to continue to grow its VMI and I/S business while still remaining profitable. Customer expectations, however, were steadily increasing, and even if VMI or I/S turned out to be a passing fad, he knew that something else would be next. All customer attention was focused on inventory and fill rates and Jay knew from his recent graduate study courses that there were only so many ways to deal with these types of problems. One either had to streamline processes through information automation or increase inventories. MLPT had already done the latter and was suffering the consequences. The firm simply could not continue down that path. Other than hoping for a miracle, the firm had no choice, Jay felt, but to begin information-automating its processes.

Last year Jay approved the purchase of a distribution package focused on middle-market distributors. The implementation had been difficult but was completed nearly on time and the system was now operational. Jay was becoming concerned, however, by comments he was receiving about the system's true capability and how it was being used. On a routine visit to MLPT branches, he had heard comments like

- "We still have to have our outside salesperson count inventory at customer X's location since they have a highly variable demand that we cannot track well enough to respond to in time to meet customer needs."
- "The new ERP system is great, but we bought a Hummer and drive it like a Neon."
- "We've encountered problems using the system but our people have found many solutions to system failures and get the job done."

Jay knew his people were simply trying to meet expectations and please the customer, but the comments indicated that his goal of information automation was not being met. If people were counting customer inventory without any tracking capability, they would introduce error into the system and defeat the purpose of automation anyway since the system was supposed to cut down on redundant activities. The comments about underutilizing the system or working around it were even more worrisome as they clearly indicated that the system was not being used properly and that the firm could be worse off than before MLPT shut down the legacy system.

Jay was concerned. If he had taken the firm's limited resources and bought a system that actually did not change or, worse yet, actually degraded the firm's competitive position, then he had hastened the demise of the firm beyond his initial fears. The firm's financial position was now in peril, and if a major recession hit the farm belt, leading to cancelled orders for their customers, MLPT would not survive. MLPT had to get the envisioned performance out of the system fast. Jay wondered whether the problem lay in the system itself or whether the firm simply did not understand the system.

Introduction

As described in Chapter 3, an ERP system is simply a centralized database surrounded by application programs. The application programs take stored data from the database, manipulate it with procedures that generate new information, then return new data to the database. This exchange of data between the database and the application programs is critical to successful ERP system operations. When an application program takes data from the database and uses it in analysis, the program requires that the data received be accurate and in the correct format and other programs that rely on that information will require that information (data) returned to the database be in a format that is understood by the next application program. Accurate means that the data must be complete, up to date, and error free. Formatting means that the returned information is in a form that facilitates the next application program to perform its analysis. Take, for example, inventory replenishment. The system will routinely take shipments and update inventory status each day or, in the case of real-time or batch operations, instantaneously or every few hours.

As discussed before, real-time means that information updates to order and inventory status occur as each action takes place. A common method used for achieving real-time tracking is RF (radio frequency) bar coding. In an RF environment, the product is scanned every time it gets moved—from the shelf to the picker's cart, from the cart to the staging area, from the staging area to packaging, from packaging to the shipping dock, and from the dock to the transportation means. Each scanning transmits the position of the product in the warehouse to the ERP database until it is finally removed from inventory either when it goes on the truck or when the customer receives and is invoiced for the order.

Batch operations collect information for a time before updating the database. A good example is a bar code reader that, although it scans the product, does not update the movement status until the scanner is downloaded into the information system. The size of the batch transfer and the closeness to real time for the system is dependent, therefore, on how often the download occurs. The system, in effect, does not know what the current sales order and inventory status is during the batching period.

The input process uses the scanners as the input devices and the collected information is stored in the database with inventory and order status updated accordingly. The inventory replenishment application program will take the product status data from the database and then calculate where inventory replenishment should occur (that is, a reorder point has triggered). After identifying items that need replenishment, the system will either automatically generate a purchase order (if configured to do so) or will issue a warning to the inventory planner that action should take place through a recommended buy amount or some other sort of signal (see Chapter 8 for replenishment program procedures). Once the action is taken, the database will be updated with on order status for incoming products. The routine exchange of data between the application programs and the database increases the amount of stored data, which, in turn, increases the richness of data for analysis by other programs or future iterations of the same analysis from the same program. The accuracy/formatting for future-use cycle is completed as the program gathers on-time information for the database and then updates it after the sales order processing programs change status. As inventory status changes, other application programs access the output to carry out their activities (modules like forecasting, replenishment, and so forth; see Figure 6.1).

The operation described above contains all of the elements present in any input/analysis/output activity in any set of application programs carried on by an ERP system. The system takes input from external sources interpreted through some device like a scanner, keyboard, EDI, or other method and formats the input for the database and use by application programs. A growing technology as of this writing is radio frequency identification (RFID), where the bar code itself is a transmitter. The ERP system is able to read the position of product in the warehouse without the use of scanners. Prices for RFID continue to decrease and, as a result, more firms are adopting the technology. RFID can give the smallest information batching possible since the bar codes are in constant communication with the ERP or warehouse management system.

| fig. 6.1 | **The Database/Application Program Exchange Cycle** |

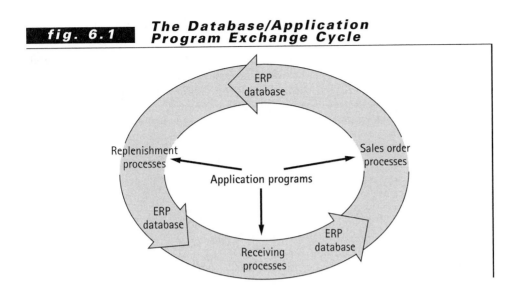

Application programs are numerous and differ from ERP system-to-system depending on customer needs and the IT company's competitive posture. ERP providers tend to focus on specific business channels and eventually branch out into similar channels. If the channel has a specific need, such as managing a private transportation fleet, the system will offer it. Other channels may not value that capability and, therefore, the systems will differ, making a true definition of ERP components difficult. Certain basic categories tend to be present in virtually any ERP system, however. For the purpose of discussion, here are five basic categories that tend to be present in all systems but that will differ in their subprograms from one package to another:

1. Sales order processing

2. Distribution systems planning

3. Warehouse operations

4. General ledger and financials

5. Executive information systems

Many application programs fall under each of the different categories and will be discussed in this and succeeding chapters. Some systems may define the categories differently as well, with human resources treated as a separate category from general ledger and financials, or other such frameworks. The intention is not to define the structure of ERP since it is constantly changing, but to offer a framework for illustrating how the system interacts with the various application programs.

Sales Order Processing

Most firms will place the greatest emphasis on sales order processing since it directly touches the customer. ERP firms have long recognized the significance of this function and have, therefore, developed programs that are easy to use and access for the sales force. Most effort to date has been focused on the inside sales force, however, due to problems with bandwidth and customer preferences. The problems tend to revolve around shortcomings in the technology (bandwidth problems) and customer capability or programs the customer is putting into place that differ from customer to customer (customer preference issues). The newest technology designed to overcome these constraints is examined in later chapters; for now the focus shall be on how sales order processing evolved and how it works in most firms' ERP systems today.

The sales order processing module in most ERP systems consists of customer information, billing instructions, order-processing options (recurring, transfers, direct ships, blanket orders, etc.), different order types (standard transaction, kitting, work orders, etc.), quoting, shipping, and invoicing.

Customer information is contained within the ERP database and will be accessed by the application program. Customer address and delivery requirements are generally entered in the first transaction and can then be accessed in an automatic (EDI or e-commerce) or semiautomatic process by the inside salesperson (in the case of a phoned or faxed order). For EDI or e-commerce, the system will enter the data directly into the standard format for the database. The system will access information for billing instructions (some firms will have a different billing address than delivery address) and pricing (some customers often get different prices based on contractual agreements or volume purchases).

The salesperson or direct-entry method will also access the order-processing options. Some orders will be part of a consolidated billing program where an agreement is placed for a total purchase of goods but the goods are delivered periodically, on an as-needed basis or according to a preset schedule. The system will issue invoices on a monthly or other regular timely basis that may not correspond with the delivery of goods. These "blanket" orders are designed to simplify the purchasing process since the person who needs the product will be able to order without the purchasing department getting involved and billing can be consolidated to fewer invoices for accounts payable to process. Other special-order processing conditions include direct ships, where the supplier ships directly to the customer but bills through the distributor, or transfers, where the company bills one operation for the delivery of goods from another operation. Many distributors routinely sell products and have the supplier ship directly in order to avoid carrying excessive amounts of inventory. The direct-ship process is different from the typical order/stock/sell/ship process and requires a different sales order methodology.

The system also typically maintains different order types. Common order types include standard orders that process a typical sale (see Figure 6.2). A standard order input form will have a header that includes the customer's information and billing. The next field will include the products ordered, quantities, and so on. The inside salesperson will access this form to enter the order either before or after pulling the customer information. If the customer account information has already been accessed by the inside salesperson, the header may already have been filled in by the system, leaving the salesperson simply to fill in the products, amounts ordered, and shipping instructions.

Other order types include kitting and work orders. The kitting process involves bringing together multiple products that are used together by the customer under a new stock keeping unit (SKU). One major computer manufacturer requires its distributor to put all components going onto a motherboard into a bag with its own

fig. 6.2 — A Typical Sales Order

Sales Order Entry					
Examine Review Prod Func Order Func Notes User Info					

	Order Number	102768		Customer	001000 A-1 MAINTENANCE SERVICE

Ln#	Product# / Description	Quantity U/M	Whse	Price
1	KLE 10000 SCREWDRIVER KIT	20 EA	10	76.0000
2	KLE 600-1 HD SQ SHK SCREWDRIVER 1-1/2	15 EA	10	5.5500
3	KLE 600-8 HD SQ SHK SCREWDRIVER 8"	12 EA	10	10.4500
4	KLE 603-3 #1 PHILLIPS SCREWDRIVER	25 EA	10	7.6950

Enter product number, customer product number, alternate product number, non-stock product number, comment line code, or miscellaneous code. (F3) (F1-More)

Quantity	Weight	Profit	Gp%	Amount
72	103.5000	970.38	51	1921.03

F2-Save	F4-Del	F5-Hdr Scr	F6-Totals	F8-Order Pad	F9-Goto Line

Source: Prelude Systems Inc.

separate SKU. The bags are then delivered to the manufacturing line with all the necessary components grouped together for installing on a board. Kitting can make manufacturing more efficient since all components are already in one place, and it improves the delivery fill rates since all necessary products are in the kit or it will not be delivered. Since the kit requires a new SKU, the information system will need a special process to create kits.

Work orders are essentially a manufacturing process carried out by the distributor. The typical work order will follow a process that accesses all the subcomponents, pulls them from inventory, and then converts them into a new SKU that reflects the changed product after conversion. Some work order processes use a bill of materials (BOM) like the ones used in materials requirements planning (MRP), while others allow the salesperson to custom-build the end product/service.[1] If the product is a standard offering, the former applies. When the product is customized to customer specifications, the latter is more appropriate.

One building materials distributor manufactured standard products that were sold by large home center stores. A BOM existed for each of the products and was accessed by the work order process to determine what should be taken from inventory to manufacture the scheduled products. Contractors required custom-made products that could be installed in customized homes or businesses. These products would be "constructed" in the work order by the salesperson. The salesperson, as part of the sales order process, initiates the work order process (see Figure 6.3).

The salesperson may also access the quoting process if the customer initiates a request for information (RFI) or request for quote (RFQ). An RFI or RFQ is an inquiry as to pricing for a group of products and/or services delivered by the distributor. The

fig. 6.3 Work Order

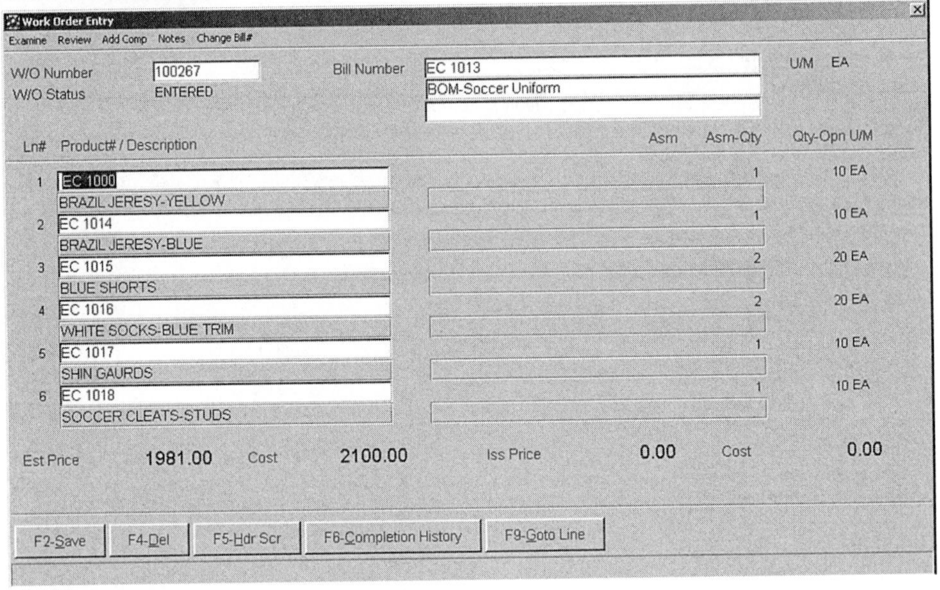

Work Order Entry

Examine Review Add Comp Notes Change Bill#

W/O Number	100267	Bill Number	EC 1013	U/M EA
W/O Status	ENTERED		BOM-Soccer Uniform	

Ln#	Product# / Description		Asm	Asm-Qty	Qty-Opn U/M
1	EC 1000			1	10 EA
	BRAZIL JERESY-YELLOW				
2	EC 1014			1	10 EA
	BRAZIL JERESY-BLUE				
3	EC 1015			2	20 EA
	BLUE SHORTS				
4	EC 1016			2	20 EA
	WHITE SOCKS-BLUE TRIM				
5	EC 1017			1	10 EA
	SHIN GAURDS				
6	EC 1018			1	10 EA
	SOCCER CLEATS-STUDS				

Est Price	1981.00	Cost	2100.00	Iss Price	0.00	Cost	0.00

F2-Save	F4-Del	F5-Hdr Scr	F6-Completion History	F9-Goto Line

Source: Prelude Systems Inc.

salesperson will take the entire order and will put together the quote for the customer. If the customer accepts the quote, the salesperson will turn the quote into an order. If not, the salesperson will either cancel the quote (some systems will track cancelled quotes for analysis purposes) or modify the quote to save the sale (see Figure 6.4).

In a sense, each of the foregoing acts as an input device for the ERP database as it withdraws data to either carry out its procedures or assist the salesperson. The procedures create the sales order, quote, work order, kits, and so on, and as those forms are filled out by the sales force, the database receives new data that can be used for future such transactions or for the purposes of other analysis programs to be discussed in later chapters. The future transactions will use the input from the current ones as a history file that can be accessed for credit decisions, advising customers on their needs, or writing future quotes.

The credit department requires a history on the customer to make decisions about credit limits or leniency in the case of late payments. The salesperson can use past history to better advise the customer on current purchases. Salespeople serve the interests of their customers and the distributors if they can suggest items that the customer has needed in the past as likely to be needed for the current project. For quoting purposes, it is useful for the salesperson to be able to access previous quotes to design more effective ones for the future.

The number of transactions associated with sales and the critical importance of correct data entry mean that the process must be well designed from both a system and human interface perspective. Failure to create stable system procedures will lead to a database full of inaccuracies that will flow into inventory status problems, customer history problems, and, perhaps worst of all, invoice problems.

fig. 6.4   A Sales Quote

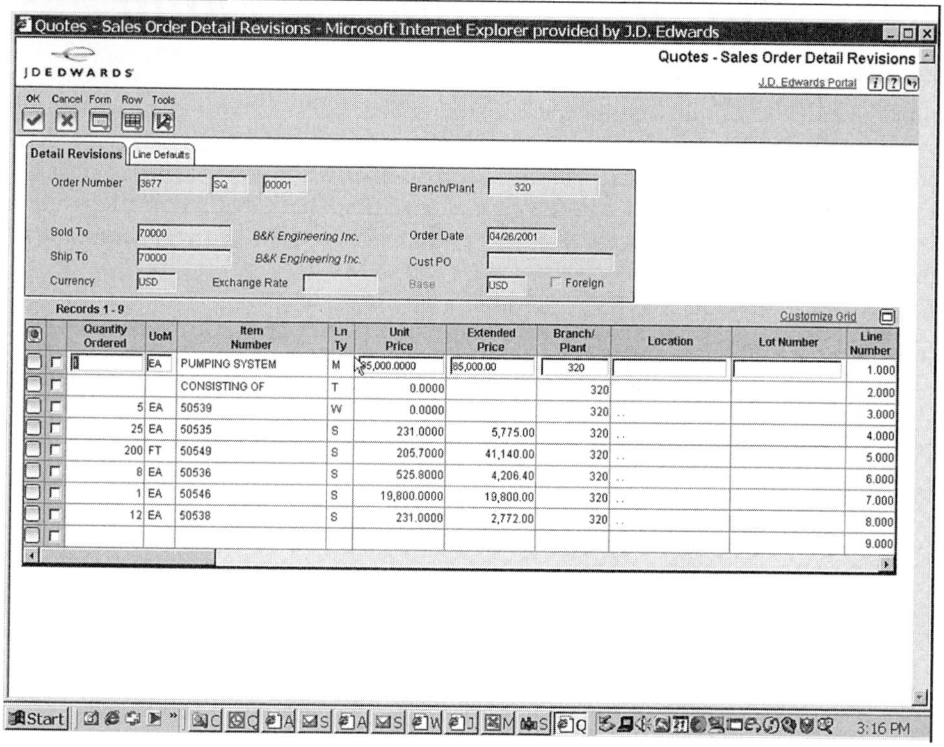

Quotes - Sales Order Detail Revisions - Microsoft Internet Explorer provided by J.D. Edwards

Quotes - Sales Order Detail Revisions
J.D. Edwards Portal

OK Cancel Form Row Tools

Detail Revisions | Line Defaults

| Order Number | 3677 | SQ | 00001 | | Branch/Plant | 320 |

Sold To	70000		B&K Engineering Inc.	Order Date	04/26/2001
Ship To	70000		B&K Engineering Inc.	Cust PO	
Currency	USD	Exchange Rate		Base	USD	Foreign

Records 1 - 9   Customize Grid

		Quantity Ordered	UoM	Item Number	Ln Ty	Unit Price	Extended Price	Branch/ Plant	Location	Lot Number	Line Number
		1	EA	PUMPING SYSTEM	M	85,000.0000	85,000.00	320			1.000
				CONSISTING OF	T	0.0000		320			2.000
		5	EA	50539	W	0.0000		320	..		3.000
		25	EA	50535	S	231.0000	5,775.00	320	..		4.000
		200	FT	50549	S	205.7000	41,140.00	320	..		5.000
		8	EA	50536	S	525.8000	4,206.40	320	..		6.000
		1	EA	50546	S	19,800.0000	19,800.00	320	..		7.000
		12	EA	50538	S	231.0000	2,772.00	320	..		8.000
											9.000

Start   3:16 PM

Source: PeopleSoft

Invoicing is the final step in the sales order process since a sale will generate a need for billing. The invoicing process is very dependent on accuracy since an inaccurate invoice will either damage the company's profitability or its relationship with its customers. The invoicing process can involve a simple one-time transaction or (as stated above) can be part of an ongoing special billing procedure like a blanket order or some other consolidated purchasing technique (see Figure 6.5).

fig. 6.5   An Invoice

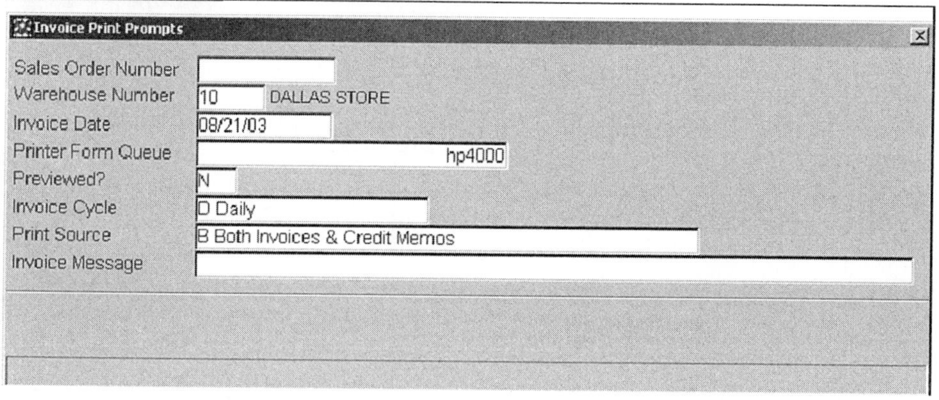

Invoice Print Prompts

Sales Order Number	
Warehouse Number	10 DALLAS STORE
Invoice Date	08/21/03
Printer Form Queue	hp4000
Previewed?	N
Invoice Cycle	D Daily
Print Source	B Both Invoices & Credit Memos
Invoice Message	

Source: Prelude Systems Inc.

Distribution Systems Planning

Once the sales order has been initiated, it gets passed to the distribution group for processing. Distribution activities are driven by the ERP system. The distribution steps detailed in Figure 6.6 (also seen in Figure 3.8 in Chapter 3) include the decision as to whether the order is a stock or nonstock item and the system response for each. In the case of a stock item, the system will first check availability. If product is not available, the salesperson is notified and the customer may be given some of the following options:

1. Backorder—The customer is asked to wait until the order can be received from the supplier as part of the standard replenishment process. The system will record the backorder and place it in queue for when the inventory arrives.

fig. 6.6 **Distribution Systems Planning**

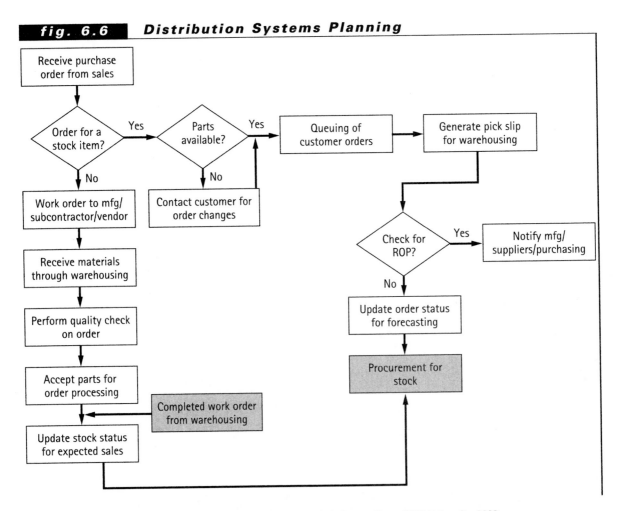

Source: Best Practices in Enterprise Resource Management, Research Report, Texas A&M University, 2003

One distribution warehouse supported both a manufacturer of heavy equipment and its customers for parts (called the "aftermarket" goods). Aftermarket goods were far more profitable than the initial equipment sale, but the initial equipment was the mechanism that created the aftermarket demand. The warehouse would not allow product to be shipped directly from its suppliers unless the supplier would relabel the product under the manufacturer's logo so that future sales would be protected. Since most suppliers were unwilling to relabel, the direct-ship process was rarely used and the ERP system would bring the product in for relabeling and cross-docking.

Incoming product, whether shipped from external vendors or modified through distributor value-add processing, is then received into the system. Inventory and order status is then updated, and the process continues. The next step is for the warehouse to respond to the customer's delivery requirements.

Warehouse Operations

Pick/slip/drop is the process of issuing the order to the warehouse. The phrase comes from the pre-ERP systems days of warehousing, where the paper managing process would have someone in the front office "drop" the pick slip into an in-basket that pickers would check and then pull out the orders due to go out that day. Since that time, ERP and other IT systems have brought considerable improvements to the picking process. The warehouse is typically laid out with the picking process in mind, and the pick slip will often reflect the layout.

Identification of primary activities and their interrelationships are important in determining facility layouts. One of the first steps in determining primary activities is to determine the primary products to be shipped. In one fencing materials supplier's case, pipe, tubing, and chain link were all important. These products were stored in the yard (an extension of the warehouse) and did not necessarily require under-roof space. The majority of shipments also included fittings to put the fences together and fencing gates. Fittings, however, were stored inside (see Figure 6.9).

The primary activities associated with these products included receiving, storage, material flow, information flows, truck loading, and shipping. The primary activities were not based on one identifiable characteristic like a product line. Instead, as is the case for most distribution sites, the primary activities were a blending or a mix of several considerations. They could be related to a product like chain link or pipe or tubing. In other cases, the primary activities included the type of work to be done, like receiving or shipping the product, or they included value-add operations.

Most ERP systems have some warehouse management capability. The level of functionality, however, can vary considerably. A full-blown warehouse management system (WMS) can offer tools that are not commonly available in most ERP systems. Due to the wide variance between systems, we will discuss the most basic of warehouse information management tools and the processes they match at this point. Chapters 9 and 14 will continue the discussion of WMS in more detail.

In a nonautomated environment, the pick slip will drop in printed form for pickers to collect and begin working their way through the warehouse (see Figure 6.10).

fig. 6.9   *A Typical Warehouse*

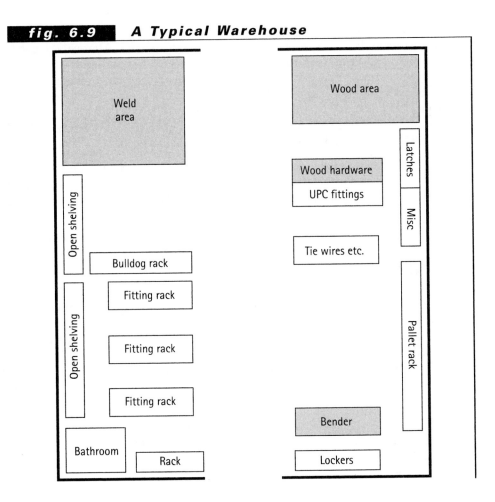

In a fully automated environment, the pick slip will show up on the picker's scanner and direct the picker to the next item via as efficient a route as possible. There are multiple potential routing and picking methods available that the system may or may not support.

The best-known method has the picker take one pick slip and through memory select the shortest/most efficient method to go through the warehouse while picking the items. Another method is called batch picking, where the picker will take multiple orders and pick them at the same time to save on having to cover the same ground again and again. The ERP system can support this type of picking by grouping orders together that follow a similar pattern or, in a fully automated environment, by minimizing effort through having pickers pick from multiple orders by directing them to the next-closest item regardless of the pick slip it comes from.

A more sophisticated method is wave picking, where the pickers stay in one area they are very familiar with and, as the order moves from zone to zone (like a wave moving through the warehouse), pick only from their area and pass the order down

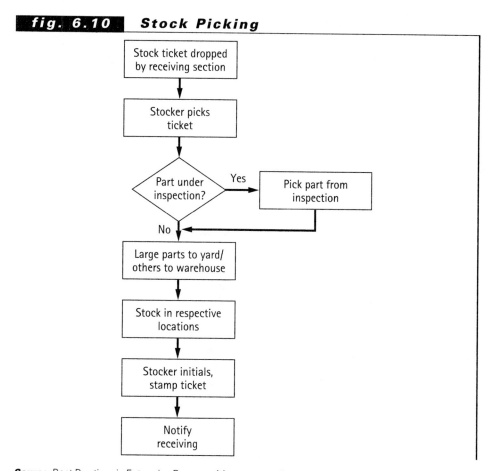

fig. 6.10 *Stock Picking*

Source: Best Practices in Enterprise Resource Management, Research Report, Texas A&M University, 2003

the line. The wave pick works very well with automated warehouses (where conveyers and carousels are available) but requires a great deal of discipline and, therefore, is ideally suited to information management automation since product must be tracked throughout its movement to guard against human error. The warehouse will typically be laid out to support the picking procedures with high-volume items and products requiring special handling grouped together. The information system will need to support the warehouse layout through the receiving process. Figure 6.11 shows a typical receiving process.

The receiving process checks in goods and changes inventory status in the system. The process also determines when and where product will be put away. The putaway activity requires the picker to determine where product will go, or if the ERP system maintains the warehouse layout, it will direct the picker to fixed locations or randomly assigned ones. The putaway process is determined by the system's capability and the organization's utilization of the system (see Chapter 9 for more detail). The system will track the time product is checked in and its movement starting from receiving into the main warehouse. The receiving process is critical to ERP success

fig. 6.11   **A Receiving Process**

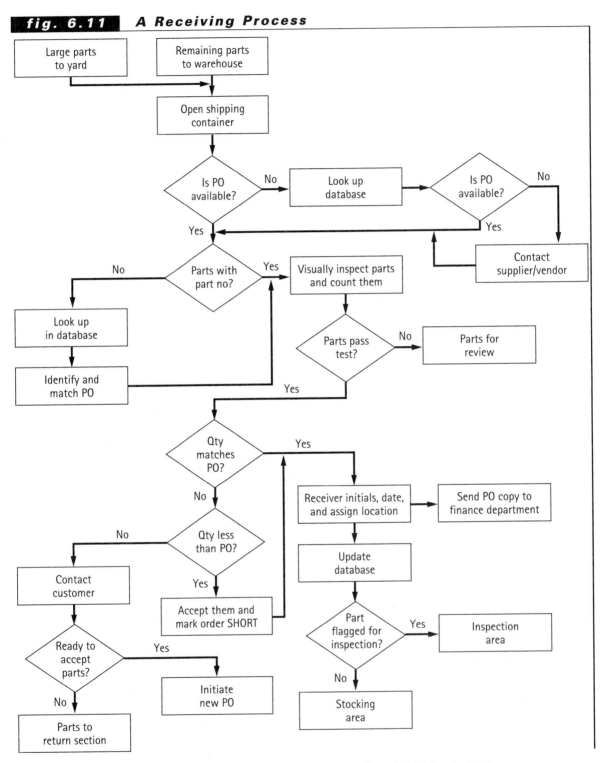

Source: Best Practices in Enterprise Resource Management, Research Report, Texas A&M University, 2003

since a product that is checked in incorrectly will likely not be corrected for a long time, if ever. Receiving, therefore, is frequently one of the first areas considered in information automation as firms try to eliminate data integrity problems. Scanners also play a role as will more stable human/ERP system interfaces (see Chapter 9 for more on inventory tracking and accuracy issues).

General Ledger and Financials

The general ledger (G/L) is the company's historian. It keeps track of all financial, human, and material resource changes in status and balances performance into the financial reporting mechanisms. The G/L, therefore, is the final arbiter of what the company has accomplished, and correct data input to the G/L is critical to corporate success. Within the financial arena, the G/L supports several decision-making tools and tracks a number of financial processes in addition to the inventory movement activities (see Figure 6.12).

Human input processes are a significant factor in G/L accuracy. As data is entered into the system, the G/L is updated. Invoicing and other processes are heavily influenced by the accuracy of the G/L records in the system database. As the figure demonstrates, the last action in each of these financial transactions is to update the ledger. ERP systems automate a great deal of the work, but many firms still leave much of the financial processes up to human decision making and manual entry.

Executive Information Systems

Executive information systems (EIS) are the reports generated by the ERP system to track the company's success in reaching its goals. The company strategy ties the firm to its goals, and those goals must be tracked by the ERP system. The EIS will issue reports that connect the metrics and systems together with reporting to management so that the firm can track and achieve its objectives. EIS is examined in detail in Chapter 10.

Conclusion

To the greatest extent possible, the ERP system is a mirror image of the firm. The different ERP modules are intended to match up with key distribution functions:

O Sales—sales order processing module

O Operations—distribution systems planning and warehouse management systems

O Financials—general ledger

O Management—executive information systems

fig. 6.12

Financial Activities Tracked within the G/L

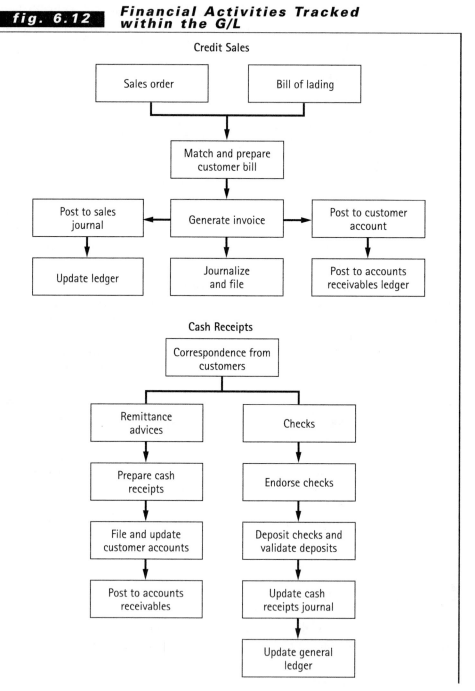

Source: Best Practices in Enterprise Resource Management, Research Report, Texas A&M University, 2003

These modules do not represent all the critical distribution functions (note the absence of marketing and transportation at a minimum) and reflect the evolving nature of ERP for distribution. ERP started in distribution with basic operational needs and has been growing ever since. Warehousing is a fairly new module and is still developing since so many techniques and technological tools are being applied here. Transportation is also rapidly being introduced into ERP, and customer relationship management (CRM) tools are greatly enhancing the ability of distributors to support sales and marketing.

ERP may continue to grow until it covers the entirety of distribution operations, but those operations have also grown over the years, and new techniques for optimizing distribution are also being introduced by researchers regularly. With the many distribution channel needs and the many opportunities for ERP upgrades, it seems likely that the definition of a base ERP system will continue to change. Now that we have formed a base ERP system, the succeeding chapters will address the richness of functionality in the base programs, discuss new functionality, and address whether ERP will continue or whether bolt-ons will develop to the degree that the functionality they offer is more important than the convenience of a single system. Commonly called the "integration versus best of breed" argument, the book ends with an examination of when bolt-ons make sense and what the future of ERP might be.

Distribution Retrospective

Jay decided that moving further along this path was sure to end in disaster. He decided that, as painful as it seemed, he would have to invest in further training. He hired consultants from the ERP provider and ordered that henceforth no activity would be carried out unless the ERP system was used as designed. The consultants were instructed to investigate all likely areas where data integrity problems might have been introduced and to support any questions that came out of the field once the work arounds were shut down. Another group of consultants were to go branch by branch through the firm and to be sure everyone was fully trained and to identify any customer-critical functions the system could not support. If the system could not support a customer-critical function, they would pass the problem back to the consultants and firm IT people chasing the data integrity problems, who were to come up with a solution ASAP.

The high service projects (VMI and I/S) were the first problem. The ERP system was not properly configured for them, and the IT people did not have the expertise to adapt the system for such complicated business processes. Jay ordered his top operations manager to get involved and hired yet another consultant who specialized in I/S. As the program rolled out, Jay held his breath. In a preemptive move, he went to the board of directors and explained his plan and the reasons behind it. Although they gave him their blessing, he could see the doubts on some members' faces.

Problems started rolling in, and the consultants and IT team were quickly overwhelmed. Jay watched for the most common and damaging problems and targeted his resources at those problems first. After a few months, things got a little better. Salespeople were no longer screaming every day, and some of the new processes were working pretty well. Testing indicated that the data integrity effort was also bearing fruit. Consulting and internal personnel costs (people pulled off their usual tasks) were escalating, however, and Jay wondered how long the board would stand by and watch the company lose sales and bleed red ink.

Jay decided that whatever the outcome, he would not back down. He had made the right decision and would see it through or leave. He decided he would rather be fired than hang on for a slow death of the firm. He focused his attention on keeping morale up, trying to convince his employees that the worst was over, and finishing the transition of MLPT.

Issues to Consider

1. What are the differences between real-time and information-batching techniques?

2. What is cross-docking and why do distributors use it?

Case Study: What to Activate?

Note to the reader: The following case is based on an actual distributor.

The name of the firm has been changed for confidentiality reasons.

Douglas Plumbing Supply (DPS) had adopted a new ERP system in an attempt to automate its information handling processes. After initial implementation, however, there was still much to be done. The company was particularly concerned with its work order, inventory management, and financial processes. The firm had a complex product-modification process that was being handled offline and needed a work order process that could track all product modifications and make accurate adjustments to inventory status. The inventory processes were dependent on cycle counts and a paper-based picking system. The financial process was dependent on standard costing techniques that were updated at the end of the year.

Each set of processes represented a gap in information handling connectivity. The work order process had many work-arounds associated with it that caused inventory inaccuracies. The inventory tracking processes batched information that led to the sales force and purchasing groups having to guess at true inventory status. Finally, the financial system problem led to the company not being able to accurately report earnings until the end of the year. The guesswork led to a general feeling of insecurity at all levels of the firm.

Terry Daniels, head of distribution planning, was responsible for rolling out the work order process in the new system. The current process was entirely paper based and differed from location to location. A salesperson would receive an order that required some modification of existing products to create another product that the company routinely sold. The modification was usually rather simple (cutting pipe to length) but sometimes could be more complicated (cut pipe to length, bend the pipe for a length that was custom to a particular job, and add special fittings to create special joints). Some contractors might do the work themselves, but often (especially when specialized tools were needed), a contractor would ask DPS to do the modification and deliver the parts ready for installation at the site.

The modifications had an impact on inventory status. An 8-foot pipe might be cut into two 4-foot pieces; one would go to the customer and the other into inventory. This action required one 8-foot length be taken from inventory, one 4-foot to be sold (withdrawn from inventory), and one 4-foot to be returned to inventory. Essentially the system had to withdraw one SKU, sell one it did not remove from inventory, and receive one that did not come from a supplier. The process was considerably different from standard shipping and receiving processes. The fact that the modifications could take so many forms made it difficult to define all the possible incoming and outgoing combinations.

The modification of materials was currently different at every branch. Some branches modified the material and changed inventory status to reflect the changes every day. The system status was simply overridden when the transaction did not follow the process the system understood. These branches stayed up to date but confused inventory planning and actual product sales since the changes did not follow a true ordering pattern. Other branches made modifications and updated the system when at a cycle count or year-end inventory. These branches had consistently inaccurate inventory status. Still others sold some products and returned some under special-order SKUs (stock keeping unit numbering system set aside for special orders that are not made part of inventory) that did not necessarily match what had taken place. These branches had sales in products that could not be tracked and built up inventory under the special-order SKUs that could not be located since the product was not in fact a special-order product. At the end of the year, these special SKUs would be identified as dead inventory even though they might still be sellable merchandise.

Terry knew that each branch considered its solution to be the best practice. Most had people who had worked at other branches and seen what problems occurred with work orders at their former locations. These employees were certain their solution was better than other branches, and unquestionably better than some unproven IT solution. They had, after all, found their current IT system was not up to the task. Terry knew he could not force them to change; he had to convince them the new system was better. He would have to demonstrate the losses associated with each branch's approach to work orders and then demonstrate, branch by branch, how the new system could improve the profitability of that branch. He wondered whether this process could succeed at all and whether his and others' energies would be better spent on implementing other processes and leaving the work order process until basic processes like inventory management and financials were under control.

Meanwhile, the logistics special products manager, Cary Davis, was trying to implement the new inventory tracking processes. The company had quickly implemented the replenishment processes (forecasting, economic order quantities, and automated purchase orders) but had not seen much improvement. Cary was sure the problem lay in the inventory updating process. The company had completely automated the sales order process and inventory was committed to orders in real time, but the status of inventory in the warehouse was anything but real time.

The warehouse got its pick tickets when the system printed them for shipping and someone carried them to the warehouse. The warehouse then picked the order using a three-copy system: the white form was returned to accounting after the pick (usually at the end of the day), the yellow went in the box as a packing slip, and the pink was given to the driver for the customer to sign. The pink would be returned at the end of the next day to reconcile inventory and prepare the invoice. After the invoice was prepared, the inventory would be officially reduced.

Since customer disputes in order quantities or quality were common, the ERP system did not have accurate inventory status even at the end of the day, much less on a real-time basis. The result was that salespeople and inventory planners did not trust current inventory status or sales order amounts. To make matters worse, salespeople, convinced the system did not have an accurate count anyway, would go to the warehouse to check on inventory themselves. Since the system already may have allocated inventory to another sale but the pick may have not yet occurred, salespeople frequently found inventory when the system said there was none. The salesperson would then overcommit the inventory, causing a stockout. The fact that inventory was there when the system said there was none only served to further convince the sales force the system was not working correctly, and such overcommitted inventory scenarios became commonplace as more salespeople started going to the stockroom.

The lack of verifiability of system information convinced planners that the forecast was not accurate—garbage in, garbage out—and therefore, the reorder point triggers could not be trusted either. Cary felt the lack of confidence in the replenishment system meant the firm was operating in essentially the same mode as it had before the ERP adoption. She believed the firm had to get all information to real time in order to build salesperson and planner confidence and ensure data accuracy for the forecasting and replenishment tools.

Cary advocated the firm activate the warehouse management system (WMS) contained within the ERP system. Tom Jackson, the warehouse manager for the company's regional distribution center (RDC), was virulently opposed, however. Tom believed the WMS was an unnecessary expense since his warehouse accuracy, according to cycle counts, was consistently good enough to eliminate the need for a year-end inventory count. A cycle count is a count generated by the information system where a group of products is selected at random or through a system designed to cover the entire warehouse within a year to be counted. The person designated to count locates the product and, if the system count is inaccurate, updates inventory status. If a certain level of accuracy is maintained throughout the year, the firm may not have to conduct a yearly inventory count.

Tom's view was that implementation of the WMS would be expensive and could hurt customer service while the warehouse was being set up on the system. If the RDC did not need a WMS, then the expense of small warehouses at branches implementing the system did not seem justified either. Tom had been with the firm for 25 years and was acknowledged as the go-to warehousing expert by most. His opinion carried great weight with management and had the support of the sales force, most of whom were not anxious to see the warehouse paralyzed during a WMS implementation. Cary, on the other hand, was fresh out of college and, while she had been hired specifically for this purpose, still had much to prove.

Eric Miller, an internal financial analyst, was responsible for bringing the financial processes online. The ERP system could support either standard costing or actual costing in determining sales margins. The company currently used standard costing, where a standard cost was established for each product. Most products were purchased at many different prices and different times throughout the year, however. Sometimes the product was bought at a discount due to large-volume purchases or manufacturer discounting. The firm was not anxious to make this information known, however, since the sales force might see the discount and push to pass it along to their customers.

Eric, however, was having difficulty reporting accurate profitability numbers. The standard cost would be reconciled with the actual cost at year-end but quarterly or shorter-term profitability forecasts were a best-guess effort. He felt the sales force had a feel for the discounted deals anyway and were probably underpredicting the actual value of products to the company's detriment. He wanted to enact actual costing and have management design a better process for controlling sales force discounting rather than hiding the real cost of the item from the firm. Management was worried, however, since it did not know what profitability would look like in the short-term and might get uncomfortable questions from ownership.

The firm was at a crossroads. The system was up and running but was not achieving expected results. Activating further changes would require more implementation with personnel who were already exhausted from the initial setup and thought the process was complete. The steering committee was trying to decide which changes to make and when. Frustration was running high, and the committee feared turnover or customer revolt if things did not settle down soon. The committee was trying to be realistic but supportive of its specialists (Terry, Cary, and Eric) as well. The system had to meet expectations but the committee could not tell whether these were the appropriate changes or there were still others that might do more. Paralysis was setting in as no one was quite sure what to do.

Case Challenges

1. What benefits would an improved work order process bring to the firm? Is it worth the implementation?

2. Has Cary fully considered the difficulties associated with a WMS implementation? How should she respond to Tom's objections?

3. How would you control sales force discounting if actual costing were implemented?

References

1. Thomas E. Vollmann, William Lee Berry, and David C. Whybark, *Manufacturing Planning and Control Systems,* 4th ed. (New York: McGraw-Hill, 1997).

ERP Implementation

part

3

7

Automating Sales and Marketing

Distribution Perspective

Bob Jackson called the meeting to order. Bob was the Vice President of Sales for Dartmouth Equipment Corporation (DEC), a $400 million fluid power distributor. DEC specialized in fluid power and other motor systems for the oil industry. The meeting had Phil Davis, Regional Sales Manager for Texas; Don Addison, Regional Sales Manager for Oklahoma and Louisiana; and Diane Brown, company President. CEO Jeffrey Dartmouth and his sister Karen, the CFO, were also in attendance by conference call. Bob was uncomfortable with not being able to see their faces during the meeting since he would be unable to read their reactions to his radical proposal. Diane had already approved the proposal, though Phil and Don did not know it, and had prepared Jeffrey and Karen in an earlier meeting, but Bob was not at that meeting and was unsure what had transpired and how the CEO and CFO really felt about automating the sales force.

The systems DEC supplied had to operate under many different conditions, such as extreme heat or cold, and were frequently exposed to the elements. Since the systems could go virtually anywhere, it was impossible for DEC's suppliers to make custom products for every application. DEC, therefore, would provide housings for specific applications by using local metal fabricators (firms that did welding and shaping of metals) into which they would insert the motors and other required equipment. The sales process required a sophisticated quoting system and a highly trained sales force that understood the applications of such systems. DEC hired professional engineers and put them through a rigorous sales training program to prepare them for the difficult task of selling engineered solutions. That made the sales force highly skilled, and competitors with less effective training programs were always looking to "pirate" DEC's salespeople, both for their skills and for the opportunity to take some of DEC's customers along with them.

"We've been in discussions with our ERP provider about activating the sales quoting and contact management systems," Bob said. "They feel they can support both the inside and outside sales forces with real-time information if the system is activated and used."

"What do you mean by support, activate, and use?" Phil asked.

"Support means that technical information like manufacturer's specifications would be available for quoting purposes, old quotes would be accessible from the database to help with new applications, and contact management tools would be made available," Bob explained.

"Whoa, one thing at a time there, Bob!" Phil protested. "You're talking about a full-blown CRM system! You know what that did to Morgan Oilfield Supply (DEC's largest competitor). Customers refused to cooperate, salespeople got frustrated and quit, and their IT department was overflowing with consultants. They almost went under! We snagged a couple of their best salespeople and took business from them as well. Do you want to give our competitors the same opportunity?"

"Of course I don't, Phil, but you know as well as I do that we're killing ourselves with inaccurate quotes and that our sales force is missing opportunities with all those date books and contact management software systems they're using. Salespeople forget things and if they're not available, no one can follow up for them since the customer

information is in their private books," Bob said. "We can't link customer actions to our purchasing activities either, since we frequently don't know what the customer is doing until the quote is formally accepted."

"What's CRM?" Jeffrey asked over the phone.

Oh, no, Bob thought, Diane did not explain this thoroughly to the owners. He turned and looked at Diane but her face betrayed nothing. He felt isolated and was unsure how to continue.

"CRM is customer relationship management software, a system that manages all contact with the customer," Bob said.

"Sounds like a good idea," Karen volunteered hopefully.

"It should be," Phil said, "but it has a poor track record. The applications I've heard of are too slow and salespeople resist them since they view them as an intrusion into their relationship with the customer. Even if you can overcome the technology problems, we'll never get our sales force to cooperate."

"Is that true, Bob?" Jeffrey asked.

Bob looked at Diane, who shrugged. "It can be, but we intend to limit the applications we use and introduce it slowly."

"What will you activate first and what will its effect be?" Karen asked.

"We'll start with contact management and then move to quotes," Bob said.

"Contact management will be the most controversial segment with the sales force," Don finally spoke up. He was the new guy and felt less confident opposing Bob than Phil did. "They'll think you're trying to take their customers away."

"Quoting will have all sorts of technology problems," Phil said. "Suppliers may not have the ability to give electronic versions of their specs, for instance."

"We need more information before making this decision," Diane said. "I want Bob and Phil to form a committee of salespeople, investigate this thoroughly, and come back with a detailed plan."

"And yanking our top salespeople from the field?" asked an irritated Phil. "That's going to ruin our customer relations—and our bottom line!" Don nodded grimly in agreement. Diane's face hardened and Phil knew the answer: "Make it happen."

Bob and Phil looked at each other in wonderment. How could they even reach agreement between themselves—much less with several salespeople involved?

Introduction

As the opening perspective suggests, automating the sales force is a difficult and frequently emotional task. Salespeople are often very protective of their customer information, and the technology challenges associated with automating the sales force are significant. The sales force is at the front end of the distributor's supply chain, however, and must buy in if information automation is to succeed. Failure to integrate full and accurate sales information into IT systems triggers the bullwhip effect.[1]

The outside sales force maintains the customer relationship through direct contact with customer representatives (like planning and operations personnel directly responsible for replenishment decisions or strategic purchasing), management, and financial people responsible for supplier relationship programs. This contact management function requires the salesperson to keep track of customer requests, unmet needs, and new projects requiring quotes or formal proposals. Most salespeople use personal calendars, card files, or some sort of customer maintenance software they can run on their laptops or palm computers. Paper-based systems are difficult to transfer to the ERP database since they require manual entry, frequently by someone at the home office rather than the salesperson who first recorded the information. While data and other information collected in a software program is often easier to load on the ERP system, the fact that it is stored in so many different places and formats virtually guarantees it will not be fully or accurately collected.

The inside sales force services the day-to-day needs of the customer and follows up on orders or other customer needs. The inside sales force is essentially "always on the job" in the customer's eyes and should be able to respond to any short-term need as opposed to the longer-term project quoting or face-to-face relationship work of the outside sales force. The most likely customer-contact personnel for the inside sales specialists are inventory planners or operations personnel directly responsible for replenishment. The inside sales force, therefore, will interact with the system on a regular basis to access order status information (supplier lead times, inventory, or expediting activities) or to respond to other immediate needs for the customer. An inside salesperson will also frequently back up the outside salesperson by maintaining the customer's needs after the outside salesperson has moved on.

Between the two—inside and outside sales—the typical distributor will collect a great deal of information about the supply chain. The sales force is privy to which products are meeting customer requirements in terms of delivery or product quality and which ones are not. While ERP tracking mechanisms can make an educated guess as to whether a new product introduction would be successful based on performance of similar products or how much business is lost due to stockouts on some products, the sales force often will have more information to add that can further improve understanding of what must be done. If that information is not recorded in a consistent manner, much of it will be lost due to faulty memories or an inability to connect what one salesperson has learned at one customer location to what another has learned elsewhere.

If complete sales information could be collected in a timely manner, there would be many opportunities for most distributors to add value for customers and suppliers as well as improve their own operations. The opportunities run the gamut from improved forecasting that leads to better planning for suppliers and higher fill rates for customers to improved technical information exchange leading to detailed product needs for manufacturing (product upgrades or new introductions) and improved functionality or optimization of existing functionality for customers.

One large automation equipment company manufactures products with a wide range of technical functions. The distributor sales force, therefore, is extremely important to the supplier and customer since they provide technical support by assisting the customer in making the best use of the manufacturer's systems. The result is a customer pleased with the manufacturer's products and a reduction in effort for the manufacturer's engineers who no longer have to support many customer applications. As the manufacturer's systems become increasingly sophisticated, the need for a seamless flow of information to the distributor's sales force that they can in turn use to assist the customer and send back new customer need information to the manufacturer becomes ever more critical to the manufacturer's success. Connecting the sales force to the ERP system, therefore, has become a high priority at many firms.

The Challenges

The sales function is critical to most firms but its significance is magnified in distribution firms since distributors are essentially market-driven service organizations. The distributor maintains—through its sales force, facilities, inventories, marketing, and financial activities—essentially a marketplace for its suppliers to service existing and potential customers from a convenient one-stop-shopping experience with technical support and available credit for purchases. The two different forms of sales functions are at the forefront of this mission and have considerable information technology support requirements that continue to grow constantly.

1. Insides sales—requires real-time inventory status, purchase order, and customer order status as well as a strong technical database to support product queries.

2. Outside sales—at a minimum, requires quick access to technical product information and customer maintenance information or, at the maximum, real-time access to the same information as the inside sales force.

Many distributors have started supporting either their sales force or their customers through the Internet, presenting new challenges and opportunities. One big challenge is sales-force compliance since no information system will be successful unless it receives complete and accurate input and the capability of technology to support the sales effort. If the sales force resists entering information into the system, the system will fail. Whether the system consists of a few applications on the front end of the ERP system or a full-blown CRM system (as described in this chapter's opening perspective), it cannot succeed without the full cooperation of the sales force.

The technology problems are driven by data and networking issues. Software is also a problem but will likely be solved as the hardware becomes available and the data problems are cleaned up. The data problems are driven by the standardization issues, discussed in Chapter 10. As of the early 2000s, many suppliers were still using multiple numbering and formatting methods that made it difficult for a distributor to enter the supplier's data directly into its ERP system without data scrubbing or reformatting the incoming information so that the ERP or other distributor IT system could interpret it for inclusion in sales or customer supporting applications.

The networking problems are mostly focused on bandwidth. Bandwidth refers to how much information can be sent and how quickly. If you send e-mail through telephone lines with an attachment on it, it will take considerably longer than if you use a DSL, cable modem, or some other form of high-speed connection. If the attachment is too large, the e-mail may not make it there at all. Most firms, large or small, have access to such high-speed connections now, so the issues surrounding suppliers sending large files with vital technical support become less about technology and more about data standardization. For most firms, the problem comes down to wireless bandwidths. The outside sales force finds itself in many remote locations and cannot enter its information in real time without high-speed wireless access. While some attempts to increase wireless capacity were underway, especially in Europe, the problem was still unresolved as 2003 drew to a close.

In the early 2000s, sales support software still lacked functionality. CRM systems had come a long way but the tremendous amount of variation associated with sales work mandated that adding functionality and upgrading sales software packages would never end. Once the technology problems are overcome, we can expect to see rapid development of new functionality in sales IT support since automation of sales effort will offer many opportunities to increase sales for the distributor and suppliers as well as increase customer satisfaction.

Whether the sales force becomes automated or not, customer expectations will continue to increase, particularly in information management. Inside sales will be expected to know more about customers and be able to respond to their needs without being requested to do so. If a problem is occurring in the supply chain—a truck breaks down, for instance—the inside salesperson will be expected to know about it immediately and be communicating with the customer. If the product is critical, say, a factory line could get shut down, the inside salesperson could be expected to have an immediate solution at hand, and the customer could expect a real-time response.

One transportation company tells of a factory that had a downed power unit in it that was crucial to get a manufacturing line running again. The customer was losing $100,000 per hour due to lost production, so the transportation firm located the truck through a global positioning system (GPS) and sent a helicopter to shuttle the power unit. While few scenarios will need such a drastic solution, the inside sales force and their customers will find many mutual benefits to real-time information handling. A distribution example would be for an inside salesperson to get a real-time warning from the supplier that a particular item would not be delivered on time due to a line shutdown causing a one-day delay. The salesperson would immediately contact the customer to find out whether the product is critical and, if so, expedite the product by overnighting it as soon as production is complete rather than using standard shipping.

Outside sales will be expected to have captured all pertinent information ever given to the firm by customers and to not have to be reeducated every time they make a call. This means all previous transaction history, service successes and failures (and why they were successful or not), sales quotes, maintenance schedules, pricing agreements, transportation needs, and on and on must be available on the system and accessible in real time by a salesperson at any location. All salespeople will be expected to have full information about their firm's support of the customer in the near term and about the supplier in the longer term (see Figure 7.1).

fig. 7.1 **What the Outside Sales Force Needs to Know**

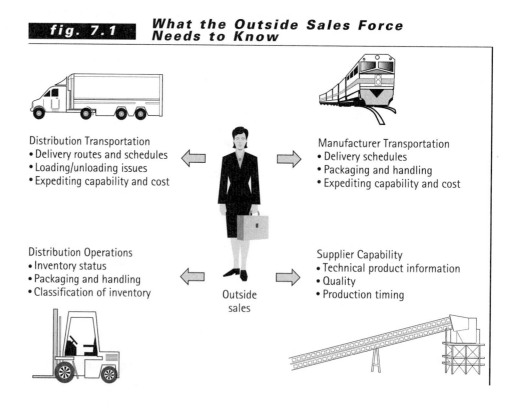

Distribution Transportation
• Delivery routes and schedules
• Loading/unloading issues
• Expediting capability and cost

Manufacturer Transportation
• Delivery schedules
• Packaging and handling
• Expediting capability and cost

Distribution Operations
• Inventory status
• Packaging and handling
• Classification of inventory

Supplier Capability
• Technical product information
• Quality
• Production timing

Outside sales

Supporting the Sales Force

Many tools have been created to support the sales force and most fall under the category of customer relationship management (CRM). The process of customer relationship management consists of contact management, quotes, and delivering customer support information. Many tools fall under CRM, such as contact management, sales order processing, customer pricing and billing, quoting, technical data, catalogs, call center, and data warehousing tools (see Figure 7.2).

Most ERP systems offer varying levels of CRM tools while other systems may interface only with partner bolt-on CRM systems. CRM for most ERP systems started at the crucial sales order processing function, in which the inside salespeople or support clerks would enter their sales or those of the outside sales force taken from written orders. In time it became necessary to offer searchability of inventory status, customer shipping and billing information, and pricing on the system to make the salesperson more effective at answering the most important questions the customer might ask. ERP providers, however, were trying to meet their customers' CRM needs and all other information needs (warehousing, reporting, production, etc.) at the same time. The process of adding CRM functionality was not proceeding quickly enough, causing some firms to begin developing their own CRM bolt-ons. The concept was very popular in theory, but many early implementations did not fare well.[2] The principal problems described above, technology and firm compliance, were magnified since the sales force and customer were directly involved in the implementation and maintenance of the CRM system. The closeness to the customer tended to make failures more visible and powerful than before, when they could be rectified before the customer could notice.

In spite of the problems, CRM inside or bolted on to ERP would go forward. The first step for a firm looking for customer relationship information automation was to understand which tools would have the maximum impact and which could be

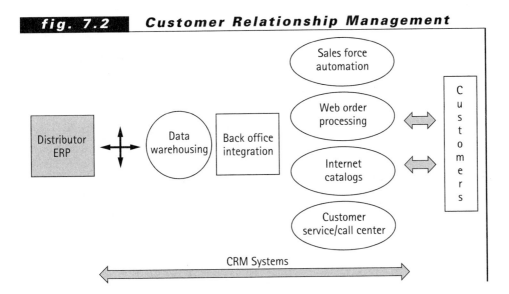

fig. 7.2 *Customer Relationship Management*

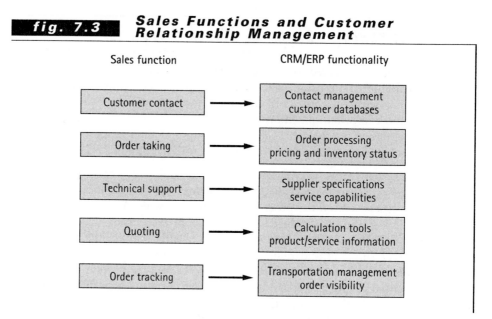

fig. 7.3   ***Sales Functions and Customer Relationship Management***

most effectively implemented right away. One way to look at CRM tools is through examining the functions carried out by the sales force and making a logical connection to information automation (see Figure 7.3).

Inside salespeople will man telephones and are the main support for existing customers. Tools that support the inside sales force would include

1. Sales order processing tools like inventory and incoming order status.

2. Customer account status tools like credit reports, pricing, and ship to/bill to instructions.

3. Product information support.

4. Customer inquiry and quoting tools.

Putting the tools to work requires a thorough understanding of the inside salesperson's activities and how they tie together. Most inside salespeople work through a fairly standard set of processes that can be documented and mirrored by ERP or CRM bolt-on tools.

The typical inside sales process with limited automation consists of several steps requiring research and interaction with different information sources. The customer order comes in through the phone or a fax machine. Phone orders require the inside salesperson to interact with the customer. If the system cannot provide fast-enough support, the salesperson will write down the customer's request. Faxed orders are typically purchase orders that are faxed into the firm from the customer. The salesperson will need to read the order and ensure there are no errors before beginning to investigate whether or not the order can be filled.

Customer order errors are as least as frequent than those of an inside salesperson, or more so, since the customer typically knows far less about the distributor's offering or processes and does not process nearly as many transactions. While taking an order directly from the customer may seem more efficient, the customer's representative will often need a quality check from the distributor's sales force to prevent errors. A common fallacy is believing the inside sales force could be eliminated if customers were able to enter their orders directly into the distributor's system. Many distributors report that the sales force must check all incoming electronic orders to protect customers from their own errors.

Once the order is confirmed as accurate, the salesperson will investigate pricing and availability. The price of the items will depend on the customer relationship, order size, and any promotions the firm may be running at the time of order. The salesperson will need to investigate the status of each and put the total together into a single quote for the customer. The complexity of this task forces many salespeople to note the customer's request and then call back. During the time the salesperson is doing this research, sales may be lost because the customer may take the opportunity to shop around by calling other distributors.

The customer relationship includes any prearranged pricing that is specific to the customer and may include discounts for a variety of reasons. Some discounts are due to the customer agreeing to buy a predetermined amount over a specified period of time: a blanket order. Blanket orders are similar to volume discounts because the customer has agreed to a large purchase but does not want it delivered all at once. Smaller deliveries will come in over the length of the blanket order period at a lower price than that volume would normally justify. Blanket orders are commonly used to buy products that need to be bought when parts or supplies for supporting normal operations run low, as in maintenance, repair, and operations (MRO), or when resupply is a set schedule of small deliveries as a just-in-time (JIT) agreement. The total volume of purchases may be significant but the individual ones may be small. The blanket order may also allow orders to be made by individuals outside the purchasing department and billing to be consolidated to a single order (the blanket order). Salespeople may need to refer to the blanket order in their pricing.

Other discounts may be generated by contractual agreements with the supplier or distributor. Some customers will buy in volumes that may justify discounts well beyond the typical volume discount schedule. These customers will sometimes negotiate special pricing with the distributor or the supplier. In the case of distributor discounting, the salesperson merely looks up the price for such a customer. In the case of a manufacturer discount flowing through to the customer, the salesperson will access that price and then also record the sale as requiring a rebate from the manufacturer. Rebates can add up to a substantial amount of the distributor's profitability. Properly tracking and reporting them to the supplier is critical to the firm's success.

One manufacturer made agreements with the large automobile companies for significant volume amounts bought through multiple distributors. For the manufacturer, the volume more than justified the discount, but since the order went over many distributors, the discount would result in the distributors having to sell below cost in order to meet the customer's desired price. To compensate the distributors for their services, the manufacturer would rebate the difference back to them. The customer was aware of the volume for the manufacturer but wanted local distribution services, so they negotiated with the auto companies for pricing.

Discounts for order size refer to classic economies of scale that suppliers (distributors, logistics providers, and manufacturers) will give customers for buying more. The logic is that a higher volume order requires fewer line changeovers (manufacturer discount), less handling effort per item (distributor discount), and less transportation cost per unit (logistics carrier discount). A customer who places large orders will cause the distributor to order in larger amounts, leading to lower manufacturing and inbound transportation costs to the distributor, and to handle material in larger amounts, leading to lower warehousing and outbound shipping costs. The distributor will typically pass on these savings through a predetermined pricing schedule that the salesperson will access in determining pricing.

Finally, the salesperson must watch for discounts driven by special marketing or other promotions. Marketing promotions are often launched to capture new market share or to promote a new product line. Sometimes products are discounted because the supplier or the distributor has discontinued them due to poor performance. In recent times, product life cycles have gotten shorter, causing more aggressive pricing adjustments to inventory. The process has greatly complicated the pricing issue for distributors since many items will go through pricing discounts at a rate faster than the sales force can keep track of without significant information automation support.

Electronics distribution makes a good example. The electronics collapse during the recession of 2001 to 2002 was first driven by a slowdown in consumer demand likely caused by the stock market crash. The slowdown in the face of a 10-year buildup of electronics production and inventory first caused an inventory explosion that took nearly a year to work through. After inventories were brought under control, the increased production capacity issue remained, however, and was exacerbated by a major new buildup of capacity in China. The result was too much capacity chasing too little demand.

When added to the natural short product life cycles, which were getting shorter in the electronics market, the result was a pattern of products being released and sold to the distributor at a price that would drop within weeks. To protect the distributor, the manufacturer would offer "price protection," wherein it would guarantee rebates if the price dropped before the distributor sold the product. The guarantees would be captured through rebates or a ship-and-debit process wherein the distributor would ship the product and debit its accounts payable for that particular supplier. In a market as dynamic as electronics, the distributor's salesperson had to carry out considerable research to be sure price quotes were accurate, and processes for reporting ship and debit had to be verifiable and accurate.

The most common form of inventory discounting, however, involves items that were either overbought, are not in prime condition, or have become obsolete due to age or seasonal changes. This sort of discounting is common to all distribution channels. The sales force has to be made aware of the discounts to facilitate sales and assist in reducing these inventories before they have to be scrapped.

Next, the salesperson has to check inventory status. In a nonautomated environment, the salesperson may physically go to the warehouse or call a warehouse person to check for availability. This manual check can lead to considerable problems with inventory being sold to multiple customers since people checking availability may not know whether the inventory they found has already been sold or not. Other problems arise when salespeople do not properly document the inventory withdrawn. One manufacturer suffered many stockouts causing line shutdowns because salespeople would take inventory planned for production off the shelf to give to important customers without informing the planners. Many distributors have made inventory status available on their systems even where a complete ERP system is not present. Nevertheless, the questionable accuracy of such systems (including some ERP systems) still causes many salespeople to reconfirm with a manual check.

After confirming availability and price, the salesperson may need to access delivery schedules, technical information, and freight costs. Delivery schedules are tied to the routes that the distributor's fleet runs to when delivering to customers. Most distributors with private fleets will run regular routes to the same basic locations. If a customer delivery is on a fixed route, the salesperson will need to check whether the truck on that route has the capacity to carry the customer's order. If not, special arrangements may have to be made or the customer may have to wait until the next delivery date. If the product is to be delivered by a third-party carrier, the salesperson may need to determine the freight costs. Third-party freight costs may be included in the price of the product or may need to be collected from the customer. In the case of collection, the salesperson will need to determine the delivery expense before contacting the customer with the final quoted price for the order.

Technical information—such as installation directions or material safety data sheets (instructions for safe handling of hazardous materials) that must accompany the product—will often have to be included with the order. The customer may need to be advised about this information when the salesperson calls back to confirm the sale in order to prepare its warehouse and transportation systems.

After this research process is complete, the salesperson can call the customer back with the quote. The customer may then wish to change the order to add on additional products, take some off, or somehow change the order pricing or delivery status. The changes may require another round of research for the salesperson. Increasing the order could require the salesperson to go back through the pricing and availability investigation or check for transportation capacity.

Before the advent of sophisticated information systems, the salesperson had been given a great deal of leeway on pricing and was supported by manuals designed to make searching as simple and speedy as possible. Warehouse personnel had to be very creative in scheduling, staging, and loading materials. As margins have gotten tighter, this slower, winging-it approach has become too costly for many firms and the demands for an information system that can support insides sales activities in real time has led to considerable investment in ERP and CRM systems, built by either IT providers or individual firms or developed in-house.

An automated sales order processing system utilizes technology like electronic data interchange (EDI) and e-commerce for standard replenishment, and reserves other support for more-complicated orders. Standard replenishment is the day-to-day fulfillment of regular inventory items that the customer orders routinely from the distributor. The process can be automated by establishing rules for replenishment that the distributor will observe or the customer's system will automatically enact. Take, for example, a product that has a reorder point of 100 units and a

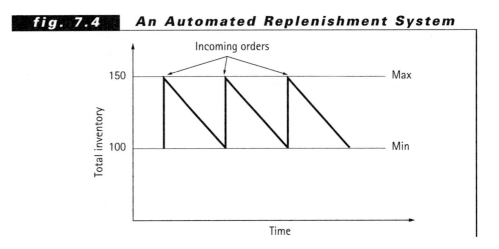

fig. 7.4   *An Automated Replenishment System*

standard order size of 50 units. The customer's system can either keep track of the inventory depletion and place an order for 50 units when the reorder point is penetrated or can merely pass inventory status information along to the distributor's system that calculates when to reorder based on the customer's instructions (see Figure 7.4).

The system simply tracks the level of inventory (as indicated in the diagram) as it is consumed and then orders either the 50-unit standard order or takes the difference between the max (150) and the actual inventory level and orders back up to the max. For example, if the inventory level drops to 85, the order size will be either 50 units (the standard order size) or 65 (the difference between the max of 150 and the current inventory level) depending on what the systems have been instructed to do.

Standard replenishment of stock items can follow a simple set of rules like min/ max or can be programmed to handle more-complex tasks and higher-level reasoning. The system can utilize advanced algorithms to determine the optimal reorder point or the economic order quantity (discussed in Chapter 8). The key issues are who should determine that the reorder point has been penetrated, what that reorder point should be, and which order policy to follow once a reorder point has been triggered.

While standard replenishment can be automated, special buys or special orders cannot be handled quite so easily. Any process that requires considerable research before a decision can be made will require, at minimum, interaction between the customer's agent and the distributor's website or extranet. The customer may also need to access assistance from the inside sales force or call center.

The foregoing does not necessarily imply that the inside sales force will be automated away by e-commerce. websites, extranets, and EDI. (An extranet is a company's private network where access is limited to the firm and approved customers.) Many firms, in fact, believe the inside sales force will remain the same or actually grow in size. These firms argue that the inside sales force could add more value in customer product selection, technical information, and logistical support if they had the time. These firms believe the inside sales force will develop these new

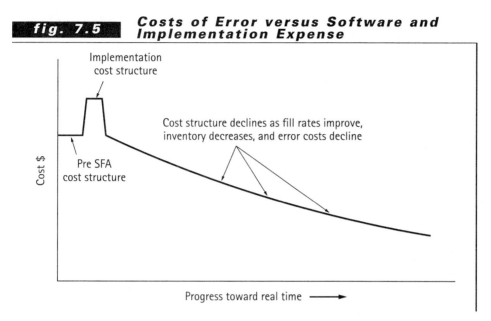

fig. 7.5 *Costs of Error versus Software and Implementation Expense*

force, therefore, can be justified by demonstrating the savings associated with real-time information exchange.

The benefits of real-time exchanges of information with the sales force are even broader. For the distributor, real time shortens response time to the customer, increases forecast accuracy, improves supplier performance, and reduces inventory. Increasing forecast error will either increase inventory or decrease fill rates. The cost associated with the increased error should be totaled across the inventory increase, fill-rate failures (stockout costs), and transportation (expediting, premium freight).

The cost structure associated with errors, customer service failures, and inventories differ from firm to firm as do implementation and training costs. Before implementing sales force automation (SFA) or other forms of sales process improvement toward real-time exchange of information, the costs of error should be compared to the costs of buying the software and the implementation costs (training, installation, data scrubbing, etc.). Each firm will also have a different savings structure associated with information handling improvements based on training needs, firm size, level of automation currently in use and/or planned for future implementation, and corporate culture. The cost and savings structures should be estimated and used to both justify the new processes and plan goals and milestones of the system implementation (see Figure 7.5 for an example using sales force automation, SFA, software).

For suppliers, real-time POS information has the same effect but also increases the firm's agility to market through reduction of the bullwhip effect. Agility to market refers to the manufacturing firm's ability to respond to surges in demand for established products and the rate of speed to design and introduce new products. Real-time information and reduction in distributor forecast error reduces the need for manufacturing line changeovers and expediting. Changeovers and expediting

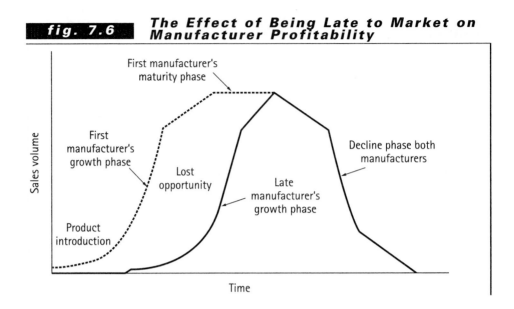

fig. 7.6   *The Effect of Being Late to Market on Manufacturer Profitability*

use valuable resources that then may not be available for emergencies that cannot be prevented and, therefore, reduce the manufacturer's responsiveness. The reduction in supplier performance will either lead to distribution fill-rate failure (stockouts) or force the distributor to increase inventory.

The advantages are driven not just by the speed of information flow but also by its richness. If the distributor provides richer, fuller information through effective use of contact management and quoting software, the manufacturer will be able to better understand the market. In a sense, if the manufacturer "sees" what the distributor's outside sales force sees in real time, it can determine product shortcomings or the need for new products that might not be discovered until after the competition does, if ever. The ability to identify these needs ahead of the competition and get the product to market faster (agility) is a key to manufacturer success (see Figure 7.6).

The effect becomes especially magnified when product life cycles continue to shorten (see Figure 7.7). The lost opportunity area remains the same size but the total sales volume area decreases in size, leaving the late manufacturer with little time to make a profit or possibly even recover its investment. For many distributors, especially those selling high-technology products under a franchise agreement (the manufacturer allows only one distributor to sell its product in a geographic zone), the ability of suppliers to introduce products faster than their competitors can have an effect on the distributor's profitability as well. While supplier agility is difficult to measure, it is another benefit of real-time rich information flow through the distributor.

The difficulties associated with reaching real time include the complexity of distribution processes, technology shortcomings, and cultural (trust) issues within the firm and within the channel. The complexity issue is best dealt with through strategic/tactical planning before the system is implemented as described in Chapters 2, 3, 4, and 5. The technology shortcomings are still significant but are being solved rapidly by IT firms. Organizations like the Industry Data Warehouse in the electrical

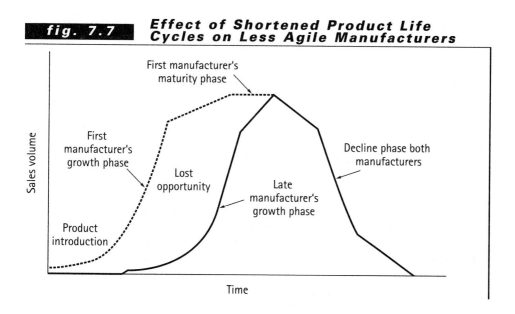

fig. 7.7 *Effect of Shortened Product Life Cycles on Less Agile Manufacturers*

channel[3] and RosettaNet [4] in the electronics channel have worked to reduce standardization problems at the same time IT firms and governments have been working on the technology and bandwidth problems.

The longest-term problems will come from cultural and trust issues. Between supply chain members and even within the four walls of a firm lie many trust issues affecting the ability of firms to practice information sharing. In supply chains, competition for margin leads to problems with information sharing as distributors fear suppliers will use real-time information to eliminate the distributor function. Most firms, however, have problems within their own organizations. The sales force does not want to share information for fear of having their activities devalued. Others fear that full capture of information will lead to measurements and objectives they cannot meet. More complete information implies new performance metrics (see Chapter 10 for a discussion of ERP and performance metrics).

Data Collection and Integrity

Procedures at the distribution firm will be one of the greatest challenges to connecting the sales force. Inadequate or overly complex processes drive data integrity problems since complex processes are the most difficult to carry out for inexperienced people or for those dealing with a new system with which they are unfamiliar. The sales force will require considerable training and processes that are well understood and thoroughly supported by the system.

The sales force's mission is chiefly customer satisfaction. As such, the average salesperson is typically willing to go the extra mile for the customer, which frequently means conducting transactions in a fashion not envisioned by system designers. The result is a need to go offline to find the solution for the customer. The offline activity will introduce data integrity problems since some data may not be captured and other data may not be a good fit for the information system.

Lost Sales and Backorder Tracking

Improper tracking of lost sales and handling of backorders, while not a traditional data-integrity problem, do introduce error into forecasting and capacity planning. When a stockout occurs, the system records inventory status as zero but might not capture the lost sales since these can be difficult to estimate. Some systems will record the lost sales by replacing the missing sales with forecasted ones, in a sense assuming that the forecast is the most accurate estimate of what would have been sold if the inventory had been there. Others offer salespeople the opportunity to record the cause of stockout and to project what they would have sold. The data is used only for next year's forecast since it is not in fact real sales and, therefore, does not contribute to profitability or other activities requiring notation.

Sales Force Data Entry

The sales force needs data collection procedures that decrease data integrity problems. An example is the PDA technology that allows salespeople to scan product and prevent transcription errors. In addition to automatic collection technology (like scanning ability), data collection techniques need to be simple and easy to understand. Processes that take a great deal of time or that can be interpreted in different ways by different people introduce data omissions or errors.

Data omissions occur when a process is not completed and critical information is left out. When a process takes too much time or effort and cuts into the time the salesperson needs to communicate effectively with customers, the salesperson is going to circumvent the process. Data entry must be quick, efficient, and easy for the salesperson. The process should also minimize confusion as to what is to be collected and how it is to be recorded. Lengthy forms that are difficult to read should be replaced with simple check-off systems (preferably a series of on screen prompts). The sales data collection system should be thorough and simple, and have minimum impact on the salesperson's customer interaction time.

Customer Data Entry

Customers are being connected by e-commerce, a trend widely predicted to grow. This e-commerce technology requires procedures at the distributor's operations to ensure quality data entry. Some customers are using supplier websites or extranets to connect and place orders. The website/extranet approach is little more than an electronic version of what already exists between the inside sales force and the customer's purchasing department. E-commerce, therefore, is not likely to improve data integrity unless the customer uses automated tools to pass information straight through to the distributor. As stated above, if the information is entered into the distributor's system by a person rather through automatic capture (scanners), the level of error may be as high as or higher than before since the distributor's salesperson may be better qualified to identify common errors than the customer's buyer.

Some distributors and their customers have set up vendor managed inventory (VMI) arrangements wherein a pick in the customer's warehouse updates the customer's ERP system while the supplier receives regular updates. If the distributor has a reorder point trigger for the customer's inventory, the distributor can refill inventory when necessary without a human exchange or keying and rekeying of data. The entire transaction becomes electronic, reducing the opportunity for human-induced data integrity problems.

Conclusion

For distributors, the work to automate and integrate the sales force into its ERP systems will be a long-term, difficult task. The benefits, however, are immense. In fact, one could argue that without a fully integrated sales force, the greatest benefits— forecast accuracy, improved fill rates, decreased order errors, and decreased inventory—will not be realized. The tools are only partially available, but customer relationship management (CRM), whether integrated into the ERP system or bolted on, has come a long way and is growing rapidly.

The distributor will need to plan carefully and proceed first with the CRM tools that make the most sense and offer the greatest benefits. The final integrated product should be designed in theory first, and all implemented procedures should be directed toward putting the finished product together. The distributor sales force affects all aspects of the business—far more than most other members of the supply chain—since they determine all product movement in a direct sense. Manufacturers have their production scheduling issues, retailers have their walk-in trade; distributors have a sales force that must be integrated into the system or the system will not be effective.

Distribution Retrospective

Bob and Phil managed to put aside their differences and pull together as talented and objective a sales team as possible for the project. Phil could see the writing on the wall: He knew Diane's silence meant at least that she believed this was necessary and he knew the owners were interested in better utilization of new information technology. Truth be told, he thought so himself but was nervous about what had happened to their competitor (Morgan). He just wanted to express his concerns so that the firm would take all due caution in proceeding. This committee was a good idea, he thought.

For Bob's part, he was frustrated at having to delay the project since he felt time was of the essence. He was also angry with Diane for not coming out verbally in favor of the plan. He feared Phil would use her silence to unsettle the sales force. He had to admit, however, that getting sales force buy-in was very important and that this committee was a good idea.

Bob and Phil charged two of the members with coming up with a procedure where salespeople could enter their contact information into the system faster than into their own personal files. Two others were to identify every step of the quoting process for 90 percent of all quotes and compare those steps to the quoting process offered in the ERP system. Where the system could not support an activity, they were to suggest an alternative approach that was simple and effective.

When the committee finished its work, Bob and Phil examined the results. The contact management team had indeed found that the ERP system could be faster than virtually anything the sales force was using, but they would need faster hardware (a laptop upgrade) and better access to the ERP system. They suggested the company start housing people only at hotels with high-speed access or wireless ports and that all laptops have Ethernet capability. They estimated the cost at $2,400 per salesperson for a force of 25, a total cost of $60,000.

The quoting team was overwhelmed at the complexity of its task. It was able to prove that at least half of the firm's quotes could take place on the system and that another 30 percent could go on with minor modifications to the salesperson's quoting processes. The other 20 percent, however, looked impossible. Bob and Phil decided that rather than enacting the system for 80 percent of their transactions, they had better bring in the ERP provider and design a process that could capture the entire 80 percent with minimal impact on the sales force. The remaining 20 percent would be addressed by a team of salespeople and the ERP team. The team's mission would be to find a solution that maximized use of the system and put solid procedures in place for any remaining offline activity.

Issues to Consider

1. What are the likely information technology requirements for the inside and outside sales forces?

2. How will wireless capability change the sales force?

3. What impact is shortening product life cycles likely to have on the need for information connectivity?

Case Study: Automating the Sales Force

Note to the reader: This case is a continuation of the Ray Distributing case, Chapter 14 of the first edition of eDistribution[5] (Lawrence et al., 2002) and continues the story. In addition to presenting a study in sales force automation, the continuation of the Ray Distributing case sets the stage for complete supply-chain information handling that is continued in further chapters in this book.

Keith pondered his fateful decision. He had purchased Ray Distributing in the early 1990s with the intent of steadily growing the organization into a major regional distributor. He had succeeded in growing the firm, but came to believe that the manufacturing branch of his firm was stronger than distribution. Now he was considering closing Ray Distributing and becoming a manufacturer instead. On the surface it sounded crazy but the numbers added up. If he was going to do this, however, he had better be prepared. He wanted to redesign his entire supply chain so that he could manage all processes from beginning to end. He decided to step back and examine a whole new supply chain strategy.

Ray Distributing was a successful small distributor when Keith purchased it. He grew the company over the next few years with an aggressive distribution sales force and a fledgling manufacturing division he called Ray Manufacturing. Ray Manufacturing produced lures and leaders for Ray Distributing's customers. In the late 1990s, however, Ray Manufacturing's products were growing much faster than the rest of Ray Distributing. Keith decided to give the manufacturing division its own name to differentiate it from the distribution group and possibly attract sales from other distributors.

He named the manufacturing division the Texas Tackle Factory. Texas Tackle Factory (TTF) proved even more successful than Keith had imagined and its growth took off. Before he knew it, TTF was accounting for a third of his sales at twice the margin Ray Distributing produced. Although TTF did attract sales from other distributors, it was unable to get much business in Texas (Keith's primary market) due to competitive issues with Ray Distributing. Other Texas distributors viewed Ray Distributing as a competitor and would not carry products from a manufacturer it owned.

In early 2001, a sales manager from one of Keith's best suppliers, Team Nu-Mark, approached him with a suggestion. Team Nu-Mark made a highly successful complementary product line to Texas Tackle Factory. Since Team Nu-Mark made products for carrying fishing gear, such as belts and kits, it did not compete with TTF on any products. The sales manager knew that the time was right for Team Nu-Mark to be sold and he thought Ray Distributing was the perfect buyer.

Keith examined the concept and decided it was a good fit. Further, Team Nu-Mark would add nearly another million in sales. He decided that the manufacturing margins were so good that he would shut down Ray Distributing and become a manufacturer full time. His plan, however, was not quite that extreme. He would shut down Ray Distributing but would outsource production to a Chinese manufacturing firm that would produce the products while TTF and Team Nu-Mark would design and distribute the products.

Keith's goal was to keep sales at $2 million (current manufacturing sales), a decrease of approximately $1 million over last year's sales, and grow them to their former level (when Ray Distributing sold other manufacturers' lines) within two years. As soon as he announced he was shutting down Ray Distributing, however, he was approached by large Texas distributors now willing to carry Texas Tackle Factory (many were already Team Nu-Mark customers). He also hired the sales manager who suggested the sale. The new sales manager immediately went to work on attracting new retail accounts to TTF with whom Team Nu-Mark already had established strong relationships. To Keith's surprise, the total volume remained nearly unchanged when he shut down Ray Distributing. Since the manufacturing divisions had better margins than distribution, the company was actually in better shape after Ray Distributing went away.

A problem remained, however: The firm did not have a strong ERP system and would now be challenging the system with a new supply chain. Instead of a sales force that called on small bait shops and a few large retailers, Texas Tackle Factory and Team Nu-Mark would be calling on larger retailers and distributors almost exclusively. The customer base would shrink in size but would require more expertise and support from Keith's sales force. The new sales manager brought some new expertise in managing these types of relationships but Team Nu-Mark (his former employer) was even less technologically advanced than Ray Distributing had been. Keith needed a new system that would support his new customer base and help him develop a more connected and informed sales force.

His typical customer accounts would be distributors with low levels of technology (no ERP or one with very limited ability) and little to no ability to deliver POS data and large retailers with anything from bar coded point of sale (POS) capability to no better technology than most of the distributors had. He decided the first step to sales force automation and integration to the ERP system would be to understand the process. He developed a map of how his sales force currently operated and used it to strategize as to how a more automated process would work (see Figure 7.8).

When the process map was completed, Keith was surprised at how complicated his sales process had become over the years. He knew that to transfer it completely over to his information system, he would have to do some redesign. Keith decided to start with the customer's initial contact with the firm and redesign backwards from there. He had two interfaces: inside and outside sales (see Figure 7.9).

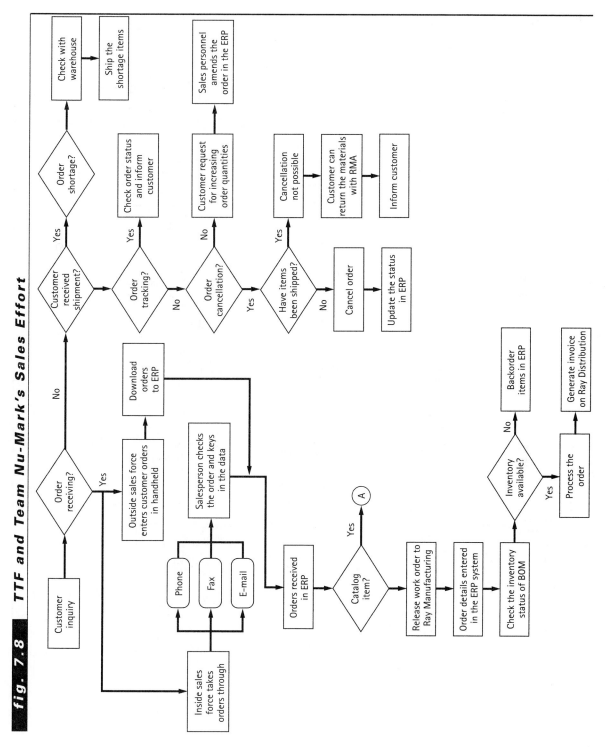

fig. 7.8 **TTF and Team Nu-Mark's Sales Effort**

(continued)

fig. 7.8 (*Continued*)

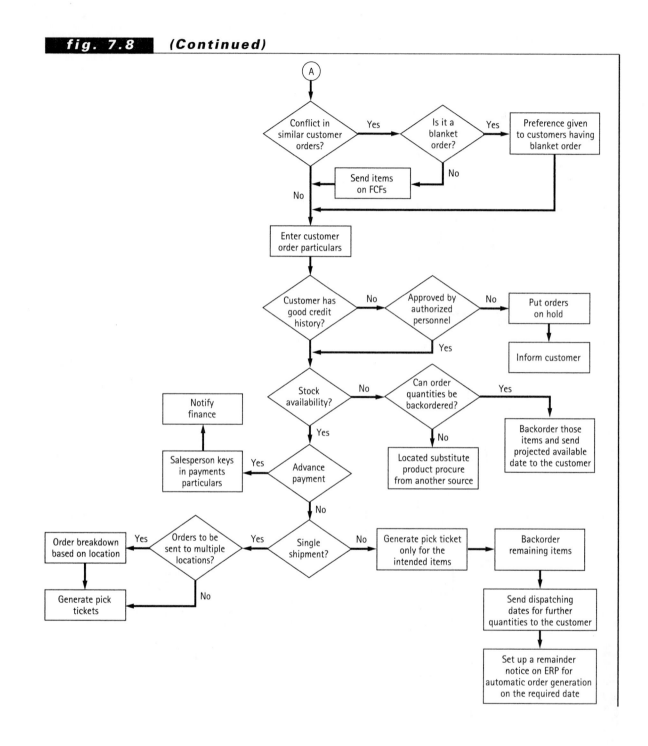

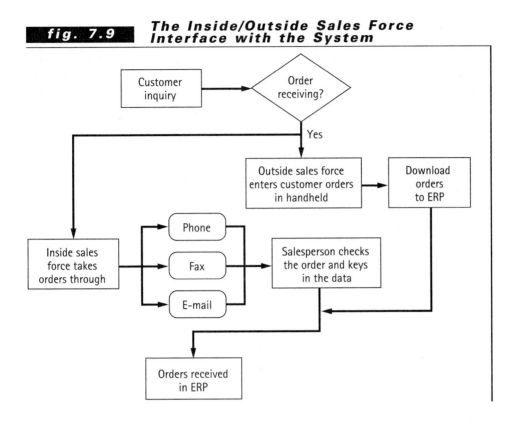

fig. 7.9 *The Inside/Outside Sales Force Interface with the System*

Outside salespeople used their palm devices to enter customer orders. Items could be scanned with these devices, which allowed the sales force to automatically capture sales without keying. This was a considerable improvement for Ray Distributing to maintain inventory for its smaller customers. These customers allowed Ray Distributing to decide when to reorder via vendor managed inventory (VMI). Larger customers usually maintained their own inventories and sent orders to Ray Distributing. Since other distributors would now maintain smaller customers, Keith was unsure whether there was any continued value from the scanners.

Inside sales was taking orders through three media: phone, fax, and e-mail. The phone (40 percent of total orders) and fax orders (50 percent of orders) would require the inside sales force to key in their orders, which meant they needed access to inventory status and pricing. The system provided this information but was somewhat cumbersome. Keith believed he could speed the process through making the system issue special reports that would give pricing, inventory status, and customer credit standing to the salesperson after the products and customer information were selected. The reporting system would require about $30,000 in programming expenses and a new, faster server at about $25,000. Keith employed two inside salespeople at a cost of $60,000 each per year after fringes and all other expenses to man the phones. He felt the new manufacturing operations might need less sales support since he would have fewer, larger customers. He planned to keep his two salespeople for the short term, however, to see whether they could grow the business enough to justify both staying.

Keith was also considering using a standard form for faxes and e-mail attachments (10 percent of sales and growing) that could be automatically converted to a sales order. To be worthwhile, Keith thought that faxes would have to be converted to an electronic format as well. New software was available that could be used to capture faxes in electronic format. Keith was interested but its $10,000 price tag made him unsure whether the investment was justified.

Keith saw this insides sales force effort as a first step toward sales force automation. He knew taking the scanners away was a step backward for the outside sales force but felt that the palmtops could now be used with contact management software. To set up contact management, he would have to buy the software ($7,000 to $15,000) as a bolt-on since his ERP provider did not have an internal program. He would then need to program an interface into his ERP system. At a minimum, he would need to find a way to dump the data into the system. His ERP database was not very friendly so he planned to use a third-party database to set up his contact management program ($49 to $59 per user per month). He was sure that larger customers meant more-significant relationships and was sure he needed to track them but still wanted to identify the cost/benefit relationship so that he could track how successful the firm was at meeting the goals of the new system.

As Keith examined the process map, he realized that he was dealing with only the customer sales contact portion; he still had to address the order-tracking, warehousing, purchasing/replenishment, and ERP system metrics that would drive all operations. He felt frustrated at the size of the task in front of him but knew it had to be completed to assure success.

"I have to start somewhere," Keith thought. "The customer seems the logical place and I can work backwards from there. In the end, I will evaluate the entire chain and fine-tune from there."

Case Challenges

1. Is there any opportunity to take advantage of the scanners? Should Keith dismiss this option so quickly?

2. Is the report for the inside sales force to check pricing, inventory, and credit status a good investment? Should he buy the fax software? Does the fax software decision affect the inside sales force report decision? If so, how?

3. Discuss the cost/benefit relationship of the contact management software. Draw up a plan for implementation that will keep Keith on track in achieving his contact management benefits.

References

1. Hau L. Lee, V. Padmanabhan, and Whang Seungjin, The Bullwhip Effect in Supply Chains, *MIT Sloan Management Review* 38, no. 3 (Spring 1997).

2. Ian Corner and Matthew Hinton, Customer Relationship Management Systems: Implementation Risks and Relationship Dynamics, *Qualitative Market Research: An International Journal* 5, no. 4 (2002).

3. Industry Data Exchange Association, http://www.idea-inc.org/ (accessed January 22, 2003).

4. RosettaNet, Electronics and Semiconductor Standards Organization, http://www.rosettanet.org.

5. F. Barry Lawrence, Daniel. F Jennings, and Brian. E Reynolds, *eDistribution* (Mason, OH: South-Western Publishing, 2003).

8

Replenishment

Distribution Perspective

Chuck Collins was frustrated with the entire process. He was head of purchasing for Canada Plumbing Supply (CPS), a $200 million distributor of plumbing supplies for home construction. The firm primarily served small and mid-sized contractors who built large residential neighborhoods and plumbing firms that serviced the homes after they were built. The contractor tended to order on a next-day basis and did not always plan material needs well. Forecasting demand was a constant challenge for the inventory planners.

CPS had brought in an ERP system a few years back and had been implementing it step by step. The sales order process was in place but the sales force continued to operate mostly offline. The purchasing process had also stayed offline because the information in the system was so bad that forecasting was considered a joke and all data in the system was suspect. Salespeople tended to do whatever worked quickest and easiest with little regard for the effect their actions had on data integrity.

Whenever purchasing tried to eliminate data integrity problems by insisting the sales force use the system as designed, it ran into a brick wall. The sales force was king since they brought the money in and the purchasing department was supposed to support them, not the other way around. What Chuck could not get across was that until he got

---

good information, he could not provide the sales force with the fill rates their customers wanted.

Now management was telling him that it wanted all replenishment to take place through the system. However, it was not willing to demand that the sales force do the same. Chuck was faced with data integrity problems, a system he did not understand, and a sales force that would not cooperate. His first problem was the data the mathematical model would have to use. For some reason, the data never seemed to make any sense. Sometimes the extract left out sales periods, which resulted in July's sales being placed in June and so forth. The second problem was the mathematical models in the system, which seemingly went crazy if a zero-demand period was encountered. Even if these events did not occur, the inventory planners could not be sure whether a forecast was performing well or not.

The planners and the sales force had battled for years, with the planners asking for more information and the sales force claiming they did not have it or were too busy to respond. The result was a group of planners that primarily responded to the sales force by making educated forecasting guesses and raising the inventory minimums whenever someone yelled loudly enough. Through trial and error, they had established inventory levels and forecasts that at least kept problems at a dull roar. Chuck was not anxious to go back to the way things were before.

Top management was not satisfied, however. It felt inventory levels were too high and that the system was not being used properly. The sales force needed to stay motivated, so instead of burdening them further, management looked to the planners to solve the inventory problem without damaging fill rates. In fact, management wanted Chuck to use the system to reduce inventory and increase fill rates at the same time! It had brought in consultants who claimed it was possible to have both, if the system was used correctly, and then went off to their next project, leaving Chuck holding the bag.

Introduction

The replenishment function is very important to meeting customer service objectives. The fastest-moving products for most firms tend to be standard stock items that are reordered on a regular basis. There is generally a correlation between how fast a product moves and how regularly its replenishment cycle occurs. The relationship is not only important from a customer service standpoint, however. Items that go through rapid replenishment cycles also tend to be the most profitable ones the firm carries, since they generate the highest sales and rarely, if ever, go obsolete.

Customers do look to distributors for new products and solutions but the relationship is usually built off a core set of products that customers require to carry out standard operations. The most important products are ordered at a steady rate for the customer's firm to consume. Standard replenishment items are often associated with raw materials like items for production or inventory for the retailers to sell. The rapid volume of these "A" items mandates that they be supported with inventory and high fill rates.

Other important standard replenishment products include support items for sales or production line maintenance. These items are often needed to sell or make high volume products. Some are B items that do not sell as well as the A items but are needed to support the sales of the faster-moving products. Others are maintenance, repair, and operations (MRO) products used to keep the manufacturing lines running that produce customers' products.

The final group includes rarely needed but still necessary items for customer service—often emergency products or items customers need for their own special orders. Sometimes these are C items that the distributor would like to eliminate but cannot due to customer demands they be kept in stock. In other cases, the distributor will reduce the inventory for these items by consolidating them to hubs rather than carrying them at every location or expediting them from suppliers. Products expedited from suppliers, often called "drop ships," are more expensive than standard distributor deliveries but save the distributor the cost of carrying the item in inventory.

In replenishment terms, the greater the volume, the easier an item is to automate. A items are prime targets for replenishment automation through connecting the forecasting module, reorder point setting, and buying functions of the ERP system. The connection does require a well-planned system built off reliable data and well-managed processes. The replenishment processes offered by many ERP systems are designed to connect these activities but must be well understood by planners and others accessing the system in order to be successful.

Automation is also frequently associated with high-service programs like vendor managed inventory. Many tools have been developed for VMI that allow the customer to pass inventory utilization activity directly to suppliers as inventory is taken off the shelf. Inventory utilization goes automatically to the distributor's system for replenishment processing.

Electronic distributors were pioneers in auto-replenishment programs where the customer provides point-of-sale (POS) changes in inventory status using high-technology tools like scanners and electronic data interchange (EDI). As VMI and other related inventory management programs grow, distributors will find it increasingly necessary to automate their own replenishment processes. The end goal is a supply chain that handles all replenishment from the end user to the raw materials manufacturer automatically in real time. Before this ultimate goal can be reached, however, each member of the supply chain must automate its own processes and link with its immediate customers and suppliers.

In a typically automated information flow system, the customer scans the item as it is taken off the shelf. The scanning device passes the inventory consumption to the customer's ERP system, which automatically sends the utilization to the distributor's system via EDI or e-commerce. Batching can occur when the scanning take places (a scanning gun that stores data until transferred into a download device) or at the ERP system (holding the data until a nightly update or regeneration of the system takes place). The batching process slows the ability of the supply chain to respond but, if kept to a minimum, may not have too adverse an effect. The problem with batching is that when the total batching time is added throughout the supply chain, it can add up to days or even weeks. Each day information spends in batching may add as much a day or more of inventory to the supply chain or an equivalent loss in sales.

The next step is the automatic updating of the distributor's sales order process. The distributor's system needs to have a set of rules that determines when to convert customer consumption to an order and pick slip. The logic has to be agreed upon by the distributor and the customer. A simple example would be for the distributor to track the customer's consumption of a product until it hit the distributor's minimum order size for the customer to get free delivery, say, 100 units. The distributor would accumulate customer usage until 100 units have been absorbed and then ship. More-sophisticated models could be set up to change the reorder point during seasonal swings as well.

At the distributor's site, the pick will go to the warehouse through electronic notification. The warehouse will then take items off the shelf, ship them, and automatically notify the supplier of the distributor's changes in inventory and the customer of the shipment. An example again would be scanners that download the pick slips from the ERP system that then directs the picker to the product's location. As the pick takes place, the picker will scan the item, which records it in the ERP system and notifies the supplier of the transaction and change in the distributor's inventory status. The product will proceed to shipping, where it gets scanned again as leaving the distributor's site, and the ERP system updates the customer's account (invoicing) and sends the customer an advanced shipping notice (ASN) that the product is on its way. The customer's system will record the product in transit so that the customer's sales force can sell off in-transit products.

The process requires information technology that many firms have already enacted and is becoming more accessible all the time. The case study at the end of this chapter demonstrates its use in the replenishment function with a small firm (Ray Distributing). The affordability of such systems is becoming less of an obstacle. Firms that wish to connect their supply chains through e-commerce now need to look to proper implementation of these procedures.

Forecasting

Forecasting is at the front end of the replenishment process for the distributor (see Figure 8.1). Failure at forecasting leads directly to increases in inventory since the fear of inaccuracy will cause the firm to build safety stock in order to protect against stockouts. Safety stock is the most expensive form of inventory since, in theory, it never leaves. The safety stock may be part of a calculated minimum inventory status that includes inventory for customer demand during the supplier's fulfillment lead-time or be treated as a separate calculation in the system. Even if the safety stock is calculated through a planner's best-guess estimate, however, the result is the same. The planner or the system will increase inventory to guarantee customer service. People tend to be risk-averse, in fact, and will likely add more inventory than a mathematical calculation would to avoid customer dissatisfaction. The forecast,

fig. 8.1   ***The Planning Process***

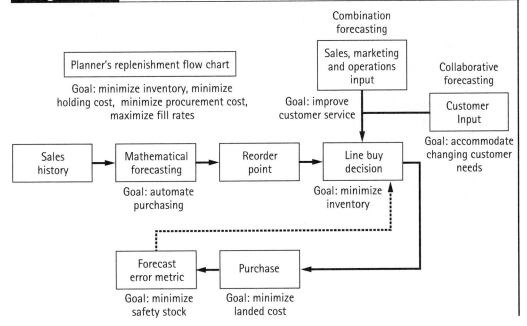

fig. 8.2 **An Incomplete Data Extract**

Actual Sales		Data Extract	
January	100	January	100
February		February	130
March	130	March	122
April	122	April	114
May	114	May	0
June	0	June	128
July		July	113
August	128	August	144
September	113	September	0
October		October	
November	144	November	
December	0	December	

therefore, is where inventory management begins and will increase inventories if not properly executed. Forecast error, in fact, is one of the biggest contributors to inventory.[1]

Data Extracts

The ERP system will have tools for forecasting, but the process starts with the data extraction for forecasting purposes. If the extract is not correct, the entire process will fail. Data extraction must be planned to meet the forecast model's needs. A common extract will use three years of data. The extract must pull all periods regardless of whether any sale occurred during that period (zero demands cannot be dropped out) since the forecast calculation may treat empty periods as not existing and shift data upward (see Figure 8.2).

In an incomplete extract, the data gets shifted upward into earlier months. In a nonseasonal environment, the result will be some forecast error based on any trends that may be present in the data being shifted back. In a seasonal environment, the problem becomes even more pronounced as the shifting could result in high-season sales being forecasted into low-season months. The resulting error could be very large and lead to inventory buildup in slow periods, stockouts in high-demand periods, and a lack of confidence in the system by planners and others within the firm (see Figure 8.3).

As the figure demonstrates, the forecasting model will be operating off very poor information. The shifted data will cause the model to predict high sales in a time when there should be little or none (months 1, 2, 3, and 12) and low sales when there are significant sales (months 7, 8, and 9). The result will be, at a minimum, too much inventory in the early part of the year. Unless planners intervene, however,

fig. 8.3   *A Shifted Data Extract*

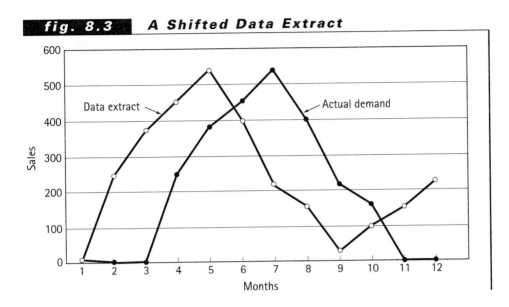

the system will not respond to the high-volume months either since reorder points will not be penetrated, rendering the higher forecasts in months 2 and 3 irrelevant. By the time reorder points are broken, the model will have moved on to its lower forecasts towards the later part of the year and will recommend lower buys, leading to stockouts in months 7 through 9, at least.

Data extracts, therefore, must be planned based on the length of the forecasting model's calculation period and capture all periods correctly. Seasonal models use three years' worth of data, in order to establish the seasonal pattern. Other mathematical models may get by with less data but the performances of these models have not been as strong as those using more data and are, therefore, becoming less common or are getting phased out of many systems.

ERP Forecasting Tools

Common ERP forecasting tools include many different forecasting techniques, any of which may perform better than others under the right conditions. Most systems will also include a method that simulates which model is performing best for a particular product at a particular time. Common forecasting techniques include the following:

O   Moving Averages—While moving averages tend to be data intensive since they require more periods for each calculation, they have been modified for use in ERP systems[2] and are commonly found in many distribution-focused ERP systems. Moving averages can be modified for seasonality and trend. Although easier for most people to understand, training for proper use is still advisable, especially if seasonal or trend models are to be used.

○ Exponential Smoothing—These forecasting methods have been proven very effective compared with other models[3] but are often difficult for laypeople to understand. Exponential smoothing includes models that are designed for trend and seasonality. If exponential smoothing models are to be used with combination forecasting (discussed later), planners should receive training to understand what the techniques do and how they respond to data integrity or other issues.

○ Regression and Other Models—Most other ERP-supported models are based on fitting a line to the data through linear regression techniques. These methods have not been proven superior to exponential smoothing[4] for historical data and are harder for most laypeople to understand. Where regression does offer hope of improved performance is in combination and collaborative forecasting where inputs other than system-stored historical data can be included. This technique is called "multiple regression" (as opposed to simple linear regression) and, at the time of this writing, is still not in common use as a forecasting technique. When available, it will require considerable training for planners to use effectively.

○ Simulation (also called Box-Jenkins, Best Fit, etc.)—Simulation models come in two forms. The first and most common model will take all the forecast models it has available, test each on past data, and find the one that most closely fits the series. The technique is based on the Box-Jenkins model,[5] which is more sophisticated than most simulation models on ERP systems. Box-Jenkins was the only model to beat exponential smoothing.[6] The simulation models on ERP systems have not been put through the same testing and it is not known whether they can consistently outperform stable models like exponential smoothing. Given the quality of data in most systems and the difficulty in training planners to use one or two sets of forecast models, firms may wish to consider learning and effectively using one model before attempting to use simulation.

The second form of simulation is an exact computer model of the distributor's environment. Such models take a great deal of time to program and rely on assumptions that may or may not hold. As a result, simulation models based directly on individual firms are rarely used in distribution forecasting.

Proper use of forecasting models requires a system whereby the data extract is collected and the forecast model is called up to calculate a forecast for a specified number of periods into the future (12 months, for example). The forecast is then presented on the planner's buying screen (see Figure 8.4) and/or used in generating orders automatically. The planner or the system uses the forecast when the reorder point is triggered to determine how much to buy.

The reorder point is set using estimates of forecast error, supplier lead-time variability, and the forecast itself in setting the amount needed to meet customer needs during the time it takes the supplier to ship. Before addressing how the forecast is used in determining how much to buy, we will look at how this reorder point is determined. We will examine each calculation in light of how the process should be automated and how purchasing, sales, and other professionals should interact with the system. The first input to the reorder point examined is forecast error.

fig. 8.4 *A Buyer's Screen*

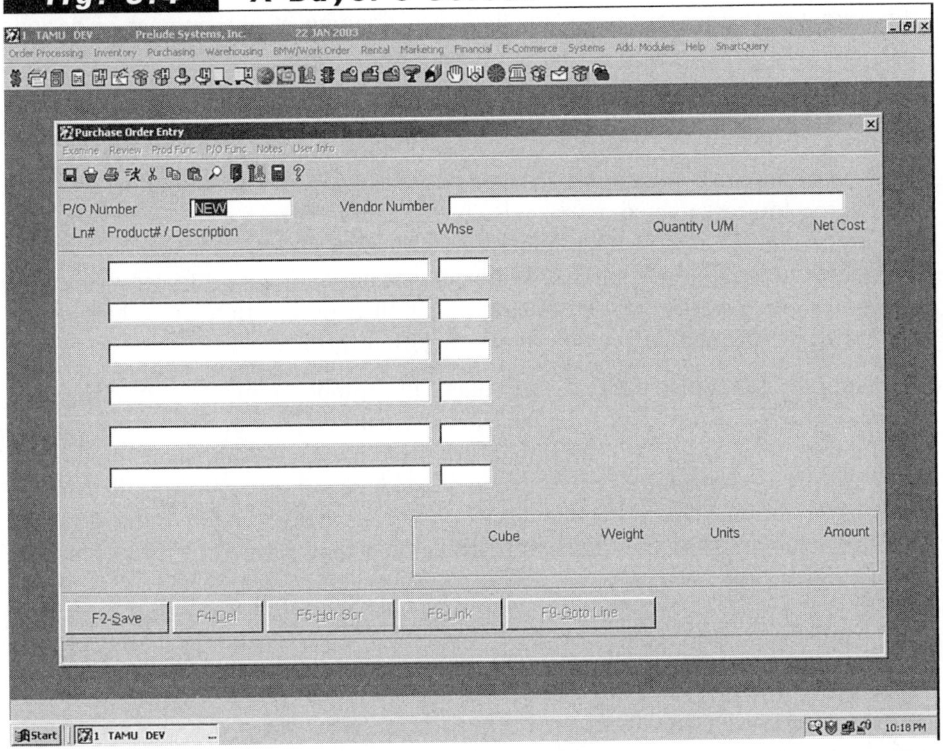

Source: Advanced Distribution System, Prelude Systems Inc.

Forecast Error Metrics

Forecast error metrics are critical to determining whether a forecast is operating as it should or needs modification. Planners can review error metrics or, in a more automated environment, the system can notify them that a forecast is not performing well. The planner will look at the error metric, make an estimate of what may be driving the problem, and then investigate the cause. If the cause is a nonrecurring event, the planner may choose to adjust the forecast or the data extract to bring the forecast in line. If the event will reoccur, the planner will likely try to find a way for the forecast to give it proper consideration by changing forecasting models, adjusting parameters that affect the forecast's performance, or set up the product for combination forecasting.

Common metrics include mean absolute deviation (MAD), bias, and mean absolute percentage error. Many others will be offered by varying systems and each takes a different view of the forecast and its performance. Each of the forecast error metrics is designed to capture certain characteristics that can be interpreted in order to guide inventory professionals to the cause of the error and make appropriate adjustments before the forecast negatively impacts the inventory level.

To demonstrate how to use a forecast error metric and automate the process, we will set up a statistical process control chart with mean absolute deviation (MAD).

MAD is calculated by adding together the absolute value of the differences between a forecast and the actual sales value and then dividing by the number of periods used. If the forecast for January is 120 units and the actual sales are 100 units, the error is 20 units. If February's forecast is 110 and actual sales are 120, the forecast error is 10 (the absolute value of 110 minus 120). If the forecast error for March is 15 units and we take the MAD across three periods, we get an MAD for April of 15 (20+10+15/3=15). What the MAD tells us in April is that for the previous three months, the forecast missed actual sales by an average of 15 units. Depending on how critical the product is, the planner may decide to accept the forecast as it is or investigate the cause(s) of the error. Products that have a low cost to carry in inventory or low-risk priority with customers might elicit no reaction from the planner. Those with high cost or risk would be investigated further.

If planners preestablish the error rate that will prompt an investigation, the entire process can be set-up to flag forecasts that need investigation. This process automates forecasting since forecasts that are performing within error limits will automatically be accepted and only those outside the limits will be called to the planner's attention. The system is analogous to statistical process control (SPC) where errors are tracked over time and plotted on a chart to alert process owners to out-of-control processes.[7]

The MAD is calculated for each of the months off the preceding period's forecast error. The number of periods included in the MAD calculation determines how responsive it is to errors. A large error will be "smoothed out" if too many periods are used. A relatively small error may cause an overreaction if too few periods are used. Many firms use three periods to balance the stability with the responsiveness of the MAD calculation. A running calculation of MAD values is established (see Figure 8.5).

fig. 8.5   A MAD Series

	Actual	Forecast	MAD
January	124	120	
February	135	140	
March	161	165	
April	178	177	4.33
May	325	205	3.33
June	210	220	41.67
July	215	195	43.67
August	180	176	50
September	150	155	11.33
October	120	115	9.67
November	110	111	4.67
December	105	90	3.67

The MAD values are then tracked against the limits established by the planning group. If a MAD value falls outside the boundaries, the planners receive a warning flag that this forecast is suspect. Planners can then go into the data and other processes backing up the forecast to determine why it is performing poorly. Figure 8.6 demonstrates that the first warning for the planners from the previous example would occur at June's demand spike. A planner investigating this spike may find that there was a promotion for that item that is not planned again. The planner may decide to take the demand spike out of the extract and replace it with the average demand for that product.

On the other hand, the marketing department may run this promotion every year. In that case, the demand spike would reoccur and is, therefore, a seasonal pattern. The system may not be using a seasonal forecasting model. The planner would have to change the forecast model in order to improve the forecast. The flag sets in motion planner investigation of the forecasting problems and focuses the planner's attention on the items needing attention rather than having to search through all products.

One firm started tracking forecast error and discovered that MAD values were in the 80 to 300 percent of forecast value range. The percentage of the underlying product's typical demand that MAD constitutes is called the mean absolute percentage error (MAPE). The MAPE gives the firm an idea how the forecasting model is performing across products with differing volume levels. The planners investigated the cause of the high error rates and found that the data extract was leaving out demand periods that had no sales. The firm had not set up the system to put zeroes into periods with no demand and the system did not recognize an empty period, so the demand was being shifted. The firm corrected the problem by making sure a zero was dropped into all periods with no demand.

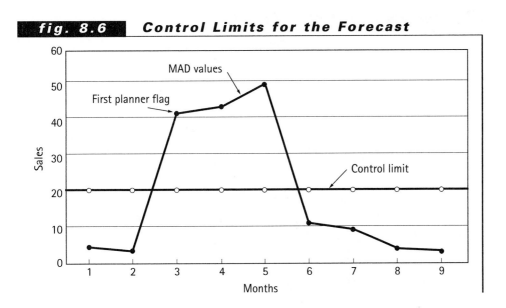

fig. 8.6 *Control Limits for the Forecast*

Another firm found that error metrics were declaring the forecast as working well but planners examining their buying screens saw actual demand that was well below forecasted demand. On further investigation, the planners found that items used in production were not being placed on the planner's buying screen. When the production items were added to those sold directly to customers, the totals matched the forecast. The forecast, as the error metrics suggested, was performing correctly. Without the error metrics, the firm would have underbought. The planner's screen was updated to include production parts.

Mean forecast error (MFE), commonly called bias, is another important measure. Bias tells the planner whether the forecast is consistently higher or lower than actual demand. Bias is simply the total of the forecast error divided by the number of periods. Using our previous example, to calculate bias we would leave out the absolute value, which makes February's negative error stay negative. The bias for this series is +8.3 (20 − 10 + 15/3 = 8.333). The forecast for these three periods has been on the high side. If bias stays positive, the forecast will drive inventories up as we overbuy. If consistently negative, we may face stockouts. A common cause of bias is a forecast that does not properly capture seasonality (see Figure 8.7).

The biased forecast has multiple positive or negative periods in a row. A nonseasonal forecasting model being applied in a seasonal environment is one potential cause. Another could be a surge in demand caused by a new customer being added. The surge might outstrip the forecasting model's ability to respond for a time. The planner can respond to these problems by taking over forecasting until the product demand settles down or by changing the model or its parameters to better reflect the environment. Figure 8.8 shows a nonseasonal model reacting to seasonality.

Planning a methodology that combines the planner's and others' decision making with the system's capability is called "combination forecasting" and is used by many

fig. 8.7   *A Biased Forecast*

	Actual	Forecast	Bias
January	124	160	
February	135	155	
March	161	140	
April	178	152	11.67
May	190	148	−9
June	210	166	−29.67
July	215	170	−37.33
August	180	175	−43.67
September	150	188	−31.33
October	120	170	−4
November	110	168	27.67
December	105	165	48.67

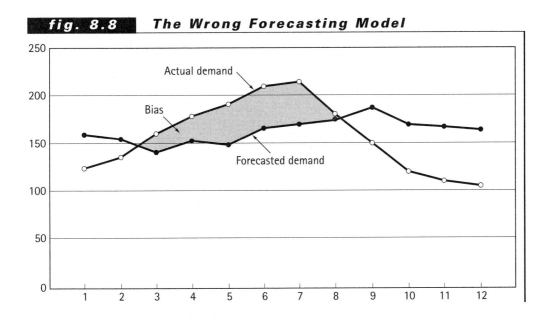

fig. 8.8 *The Wrong Forecasting Model*

firms to improve forecasting. A combination forecast occurs when the system notifies the planner that the forecast is not performing well or outside information comes in that gives the planner reason to believe the forecast will not be accurate. The warning or flag the system issues to the planner has already been discussed in Chapter 6. The planner needs only to follow a standard procedure for investigating what the probable causes for error are and what response should be used to correct the problem. Planners should be trained for the process and a consistent response methodology developed. If each planner follows his or her own instincts to solve the problem, varying approaches will be used that may not improve forecasting and could, in the case of changing a data extract, actually introduce more data integrity problems into the system.

The other signal that a forecast may fail is the introduction of information the system does not have. The sales force, management, planners, suppliers, and marketing each may have information not in the system. The data in the system is historical, called a "time series," and does not, therefore, have a forward view of events. W. Edwards Deming compared time series (historical) forecasting to driving a car with all the windows painted over and trying to steer by looking out the rear view mirror.[8] As long as the road ahead is no different from that behind you, the forecast should be sufficient. If any changes occur, however, the firm will be unprepared for what lies ahead.

The key to combination forecasting is establishing a method to both understand what is ahead and capture it in a consistent fashion. For example, take the sales force's information: A salesperson may learn that a new customer is very interested in making her firm a key supplier. If the customer buys in large volumes, the affected products will need to have their forecasts adjusted by the planners until such time as the mathematical model has caught up with the new demand pattern (see Figure 8.9).

Notice that the forecast has to chase the demand pattern after the new customer essentially increases the average demand for the product. This pattern is more than just trend. A trend represents a gradual increase and is usually based on incremental increases in demand through adding small customer accounts, or through a steady increased consumption on the part of all customers, or both. The pattern suggested in Figure 8.9 is a substantial leap in demand coming from a major customer who can swing a large portion of any product's sales by simply adopting the product. If a small distributor like Ray Distributing added a large customer like Wal-Mart, for example, all products bought by Wal-Mart would be affected as pictured in the graph.

Patterns like the one in Figure 8.9 are rarely a surprise to all in the company. If a new customer is the cause, there is a good chance the salesperson for that region knew about it in advance. If the cause is an upgrade in the product that will increase its utility to key customers, marketing or management should know about it. If the surge is caused by a liquidation of inventory, the planners should know and should prevent any more purchases of the product as the liquidation renders the forecast irrelevant.

How to react to predictions of demand changes by other experts is important. Even more important is to accurately capture those predictions. The firm needs to encourage reporting of pattern-changing events from all parties and provide for those predictions with a documentation trail that both reports to the planners and records the expert's input for future use. The process can be set up as a report in the system that is filled out by branch managers after polling the sales force, and by marketing and management experts periodically. The key to the reporting system is that it must be consistent (not open to different interpretations from different people), easy to complete (to encourage compliance), and issued on a regular schedule understood by the planners (to ensure proper utilization of results).

Once the predictions are delivered to the planners, the firm still needs a process by which the planners can convert the estimates into forecasts. Combination fore-

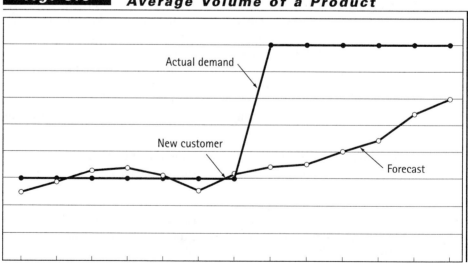

fig. 8.9 *A New Customer Increases the Average Volume of a Product*

casting has the planner use the mathematical forecast and its error metrics to establish a baseline from which to add or subtract the effect of this external information. In the early going, the firm may use the planner or other expert's best guess as to the increase or decrease caused by the change. In time, more-sophisticated techniques can be adopted that allow the system to identify similar circumstances from the past that may give the planner a good estimate of what will happen now.

Collaborative forecasting includes the customer in the process and is difficult to achieve without solid combination forecasting and error metrics backing it up. To include the customer, the firm must first do a good job with the combination forecast. This means that error metrics should be collected after the combination forecast as well as after the system's mathematical model to see whether the combination forecast has improved the system model. If so, the combination forecast should proceed. If not, the combination forecasting technique should be investigated to see whether improvements could be made to make it more successful than the math model.

If a product's forecast cannot be improved upon by combination forecasting, the firm should suspend this expensive and complex process. Information automation plays an important role by narrowing the combination forecasting effort to those products with high forecast error and those predicted to have accuracy problems unless new information is included in the forecast. Category A items tend to be relatively stable and therefore are rarely in need of combination forecasting (provided any potential data problems have been fixed in advance). This leads to considerable savings in planner effort, which will be demonstrated later in this chapter (see "Buying Decisions").

Only customer-critical products that cannot be accurately forecasted through math models or combination forecasting should be considered for collaborative forecasting. Collaborative forecasting requires the customer to report unusual developments in the same fashion as the experts do in combination forecasting. Some customers will be unwilling or unable to participate. Others may be willing to help but will require some sort of quid pro quo from the distributor (discounts or guaranteed fill rates). For these reasons, collaborative forecasting should be limited only to customers constituting a large percentage of the distributor's business and then only on products where the customer can actually add value to the forecasting decision. This means that collaborative forecasting will constitute a very small portion of the forecasting activity (see Figure 8.10).

The error metrics applied to combination and mathematical forecast modeling should also be applied to collaborative forecasting. Due to the customer inconvenience, the need to eliminate unnecessary forecasting effort is even more important under collaborative forecasting than combination. In general, mathematical models, if reading good data from well-designed data extracts, will outperform human estimates or what is commonly called "expert forecasting." Combination forecasting will typically offer significant improvement over mathematical models if the math model is underperforming. Collaborative forecasting has a short history and limited use. Because it is the most expensive and difficult technique from both technology and customer-relationship standpoints, collaborative forecasting should be used only under special circumstances.

Minimizing forecast error is an important first step in minimizing inventory since forecast error is calculated, directly or indirectly, into the reorder point in general and

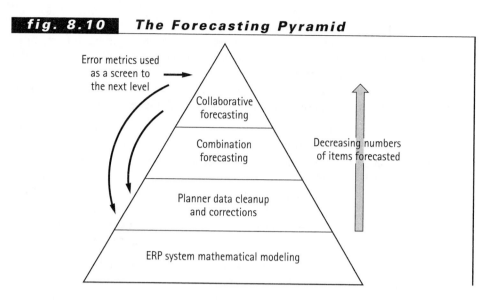

fig. 8.10   *The Forecasting Pyramid*

safety stock in particular. The next factor for capturing safety stock calculation is the supplier's performance. An accurate forecast will not be enough to support customer service if the supplier cannot be depended upon to deliver on time at high fill rates.

Lead-Time Tracking

After forecasting customer demand, the firm must forecast suppliers' performance as well. The goal of tracking supplier performance is twofold. First, we want to make an accurate estimate of suppliers' delivery times and the variability of those times. Second, we should use what we learn to assist suppliers in improving their processes. Some supplier lead-time failures are driven entirely by supplier issues; others are driven by distributor actions like poor forecasting, uneven buying patterns, or a lack of information sharing with the supplier.

Supplier performance metrics are critical to setting safety stocks and demand during lead-time inventory needs. Safety stock calculations use an estimate of supplier variability (reliability) to determine how much safety stock is needed to protect against stockouts when suppliers miss delivery windows (or fail to ship completely). Statistical analysis can and should be applied to supplier performance, but many firms use planner estimates instead. As with forecast error, planners are likely to err on the high side to avoid upsetting the sales force. The result is too much inventory in products that have suffered recent supplier failures.

The ERP system can easily track supplier performance by collecting lead times. One method is to take the date on the purchase orders (POs) and subtract it from the receipt date to determine delivery time. The delivery times can then be collected across all shipments from the supplier for a specified period of time. This is the simplest but not necessarily the best method. If the supplier and distributor frequently have to negotiate lead times or if the supplier has different fill rates at different plants, the distributor may want to develop a more sophisticated lead-time collection tech-

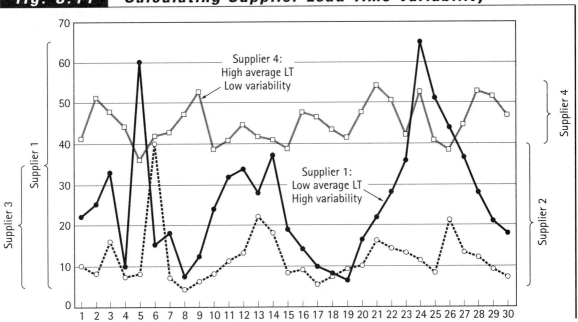

fig. 8.11 **Calculating Supplier Lead-Time Variability**

nique. One distributor chose to find the variability of a supplier's lead time by collecting all delivery times and finding the variance of their lead times (see Figure 8.11). In addition to variance, the distributor also calculated the average lead time.

Notice that a high average lead time does not necessarily mean a high variability level or vice versa. The product with the highest variability comes from supplier number 1 (226 days), but the product with the highest average delivery time (46 days) was from supplier number 4, who also had the lowest variability. The variability tells us how reliable the supplier is and is a key component of safety stock calculations. The average lead time lets us know how much inventory we need to carry to get us through the supplier's lead time (on average). The average lead time is multiplied by forecasted demand for the period to get this demand-during-lead-time number. If a supplier has a longer lead time, the firm has to carry more inventory to cover that longer lead time. If, however, the supplier's deliveries are hard to predict (highly variable), the firm will need inventory not only for the average lead time but for worst-case scenarios as well. This worst-case-scenario inventory is rarely used and, therefore, decreases the distributor's profitability.

Setting the Reorder Point

Once the supplier and forecast performance is known, we can make a reasonable attempt to set the reorder point. There are four common methods for setting the reorder point:

1. Guess—That's right, many firms just apply the planner's or branch manager's best guess.

2. Educated Guess—The planner or branch manager will take the supplier's stated lead time and the average demand for the product, multiply them together, and then add a "fudge factor" for a safety stock.

3. Let the Supplier Decide—The branch will order in the supplier's minimum order size. One box is the min and a second is the max. When the max goes empty (i.e., the min has been penetrated), the branch reorders a box.

4. Have the ERP System Calculate and Maintain the Reorder Point—This methodology differs from the min/max system but revolves around the same principles explained previously: the forecast, forecast error, supplier average lead times, supplier lead-time variability, and firm's desired fill rates. Next we discuss fill rate selection.

Selecting the Fill Rate

The final important component for calculating the safety stock is the desired fill rate. Until the firm establishes the fill rate, there is no way to know how much safety stock to carry. A high fill rate requires higher safety stocks. Since the safety stock is part of the reorder point, the reorder point is also affected by the fill rate. As the fill rate increases, the safety stock and, hence, the reorder point increase as well (see Figure 8.12).

Demand during lead-time inventory is the forecasted demand for the average projected lead time, unaffected by fill rate. The safety stock is the inventory for surprises

fig. 8.12 **The Relationship Between Fill Rate and Reorder Point**

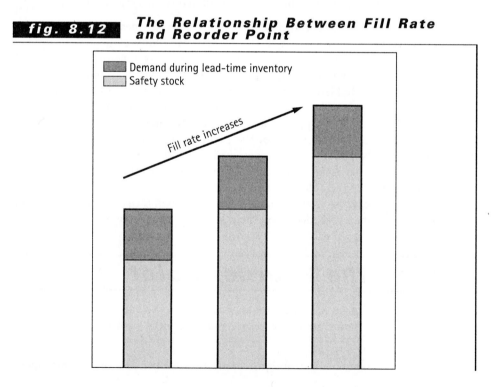

like supplier lead-time variability and forecast error. Therefore, increasing fill rates requires higher levels of safety stock. To set the reorder point, the management must decide what fill rate is appropriate. Most firms determine fill rates in one or more of the following ways:

1. Guess—The planners and the sales force fight it out to set the minimum or reorder point. No one is quite sure what the actual fill rate is—just that customers are not complaining as much as before.

2. Set a Blanket Policy—Management decides on a fill rate that will then be reported to customers as the firm's policy. One firm set a 98 percent fill rate policy. It was not clear, however, whether the fill rate should apply to all products or only to core products (A items). The firm quickly found that a 98 percent fill rate would build inventories more than anticipated. This method is easy to decide upon but very difficult to implement.

3. Physically Simulate the Fill Rate—Some firms will change the fill rate and measure costs (stockout and expediting versus additional inventory holding costs). One firm found it minimized costs for a group of products at a 96 percent fill rate after raising the fill rate until inventory costs began to push total costs higher (see Figure 8.13). This method is effective but time consuming and expensive.

4. Use Computer Simulation on the Fill Rate—If the firm has determined its holding cost and stockout costs, the fill rate can be simulated by applying different fill rates and determining the least-cost policy under each of the potential fill rate levels.

fig. 8.13 **A Firm Simulates Its Fill Rate**

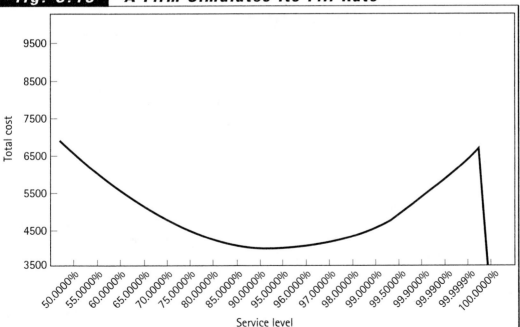

The fill rate that minimizes inventory costs as opposed to stockout costs is selected for each product. This method requires the firm to determine holding and stockout costs. The former is relatively easy; the latter can be very difficult.

Assuming the firm can agree upon a fill-rate policy, the next step will be to determine what the system can support. The system will have to be evaluated as to which processes it makes available and how those processes match the firm's goals.

1. Min/Max—Some systems will support only a simple min/max approach where the min and max are established and set by the planners. Planners need to examine the fill rate expectations, supplier performance, and forecast error in deciding what the min and max should be. The method could be made more accurate if the reorder points were estimated statistically in spreadsheets, but the process would have to be repeated periodically to assure accuracy.[9] (For details on statistically setting reorder points, see Lawrence *et al.,* 2002, or Ballou, 1999).

2. Dynamic Reorder Points—Some systems support dynamic reorder points, where the system tracks the error measures and then calculates and adjusts the reorder point as conditions change. Since supplier performance, demand during lead time, and forecast error change continuously, a dynamic reorder point is preferable for both accuracy and human efficiency. Many different systems and bolt-ons use different ways to calculate reorder points. Some focus on lead times, others on forecast error, and others on both. Some systems consider fill rates and some do not. A firm should thoroughly investigate how the system works and determine the effect it will have on the firm's objectives.

Buying Decisions

Most college students learn about the purchasing decision as a single-item order where all that needs to be determined is how much to buy. The decision is based on the holding cost of inventory versus the cost of placing an order. In reality, virtually all buys are what we call "line buys." Line buys are a more complex form of purchasing since they require the planner to consider freight and other costs in determining the amount ordered. Freight is considered, as are quantity discounts since a driving reason behind making a line buy is to reduce the per-item landed cost.

The most common form of line buy is where a single supplier makes multiple products for the distributor. The planner, when buying a product, must consider whether to buy the one product or to buy other products from that supplier as well to economize on freight costs and other economies of scale. Freight costs can be saved if two or more products are purchased since the freight company will charge less for each additional item if the total exceeds a certain minimum.

Other economies of scale include handling costs of the order by both the purchasing and warehouse personnel. The larger the order, the less effort on a per-part basis, so the total landed cost per item will be less than it would be for a series of smaller orders. The balancing cost will be the inventory costs, which provoke another question: If only one item has triggered its reorder point but a substantial savings could be achieved if the order size were increased beyond what is needed for that item, what do you add? The problem is called "coordinated replenishment" and includes virtually every purchasing transaction of any size. The coordinated aspect refers to multiple products being coordinated together in the decision.

Take the following example: A purchasing person needs to buy a product from a supplier that provides five stock items. A certain B item has penetrated its reorder point but the planner would like to add more to the order. One A item is fairly close to its reorder point. One B is even closer. Two other A items are not close at all (see Figure 8.14). Should the planner buy more of the B item that has triggered, or add some A items, or buy the other B, or some combination of the foregoing?

The answer will depend on how big the discounts (freight and supplier) are for more items and how far from the minimums the single-item purchase will be. The decision can involve many variables and add up to considerable costs. Many firms have a policy against buying in anything less than truckload quantity because the transportation savings is so significant. Under this type of restriction, the coordinated replenishment decision will dominate nearly every buying decision.

Different ERP systems and/or bolt-ons can support buying decisions to varying degrees. Most will offer the single-product recommended buy. The simplest form of buy is the one product/one supplier buy and is often available in systems under the economic order quantity (EOQ). The EOQ is a well-known, proven method for buying a single item. Many firms do not use the EOQ since it is not designed to handle line (coordinated) buys. The line buy requires more complex analysis like EOQ for quantity discounts or coordinated replenishment approaches. Even though line

fig. 8.14 *A Coordinated Replenishment Decision*

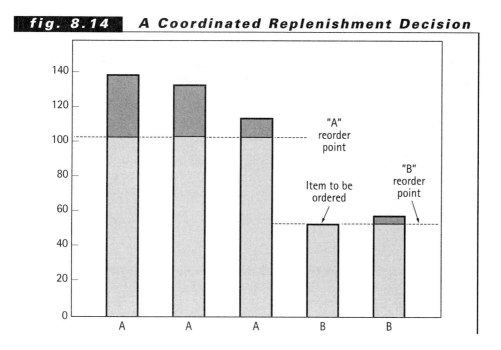

buying is by far the most common, many systems are not set up to handle this complex environment.

To automate the buying decision, therefore, a firm must either be willing to accept the shortcomings of the EOQ or use a line buy program. The line buy decision is so complex that many line buy programs will simplify the problem (that is, leave things out or limit the number of products that can be considered). The firm should evaluate the shortcomings of each process and how they affect the outcome of most decisions before determining how the planners should use the system.

Inventory Classification

A powerful and simple concept, classification schemes can be set up to evaluate how inventory is being used and what its future should be. ABC is the most common classification scheme and takes on different forms for different purposes:

1. Gross Margin Return on Investment (GMROI)—Equivalent to the "turn and earn" metric, it allows the firm to put the largest investment in the inventory that provides the highest profit. The calculation equals the total gross margin dollars for a specified period (a year is common) divided by the average inventory value in dollars.

2. Sales Volume—The sales-volume ABC ranking allows the firm to watch cash flow since items are ranked based on total sales.

3. Hits—The hits ranking allows the firm to watch products that would disappoint the most customers if they stocked out. Calculated simply as how many times a product was pulled for any customer, this metric is also popular for warehouse layout purposes (see Chapter 14 for more on warehouse layout).

When combined with purchasing policies, the ABC system can improve profitability and reduce effort (automation). One firm used GMROI in the following fashion:

A items—Reorder when necessary, carry a safety stock for a 98 percent fill rate at all locations.

B items—Reorder when necessary, carry a safety stock for a 90 percent fill rate at all locations.

C items—Consolidate to regional distribution centers (RDC) or other hubs. If the hub does not achieve A or B status with the item, eliminate from inventory.

D items—Eliminate.

The rules as to what constitutes an A versus B versus C versus D item will differ from firm to firm, but our example firm used the following rules:

A item = 200 percent GMROI or greater

B item = 100 percent < GMROI < 200 percent

C item = 0 percent < GMROI < 100 percent

D item = GMROI < 0 percent

Some firms prefer to use another classification method like total sales or a combination method like GMROI/sales volume/hits where the best ranking among the three is used. The ranking system not only reduces inventory by eliminating slow movers that might not get recognized otherwise, it also reduces the planner's workload. C and D items do not have to be forecasted (combination or otherwise) or tracked anymore. Since C and D items often constitute as much as 50 to 80 percent of a firm's SKUs (stock keeping units), the workload is reduced by all of the D items and by the number of locations from which the C items are consolidated out.

On the other hand, A items tend to have stable patterns and, therefore, frequently do not need combination forecasting. Planners will find the forecast error metrics will not flag as many A items. Planner forecasting activity will be limited to a few A items and more B items. Combination forecasting takes time, so the planners will be more effective if they are not handling the entire inventory.

A final benefit of the automated ABC system is obsolescence control. An item tends to start in A or B status and then eventually move down the hierarchy. An A item that drops to B status will have its safety stock automatically reduced. When it moves from B to C it will be consolidated. By the time it hits D (obsolete), virtually no inventory remains, as opposed to the large markdowns so many firms go through every year when these products are scrapped or sold at a loss.

Automating Purchase Orders

Assuming the above processes have been made available, the system may be able to automatically produce POs without planner intervention. The system will use the rules established with the ABC system and the reorder points from the supplier performance, forecast error metrics, and fill rates to determine when to issue a purchase order. How much to buy may be taken from the EOQ or a line buying program, or the system may prompt the planner for assistance.

Automated purchase orders are offered on many systems, but many firms do not use them. Data integrity concerns are the principal concern since the steps to the automated purchase order contain many places where inaccurate data could lead to problems with the order process.

Aggregate Planning

Aggregate planning is often associated only with manufacturing but is actually the planning of needs and placement of resources. A distribution firm will make long-term decisions based on long-term aggregate forecasts for the placement of major assets like warehouses or transportation or automation equipment. Since inventory is one of the distributor's largest assets, it should be included in the distribution aggregate plan.

The aggregate plan must direct and drive replenishment processes through a combination of management thought on desired fill rates and the cost of resources. For distributors, most facilities and other assets are driven by inventory. This means that ABC and fill-rate policies are key components of the distribution aggregate plan. The aggregate plan, therefore, draws information from the ERP system and drives the replenishment process through the system by the long-term strategic decisions made as part of the planning process.

Conclusion

Replenishment decisions and the processes that support them are among the most significant activities carried out at a distribution firm. The repetitive nature of replenishment means that information automation can play an important role in replenishment process improvement. ERP or other information systems will likely come to control all aspects of the replenishment process. Failure to implement stable processes with a high degree of data integrity will force many firms to use error-prone, human-based processes that are more expensive and less effective than automated processes.

The replenishment process has received considerable attention from the distribution and information technology communities in recent years. The area will continue to grow in importance, and many of the remaining problems with replenishment automation will be addressed. Distributors should focus their planning efforts on understanding these processes and training their planners to work with an automated process. Operating in manual mode while your competition is automating processes will be a difficult position to maintain.

Distribution Retrospective

Chuck realized he could not get anywhere unless he proved the system would fail without more cooperation from the sales force. He decided that he would need to implement a process using forecasting from the system to drive firm activities. He was sure that once management saw the results of the forecasting module, they would put more pressure on the sales force to use the system properly. His problem lay in his own planners: He would have to train them on the system, discontinue their expert-based current process, and switch to combination forecasting. While he wanted to show management how poorly the forecasts were performing, he could not afford to sacrifice customer service. Combination forecasting would protect the customer, but checking every forecast would put a huge burden on his planners. He simply did not have the resources to carry out combination forecasting, much less pull his people off their current jobs to go through forecasting training.

After thinking it through, Chuck hit on something. He did not have to have the planners investigate every forecast. After all, management was always complaining about how much inventory the firm was carrying. They thought the problem was poor forecasting, but Chuck knew that most of the problem was products he was forced to carry by the sales force but that did not produce any profits. The system had something called "turn and earn," which was supposed to evaluate the profitability of products. He decided to start by evaluating all products and then suggesting that only a subset should continue in inventory.

The results shocked even Chuck. Less than 5 percent of the inventory qualified as A items, and those items accounted for more than 85 percent of all profits! He wanted to wake management up, not give them heart attacks! He swallowed hard and took the results into the Vice President of Operations, Jared Helms. He figured he would either get the support he wanted or get fired for letting it come to this on his watch.

"You have got to be kidding me!" Jared shouted. "How did this happen?!"

"Reactive purchasing is my best guess," Chuck said. "The customer or salesperson says, 'Jump,' and we ask, 'How high?'" Chuck was not going to shirk his responsibility but he was ready for what was coming.

"This is how you run things?" Jared knew the question wasn't fair, but he wanted Chuck to squirm some.

"You tell me where this company's policy lies!" Chuck had expected the question but was surprised at how angry it made him. "How many times have I protested and been told the sales force knows the customer better than we do or a hundred other reasons why we should be more flexible? This is the result!"

Jared sighed. He knew it was all true. In fact, he had fought this same battle many times with his boss when he was the one in Chuck's position. As Vice President of Operations, he was actually on Chuck's side. It was time to say so.

"You're right," Jared said, to Chuck's surprise. It wasn't supposed to be this easy. Chuck had brought all kinds of documentation to prove his point. "What do you want to do?"

"I want to stop buying all C and D items. That will lighten our load and the company's inventory will drop rapidly, proving our point." Chuck said. "Then I want to design a combination forecasting process and pretest it with our data. Unless I miss my guess, it will look horrible, and then we can go to the sales force to begin eliminating the data integrity issues. I'll need an IT consultant to assist us with the ERP system."

"Wow, you want to blow the roof off the place," Jared said. "All right, I'll approve the immediate hire of a consultant. Discontinuing C and D items is going to be ugly but I'll put my neck on the line if I have to. I'll also take everything you learn to the executive committee. That's my fight, not yours. Just keep me informed."

Issues to Consider

1. Explain what batching is and its effect on the supply chain.

2. What are the effects of inaccurate data extracts?

3. Why are forecast error metrics so important?

4. What effect can ABC classification have on inventory levels?

Case Study: Demand Management

Keith considered the Ray Distributing ordering process. He had been operating as a distributor and been reordering product from suppliers through a purchase order system. The system treated items according to a GMROI classification system where he would reorder only products in the A and B categories. He had adopted the process a few years ago and had seen a tremendous decrease in his inventory. He wanted to use a more reliable forecasting system than his best guess, but his ERP system did not support forecasting or dynamic reorder points, so he had been stuck with setting his own mins and then reordering based on his expert opinion and supplier minimum shipping sizes.

Keith had spent the better part of two years trying to improve on this system but now realized that it did not matter anymore. The manufacturing operations would have 500 to 600 SKUs whereas distribution had 3,000 to 5,000. The forecasting problem had been simplified from a sheer numbers perspective but the time involved had lengthened considerably. The longer production time window meant that Keith's forecasting period would be much more difficult. A longer forecast is inherently less accurate, Keith knew, so he had to first forecast as best he could and second, take advantage of every opportunity to minimize inventory.

He thought about the problem and decided to sketch the supply chain (see Figure 8.15). It looked simple enough but the time windows were worrisome. He also did not understand how he could get the ERP system to manage the bill of materials for the products with such long time windows. One step at a time, he told himself. He decided to address the top-level forecast first. He would have to add up all lead times and make sure the forecasting period covered the entire length of the production cycle time. He would also have to address ABC status of products and their product life cycle since his products followed a very definite cycle. He would need to determine how to manage customer demand under his product life cycle/forecasting/long-lead-time scenarios.

Further complicating the forecasting problem was product life cycles: Products would go obsolete over time through the application of different forces than what might be seen in other distribution channels. The product life cycle followed a pattern

fig. 8.15   ***Texas Tackle Factory and Team Nu-Mark's Supply Chain***

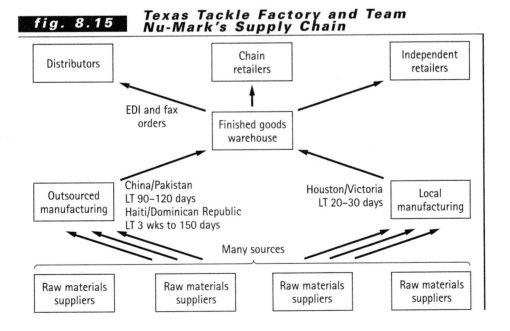

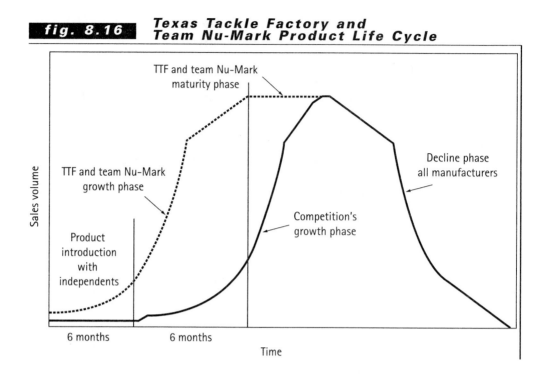

fig. 8.16 **Texas Tackle Factory and Team Nu-Mark Product Life Cycle**

that had a great deal to do with competition. Once a new product was introduced, the competition would try to copy it. It normally took about five months for them to respond. After the competition introduced the new product, they needed another six months to penetrate the market since retailers bought new products on a biyearly basis.

Keith used the independent retailers to test new products since they were more loyal and flexible. He could test a new product for about six months and, if it proved successful, take it to distributors and larger retailers next. After the larger customers got the product, he had about one year until it went into decline due to competitive pressure (see Figure 8.16).

Keith realized his products had to be forecasted differently at different points in their product life cycle. Given the lead times associated with imported products, he would have to watch these stages carefully or he could get caught with no product during a growth phase or with too much coming in during a decline. Some products could be sourced through his operations in Houston and Victoria but many could not. He decided on a multitiered ABC system to guide his forecasting and replenishment systems. The process would depend on whether a product was a standard item not likely to go obsolete (no product life cycle issues), or a nonstandard product, and whether it could be sourced locally in an emergency. The product's contribution to profitability would be reflected in its first classification digit (A, B, or C); its status as a standard or new product would be reflected in the second digit (S for standard, N for nonstandard); and the third digit would indicate whether it could be sourced locally or not (L for local sourcing available, I if international were the only available alternative). He then set up the following policy:

A = 200 percent plus GMROI for standard products, 100% to 200% GMROI from similar products for nonstandards in their growth and/or maturity phases.

B = 100 percent to 200 percent GMROI for standard products, 100 percent to 200 percent GMROI from similar products for nonstandards in their growth and/or maturity phases.

C = <100 percent GMROI for standard products, <100 percent GMROI for nonstandards.

Any product released over a year ago that was still below 100 percent GMROI was considered to be in decline. Keith now put the following policy in place for forecasting and replenishment:

ASI—Forecasted with mathematical model and automatically goes to combination forecasting, carries safety stock for a 99 percent fill rate. Reorder when necessary.

ASL—Forecasted with mathematical model and passed to planner only if error exceeds limits, carries safety stock for a 95 percent fill rate. Reorder when necessary.

ANI—Forecasted by expert analysis using comparison to other products' performance at this point in their life cycle, carries safety stock for 99 percent fill rate derived from similar products. Reorder when necessary.

ANL—Forecasted by expert analysis using comparison to other products' performance at this point in their life cycle, carries safety stock for 95 percent fill rate derived from similar products. Reorder when necessary.

BSI—Forecasted with mathematical model and automatically goes to combination forecasting, carries safety stock for an 85 percent fill rate. Reorder when necessary.

BSL—Forecasted with mathematical model and passed to planner only if error exceeds limits, carries safety stock for an 80 percent fill rate. Reorder when necessary.

BNI—Do not reorder.

BNL—Do not reorder.

All C items—Do not reorder.

Keith felt this policy would force him to be agile and introduce new products quickly and avoid obsolescence problems. He now needed to figure out how to automate the process. He could have some programmers write the policy into his ERP package and code a solid forecasting and safety stock methodology, or he could adopt a bolt-on that had the forecasting and safety stock models in it that would pull the ABC status from the ERP system and the data for analysis. He decided on the latter since coding such complex processes would be expensive.

When he looked at bolt-ons, however, he was not able to find one in his price range that would consider both forecast error and supplier performance. He did find one that could figure based on lead times. He thought that lead times could be more important than forecast error, especially since he was doing combination forecasting. He bought the package and instructed the ERP provider to start programming the ABC policy.

Case Challenges

1. Why is Keith planning to use expert forecasting on the nonstandard products? Is there a better way?

2. Why is Keith eliminating the B items on nonstandards? Is this wise? What about the C items going away? Will important customers be lost?

3. Help Keith automate this process. Draw a model that shows where the ERP system ends and the bolt-on begins. Be sure to show what data should be exchanged and when.

References

1. Spyros G. Makridakis, Steven C. Wheelwright, and Rob J. Hyndman, *Forecasting: Methods and Applications,* 3rd ed. (Hoboken, NJ: John Wiley & Sons, 1997).

2. Richard B. Chase, F. Robert Jacobs, and Nicholas J. Aquilano, *Operations Management for Competitive Advantage,* 9th ed. (New York: McGraw-Hill/Irwin, 2001).

3. Makridakis, Wheelwright, and Hyndman, *Forecasting: Methods and Applications.*

4. Ibid.

5. Ibid.

6. Ibid.

7. Mary Walton and W. Edwards Deming, *Deming Management Method* (Farmington, UT: Perigee, 1988).

8. Ibid.

9. F. Barry Lawrence, Daniel. F Jennings, and Brian. E Reynolds, *e-dDistribution* (Mason. OH: South-Western Publishing, 2003); Ronald H. Ballou, *Business Logistics Management,* 4th ed. (Upper Saddle River, NJ: Prentice Hall, 1998).

9

Operations Management

Distribution Perspective

Crouch Steel was a half-billion-dollar metal service center in 2000. Kevin Maddox was the warehouse manager for the Dallas operations. Crouch had adopted an RF tracking system in 1997 and had implemented it at the Dallas warehouse to test its capability and establish processes before rolling it out to the rest of the company. The system had performed better than expected with inventory accuracy improving so much the firm had been able to do away with its yearly inventory at the Dallas operations.

Kevin was now considered to be the firm's RF expert since he had managed the entire implementation process. Management was now considering whether the system should be rolled out to all branches or shut down to save on licensing fees. Since rolling the system out to other branches would increase the licensing fees (several licenses were required for each site), management wanted to see what savings had been achieved at Dallas. Kevin felt sure a great deal had been accomplished through more accurate inventory status, reduced picker effort, increased fill rates, and decreased warehouse cycle times. He did not know, however, how to demonstrate the savings to a sufficient degree to justify extending the system to other branches since many of the gains had been associated with other processes.

Improved fill rates and increased inventory accuracy, for instance, were often credited to the inventory planners' efforts. The system did not track warehouse cycle times or picker productivity, and Kevin was unsure how to capture those savings. He decided he needed to know more about how the ERP system supported the RF system and vice versa before he would be able to project what savings had been gained to date and what additional savings would come from the extension of the system to other locations.

Introduction

The ERP system controls and drives the operations division's processes and activities. The needs of the distributor's operations information handling processes differ from sales, marketing, and purchasing, which are all purely informational. In spite of the physical human and equipment components, the operations of facilities and inventory handling still rely on the ERP system for support, tracking, and measurement. The organization of these activities takes on a different pattern since the system is now tracking and driving a different set of processes.

The operations division of a distributor is largely physical in nature, but to support the sales, marketing, purchasing, and managerial functions the operations division must be plugged into the ERP system. ERP tracking of activities keeps the other functions informed so that they can respond to changes in business conditions. If conditions change in the warehouse or transportation fleet, either customer service or distribution replenishment needs, or both, may be affected. The functional area (sales, marketing, purchasing, etc.) associated with the impact of the change needs to be informed so they can make adjustments.

For instance, if the warehouse learns that products for a customer listed as in stock when the customer placed the order are not available at picking and shipping time, the salesperson responsible for that customer account should be notified so that he or she can contact the customer and be sure appropriate adjustments are made. If the warehouse discovers misplaced inventory that has been removed from the ERP system, the inventory planners would need to know before they placed additional orders against those products. If a supplier has missed a delivery time window, sales and planners would need to be updated. The salesperson needs to be notified because the products that are being shipped might not arrive in time to meet future orders. The customer or the salesperson may be able to introduce an alternative product or reschedule activities associated with the missing product. The planners need notification because they may need to expedite the order through another supplier.

Order tracking is becoming more important as customer expectations increase. Customers are moving to just-in-time deliveries or, at least, to reduced inventories in general. These reductions in supply chain inventories mean that customers have less room for error as well as faster notification if the errors do occur and the supply chain will not be able to respond. If a glitch occurs anywhere in the order delivery process, customers will want to know immediately so that they can plan for any increased lead times or incomplete orders. In a perfect world, the distributor will have already solved the problem without inconveniencing the customer at all. This process will continue to grow in importance.

System capacity and activity level are also key. If the warehouse is operating at or near its capacity level, other members of the firm—and, possibly, of the supply chain—need to understand that capacity constraints may slow the flow of materials, affecting all downstream activity. If we think of the supply chain as a fluid flow problem, the distributor's warehouse operations are storage tanks along the line. Capacity limitations can be encountered in throughput (how much the warehouse can ship at full speed) or storage limitations (how much can be kept in the warehouse at one time). The warehouse, therefore, is a key link in the supply chain.[1]

The goals of the distribution warehouse and operations are to

○ Create an equilibrium/balance between the supply and demand of products. Distribution operations create a "smoothing effect" to the flow of orders and materials through the supply chain. The operations division employs inventory, expediting, personnel, transportation, and other means to create this balance.

○ Respond to demand patterns and work to increase customer satisfaction levels. Increasing service levels (fill rates) has become one of the most significant attributes of supply chain management (SCM).

○ Act as reservoirs for the supply chain to store and consolidate products. The warehouse increases product value by increasing proximity and accessibility for the end user. The branch warehouse provides the most expensive and most accessible inventories. The regional distribution center is the next step back in the chain. The distributor's warehouse principal value-add is location.

○ Act as buffers for manufacturing systems. Many distribution professionals poorly understand this activity. The manufacturer's production processes are very expensive and highly inflexible when compared to inventory with multiple sources of supply. The inventory stored in distribution warehouses acts as a buffer for supplier's capacity restrictions and must be managed as such. This buffer management role requires the sales and operations divisions to properly understand and be kept up to date on the manufacturer's production status. The distributor's operations, therefore, are critical to the success of the supply chain.

The operations division's functions fall into two basic categories: inbound and outbound materials management. Inbound processes include receiving (with inspection), putaway, and replenishment. Outbound processes include: processing orders, order picking, checking, packing, and shipping (see Figure 9.1). All processes are controlled through the ERP system's warehouse management module. The control of operations' processes is a largely information-based task. The tracking and control of the operations division allows other divisions that support operations' processes to respond more quickly and, perhaps more importantly, allows the operations division to control its own performance.

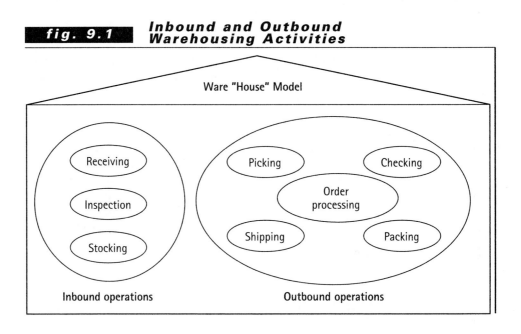

fig. 9.1   **Inbound and Outbound Warehousing Activities**

Ware "House" Model

Receiving
Inspection
Stocking

Picking   Checking
Order processing
Shipping   Packing

Inbound operations

Outbound operations

Inventory Tracking

Tracking inventory movement throughout the distributor's operations is both an asset control and a customer service issue. Asset control refers to keeping the investment in material and equipment to a minimum while still meeting customer service objectives. Warehouse throughput depends, in large measure, on the equipment the warehouse has available, and customer service depends on inventory availability. Lack of visibility, as noted in earlier chapters, results in an increased need for inventory due to errors in forecasting and order handling caused by time lapses in discovering problems. The increased inventory and frenzied activity levels in the warehouse (see Figure 9.2) lead to increased need for warehouse space and handling equipment. Since inventory and the warehouses to support it are the principal non-financial assets for distributors, the firm's success and return on investment (ROI) depend on controlling these assets. Increased visibility (better information capability) will lead to a reduced need for assets, increased throughput, and increased customer service. The problem extends beyond the warehouse alone, however, and into the supply chain.

The flow pattern through the warehouse is merely a microcosm of the supply chain. Receiving is the internal supplier, the picker is transportation, and the shelving areas are warehouses. This internal supply chain then links itself to the external supply chain. As the distance material is being moved and the control of customer orders throughout the broader supply chain becomes an issue, the importance of information and its movement velocity increases. Supplier and logistics firms will be black holes to the supply chain if they are not linked into the information exchange and movement up and down the channel (see Figure 9.3). Supplier purchase order information status or logistics carrier material movement status is, therefore, signif-

| fig. 9.2 | *The Frenzied Routes of the Warehouse* |

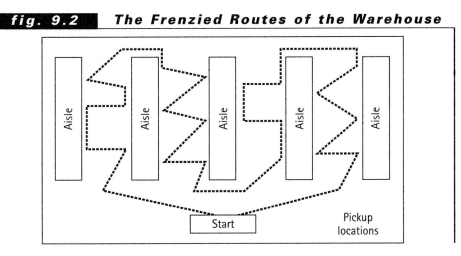

icant to asset control and customer service and involves interface among information systems of all players: distributor, logistics carrier, and supplier.

Transportation providers like FedEx and United Parcel Service have developed transportation tracking software that will allow customers to schedule and track their freight. Small orders (UPS and FedEx specialties) are frequently "hotter" than larger shipments, however, so these systems had been slower to develop with other carriers but were rapidly being rolled out in the early 2000s. The key issue is setting up the ERP connection and establishing processes that give the sales and purchasing group visibility to where product is and when it will arrive at its destination. The supplier has a role to play as well by using advanced shipping notices (ASNs) that notify the distributor that the product is now in transit and what is contained in the shipment.

The greatest degree of control will be over the distributor's operations from pick slip issue through invoicing. The distributor can bring visibility to these processes. The control of internal processes is a function of well-designed processes and completely connected information handling. Many ERP systems use distribution requirements planning (DRP) to maintain inventory placement throughout the

| fig. 9.3 | *The Supply Chain Black Hole* |

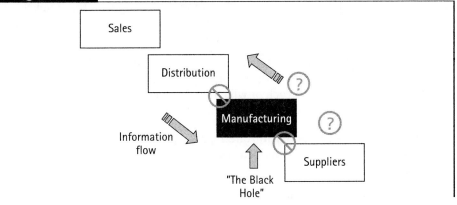

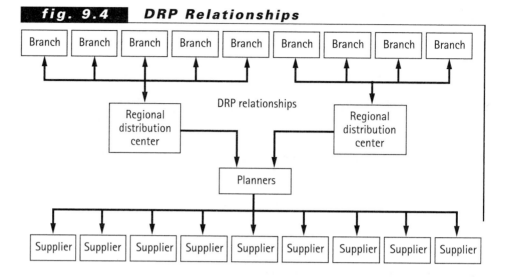

fig. 9.4   **DRP Relationships**

distribution network. To be successful, DRP must be connected to work order processes or material requirements planning (MRP) processes and must establish relationships among branches, regional distribution centers, and purchasing/planning activities (see Figure 9.4).

The relationships resemble an inverted MRP Bill of Materials (BOM). Every box represents value added to the product. The supplier transforms the product from raw materials to finished goods. The planners arrange for transportation to the regional distribution centers. The movement of material is further value-add since the product is now closer to the customer and, therefore, more valuable. The DRP program tracks this movement and, as an MRP program does by building products through the bill of materials, positions product at varying stages of closeness to the customer. The next level is the branch, which represents the final stages of value-add.

The DRP module uses stock levels and order quantities established in the inventory-planning module (see Chapters 8 and 14). The system triggers reorder points and moves inventory from the supplier to the RDC and from the RDC to the branch. Customer demand relieves inventory at the branches until the reorder point is triggered. The branches then act as the customers and pull their demand through the RDC. Finally, the RDC triggers its reorder points and buys from the suppliers. The relationship between the RDC and the branches, therefore, is essentially no different from that between the supplier and the RDC.

As systems like DRP track and move material through the distributors' operations, the system will track fill rates to operations' systems performance for the customer. Fill rates come in two forms, each of which tells us something different and requires different actions from the system and personnel:

1. Order Initiation—The initial fill rate represents a level of preparedness for the operation and is focused on purchasing.

2. Ship-Confirm—The final fill rate represents actual customer service and includes purchasing, transportation, and operations performance.

The order initiation fill rate represents what is in stock when the customer calls. Although useful in demonstrating how well prepared the firm is, this fill rate is not always optimal for cost minimization. Some products can be accessed quickly from other branches or suppliers and should not be in stock at all times. The second fill rate that is more commonly tracked by ERP systems is the ship-confirm one that tracks fill rates as products go out the door (shipped). This fill rate is the only relevant one to the customer but may hide a great deal of cost. The effort on the part of planners and operations personnel may have been so great as to raise costs to prohibitively high levels. Expediting costs are the price of too great a difference between the order initiation fill rate and the ship-confirm rate.

Many systems can track multiple fill rates but analysis is necessary to determine the best fill rate at order initiation versus ship-confirm. The focus in recent years on customer service has led to ship-confirm getting the most attention, which in turn causes large inventories if the firm equates ship-confirm fill rates with order initiation fill rates. The fill rate at ship-confirm is the end of direct control for the distributor but does not end the monitoring of orders as part of the customer service process. Tracking the movement to the customer is a function of working with the logistics carrier and, in the case of vendor managed inventory, the receiving process at the customer's location. The exact meaning of what truly defines customer service was still unclear in many supply chains in the early 2000s.

ABC Layouts

In addition to inventory control, ABC classification can be used to lay out the warehouse in such a fashion as to increase picking efficiency and safety. Picking efficiency requirements typically drive the layout decision. There are three commonly used or misused layout philosophies: popularity, similarity, and size and shape.

The "popularity" methodology puts the fastest-moving items in the most accessible places. Items are ranked based on the number of hits (number of times picked) and then placed where they can be accessed most easily and quickly: at the head of rows in an endcap (set of shelves at the end of the row), and/or in the "golden zone" (those shelves between the knees and shoulders), where product can be picked quickly with less risk of injury.

The popularity philosophy seeks to minimize the amount of time a picker spends in transit by putting those items that are picked most often closest to the picker and/or the shipping area. Pickers spend the majority of their time in transit.[2] Reducing the picker's travel time leads to increases in productivity per picker (more lines picked) and/or decreases in the necessary warehouse workforce. The warehouse throughput (amount of product picked in a specified period of time) is directly influenced by picker transit time. If the firm increases throughput, the firm becomes more agile: better able to meet customer needs with fewer resources (labor hours) consumed. A higher throughput can also lead to other efficiencies like reduced obsolescence and higher inventory turns since picker transit time is a part of the supply chain lead time.

The "similarity" methodology puts items that are commonly picked together next to one another. An example would be roofing nails placed next to shingles that require that length of nail. The similarity method reduces picking time since the picker will be in the same place to pick the entire order. The objectives are the same as for popularity, but the process focuses more on the order type than on the turnover of individual items. Orders have to be analyzed to determine what common order types are and which items should be stored together. Similarity can be difficult to achieve if the parts are used for multiple purposes.

Similarity is often confused with matching all items of similar characteristics (all screws together), which leads to picking errors. Many firms maintain stock keeping units (SKUs) that identify parts based on similar appearance or functionality. All nails will have a common number scheme, for instance. Sometimes the number scheme is drawn from the manufacturer's part-numbering system. Placing items that have the same numbering scheme and physical appearance close to one another will lead to picking errors when warehouse personnel transpose numbers, have literacy problems, have hard-to-read pick slips, or work in poorly lit warehouses. Worse yet, this system may lead to product applications that violate engineering specifications or government regulations. For instance, screws fall under fastener legislation.[3] If an incorrect strength of fastener were sent to an automobile manufacturer as part of a kit, it might not be caught by that manufacturer's quality control. The result could be a catastrophic failure that leads to legal problems for the distributor firm.

The "size and shape" methodology puts heavy or bulky items in the places where they can be most easily accessed. The golden zone is important, but often these items are stored on lower shelves to facilitate handling equipment like forklifts and to prevent heavy objects from falling on pickers below. Safety becomes a key issue since these items may injure a picker if placed on higher shelves or in difficult-to-retrieve places.

One firm put strict procedures in place for maintaining safety in the warehouse. A logistics manager visiting a branch noticed that pickers had put a box of nails on a high shelf with broken wooden supports running underneath. Even though the shelving had steel beams on which the box rested, a shifting of the box during subsequent picking could have led to the box falling between the struts. The box itself was extremely heavy, but the greater risk was the nails falling in a shower on a picker below. The pickers were instructed to bring the nails down to a lower level or repair the wooden supports immediately.

The biggest challenge for size and shape warehouse layout processes is the maintenance of a cubic dimensions database. The warehouse layout cannot be maintained by a system unless the system knows both what bins in the warehouse can hold (sizes, shapes, weights, etc.) and the dimensions of the products. One firm decided to allow its ERP system's warehouse management system to determine where products would be put away based on popularity, similarity, and storage medium. The company carried pipe, coiled wire, flat steel, and other products of varying weights and shapes. The firm set up fixed locations for wire and pipes since they required specialized shelving and allowed the system to place the remaining material. The challenge was collecting the data on the dimensions of the various products. The firm used supplier cubic information (where available) and then measured the fastest movers to establish an initial database. The A items constituted 90 percent of volume and so the initial database did handle the vast majority of all items received but, in the early going, the receiving dock got many queries from the system for product dimensions. Nevertheless, the database eventually settled down to the point that only new products had to be entered.

ABC layouts are difficult to maintain without information system assistance. Popularity is dynamic in nature, and product status and locations will change faster than a nonautomated system can respond. Items will move from A to B to C status routinely and make warehouse layout very difficult in a manual system. An automated system will gradually change product positions as their status changes and mix picking and putaway efforts with changing product positions in the warehouse so as to save on picker efforts. This process, called "task interleaving," is used when the system identifies a picker activity that will allow product positions to be easily changed. For instance, a picker may be putting away 100 items that have moved up in status. The system will locate the remaining products in stock at the same time as it instructs the picker to put away the incoming material and route the picker to those products as part of his or her trip through the warehouse.

One firm set up a popularity-based warehouse where A items were at the end of rows in the golden zone. Other items went by the similarity method where items that got picked together with A items were located as nearly as possible to the A's. Oddly shaped items were placed against the wall so that equipment could get to them easily and where special hooks and other hanging devices could be used to store them. The company spent a few weeks setting up the warehouse based on an ABC hit-based analysis. The new setup was very efficient but slowly began deteriorating. The firm was unable to continue reorganizing the entire warehouse and did not have the ability to track product status changes and change them routinely.

Another firm wanted to keep its best-sellers on their carousels (high-speed picking shelving that rotates to the picker). Carousels have become increasingly popular due to their ability to bring product directly to the picker, thereby reducing transit time. A carousel can also increase the accuracy of the pick since it identifies the proper part location. Pickers often transpose numbers and go to the wrong location in the warehouse. The firm, however, chose not to tie the carousels to their information system. The pickers had to look at the pick slip to determine which bin the product was in and then call that bin from the carousel. The work-intensive process made moving products from the carousel to other places in the warehouse slow and laborious. The carousels were not changed out as the inventory-pick status changed, which made keeping the carousel focused on top sellers difficult. The firm came to refer to the carousels as their slow-moving-inventory storage bins.

Automated Parts Identification

Automatic identification of parts opens many opportunities for combined information and physical automation. The tools associated with automatic parts identification are scanners, bar codes, radio frequency (RF) technology, and a warehouse management system (WMS). The WMS is the brain of the warehouse and makes all decisions as to how products move and directs people and equipment through efficient handling of materials.

Carousels and conveyers can use parts tracking for pick to light systems. A pick to light system uses lights to indicate which bin is to be picked from and possibly which bin a product should be placed in. The lights act as a visual signal to increase accuracy, and the scanners and WMS will double-check to assure the pick is carried out correctly. The process seeks to minimize human error, reduce picker effort (especially transit time), and increase warehouse throughput.

One firm set up a group of carousels for small, fast-moving items at the front end of the warehouse near receiving. The carousels would be activated based on the pickers' activity. The pick slip would drop into the system and the carousel with the first part to be picked would automatically begin rotating to the picker. As the carousel stopped, the bin with the product in it would be lit by a red light on the carousel. As the picker went to that carousel, the other carousels (a total of four) would begin spinning to bring the next items to the front. The picker would pick the item, scan it (the system would then verify that the correct item had in fact been picked), and turn to place the item in a set of plastic totes (bins) that were sitting on a conveyer in front of the carousel. The red light would show next to the tote associated with that order. The picker would scan the tote and then the item, and the system would verify that the correct item was placed with the correct order. The tote then proceeded to the next picking station, where products from other storage media (nonautomated shelving, for instance) could be added to the order. When the product reached shipping, it went through a final scan as items were packed.

The process guarantees a higher level of picking accuracy: Picks are continuously checked as items move and are scanned. The process also allows the picker to pick multiple orders at once and minimizes travel distance since the product comes to the picker. The carousels and scanners allow for a paperless environment with higher throughput and significantly reduced errors. The key to the process is the warehouse management system that tracks and controls every action. Without the automatic data collection tools (scanners), however, the process would not be possible. The connection between automatic data collection and WMS is important to successful utilization of each.

Bar codes provide a quick, economical, and nearly error-free method of identifying the parts or the part type from a bin. Bar codes can be identified with an error rate of less than one character per million compared with an error rate in the thousands per million for keypunch operations. A bar code system comprises the code labels, a printer, an optical code reader, and a signal receiver for identifying the code and transmitting it to the central computer. Laser scanners are commonly used in industrial environments and are used in many WMS applications.[4]

RF (radio frequency) systems allow remote transmission of data to control computers. RF tags with thousands of bits of data can be attached to each product. Some tags are also programmable. Information can be added to and read from the tags as the product proceeds through its set of production operations. Basically a product can carry its own process plan for guiding each machine visited and the output on each operation performed can be added to the encoded data to automatically construct a process and quality audit for the individual product unit. Scanner technology continues to advance in both its capability to absorb more information and the ability to read bar codes at greater distances. As RF technology and WMS become more powerful and affordable, firms will continuously improve their information collection and tracking processes, and new applications will be developed to further speed flow and reduce error.

Advanced shipping notices (ASN) can facilitate the receiving process and assist planning and sales. An ASN is an electronic notification that a shipment has left the supplier's operation and contains a certain group of items. The receiving department at the distribution firm can use the ASN to schedule the arrival of trucks (with the carriers) and/or prepare resources at the warehouse for incoming goods.

Many firms use time windows to schedule inbound freight. The trucking firms are given a scheduled arrival time and a window for unloading based on the type of load and truck. A flat-bed truck, for instance, can be unloaded on three sides by forklifts where a van may require hand trucks or dollies to unload. The type of material can also affect the unloading process. Heavy or unwieldy items or hazardous materials may require a more time-consuming unloading process.

One steel distribution firm received shipments of flat or rolled steel in large quantities every day. The firm typically received 20 to 30 truckloads per day and shipped out approximately the same number to its customers each day. The product came in on flat-bed trucks and required special unloading/loading equipment. The weight and unwieldy nature of the product made the use of overhead cranes a requirement. The firm used a lane through the middle of the warehouse to unload the trucks in the morning. The receiving process had to start and finish early since the lane would be needed to load outbound materials that afternoon. Each morning, the trucks would be lined up along the street to go into the warehouse for unloading. The traffic jam was frustrating to the truckers and dangerous from a traffic standpoint. As business grew, the process became unmanageable.

The problem was that the firm did not know which freight would come in on which day. Some days receiving was light, but other mornings might see a major flood of inbound trucks. The firm began requiring its suppliers to send ASNs for scheduling purposes. The ASNs were transmitted to the distributor by the supplier's ERP system and allowed the firm to schedule more effectively with the trucking firms since they now had an idea how many trucks might arrive on a single day. If a particular day would receive too much freight, some carriers would be scheduled for a later day. The firm also established time windows for delivery based on the size of the load and the handling equipment needed rather than allowing the trucks to show up first thing in the morning.

If the ASN is integrated into other processes like the sales order and replenishment processes, the firm can track incoming orders with greater precision. Sales can use the ASN to determine when a product is going to arrive as opposed to when the customer needs it. If a rush order for an important customer comes in but all inventory is allocated, the salesperson might check incoming orders to see whether some orders can be pushed back without affecting customer service. If an item is on order and due to arrive in a few days, the salesperson may shift the allocated inventory to the rush order and allow incoming items to fill the other orders. If the inbound order is delayed at the supplier's operation, however, or the order is not shipped complete, customer service may suffer. The salesperson can be more certain of the order's contents and arrival if he or she knows the product has left the supplier's premises. The ASN also facilitates the receiving process since orders that are due to go out immediately can be set up to cross-dock (go out immediately rather than be placed in inventory for picking later).

Inventory planners can also use the ASNs. If an item is not going to arrive on time or is only partially shipped, the planners may need to source it elsewhere and/or may wish to cancel the remaining portion of the order. One firm had a policy of canceling the balances of all orders that did not ship complete. The firm ordered from the same suppliers weekly and, rather than track backorders, preferred to simply add unshipped products to the next order and cancel any backorders. The sooner the firm knew what had shipped and what had not, the sooner the backordered material could be added to the new orders.

Since ASNs are sent electronically, automatic electronic capture of data through bar codes and scanners will speed the process by allowing for scanning product as it leaves the company. Logistics carriers have further facilitated the process with software that connects to the supplier's ERP system. These systems allow the firm to enter shipments and track them automatically through the ERP system. Customers are also provided visibility (if they connect to the shipper's system) and can follow the progress of the shipment through the transportation network. This visibility further improves the ability of inventory planners, receiving, and sales to project the exact arrival time of inbound materials. The ERP system can take the ASN as an alert and then follow the product from source to final delivery.

Another benefit of automated data collection is the ability to use statistical process control (SPC) to measure the effectiveness of picking processes. SPC can be used to track the accuracy of picks from different zones in the warehouse. The control charts, as explained in Chapter 8, keep track of errors as product passes through the warehouse. As the product is scanned and tracked, the SPC process charts each processing area of the warehouse to determine whether any area is generating errors outside established tolerance limits. If so, the process will be checked to determine error causes so that improvement measures can be taken. These processes popularized by Deming[5] and Motorola, through their six-sigma program,[6] capitalize on an information system that can both direct activity (through scanners and pick slip control) and track it as orders move through the warehouse.

TTI, a large electronics firm based in Fort Worth, Texas, uses SPC to drive its warehouse operations. Each area of the warehouse is treated as a zone where product is picked, packaged, or modified. As product is pulled from different shelving areas, the pick is scanned and errors are tracked. Before the product gets shipped, statistical sampling is added to the continuous tracking process to further ensure quality. The information system drives all activity. The process has allowed TTI to consistently produce a higher picking accuracy.[7]

Pick Slips

The picking process can be tracked and controlled by various tools and should be designed to take advantage of information automation. Typical pickers spend 50 to 60 percent of their time in transit. This transit time has a large impact on picker productivity and warehouse throughput. The pick slip or RF scanner can be engineered to reduce the traveling distance by employing improved routing and picking techniques. These techniques are designed to reduce the total distance traveled and, as described earlier in this chapter, sometimes bring the product to the picker rather than the other way around.

A fishing distributor had a largely manual process that led to considerable picker effort. The picker would grab the pick slip at the purchasing office in one corner of the warehouse and then proceed to pick items from that order. To ensure accuracy, the picker had to go up the aisle picking from the left and then back down the other side picking from the right. The company had found that picking from both sides of the aisle created too many errors. In addition, pickers had too high an error rate if they picked multiple orders at once. The process was very labor intensive since each order required the picker to cover the entire warehouse (see Figure 9.5).

Other issues included a need for two quality checks and order add-ons. To further ensure accuracy, the order would be recounted at packaging by a different employee and again at shipping before sealing the carton. Order add-ons were a common occurrence: Customers would call in additional items for an order during the picking process. The picker would have to finish the pick and come back to the office before finding out that additional product for the order just picked had been called in and needed picking. If multiple items were added, the entire picking process might have to be started over.

fig. 9.5   *A Picker's Route*

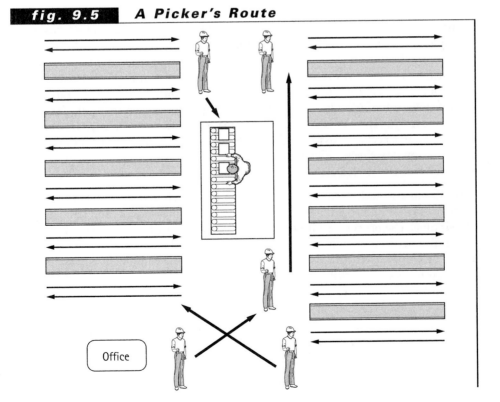

Office

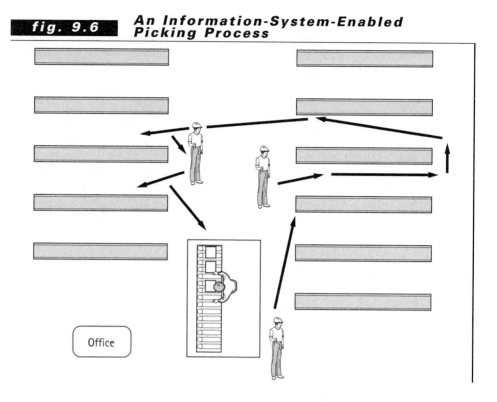

fig. 9.6   **An Information-System-Enabled Picking Process**

Office

The company decided to get a warehouse management system and RF scanners. The system maintained an ABC layout and allowed the picker to be directed right to the products to be picked. Add-ons were transmitted to the handheld scanner the instant they came in to the warehouse so that pickers could pick them as part of their routes (see Figure 9.6). The new route was not only a great deal shorter than the previous route, it included multiple orders (up to five or six could be picked simultaneously). The improved system dramatically decreased picker transit time, and the greater accuracy associated with the scanners allowed the firm to eliminate one of the quality checks. Eventually the process improved so much, the other quality check was eliminated as well.

WMS can also seek optimal routes through the warehouse. Routing optimization is the process of selecting the route through available pick tickets that will minimize transit time. The process requires the system to consider order delivery times, warehouse distances and layout, picker carrying capacity (the picker may have a forklift with a pallet or only a cart), travel speed, and so on. The routing decision is so complex that most systems will use some sort of simplifying algorithm to determine the best route.

Cycle Counts

Cycle counting is designed to control data integrity problems. As a system maintenance activity, a cycle count is used to check whether what the system records as in stock is in fact what the warehouse has on hand. The system will issue a list of items on a periodic basis for counting, and a picker or manager will count the items. Many firms prefer to have a manager or highly trained picker carry out cycle counts since errors will have a significant impact on data integrity and, therefore, system performance. ERP systems support multiple techniques for cycle counting.

Random counts use statistical techniques to ensure data accuracy. The system will choose a statistical sample for the picker to count. If the count is accurate, the system is assumed accurate. If the count is not accurate, the picker may be directed to count additional items (increase the sample size) until an acceptable level of accuracy is obtained. The count could conceivably increase to include the entire warehouse. The corrections made to the system are as important as the original data itself. If the system has the correct amount recorded but the count is incorrect, the system update may actually make matters worse.

Random counts are controlled by the system and may or may not, depending on how the system is set up, cover the entire warehouse in a year. Some firms set their system to conduct planned counts where all products eventually get counted. One method is to simply start the system count at one end of the warehouse and slowly count from one end to the other over time. Another is to use the ABC classification to count faster-moving or more-profitable items more often while making sure that all items get counted at least once during the year.

MRP and Work Order Processing

Most distributors have some manufacturing activities that require at least a work order processing system and possibly even a full scale materials requirements planning system. Distributors add value to products in a number of different ways. A popular method is kitting, where the distributor adds value through bringing together parts under a single part number (SKU). The new part number becomes a single item. The customer benefits by not having to gather all the parts together when needed from different parts of the warehouse, not having to order and stock multiple part numbers, and handling only a single product through receiving.

Electronic distributors frequently create kits for contract manufacturers that then assemble the component parts into a finished product. Other value-adds include relabeling products to carry the customer's name rather than the manufacturer's, programming devices to the manufacturer's specifications, and even actual product modifications or assembly in some cases. The line between distribution and manufacturing work is often vague and carries a different definition in different channels. Fluid power distributors will often custom-build entire assemblies to a particular environment. Building materials and metals distributors will cut, shape, or otherwise modify product to a particular use. Most distributors engage in some sort of kitting operation.

Distribution requirements planning or other replenishment tools often do not support the distribution value-add activities in ERP systems. Instead, value-add is associated with materials requirements planning (MRP) or a simple work order process module. MRP and work order process modules run off of a bill of materials

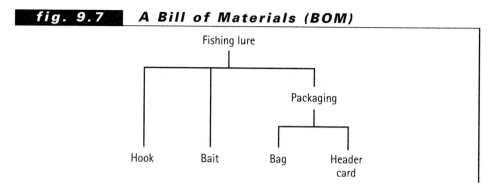

fig. 9.7   *A Bill of Materials (BOM)*

(BOM; see Figure 9.7). The system tracks the progress of the production cycle by first pulling the raw materials items from the warehouse or ordering them from suppliers if they are not in stock. The raw material inventory status is reduced or the system issues a purchase order for those items bought outside.

The next step is the subassemblies for which the system creates an inventory, which in turn will be relieved as the subassemblies and other products are taken to the next level of the BOM. Some firms maintain subassemblies in stock to speed the production process. An item that is used in many applications may have its own production process that then places the item in inventory. In Figure 9.7, the packaging is a subassembly that will eventually go into the final product. The subassembly has to be identified to the system (have a stock number) the same as the raw materials, and as the packaging gets created the system must relieve the header card and bag inventory.

Sometimes subassemblies are stored in inventory, but in many cases the subassembly will go immediately into the next-higher-level product. The work in process inventory associated with the subassemblies may not exist for any length of time and is sometimes referred to as "phantom inventory." One firm had a problem with phantom inventory since it sold both the subassembly and the finished product. The sales force could not distinguish between real (saleable) inventory and the work in process inventory.

The MRP or work order process has to be carefully managed to ensure that products are replenished correctly and that status is changed when product is modified. Distributors often struggle with work orders since the modified product may not fit into a product SKU after completion. This is especially true when the distributor may cut wood or pipe (or like products) to a customer-desired length and then have leftover material that is not identifiable.

Since distributors deal with a variety of processes that may differ from customer to customer and application to application, they frequently have difficulty dealing with work orders. To be successful, the process must match the system and be fully detailed for any eventuality. If a case occurs that does not match the system's methodology, the new product must be integrated into the system. Some companies use special product SKUs for this purpose, but the process often leads to an increase in obsolete inventory if the specials are not eventually made part of the regular inventory.

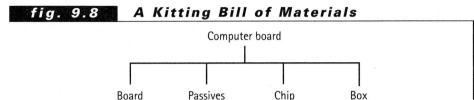

fig. 9.8 *A Kitting Bill of Materials*

Computer board

Board   Passives   Chip   Box

Most distribution value-adds are simpler than manufacturing processes. The principal difference is the depth of the bill of materials. Kitting and programming have single-level BOMs (see Figure 9.8). Assembly has multiple levels but distribution applications are usually not as deep or complex as most manufactured products.

Conclusion

The operations division of the distribution firm performs many complex tasks that can be supported by the ERP system. These processes, when linked through IT systems, can lead to higher levels of customer service and/or a reduced level of assets to support them. The tools to accomplish this linkage include warehouse management systems, scanners, and human processes that collaborate with the physical and information automation. The processes have to be connected with solid human interaction processes that limit data integrity problems.

Distribution Retrospective

Kevin decided to compare Dallas with another RDC in Chicago. He broke out his analysis to the key areas where he believed the RF system added the most value. He focused on reduced effort by pickers, reduced warehouse cycle times, increased warehouse throughput, increased data integrity, reduced inventory, and improved customer service levels. He collected information on the number of pickers at Dallas, the amount of product they pulled per hour (picker productivity), total warehouse volume (parts picked, packed, and shipped), inventory accuracy, total inventory to sales ratio, obsolescence, and ship-confirm fill rates. He put the results in a spreadsheet to show to management (see Figure 9.9).

The increased number of pickers for the lower-volume Chicago warehouse gave Kevin a simple cost to justify the RF system, but it was not enough. The higher

fig. 9.9	**Warehouse Fill Rate**	

Measurement	Dallas	Chicago
Total pickers	10	13
Picks per hour	14	8
Warehouse volume	250,000 units	180,000 units
Parts variances	5% of inventory	28% of inventory
Inventory turns	16	9
Obsolescence	6%	8%
Warehouse fill rate	99.70%	98%

obsolescence rate brought him closer, but he wanted irrefutable evidence. He wanted to establish a connection between the part variances (the difference between what the system shows in inventory and what is actually counted in a cycle count) and the inventory turns. He could then use the fill rates to pull the sales force onto his side if he could prove the Dallas fill rates were also a result of the RF system.

He queried the inventory planners and asked them how they established inventory levels at the RDCs. They informed him that inventory was first based on forecast accuracy and product volume and then adjusted for customer service failures. The planners said that when failures were outside of the tolerance limits for effective customer service, they would increase the safety stocks to ensure that company objectives were met. Kevin checked and found that the lower turns at Chicago were a direct result of higher safety stocks. He multiplied the firms' cost of capital times the excess safety stock inventory to get the cost of money tied up in inventory.

Kevin now had financial justification and he planned to take his evidence to management. First, however, he planned to send the fill rate information to the Vice President of Sales and his regional managers. He felt ready to prove the value of RF technology.

Issues to Consider

1. Over the past 20 to 30 years, inventory has been judged to be bad by many. Since warehouses store inventory, what positive role do they play?

2. Explain the two types of fill rates and the significance of each.

3. What are the types of warehouse layout methodologies? What are their strengths and weaknesses?

4. If pickers spend the majority of their time in transit, what opportunities does this present and how can distributors improve their operations?

Case Study: Work Order Processing

Keith looked at his manufacturing operations. Ray Manufacturing was essentially a small operation that built items Keith designed himself. Keith had designed bills of material for each of his products in spreadsheets. While the BOMs made planning his master production schedule (MPS) possible, he was not able to track production progress and, more importantly, raw material and work in process inventories. His ERP system had limited ability to deal with work orders or MRP-style planning.

His ERP system had a BOM module that could be used to update inventories and schedule production. The system ran off sales orders, however, rather than forecasts. Keith needed the forecasting module included because production lead times were greater than customer purchasing time windows. Customers typically bought a few weeks in advance but production scheduling could take a great deal longer. He needed to build to forecast rather than sales orders. Keith decided to divide his products into categories, pick a few items that represented his different production environments, and then design a system to support those products that could be set up for all others.

Keith's production broke into three areas. One category was outsourced production. Keith had contracted with factories in China that produced products for Texas Tackle Factory (TTF), one of his manufacturing divisions. He designed the products and outsourced the production to the Chinese factories. The lead times ran between 60 and 90 days, but the process was more of a pure distribution purchasing activity than a manufacturing process.

The second category was a group of TTF products that were partially manufactured outside and partially inside Keith's operations. The raw materials would be gathered first in Alabama and then sent to the Dominican Republic, where production would take place. Finally, the products were shipped to Victoria, Texas, where Keith's group would bring together the final packaging. The bait and packaging came from Alabama (two-week lead time) and the hooks and line were from the Dominican Republic. Once all parts arrived in the Dominican Republic, the lead times for assembly there ran about three weeks. When the finished lures arrived in Victoria, the lead time for packaging was about one week. The BOM is depicted in Figure 9.10.

The longest lead-time path went from Alabama (two weeks) through the Dominican Republic (three weeks) to Victoria (one week) and then to the customer, for a total of six weeks. Keith was unsure how to integrate the different manufacturing locations with an effective forecasting system to be sure he maintained inventory to meet customer demand.

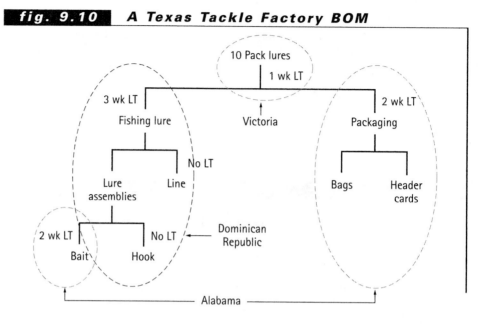

fig. 9.10 **A Texas Tackle Factory BOM**

The final scenario was for his other manufacturing division: Team Nu-Mark (TNM). TNM had a fishing belt that consisted of a stringer, a tackle box, the belt itself, and a pouch for the tackle box. The tackle box came from Florida, where it was produced with a two-week lead time. It was then shipped along with the other parts (one-week lead time) to Team Nu Mark's plant in Houston. The tackle box then had to have holes drilled in it before it could be inserted in the belt (one-week lead time). The belt could then be assembled in one week. It would then be shipped to Victoria and packaged (one week). The fishing belt BOM is depicted in Figure 9.11.

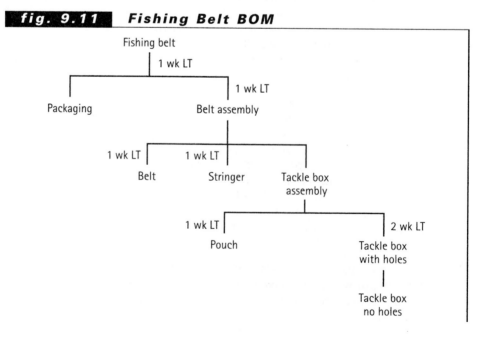

fig. 9.11 **Fishing Belt BOM**

Keith pondered how to set this up. He thought the purchasing module could handle the Chinese orders, but the combination of shipping expenses and different factories in China was somewhat bewildering. On the TTF products, he felt he would have to treat the entire system as his manufacturing operation and lay out the process as though all activity took place under one roof. He felt comfortable that the Team Nu-Mark case would work the same. He began building the BOMs into his ERP system and trying to connect the purchasing module to the manufacturing process by triggering inventory needs, wherever they were, as though the process were contained entirely at Victoria.

Case Challenges

1. Why does Keith need the forecasting module to interact with MRP rather than just taking sales orders? What solution do you suggest for the system's method?

2. How should Keith manage the Chinese purchases?

3. How should Keith treat manufacturing outside of his operations? Can he manage the process as if it were his own?

References

1. Sunil Chopra and Peter Meindl, *Supply Chain Management: Strategy, Planning and Operations* (Upper Saddle River, NJ: Prentice Hall College Div., 2000).

2. Richard L. Francis; Leon F. McGinnis, Jr.; and John A. White, *Facility Layout and Location–An Analytical Approach,* 2nd ed. (Upper Saddle River, NJ: Prentice Hall, 1992).

3. Fastener Quality Act, National Institute of Standards and Technology, http://ts.nist.gov/ts/htdocs/230/235/FQA/fqaregs2.htm (accessed October 24, 2003).

4. Intuit Eclipse Distribution Management Solutions, http://eclipse.intuit.com/products/rfbarcode.html (accessed January 22, 2003).

5. Mary Walton and W. Edwards Deming, *Deming Management Method* (Farmington, UT: Perigee, 1988).

6. Peter S. Pande, Robert P. Neuman, and Roland R. Cavanagh, *The Six Sigma Way: How GE, Motorola, and Other Top Companies Are Honing Their Performance* (New York: McGraw-Hill, 2000).

7. TTI achieves a smoother flow of operations with conveyor and carousel system, Cisco-Eagle, http://www.cisco-eagle.com/CaseStudies/TTI/Index.htm (accessed January 22, 2003).

Chapter 10

Executive Information Systems

Distribution Perspective

The Meadows Ceiling and Insulation firm was faced with declining profitability. The President and CEO, Jack Kress, did not like it but was unsure what to do. He called in the Vice President of Operations, Jerry Robinson, to discuss the matter. Jack was going to get to the bottom of the problem or heads would roll.

"Sales increased a paltry 2% this last quarter," Jack said. "That is a weak performance but my concern lies elsewhere. We have experienced declining profits with increasing sales for two years now. In the early going, you convinced me that the problem lay in the increasing service levels that salespeople claimed we needed to continue market growth. Enough is enough! If you are still right, then the sales force needs to find another way to increase sales than giving away our profits. If you are wrong and the problem lies in inefficient operations, then your group is responsible. I don't care who is to blame. I just want the problem fixed! I am not saying I'm going to fire anyone based on what you find out but I want answers now! Then I want a plan that we will hold our people to or else! Am I clear?"

The meeting was over and all Jerry could say was "Yes, sir."

"Well, that was pleasant," he thought as he left Jack's office. It would not do any good to ask Jack why he had not supported this type of investigation before. Jerry had to *find answers and develop a plan fast. He called a consultant he had worked with on IT projects at Meadows in the past and asked him for a reference on a performance measurement expert. Jerry figured the problem was the firm's inability to identify where profitability issues started and thought a strong group of key performance indicators would not only answer Jack's questions in the short term but would prevent many such problems in the future.*

Mike Jacobs was an IT consultant for the ERP system at Meadows. He was not surprised to get the call. "I told you that you needed to design a set of metrics for your executive information system a long time ago, Jerry. The company has the right tools; they just need to be pointed in the right direction."

Jerry was in no mood for I-told-you-so's. "Do you have any suggestions?" he snapped.

"Sorry, Jerry, that was insensitive," Mike said. "I think I'm your guy. I know the system and your company. The rest is just a matter of matching classic measures to your firm."

"I hope you know what you're getting into," Jerry said. "I can't fly cover for you if you don't get it right in a big hurry."

"I understand," Mike said. He began to wonder whether he had walked into a land mine.

Introduction

Once a system with interconnectivity capability (ERP) is in place and all processes are planned, the company needs a central focus, or "brain," to run the firm. In the ERP system, this brain is often called the executive information system (EIS). EIS creates reports that can be used to measure firm performance like profit and loss (P&L) statements, balance sheets, and the like. These reports essentially capture financial metrics but, when considering measurement, the firm should broaden its scope to include all operations. The ERP system's connectivity enables creating a coherent, logical set of measures that drive the firm. Measuring success in a consistent fashion has been very difficult for most firms in the past since capturing the necessary metrics and matching them to one another was work intensive. ERP can carry out this activity easily and quickly. The problem for most firms now is not the ability to measure and compare the outcomes but developing a proper set of measures to drive performance. If there is one thing information systems can do well, it is measure things.

The focus should be on achieving strategic goals like profitability, good corporate citizenship, return on investment (ROI), and so forth. Setting these goals is an important exercise well understood at many firms and is carried out through strategic planning every year. After the plans are laid, however, many firms find themselves frustrated and unable to achieve their goals according to plan. The company's operations do not seem able to meet reasonable financial goals and customer service objectives. The big gap is that financial measures often have not been properly connected to operations performance. This disconnect has yielded disastrous results at many distribution firms.

In many ways, distributors have been unable to prove the value of their activities to other members of the supply chain. This failure to demonstrate the value of distribution is linked to performance metrics since higher service claims must be proven to be accepted by customers. Internally, many distribution firms (and others) have had a difficult time even figuring out what their value is in quantifiable (believable) terms. Performance metrics are the logical way to provide such proof but require a systematic and reliable methodology to provide proof of firm effectiveness. Metrics can be used to capture the performance of a process, a new initiative, people, customer service, and even the firm itself. However, many firms are finding the development of such metrics to be problematic.

An auto-parts distributor had worked extensively to establish metrics that would guarantee high customer service levels. It developed metrics to measure fill rates, average lead time, and lead time variability. The firm had improved forecasting and inventory control and used the savings to reallocate slow moving inventory into stronger sellers (A items). In so doing, the firm had improved fill rates and reduced lead times, which was reflected in its new metrics collection. The firm was now trying to determine what its next set of improvements should be and at whom they should be directed. Customers were happy but this might further increase their expectations. Stockholders, on the other hand, were anxious to receive some additional ROI after investing in all the process improvements the new metrics were driving. The firm was unsure how to both ensure and prove that improved ROI was coming out of its new processes. The company needed to be able to link financial measures to its operational metrics.

Financial performance metrics have been in existence for many years but have been heavily influenced by tax laws. Since many financial metrics were originally designed to minimize taxes, they often do not easily translate into measures that support effective operations. The problem becomes even more extreme when taken out into the supply chain. Our traditional financial measures actually make it just as profitable to take margin away from our suppliers as it is to raise prices on our customers. Since we have more control over our suppliers than our customers, the natural inclination is to abuse suppliers (anti–supply chain management). Metrics for the firm's supply chain goals are difficult to develop since they may come into conflict with traditional financial measures.

Another problem area is investing in improvements and, after achieving them, being unable to prove the investment brought about that improvement. Many improvements, especially information automation ones, require new ways to measure their performance. In the 1990s, many pundits stated that IT systems could not be measured using traditional financial metrics. Unfortunately, new metrics were not proposed and the systems were not only unable to prove their value but often did not add much value at all since it was difficult to set objectives and achieve them without appropriate metrics in place.

In general terms, distributors have had a difficult time linking their strategic, financial, and operational objectives. Key performance indicators (KPIs)—metrics driving firm performance—are often in conflict. KPIs should support the firm's goals but poorly applied metrics can actually lead the firm in the wrong direction. In other cases KPIs are not captured or only partially measured, leading to confusion as to what influences what. When no metric is in place, finger pointing becomes a problem and opinions are thrown around with little supporting evidence. The information vacuum leads to a deadlock and the firm has difficulty moving forward with solutions. As W. Edwards Deming said, "You cannot improve what you do not measure."[1]

Setting Strategic Objectives Based on Supply Chain Goals

Executive information systems must bring together the metrics to connect the firm's internal processes and drive its performance to strategic goals. This process requires well-designed metrics that connect and are directed at strategic goals. Contrary to popular belief, financial metrics do not have to hinder this process. In fact, any set of metrics that ignores the financial imperatives of the firm is certain to fail. The firm must begin with an understanding of strategic objectives and connect those to its financial metrics. In a broader context, the firm should consider its role as a contributing member of the supply chain (see Figure 10.1).

Figure 10.1 shows just a few of the contributing factors the distributor brings to the supply chain but serves as a starting place for considering what the strategic goals of the firm should be. While profitability may be a leading short-term goal, the eventual survival of the distributor depends on its ability to contribute to the supply chain. Strategic goal setting should begin here and position the firm to support not only its own profitability but its value to the supply chain in general. On the left side of the diagram are the general supply chain goals: a desired customer service level (CSL), the cycle time of the supply chain, product quality, and market share (sales force performance).

The figure demonstrates that in order for distributors to understand their own metrics setting and selection, they must look to the supply chain's goals. Customers

fig. 10.1   *Contributing to the Supply Chain*

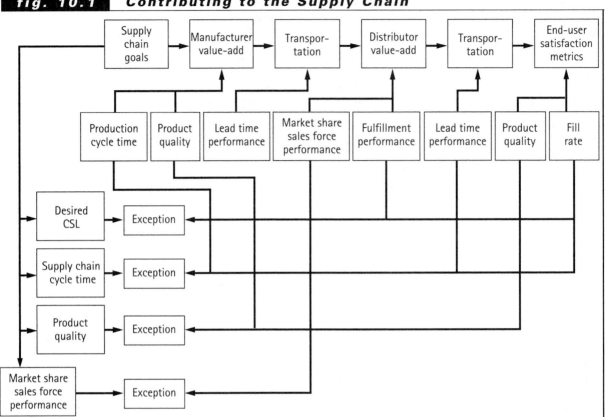

Source: Lawrence *et al.*, 2002.[2]

will select distributors based on their ability to contribute to the customer's success (CSL, cycle times, and product quality). Suppliers will work with distributors based on their ability to capture market share thereby better representing the supplier's products. Suppliers known for high-quality products frequently are able to choose among competing distributors. The metrics in the diagram are at a very high level and will have many sublevels that should be distributed to the appropriate members of the supply chain as suggested by the diagram. The exception boxes suggest there may be a disconnect between the customer or supplier expectations and actual supply chain performance. All members of the supply chain should work proactively to overcome these performance gaps.

These supply chain goals can serve as a starting point for the firm's strategic planning for metrics design. The goals are measurable and somewhat well understood in most supply chains. The desired customer service level is typically defined based on customer expectations. In many supply chains, the customer has been very clear on this metric and, where it has not been defined, most supply chain members have at least a market-based sense of which level is required to retain their customers. Many, in fact, have set a strategic customer service goal designed to increase market share.

The customer's expected fill rate, when translated into inventory, becomes in a sense a cost of doing business since firms cannot miss the mark and expect to remain valued partners. Increasing the fill rate should not be considered at odds with financial metrics any more than a buying a new forklift or opening a new warehouse. The complication arises in determining what the fill rate should be for each supply chain member. Lower supplier (manufacturer) fill rates will result in larger distributor inventories. The only way for supply chain members to determine who should do what, however, is to measure the fill rate of each and connect it to financial and operational measures that demonstrate the impact of the policy. Once the impact is understood (a major contribution of metrics), the supply chain can collaborate to reduce costs throughout the supply chain. Metrics collection does not follow supply chain planning: It leads it.

The supply chain cycle time is another customer service metric that is easily measured. The cycle time is the length of time it takes a customer to get product through the supply chain from different stages of development. Since a 100 percent fill rate is almost impossible on most products, the supply chain's ability to respond to unexpected demand on some items becomes an important issue in many cases. A graduate class visiting one of the most successful ice cream manufacturers in the country asked about its best-selling product. In spite of being a regional firm, this flavor was a national best-seller and accounted for half of the firm's business. The students asked whether the firm had ever experienced stockout on that flavor. The operations manager said it had never happened since he had been with the firm and he hoped he would not be there if it ever did. A 100 percent fill rate is possible if all resources are directed at achieving it, as the above example demonstrates. Although truck breakdowns, tornadoes, and other "acts of God" will undoubtedly play a role, they are not the primary inhibitors in most cases.

One distributor had a large manufacturing firm as a customer that purchased a motor for its manufacturing processes. If the motor failed, the manufacturer's line would shut down at a cost of $30,000 per day. The motor cost $1,500 and was considered by the motor manufacturer to be obsolete (no longer in production). The customer wanted the distributor to inventory the item, and the distributor wanted the supplier to carry it. In fact, the time the line would be down made it prohibitively expensive for anyone other than the customer to carry the motor, and possibly a backup, since the manufacturer needed a great deal of lead time to custom-build the motor. The fill rate from the supply chain on this item should be basically zero since the cost of inventorying it is too expensive from a holding-cost point of view for the suppliers. The customer would need to carry it since the stockout cost was so high. Even a slight (hours') delay getting the product from the customer would not justify the line shutdown cost.

If we put the most unusual cases aside, however, it becomes clear that most items fall somewhere in between the extremes with fill rates in the 80 to 99 percent range and a need for the supply chain to respond to stockouts (backorders) on a fairly routine basis. If the supply chain cycle time is too long, customer service will suffer or distribution will be forced to carry excessive inventories as a buffer. The resulting costs will eventually have to be passed on to the customer. Therefore, tracking each firm's cycle time and applying improvement measures to the entire chain is a critical activity that must be measured and pursued aggressively. While the marketplace may have a minimum expectation for cycle time based on the product's status, shorter is always better and each supply chain member should track and seek continuous improvement in its own cycle time.

The other metrics, product quality and market share, have been well understood for some time. Manufacturers have always pursued product quality but a renewed emphasis was placed on it during the 1980s with the total quality management (TQM) movement. Distributors have also been drawn into the process since their handling and value-add processes also affect quality. The customer generally delineates the minimum quality levels, and the costs of quality should be tracked through the metrics to determine how to improve.

Market share is less customer focused and more stakeholder focused. The distributor essentially has two sets of customers: consumers (end users) and suppliers. A distributor is a marketplace where customers come to buy based on convenience, service, and price; suppliers come to sell based on the distributor's ability to reach customers and promote their products.[3] While some suppliers will take any market they can get, many are choosy about who gets their product. The best suppliers have the power to pull their product from poor-performing markets (distributors). The loss of some suppliers can kill a distributor's business.

Electronics distributors, for instance, are very dependent on key suppliers like Intel and Motorola. The suppliers set up franchise agreements that delineate expectations for their distributors and, in return, protect territories for the distributor. These distributors are called "authorized distributors" and are expected to add value to products, technical support, inventory support, and, most importantly, market share growth for the suppliers (Lawrence *et al.*, 2003).[4] Failure to meet the suppliers' objectives can result in loss of the franchise.

Other stakeholders are interested in market share as well. Market share influences the value of the firm since it demonstrates the firm's capability to control its destiny, maintain a healthy cash flow, and capitalize on opportunities. The value of the firm, therefore, is tied to market share. Stockholders and employees look to market share as an indicator of the firm's health. Amazon.com grew market share at the expense of profitability for many years since a certain critical mass was required for the firm to compete. Stockholders stuck with Amazon throughout the process in the interest of finally getting to the point that the firm could succeed.[5]

Market share can come into conflict with other financial measures (as suggested in the Distribution Perspective above), however. Most firms recognize market share growth as a cost of doing business but do not measure those costs and compare them to the outcome. The costs should be understood and ultimately justified to avoid situations like the one in this chapter's Distribution Perspective where profitability continues to suffer without any understanding of the benefits.

Ultimately, the firm's strategic objectives will be largely driven by customer expectations. Connecting the customer's expectations to a connected set of metrics maintained within the ERP system is critical to meeting both the firm's and the supply chain's success. So, what does the customer want? Although customers want many things, they tend to fall into some general categories:

○ On-time delivery—On time means that the order is sent complete when the customer wanted it, not early and not late. While many customers still are not limiting the early arrival of goods, more and more are setting time windows for delivery. A time window is a scheduled arrival time for an order. In just-in-time deliveries to a manufacturing line, time windows can be as short as a few hours. Many retailers are beginning to require delivery on specified days and will penalize suppliers that deliver late or refuse shipments that come early. The time window forces exactness for the distributor that requires close collaboration (measured and tracked) with its transportation provider and a firm understanding of its own time windows with suppliers (to prevent its own inventory buildup). The EIS/ERP system is critical to the tracking and measurement of these processes.

○ Quick response—Even with time-window restrictions, there will be times when product is not available. The customer then wants the distributor to be able to respond quickly and fix the problem. This responsiveness involves more than just inventory. The distributor's services are often needed in emergency situations as well.

○ Ability to cover for customer or supplier failures (flexibility)—Similar to quick response, the customer will often look to the distributor to manage supplier failures. This might mean carrying extra inventory in critical parts on which suppliers have long lead times or sourcing product elsewhere when the need arises.

○ Continuous improvement and innovation in products and services—Most customers are themselves in a continuous improvement mode. They expect suppliers to be pursuing process improvements that they will benefit from on a regular basis. For distributors, this might mean collaboration with suppliers to bring new product features the customer needs to market or improving distribution processes like ordering (e-procurement), payment methodologies (electronic funds transfer), and so on.

○ Accurate invoices and shipments—Customers also require a high degree of accuracy from the distributor. Billing errors not only potentially cost the customer money but may require an expensive audit process and can introduce inventory valuation errors as well. Inaccurate shipments can cause stockouts, excess inventory, expensive auditing, freight expense, and so on.

To respond to these customer requirements, the distributor will set a group of strategic objectives that represent how the firm goes to market. A set of strategic objectives that meet these customer desires and the firm's financial objectives might look like the following:

○ The firm will maintain on-time delivery by achieving an overall fill rate of 98 percent, requiring transportation providers to meet 98 percent efficiency, and increasing supplier fill rates from 92 to 95 percent. This policy and the others that follow will drop down into tactical objectives that require the system to maintain operational metrics as (as discussed later in this chapter).

○ The firm will increase responsiveness by reducing the customer fulfillment cycle time on nonstock items from the current average of 90 days to 60 days.

○ The firm will increase flexibility by establishing an alternative source of supply for all A items and reduce customer-driven expediting by 50 percent.

○ The firm will improve the sales order process by reducing average customer ordering time (time spent on the phone with the inside salesperson) by 25 percent.

○ The firm will increase invoice accuracy from 97.5 percent to 99.5 percent.

○ The firm will increase average gross margin by 5 percent.

○ The firm will increase return on assets (ROA) by 5 percent.

The objectives are not yet prescriptive since the "how to do it" is not established—that comes in the tactical objectives. The goals are set based on a reflection of customer requirements and financial objectives. There may be conflict between the financial objectives and the others listed. Therefore, the plan must be set up to collect and track progress toward the objectives in such a way that financial objectives do not hinder the other improvement measures. In many cases, seemingly nonfinancial objectives can be turned to a profitable advantage if well understood (measured) by all.

Connecting Strategic Objectives to Financial Measures

The financial objectives represent the interests of other stakeholders (besides customers). Owners want a greater return on invested funds (ROI) and may have other personal objectives such as a chance to serve the community through the firm's philanthropic endeavors. Employees want increased prosperity for the firm since a more financially secure firm will be more likely to continue employment and offer higher wages and career growth opportunities.

The key is to match financial metrics to strategic objectives so that all stakeholders can achieve their objectives. This process requires interpreting strategic objectives into financial metrics. Once that interpretation is decided upon, the firm will determine what tactical actions and objectives are necessary to support the strategic ones while still meeting the financial goals. The tactical objectives should then lead to operational metrics that, in turn, control the processes used to meet the tactical objectives. The process pushes the strategic objectives through the tactical ones while establishing a hierarchy of measures through disaggregating the objectives into measures of individual processes. Those metrics finally have to be aggregated back up the hierarchy through the executive information system functionality to ensure the strategic objectives are being met according to plan (see Figure 10.2).

The premise of ERP is that all processes are connected to the system and, therefore, measurable. Since all are connected to one system, coordination of all activity is now also possible. A major benefit of connected systems is that they allow for planning where all of the firm's efforts can be coordinated. When metrics are treated

fig. 10.2 | *The Strategic Planning/Metrics Collection Hierarchy*

as standalone efforts of individual departments and not related in real time, processes can become disconnected and measurement sometimes evolves into a series of poorly understood or—worse yet—conflicting activities.

As the planning process goes forward, the financial and operational metrics are determined and their meaning is established. The measures must be collected by the system and the firm must be able to interpret them in a manner that makes sense for meeting the firm's strategic and tactical objectives. If the measures are not matched to the goals, the firm will be unable to determine whether those goals are being met. Many firms have large assets that are carried on the books at less than market value (for tax purposes). To optimize the return on assets (ROA), however, the firm needs to understand the true value of these assets to make rational decisions on which assets to keep and which ones to divest.

One large distributor had three branches in northern California valued on the company's books at approximately $200,000 each. The properties were in fact worth about $1.2 million each since the property values had increased dramatically over 20 years since they had been acquired. Management had to recognize their true value when it came to making decisions designed to maximize shareholder value. The firm decided the properties should be sold in favor of less-expensive sites, and the difference was returned to the shareholders.

One way to determine how to measure strategic objectives is to match them to the customer-facing financial metrics. Some customer-facing financial metrics include:

○ Sales per sales representative—This metric represents the effectiveness of the sales force and indicates the need for additional training or other support for salespeople. The stakeholders most interested in this metric are suppliers (from a market-share standpoint) and the firm itself (for both market, share and efficiency reasons). The firm should give careful consideration to how this sort of metric is collected and disseminated. Many firms seek to reduce sales territories when they believe this metric has grown too large. Salespeople view this as a punishment or betrayal since their salaries are often adversely affected. The tradeoff between sales force efficiency and morale is complicated, and policy should not be "shot from the hip."

○ Gross margin—A financial metric that demonstrates the profitability of the firm product by product. Gross margin measurement is more difficult than it might seem. Some firms measure it directly by taking the most recent cost of goods sold (COGS) and deducting it from sales. Cost of goods sold will vary throughout the year since discounts are sometimes picked up from purchasing large orders, or premium prices are sometimes paid due to expediting or by adding features to a base product. While the firm will reconcile profitability on a regular basis, business units need to understand COGS so that they can make reasonable decisions about selling prices and customer discounts. Some will measure COGS against a standard cost (a cost that is based on an average or otherwise calculated product cost), but this cost will also have to be reconciled periodically. Measuring the firm's profitability and using the metric to drive management and sales force decision making requires considerable planning and the establishment of proper metrics within the system.

○ Days Sales Outstanding (DSO)—This financial metric is used to determine how effective the firm is at collecting on debt and choosing the "right" customers. If reduced, it frees up capital and increases the return on assets (ROA). The DSO is simply accounts receivable divided by average daily sales. The connection to the strategic financial metric (ROA) is a straightforward calculation, but the policies the firm should use to reduce DSO are anything but simple. Reducing DSO is a function of decreasing the amount of and/or the length of time credit is extended to customers. Reducing DSO may require a potential loss of sales (tightening credit), increased investment in technology, and/or process improvements that either make it easier for customers who will pay early to do so or decrease the cycle time of the transaction once the customer makes payment. Many firms have started using electronic funds transfer (EFT) for their customers to submit payment or automated faxes to bill customers (reducing mailing time). Other strategies include stronger incentives for early payment, but these also have a cost associated with them (greater discounts). The executive information system must not only track the DSO but also the impact of the strategies imposed on the DSO. Further, the DSO should be connected to the hierarchy of financial measures at the next level (see Figure 10.3). As the figure shows, DSO has a place in the hierarchy that allows it to contribute to our understanding of the important financial metrics ROA and ROI. For example, if customers begin paying faster, DSO decreases, indicating that financial assets are being used more effectively. Top management can drill down through the ROI/ROA layers to determine whether DSO is contributing to or hindering financial performance. This same hierarchy exists for the foregoing measures and many others.

○ Discounts—The amount of discounting should be measured to determine where such actions are building sales enough to capture economies of scale like supplier discounts and where the only result is a loss in margins. The stakeholder goal remains the same (ROI) but the tactical resource now is the margin generated.

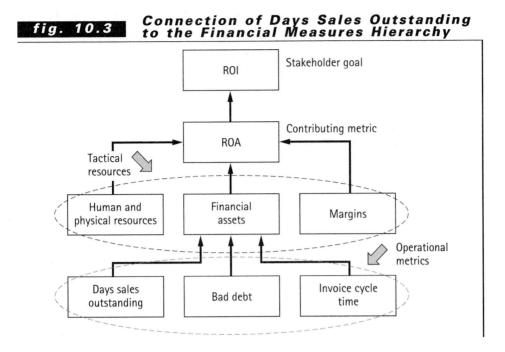

fig. 10.3 *Connection of Days Sales Outstanding to the Financial Measures Hierarchy*

- ○ Total sales—The yearly volume of a firm is very important but difficult to interpret. All firms track total sales but making increased sales equal increased profitability requires the coordination of many activities.

  - ○ *Same store sales–Sales can increase in total but be eroding throughout the firm. The same store sales metric indicates whether the firm would be growing if it were not for acquisitions or new branch openings. Same store sales will sometimes decrease because new store openings take away sales from existing operations. A decreasing same store sales where the loss in sales cannot be attributed to the same firm's other operations is generally a bad sign.*

- ○ Customer disputes (warranties, returned goods, etc.)—Customer disputes demonstrate both a direct cost and an indirect one. The direct costs are the cost of satisfying the customer by taking back or repairing merchandise. The indirect costs are more difficult—but not impossible—to measure since they involve customer perceptions and goodwill. The best way to measure the impact of goodwill issues is to improve the process and measure the effect on sales and profitability with affected customers. An ad hoc measure can then be interpreted to determine what the effect of further investments in product or service improvements will be on the firm's well being.

- ○ Market share—The total percentage of the market controlled by a firm is an indicator of power. Channel power gives a firm leverage with suppliers, resources to do battle with competitors, and name recognition to draw customers to them with a minimum of effort. This measure also has to be matched with others to understand its meaning and the value of any efforts designed to grow market share.

Connecting Financial Measures to Tactical Objectives

Connecting financial metrics to tactical objectives was considered difficult if not impossible during the 1970s and 1980s. Just in time (JIT) and other improvement programs were often stymied by accounting measures that did not recognize the savings those programs created. In more recent years, however, a great deal of work has been done to connect financial measures and tactical objectives. Kaplan and Norton[6] developed the "balanced scorecard" that specifically matched operational activity to financial performance. The DuPont model[7] was an even earlier attempt to demonstrate the hierarchical nature of metrics collection. These models demonstrate that financial performance can be directly linked to operational activity. The key is to consider all aspects of the strategic objective, where the metrics should point to achieve the objective, and which component processes should be measured and how those processes interact. See Figure 10.4 for an example using customer service improvement as the strategic objective.

The figure starts with management setting the strategic objective, such as a 98 percent fill rate. The fill rate then leads to an inventory investment that will affect the ROA and ROI. The decision also involves the outcome in terms of customer service failures and the associated costs. If the fill rate is 98 percent, the firm has a stockout rate of 2 percent. The cost of that policy can be measured by tracking the firm's reaction to a stockout. The potential responses to a stockout condition include backorders, expediting, and/or losing the sale. "Expediting" means speeding product acquisition from suppliers, upgrading the customer to a better product, or seeking alternative (more expensive) suppliers. The frequency of responses and their cost

fig. 10.4 **The Relationship Between Operational and Financial Metrics**

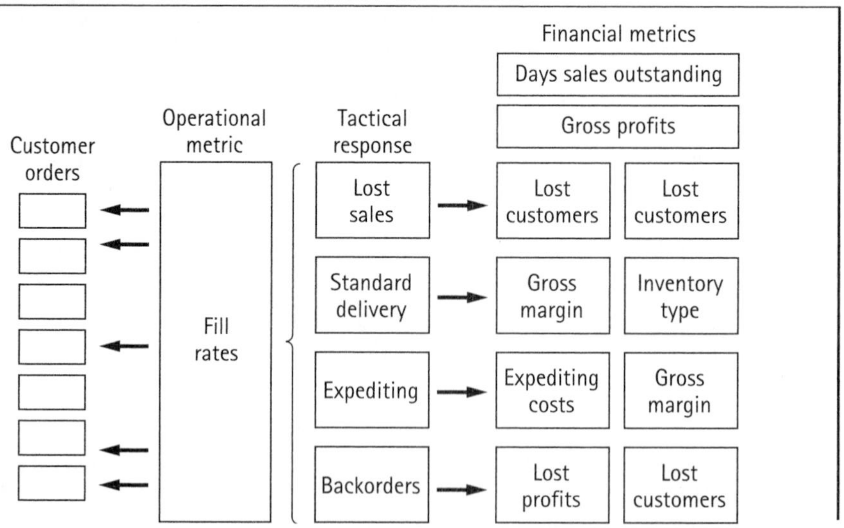

| **fig. 10.5** | ***Merging Operational, Financial, and Stakeholder Metrics*** |

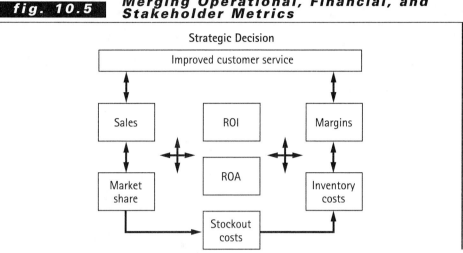

should be captured as part of the operational metrics. The operational metrics can then be aggregated through the financial metrics to determine whether the strategic objective is being met (see Figure 10.5).

Figure 10.4 shows the fill rate as the response to the customer. If the fill rate is set high enough, the most common response to the customer will be standard delivery where the customer receives the item and the firm derives a margin after deducting logistics and other expenses depending on product and customer requirements. Some products have greater profitability than others due to their logistics needs or inventory status (ABC class). If the firm does not have the requested products, the other tactical responses are to lose the sale (lost profits and customers), expedite (activity costs may exceed gross margin), or backorder. Backorders also carry potential lost customer risk since they may go elsewhere while waiting. The costs and margin generated by the responses driven from the fill rate build up to financial measures like total gross margin generated and days sales outstanding as customers the firm chose to serve pay or do not pay in a timely fashion.

Management has to tie together the metrics suggested in Figure 10.4 with a strategy that balances the positives, like higher margins, greater market share, and increased sales, with the costs like inventory and stockouts. The strategy has to tie these costs to stakeholder goals, like ROI and ROA, as seen in Figure 10.5.

Meeting customer service objectives is challenging, especially with the push from item fill rates to order fill rates now being required by many customers. As discussed in preceding chapters, meeting order fill rates requires a considerable increase in item fill rates. The fill rate of each item is multiplied by the fill rate of each of the other items in the order to reach the order fill rate. Although currently not commonly measured, the order fill rate is increasingly being demanded by customers and will likely become the next important customer expectation. The impact of adding items to an order is illustrated in Figure 10.6. For example, an individual item fill rate of 90 percent would result in a double-item fill rate of 81 percent.

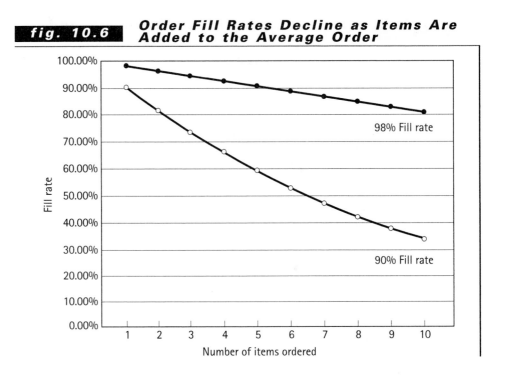

fig. 10.6   *Order Fill Rates Decline as Items Are Added to the Average Order*

Sometimes tactical objectives lead to internal conflicts. Common problems include internal profitability and metrics that can lead to downgrading customer service. Many firms use internal profitability as a method to enforce efficiency. Each division is given an objective for profitability. The method can lead to one division pushing inventory onto another or refusing to support common objectives in a consistent fashion. The concept of internal profitability came about to ensure that all parts of the firm were competitive and efficient. The system breaks down, however, when it causes misalignment of goals. Since some divisions act as suppliers of products or services to others, the internal profitability goals, especially when salaries and bonuses are connected to the goals, will often cause divisiveness with different divisions refusing service or assistance to each other in the interest of meeting divisional profits at the expense of the entire firm.

One large manufacturer with considerable distribution capability used internal profitability to control performance among divisions. To minimize product cost before shipping it to distribution, the manufacturing division made long production runs to cut down on the cost of changing over production lines from one product to another. They then shipped these large lot sizes to the firm's regional distribution centers and recorded their profits as product that had not yet been sold to end customers having been "sold" to distribution. Plant managers' budgets were met (bonuses!) but distribution was buried in inventory. The result was high obsolescence costs, stockouts when A items ran out between long scheduled runs, and a general increase in warehousing costs. Manufacturing was credited with contributing to profitability while distribution was blamed for subsequent losses.

After setting strategic objectives and aligning financial metrics, tactical objectives should be set that support strategic and financial goals. The objectives should be financially measurable and operationally meaningful. Operational meaning is drawn from the task involved and its relationship with the tactical goal. Financial meaning is taken from converting tactical process success.

Connecting Tactical Objectives to Operational Metrics

The relationship between tactical objectives and operational metrics must be exact. Many organizations express tactical objectives in vague terms:

○ "We have to reduce inventory."

○ "We have to be more responsive to customer complaints."

○ "We need to improve forecasting."

Although these are all good objectives, they do not define how the objective is to be met. Even when the objective is more clearly stated, it still may not be sufficient to drive improvement: "We need to reduce inventory by 20 percent." This objective is more prescriptive but still does not create a plan for reducing inventory. In the hands of different managers, the firm will get different results. One branch may try to dispose of its slow-moving inventory through aggressive markdowns, which may have a negative impact on profitability. Another may simply put a cap on how much it buys, which could drive A items to critical levels, forcing expensive expediting (again reducing profitability).

The tactical objective should be broken down into its components, and a plan of attack that meets strategic goals should be developed. If the tactical objective is not consistent with strategic objectives, it should be revised or abandoned. If the objective is sound but may interfere with other strategic objectives, it should be carefully planned to capitalize on its positive impact and minimize any negatives. Inventory reduction, for instance, can increase profitability through a reduction in holding costs but can negatively impact profits if carried out at the expense of customer service. The customer service and profitability goals should be firmly set and monitored by the system in real time to determine how changes in inventory are affecting these strategic goals.

The inventory reduction objective should then be examined to determine what the drivers of inventory are and how they can be reduced with a greater positive than negative impact. The principal drivers of inventory are delineated in Figure 10.7. The first inventory driver, forecast error, has been described in Chapter 8 and is very important in any inventory reduction scheme. Forecast error must be measured by error metrics that can then be directly traced to inventory levels. MAD (mean

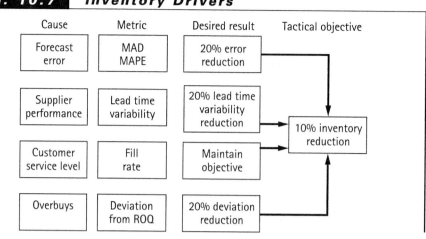

fig. 10.7 *Inventory Drivers*

absolute deviation), for instance, can be used to calculate safety stock. A reduction in MAD, therefore, can be directly traceable to a reduction in the need for safety stock. Not measuring MAD might lead to a reduction in forecast error not being captured and translated into reduced inventory.

The next major driver, supplier performance, is another major component of safety stock and can be measured by information systems in the form of lead-time variability. Supplier performance improvements can also be mathematically connected to inventory levels. Customer service levels are represented by the fill rate. Higher fill rates mean larger safety stocks. This is a good example of conflicting objectives that must be reconciled. If the fill rate is increased, inventory increases, but if it is decreased, customer service suffers. The best approach is to establish an achievable fill rate for a given level of desired inventory investment.

The tendency to overbuy is another example of conflicting objectives, namely landed cost (what an item costs after purchase price and delivery) versus inventory holding costs. Purchasing may try to minimize landed cost via bulk purchases that capture supplier and transportation carrier discounts. These large purchases increase inventory, however. The ERP system can and should make a recommended order quantity (ROQ) that balances these costs. If purchasing deviates from the ROQ, the deviations can be measured for the purpose of determining the impact on inventory objectives.

The connection between tactical objectives and operational metrics is a function of the relationship between a measurable goal and its related measures. If a tactical goal is properly correlated with the operational metrics and their relationship is understood, the ERP system through its executive information system or other reporting mechanisms can not only measure but control entire processes like the inventory reduction example above. Some other key tactical objectives (besides inventory reduction) include:

1. Reducing cycle times.

2. Reducing overhead.

3. Reducing operating costs.

4. Increasing customer service.

Operational metrics and their relationship to tactical objectives should be clear. Here is an example: Reduced fulfillment cycle times are a function of the following equation:

Receiving cycle time + picking time + packaging time + delivery time + (probability of stockout × average backorder time) = Total cycle time

Each element in the equation has its own mathematical components that will differ with different environments and places within the supply chain. As another example, to reduce inventory we examine the following equation:

Regular inventory + safety stock = Total inventory

Where: Regular inventory = Average inventory depleted between orders
  Safety stock = A function of desired fill rate, supplier performance, and forecast error

(See Ballou, 1998[8] for a mathematical treatment of these equations.)

For each tactical objective, there should be quantifiable measures developed and metrics collected. Figure 10.8 lists some common measures associated with customer service.

In addition to the customer metrics, each operational area of the firm has its own set of measures that can be developed and used for improvement. Some common measures associated with distribution and procurement are listed in Figure 10.9. The process of developing the tactical objectives from the strategic ones and deriving operational metrics from the tactical objectives while maintaining consistency with financial metrics is called disaggregation of measures (see Figure 10.2). The next step is to aggregate the measurement results for management decision making.

---

fig. 10.8 *Customer Metrics*

• Overall customer satisfaction	• % of customers sharing information
• Customer complaints	• Service system flexibility
• % resolution on first call	• Planning cycle time
• DRP performance	• Demand variability
• Perceived value	• Payment (invoice) accuracy
• Lost sales	• Forecast accuracy
• Time to market	• Shelf space
• Query time	• Utilization of POS data

fig. 10.9   *Distribution and Procurement Metrics*

- **Distribution**
  - Inquiry response time
  - Over/short/damaged (warehouse fill rate and quality)
  - Invoice accuracy
  - On-time delivery
  - Line item fill
  - Order fill rate
  - Quantity fill rate
  - Order time and variance
  - Stockouts/backorders
  - Range of products/services
  - Returns handling

- **Procurement**
  - Cost deviation from contract price
  - Supplier performance
  - Forecast accuracy
  - Deviation from primary vendor
  - Orders processed/labor unit
  - Processing accuracy
  - Order cycle time
  - Order cycle time variance

Aggregating Measures for Executive Decision Making

Once the system has been measured going down the firm, you must reaggregate it back up to useful measures for management decision making. The operational metrics have to be associated with the appropriate financial metrics and tracked in real time. If an operational metric indicates failures are occurring, the system should warn responsible individuals in the firm before financial damage is incurred. If, on the other hand, the operational measures are reading the system as operating correctly but the financial goals are not being met, the system is either not collecting the right data, the measures have not been properly designed, or the tactical goals were not correctly matched to financial ones.

Many firms struggle with designing tactical goals that properly match financial metrics. The operational metric "Deviation from primary vendor," for example, can demonstrate use of expediting (going to a more expensive source during a stockout) or "rogue buying," where a manager or planner buys product from nonapproved vendors. Proper interpretation of the metrics is critical to controlling operations. One firm found effective purchasing very difficult when its branch managers would routinely use petty cash to buy in the local market to get faster delivery rather than waiting for purchasing to make more economic deals. "Customer service needs" was always the excuse, and the centralized purchasing division had a difficult time proving these purchases were not necessary. Supplier relationships often broke down when a supplier salesperson would visit a branch and see competitors' products there after their firm had negotiated considerable discounts for the distributor.

Sometimes the operational metrics have an additive effect. Two or more measures might go together to explain changes in a financial metric. When this occurs, the firm can either try to identify the exact relationship or simply try to reduce the prob-

fig. 10.10 **Procurement Operational Linked to Financial Metrics**

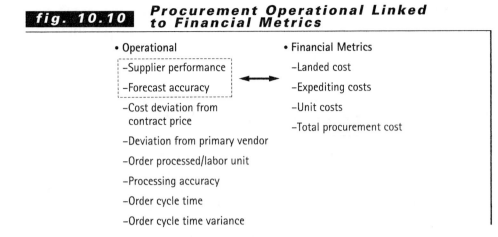

- Operational
  - —Supplier performance
  - —Forecast accuracy
  - —Cost deviation from contract price
  - —Deviation from primary vendor
  - —Order processed/labor unit
  - —Processing accuracy
  - —Order cycle time
  - —Order cycle time variance

- Financial Metrics
  - —Landed cost
  - —Expediting costs
  - —Unit costs
  - —Total procurement cost

lem through improvements measured in all contributing metrics. Figure 10.10 demonstrates a relationship between procurement operational measures and their associated financial metrics.

The financial metrics then can be built into their own hierarchy that eventually leads to a few manageable metrics for top management to review on a regular basis. If the metrics are out of line, however, the executive information system provides drill-down capability so that the metric that needs further investigation can be compared to its supporting financial metric. The supporting financial metric can be further explored through examination of supporting operational ones until all root causes for failure have been identified and areas needing attention are exposed.

The top-level metrics to examine are typically key performance indicators like return on investment, return on assets, average gross margin, earnings before interest and taxes, and the like. Dashboards and scorecards have been developed for this purpose by many information technology providers like ERP (through their executive information system capability) or bolt-on technology. Dashboards (see Figure 10.11) are a select set of metrics presented in a style that gives the executive a quick

fig. 10.11 **The Executive Dashboard**

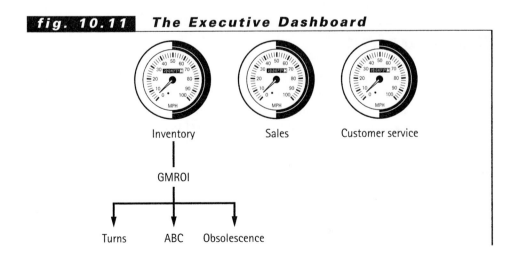

glance at firm performance with drill-down capability (like the dashboard of a car does for the driver). Scorecards are more like standardized reports that list related and relevant measures together that allow the executive to see how performance in one area interrelates with others.

Sharing Information in the Firm

Once the system is set up, employees and other stakeholders have to be given access and the power to act on what the measures are telling them. Processes should be put in place that lead to cause and effect for employee actions. In other words, measurement and reporting will be ongoing through the EIS module, but how to respond to changes in metrics has to be delineated for responsible members of the firm. The decisions made at the lowest levels of the organization will have an affect on firm performance that should be reflected at the managerial level through the reaggregation of metrics back up the executive information system.

One final note: The EIS should support reports for management to use in guiding other important influences on corporate success. Most systems are designed to support profitability for tax and other legal purposes but often have to be modified to give management other views of the corporation. Reports should be designed to demonstrate ROI and guide investors on which projects should be supported, which should not, and the relationships among each.

The long-term capacity planning activities of the firm like major property purchases, new facility construction, acquisition of competitors, and so on, frequently require new investments from stockholders, approval from the board of directors, or additional loans from financial institutions. If management cannot provide detailed financial analysis and justification for capacity increases based on real firm performance, investors and others will have a difficult time evaluating these opportunities. The result will be lost opportunity when the value of these potential investments cannot be proven well enough to get approval or lost investments when the wrong projects are approved.

Conclusion

Key performance indicators have been used and abused at firms throughout the history of distribution. Many were developed in response to tax laws and others in response to the investment community. These high-level metrics have their place but are frequently not directly connected to the lower-level performance measurements that drive the day-to-day operations of the firm. The result is confusion as to what should be done, what has been done, and how successful these actions were when completed.

Executive information systems and enterprise resource planning open the door to connected measures that move in tandem with one another and allow for real-time control of firm activities. The opportunities offered by ERP are often lost due to unconnected logic and decision making throughout the firm. To be successful in capitalizing on the promise of ERP, management must design a hierarchical set of metrics that tie to strategic and tactical objectives and that match operational and financial KPIs. The EIS, therefore, is critical to ERP success.

Distribution Retrospective

Mike was sure Meadows's problems stemmed from not knowing what the implications of their decisions were from one day to the next. He decided that the firm needed a connected set of metrics that would tell it what effect operational decision making was having on profitability and, most importantly, what the effect of discounting was on profitability as compared to the economies of scale that would be captured by increased sales. He was especially interested in drawing a connection between sales and operations that would make it possible to evaluate the value of a discounting decision in advance.

Mike knew in the short run, however, that he had to answer the question about shrinking margins. He viewed this issue as central to understanding and meeting the company's strategic objectives. The firm wanted increasing (rather than shrinking) profitability but also wanted to grow market share. In some ways these two goals were in conflict, but in others they were not. Mike thought the correct approach would be to get exact numbers from management for these goals and work backward. He checked the firm's vision statement and found it wanted an overall fill rate of 98 percent. He knew the current fill rate was 90 percent and that customer service failures were common.

On the profitability side, the firm had targeted a gross margin of 28 percent according to a statement issued to a financial institution but was only achieving a 22 percent overall margin, which was declining. Rather than ask management what the latest figures were and go through a series of meetings that could take weeks, he decided to use these as his benchmarks for the shrinking margins and to build an understanding of them that would lead to a consistent metrics collection program.

Mike had three deliverables in mind for Meadows's management team: an explanation of the relationship between declining margins and market share, a recommended procedure to improve margins, and a metrics collection methodology that could be automated on the system and prevent this problem from recurring in the future.

He examined the average discount offered customers and found that the sales force was not discriminating between critical customers and less-important sales. The average discount was cutting deeply into margins. He also found that the problems with fill rates were a function of poor forecasting and a rising level of obsolete inventory that was not in many cases being recognized as obsolete. The obsolete inventory was causing branches to hit financial or space limits on their inventory such that they bought less of everything. The decreased buying was leading to stockouts in A and B items. There were many other contributing causes but Mike felt these were more than enough for the firm to deal with up front.

Mike went to Jerry and Jack with the following suggestions:

1. *Discounting had to be tracked and a monthly report issued by the system that demonstrated to management the margin loss associated with sales force decisions. The report should have drill-down capability to allow management to rank the customers versus discounts issued. The report should be proactively used to limit discounting to customers who did not require or should not receive discounts. He also suggested the firm develop a correlation between market share and the level of discounting to determine what impact tighter policies would have on market share before making any decisions.*

2. *The margin improvement would be based on reducing discounts, but Mike also wanted to capture more market share by increasing the firm's fill rate. He suggested that fill rates be tracked in real time on all products (rather than by lines on an order) and that an ABC policy be used to increase fill rates on the fastest movers. He pointed out that the firm would have to take a hit on getting out of*

dead inventory and move the investment to fast movers. He could see the disappointment on Jack's face when he realized the short-run impact this would have on profitability. He pointed out that this would be the best way to grow fill rate and he believed a higher fill rate was the best way to grow market share.

3. *Mike then detailed how the metrics would connect and lead to financial and strategic objectives. He pointed out that unless this process was organized and put on the system to run in real time, Jack and Jerry would find themselves back in this position next year.*

Jack let out a long, slow sigh. "You are telling me that we have to basically rebuild our organization's approach to sales and operations and teach our IT system to track and report on its performance continuously?"

"How much is this going to cost?" Jerry asked nervously.

"Doesn't matter," Jack said, to Jerry's shock. "There is a right way and a wrong way to do things. We do them the wrong way and cover it up with accounting and sales band-aids. Long term, it will mean our destruction. I can protect myself or do what's right for the company. We are going to learn things about ourselves we'll wish we didn't know, but we must take the plunge."

Issues to Consider

1. In the strategic planning hierarchy, how should the firm disaggregate from strategic objectives to operational metrics?

2. What relationship should exist between financial and operational metrics?

3. How can metrics be used to drive positive change?

4. If we can assume customer expectations will continue to increase, how does one adjust metrics to anticipate future needs?

Case Study: Targeting Success

Note to the reader: This case is a continuation of a case in e-Distribution by Lawrence, Jennings, and Reynolds. The material is based on a real company from a channel other than plumbing supply. This case does not represent the state of the plumbing supply market.

David Jackson, Vice President of Operations, looked over the numbers and was not happy. He had succeeded in lowering slow-moving inventory, but the target for overall inventory still seemed far away. The decrease had come at a high price in inventory write-offs, too. He still needed to get the inventory down, but the firm could not continue to absorb inventory driven margin losses at the rate it had last year. He was also worried that obsolete inventory was being replaced at every location almost as fast as he could eliminate it.

My Plumbing Supply (MPS) was the largest plumbing manufacturer/distributor in the United States. In recent years, MPS had adopted an ERP system, absorbed its second-largest competitor, and begun a logistics program targeted at decreasing assets while still meeting or exceeding customer service expectations. The market was very tough with many of MPS's products becoming commodities that had to compete with imported goods at significantly tighter margins. The firm had to meet the increasing customer service demands on the one hand and decrease costs at the same time.

David was not the only one with a problem. The market had gotten very tight and the sales force was having a difficult time making sales without significant discounting. John Evans, the Vice President of Sales, was under pressure to keep prices up while still maintaining market share. John and David got together and decided they would develop a linked set of metrics that would control the entire process so that they could figure out how to make improvements and adjust to changes in the environment without damaging the company's current position in the market.

David wanted lower inventory, but John wanted the right stuff in place so that his sales force would not miss easy sales and would feel more confident about the firm's ability to meet customer needs. He felt more confidence would translate into less inclination to use discounts to maintain customer relationships. They decided the best approach would be to link the actions of salespeople to financial metrics and link operational responsiveness as well. They were not sure where it would lead but felt the mere act of putting the metrics together would help them understand what was going on.

John and David decided to focus their efforts on three strategic goals: one for each division (sales and operations) and one to meet the needs of the stockholders. The goal that would support the sales force would be increased market share. John and David agreed they should use increased fill rates to achieve that goal. Better service levels were the only alternative to discounting. The company had established an objective to increase market share by 2.5 percent. Currently fill rates at ship-confirm (out the door, on a truck, to the customer) were running a company average of 94 percent. Now the question was, what fill rate would get them the targeted increase in market share? They decided to shoot for a 96 percent overall fill rate and see whether that achieved their goal.

David wanted decreased inventory for the operations division. He was under pressure to achieve at least a 20 percent decrease in inventory. John was unsure how that goal could be reached without endangering the increase in market share. After some discussion, they decided to set the target for inventory decrease at 10 percent. David felt he could defend that number based on protecting customer service. The question was, how to create a higher fill rate while decreasing inventory? David had read somewhere that forecast error was a major inventory driver and that supplier lead times were another. He decided they should initiate a program to reduce forecast error by fully activating the planning module on their ERP system and start working on their supplier relationships to find innovative ways to reduce lead times. He was not sure, however, that reduction in lead times and forecast error would get him to the 10 percent reduction in inventory. He and John decided they would ask the purchasing group for its advice on the matter.

David also planned to push the ABC analysis the firm had launched. ABC would allow the firm to increase fill rates on the fastest movers, which would reduce the need for excessive inventory since an increase in A items would reduce the need for an across the board increase in inventory. A items represented about 21 percent of inventory and about 85 percent of sales. Increasing A-item inventory would have the biggest effect on overall fill rates. David was unsure exactly how the relationship would work, however.

David's biggest fear was that the dead inventory was being replaced as fast as he could eliminate it. The firm simply could not sustain the write-offs it had experienced last year. To ignore the dead inventory problem, however, would only make it worse and would lead to an inevitable day of reckoning. David wanted the ABC system to not only help him raise fill rates but lower inventory as well. He had heard that the ABC system could help prevent slow-moving inventory by automatically decreasing inventory before it became a slow mover and then consolidating it while there was still a chance of eliminating it (before it went obsolete). He wanted to "see" it happening through his metrics and adjust when the system was not producing desired results. What should those results be?

Mary Davis was the head of purchasing. When she heard what David and John were planning, she was very skeptical. She had seen these key performance indicator exercises come and go and usually it boiled down to her group getting burdened with unrealistic expectations and no power to even remotely affect their outcome. She told David that improving forecasting would be helpful and might make the inventory planners buy a little less, but she had no idea how much less since every planner was using the system differently. David was taken aback that there was such variation in the purchasing process and asked why. Mary quickly pointed out that planners were continually getting second-guessed by the sales force and, whether management wanted to admit it or not, disagreements were most often settled in favor of the sales force.

Mary also said that planners had nothing concrete on which to make or defend their decisions. If they received better forecasts, the only way inventory would go down was if they decreased safety stock. If they decreased safety stock, the sales force would question their actions. Whenever a stockout occurred, the sales force would blame the planners and insist that the inventory be restored. Without a sound methodology to demonstrate that the change in safety stock was valid and that fill rates were being met, the planners would have no choice but to restore the inventory. So the net effect for Mary's group would be a lot of work only to be criticized and forced to undo their efforts in the end. She had been through it before and did not want her team to be the scapegoat for poor planning on management's part.

David decided to look to other ways to improve fill rates and lower inventory at the same time. One way would be to improve supplier delivery performance, but that would take him back to purchasing again since decreases in safety stock brought about by better supplier performance would again have to be proven as effective. This whole thing was your classic chicken-or-egg dilemma. Then David had a revelation. The problem was that nobody could prove any move was wise since everyone had an opinion and could collect small bits of data that supported his or her view. The company was operating off scant information and did not have true measures to determine what actions should be taken or how to evaluate those actions after they had occurred. Without a set of metrics that would support those who were doing the right things and convince those who doubted those actions, the firm could not move forward on any front. A set of purchasing metrics that tracked the relationship between safety stocks and fill rates was a priority.

David and John had one more issue to consider: the stockholder's interest. The metric they felt was most appropriate was ROI (return on investment). ROI was going to be difficult to tie into operational metrics since increasing assets might cause increasing sales, which may or may not lead to increased ROI. If the investment in assets grew faster than profits, ROI might actually decrease if additional funds were required from the stockholders. If, on the other hand, the additional assets were acquired through loans or investment from internal funds, the ROI would go higher as long as the interest payments on the loans were not more than the additional profits generated through increased sales. Even if the increased investment got a higher ROI, the company might have been able to achieve a higher one if it had invested the funds in another venture. Just thinking about the measurement process made one's head spin.

David went down to John's office and the two of them put together a drawing that would capture the metrics needed to interconnect the entire process as they envisioned it (see Figure 10.12). They then began to evaluate how to reach their objectives while properly supporting and evaluating decision making with solid KPIs. They were unsure how to tie the resulting KPIs to financial measures but thought that they could try to hit the other targets and see what the outcome would be. They might do better than they expected or might find a need to tighten the other metrics as they went. They simply did not know what else to do. Finally, they decided to put all relevant metrics into their ERP system and make sure they could monitor the firm's activities in real time. They felt that if the system tracked the success or failure to reach these goals in real time, they could make adjustments as the need arose.

The next step was to develop all the relating measures and processes that would contribute to success or failure to reach the goals in the diagram. David realized that there were more measures than he and John could imagine in one sitting. He also understood that this process could introduce too many and/or conflicting measures. On top of overwhelming the firm with metrics that led them in circles, they were also concerned that if the measures were not complete or were pointing in the wrong direction, they might do more harm than good. Employees would view any measurement system as a potential compensation tool. People might become concerned about their job security or stature in the firm being affected by metrics. Some would seek to find the blind spots in the metrics and prove them invalid. Others would seek

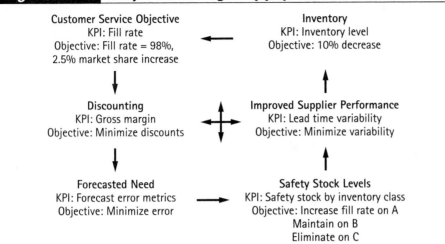

fig. 10.12 *My Plumbing Supply Metrics*

Customer Service Objective
KPI: Fill rate
Objective: Fill rate = 98%,
2.5% market share increase

Inventory
KPI: Inventory level
Objective: 10% decrease

Discounting
KPI: Gross margin
Objective: Minimize discounts

Improved Supplier Performance
KPI: Lead time variability
Objective: Minimize variability

Forecasted Need
KPI: Forecast error metrics
Objective: Minimize error

Safety Stock Levels
KPI: Safety stock by inventory class
Objective: Increase fill rate on A
Maintain on B
Eliminate on C

to use the metrics to settle scores or manipulate others. David and John talked about the downsides and almost decided to table the whole project. They decided in the end, however, that not doing anything guaranteed failure.

Case Challenges

1. John wants to grow market share while holding down discounts. What is the relationship between the two? How can he be consistent with David's inventory objectives? How does real-time metric keeping help?

2. How can purchasing contribute to this process? What can be done to keep them from becoming the scapegoat of failed processes?

3. How does ROI fit in the picture? What additional costs will be generated by David and John's plans? How can ROI be increased in spite of (or because of) the investment?

References

1. William J. Latzko and David M. Saunders, *Four Days With Dr. Deming: A Strategy for Modern Methods of Management* (Engineering Process Improvement Series) (Upper Saddle River, NJ: Prentice Hall, 1995).

2. F. Barry Lawrence, Ramesh Krishnamurthi, and Norm Clark, "Performance Metrics for a Connected Supply Chain," *Review of Electronic and Industrial Distribution Industries* 1, no. 1 (2002): 139–161.

3. IBM's Technology Roadmap for e-Distributors, 2001, IBM Corporation, http://www-1.ibm.com/medium-business/resources/whitepapers/whitepaper.jsp?contentId=4342.

4. F. Barry Lawrence, Daniel. F. Jennings, and Bharani Nagarathnam, "A Framework to Quantify the Value of Authorized Distribution Channel," *Review of Electronic and Industrial Distribution Industries* 2, no. 1 (2003): 1–17.

5. David Shook, "Remapping Amazon's Course," *BusinessWeek* (July 15, 2002), http://aol.businessweek.com/bwdaily/dnflash/jul2002/nf20020715_0591.htm.

6. Robert S. Kaplan and David P. Norton, *The Balanced Scorecard: Translating Strategy into Action* (Cambridge, MA: Harvard Business School Press, 1996).

7. Leaps and Bounds: Moving Ahead With The Dupont Legal Model, 1992, *http://www.dupontlegalmodel.com/files/leapsandbound.asp.*

8. Ronald H. Ballou, *Business Logistics Management,* 4th ed. (Upper Saddle River, NJ: Prentice Hall, 1998).

Managing the System

Distribution Perspective

Bill Black, CEO of Hill Country Sporting Goods Supply (HCSGS), a $200 million supplier of golf and fishing supplies to small and mid-sized distributors, called the executive committee meeting to order. In the room were his Vice President of Sales and Operations, Lisa Gayle, along with his Director of Information Technology, Keith Jenkins. The firm had an IT department of five programmers and one business process expert from operations, Phil Stack, who had learned so much about their ERP system that he was always being pulled into IT projects. Bill had finally decided that Phil was more valuable leading IT projects than working in the warehouse and asked him to join the IT department.

Keith was explaining that, as usual, there were far more requests for IT projects than the department could carry out. His solution was to list the projects that were being requested and let the executive committee decide which ones should be prioritized and carried out this year. Bill asked how many projects were being requested. Keith replied they had received approximately 30 and could handle about ten. He recommended the executive committee pick ten that the IT department should complete in the coming year. They might get to more but that was the most he could commit to given his current resources. Bill agreed, and the committee picked its top ten and adjourned.

Bill was not comfortable with the solution. Phil had worked for Bill when Bill was warehouse manager. Bill remembered Phil poring over the manuals when the new system came in and could not understand Phil's fascination with this IT stuff. In one of their discussions, Phil had pointed out that the ERP system would come to govern everything HCSGS did, and he was curious how the processes would look and work when the firm finished reinventing itself. Bill wasn't sure he bought into this reinventing-the-firm concept but it seemed like Phil's knowledge kept his division out of all the IT problems that continually plagued other divisions. He had grown to respect Phil so he called him in to talk about the IT prioritizing process the executive committee had committed to in the meeting.

Phil started by saying that the prioritizing method was problematic because some of the lower-priority selections would be necessary to make the higher-rated ones pay off. He had noted that projects that depended on data integrity were often prioritized over data-scrubbing or other data accuracy projects. While some benefit could be gained, the firm was suboptimizing its network and human resources. Bill asked why Keith had not explained the interdependence of these processes to the committee.

"It's not his job to know what the business processes depend on," Phil replied. "That's the job of business process experts in the firm."

"Like you," said Bill.

"Not just me," Phil said. "There are many functions in this company I know nothing about. You have to get more people involved."

Bill shifted uneasily. Most of his people were unhappy with the system, and requiring them to get involved in projects they believed to be IT's responsibility was not going to be popular.

Introduction

Once the system is in place, metrics are aligned, and processes are operating according to plan, the firm must begin the day-to-day operations of running the new information-enabled enterprise. An information-enabled enterprise is different from

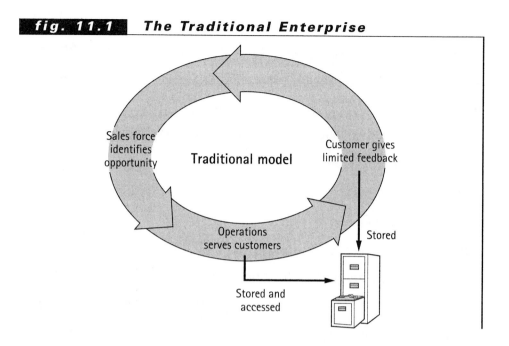

fig. 11.1   *The Traditional Enterprise*

traditional models not only in a technology sense but also in a planning and organizational one. The traditional enterprise identifies opportunity through information gathered by employees, evaluates the information, may or may not compare the new intelligence with a limited amount of recorded information, makes a decision, takes action, and then records some portion of what took place for financial reporting purposes or to use in future scenarios. The amount of information recorded and used in future decisions is limited due to the difficulty associated with collecting and retrieving it (see Figure 11.1).

The information-enabled organization rearranges the order of activity. Opportunity is still identified through employees, but those employees may have been directed at those opportunities by the analysis programs in the ERP system. Some examples might include:

○ The customer relationship management module in the ERP system identifies a possible connection between a customer type and a new product introduction that was not anticipated by either the supplier or the distributor. The distributor sales force is directed to call on more of these customers and demonstrate the new product.

○ The financial module determines that a particular customer type has a far lower rating in days sales outstanding (DSO, a measure of the length of time it takes for customers to pay) than others. Management surmises that this customer group is experiencing good financial health and increases sales efforts to them to increase sales and decrease DSO and bad debt expense.

○ Purchasing reviews its supplier lead-time report that highlights a supplier whose lead times have suddenly increased. The increase has been steady and is now threatening to cause stockouts. Purchasing contacts the supplier and discovers that the problem is not going to be a short-term one. They decide to increase safety stock and demand during lead-time inventory. Next they notify sales that the risk of stockout on this product has increased and that salespeople should consider product substitution when possible. (Purchasing's recommended substitute products are based on the same report.)

○ Inventory reports indicate to management that inventories are increasing at a faster rate than sales—a sure sign of trouble. Management decides to halt purchases on all items other than A-class until inventory balances are back in line.

All of the foregoing could be achieved in a noninformation-enabled environment but not to the same degree or in as timely a fashion. The first example, for instance, would require the sales force to notice the unusual demand pattern and to report it to management. The amount of time needed to get the issue recognized and passed up and down the management structure might number from in the months to never. This process of analyzing system information to identify new potential markets and sales is referred to as "data mining" and is restricted where data is either not collected or very difficult to access (such as buried in file cabinets). The analysis can become very complex as well if the firm does not have staff or programs with adequate computational skills.

Once the analysis is complete, the process of responding to the information often requires others in the firm to have access to that same information. Take the fourth bulleted example: Management may identify a problem, but unless analysis is done to identify the inventory stratification (A, B, or C items) and that information is delivered into the hands of all who influence purchasing, the management edict cannot be carried out. One large distributor faced inventory levels that exceeded what the firm could support financially. Lacking any ability to determine which products were most profitable or most important to profitable customers, the firm could only stop buying all products until the inventory was back in balance. The net effect was to force the firm into stockouts or expediting, both of which were more expensive than the inventory holding costs.

The information-enabled firm uses the real-time capability of ERP to store greater amounts of information in a more timely fashion. Real time also leads to the ability to access that same information and perform analysis. Analysis can then be used to enhance sales, operations, and other firm activities. The analysis itself produces information that can be stored and used in future higher-level analysis (not possible in many cases without ERP). In other words, the information-enabled firm will interact nonstop with the ERP system (see Figure 11.2).

The examples suggested in Figure 11.2 are only a few of many possibilities that many firms have already identified and many more that we are only beginning to understand. The difference between the traditional and the information-driven enterprise is that the latter relies on the system to determine what will happen and when. The collection of information in the traditional enterprise was based on records that served as historian, whereas in the ERP-driven firm, the system becomes part of the decision-making process and may even become a decision maker itself. The system can have logic embedded in the analysis programs that directs people on the proper

fig. 11.2   *The Information-Enabled Firm*

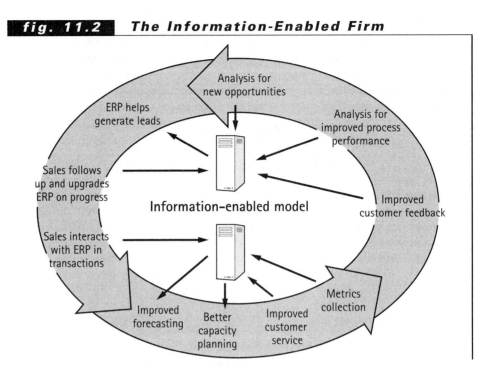

procedures for action on routine tasks to save human decision-making effort (which is inherently slower and less consistent) for the more complex tasks that are beyond the system's capability. However, these problems are numerous and not addressed in many firms due to a lack of time. In the most automated environments, the ERP system will often make the decisions and take action itself.

One firm was having considerable difficulty with forecasting. The ERP system gave a forecast using mathematical forecasting models that the inventory planners considered so inaccurate that they never used it. The result was a very large group of planners spending a great deal of time forecasting. The firm redesigned its forecasting process to include the ERP system's capabilities and ease the planners' workload. The data-extraction program was set up not only to pull an accurate data series for the mathematical model to use but to eliminate obvious problems like spikes in demand or common data-integrity issues. The forecast was then run and its accuracy was measured. If the accuracy was good enough, the system would simply make buy recommendations and not offer the forecast to the planner for changes. If the forecast was not performing well, the system had a series of screens it would take the planner through to find and correct the problem. This investigation was not possible before the system was set up for error metric collection since the planners did not have to time to investigate every data series. In effect, the system acted as a decision maker by deciding when it was appropriate to change the input data series, when the forecast could be trusted, and when to engage a planner's expertise. By taking over these mundane decisions, the system was able to conduct forecasting for the vast majority of products, leaving planners with time to investigate those products that needed human intervention.

Enterprise Thinking

The ERP system uses logic to run the firm that must parallel the same logic that management believes will optimize the firm's competitive posture. Some logic is simple and captured by most systems in a consistent fashion (we referred to this logic as noncore processes in earlier chapters). Other logic must be customized by the provider, identified in ERP packages that serve similar markets, or added as modifications to the system (the least desirable approach). This logic should be established in advance of selection and used in picking the system.

Implementation should capture the information-enabled logic and integrate it into process design. Process design consists of more than just how the system works; it also goes into how the system will interact with people and how their processes will work with the new system capability. ERP capabilities are numerous and some of those capabilities cannot be put to effective use by all firms—but the most important aspect of ERP is its connectivity. If the firm is to be successful, design should be directed at achieving and maintaining that connectivity. A good implementation will lead to internal connectivity but maintaining it requires a paradigm shift on the part of many within the firm. Maintenance will also uncover new functionality needs that were not envisioned or captured in the implementation phase. A successful implementation will capture as much as possible of the current environment, but because change is a constant, the maintenance process will frequently provoke a need to further extend the firm's competitive imperatives into the new ERP logic. The new extensions may come in the form of new revisions to the software, enabling modules not currently in use, or the addition of modifications or reports. This component of system maintenance is essentially a continuation of the never-ending implementation.

Remember that the process design will require considerable input from multiple experts in the firm who will be using the process in the system and meshing it with their own processes. This is key to successful implementation but also necessary for continuing maintenance of the system. After system selection and implementation, the firm will face many scenarios for which new functionality or reports are needed or perceived as necessary. The firm will be forced to at least investigate the value of such improvements. To do so, the firm will either use in-house IT specialists or contract for assistance from IT consultants. The proper division of labor between IT specialists and business process experts is difficult to establish and maintain.

Business process experts frequently prefer to leave IT projects to the IT specialists. They naturally believe the IT folks will know what to do with problems that seem obvious to them (how the business process actually works) and have significantly more knowledge about the technological side of the problem. Businesspeople frequently view IT specialists as having far more knowledge than would be possible for any specialist to maintain. The black box syndrome, where business process experts become intimidated by IT jargon and tools they do not understand, is largely to blame for this problem. The result is a tendency to depend on IT specialists for all aspects of ERP, both those they are qualified for (technology) and those they are not as prepared for (business process design).

IT specialists, on the other hand, frequently prefer to keep as much of the process design under their control as possible since system processes and their limitations are difficult to explain to laypeople. When integrating IT systems and business processes, many things can go wrong and some IT specialists might be tempted to keep others in the dark until they feel they have a reasonable solution. This often leads to poorly designed processes that no one really understands. The IT specialist moves on to the next project leaving the process owners (people in the department the process is designed to serve) to encounter and chase problems that keep popping up for no apparent reason.

One company maintained an internal IT department consisting of five people and regularly hired part-time consultants to handle special projects. The most experienced programmer kept many procedures entirely to himself and would often decide for the company how a process would work in the system. Operations personnel and even the IT director found discussing how the system handled certain critical functions with the programmer to be like penetrating a dense fog of technical jargon. When the programmer did eventually leave, consultants from the ERP provider had to be hired to untangle many processes that continued to function poorly. They found that many of the problems the firm had been suffering with came from decisions this programmer made based on a limited knowledge of how that business process was supposed to work.

Another firm was trying to meet its budget commitments on inventory control when a branch manager noticed that inventory was increasing and decreasing from one day to the next without any identifiable sales activity. The branch manager was being held responsible for inventory performance, so he called the purchasing division to find out what was going on. The purchasing group had no clue either and decided to contact the IT department for an investigation. An IT specialist looked into the matter and discovered a connection between how material costing for manufacturing could affect the value of inventories. If manufacturing costs increased, the value of some inventory could increase.

The IT specialist realized that changes made in the manufacturing-costing program might be affecting the inventory valuation of items that were not recently produced. He could not follow the documentation trail of the former programmer, however, and no internal process experts understood the changes since they had left it entirely in the hands of that programmer. The cost of bringing in consultants from the ERP firm to trace this problem was considered prohibitive, and the firm decided it would have to live with the problem. The branch manager was disheartened and let his colleagues know of the problem. The branch managers decided that top management did not really care about inventory management since they were unwilling to make it possible for branch management to track true inventory value. The firm soon lost the support of its field personnel in its endeavor to meet inventory objectives. Without the backing of field personnel, the firm was not able to reach its inventory goals. Ironically, the information tools prevented the firm from taking the kind of improvement actions necessary to make the system successful.

The problem stemmed from the original unwillingness of process experts (finance and manufacturing) to get involved in the original design of the program. When it comes to the relationship between IT and other firm experts, neither side fully understands the complexity of the other's environment, so the system will always be in need of changes when it falls short of basic business needs. After implementation, the firm frequently finds itself in a never-ending cycle of fixing processes again and again. The firm has to start thinking of the company and its information flows as a single, connected enterprise and begin considering how changes in one area or functionality will affect others.

IT experts think about this problem in terms of how changes affecting data or processing of that data in one area of the system will affect its interpretation in other parts of the system. Changes made in one part of the system will often have reverberating impacts in other parts of the system. ERP companies warn against changing base code for this very reason. This same logic applies to how the firm should view which changes made to support one division or function will affect others.

In a disconnected information system, firms build "silos" that are largely independent. Each division has to wait a specified period of time before information can flow from one critical area to another. When information is transferred from one silo to another, it is frequently put in a queue for inspection before use. Any information not deemed worthy of moving on by any silo is filtered out, frequently without consideration as to its value to other silos or suppliers.

Invoicing, for example, frequently requires a lengthy process during which a sales order gets processed, a pick slip is dropped in the warehouse, the material is picked/packed/shipped, the customer signs a bill of lading (or some other form to recognize delivery), freight and material costs are established, incoming documentation of the foregoing is checked in the finance department and recorded, and finally an invoice is prepared and sent. This process can take from days to weeks or longer if the process has little to no information automation (as would have to be the case in a disconnected environment).

The overwhelming amount of paperwork limits the amount of information that can be exchanged or understood. Each department receives a great deal of information to process, but much of it is not deemed valuable, while information considered critical is not included. This lack of critical information requires the department to expend a great deal of energy in follow-up and verification procedures that waste time for the receiving silo and all input sources. Each department finds itself buried in paperwork without a clear understanding of how to get the right information or how to pass on information critical to others in the firm or supply chain.

This process can become especially lengthy in an environment where there is a great deal of additional processing. One distributor had a very successful business in specialized manufacturing. This distributor would take power units that it sold to manufacturing firms on a regular basis and build larger, more powerful ones on skids that could be of considerable size and weight. The freight associated with such a unit could be very expensive since special handling and additional insurance were usually necessary. Invoicing was often inaccurate whenever the salesperson failed to properly note freight charges.

The finance department held up invoices for days sometimes as a quality check to make sure freight was captured on large transactions. The cost to the firm was very high since every day added to the invoicing process could translate into an extra day to get payment from the customer. Days sales outstanding (DSO) is a serious concern to most distributors since their accounts receivable is one of the largest assets on their books. The finance department protected itself from inaccurate information coming from sales by setting a buffer in front of their silo, where all incoming information was held until complete and checked for accuracy before invoices were processed.

The net effect for the firm was a series of silos. The manufacturing process and its tracking was one, finance another, and the sales force constituted yet another silo. The paperwork piled up between the silos much like inventory does between stations on a manufacturing line. Information automation begins the process of connecting the silos. The automation consists of a pipeline that passes information freely from one silo to the next without queuing or unnecessary inspection holding up the data transfer process. The size of the pipeline depends on the level of connectivity and organization of the process flows. If a single database is accessed, the firm manages less information at faster rates of transfer.

The effect is to create a pipeline that flows continuously and has less to transport between departments. Another benefit is to create system-based rules that ensure information critical to other departments is not filtered out before it can reach the departments needing it most. The information is passed freely, in the desired format, without multiple parties having to examine it and decide whether it holds value before passing it on. In fact, the information will not be handled at multiple points like it used to be, but rather passed to exactly where it is needed.

An interconnected information system (ERP) forces us to consider the flow between the silos since the centralized database does not recognize the boundaries and will feed bad information from one division to the next through the shared database. This requires the firm to eliminate bad or incomplete data at the source (the sales estimates, in our example). This thinking has been advocated but not implemented at many firms for years. However, until information-flow interconnectivity is established firms can and will continue resisting integration.[1] The silo approach will not work for firms seeking information interconnectivity and those that do not use information automation techniques will find competing under such conditions increasingly risky.[2]

Organizing and Deploying Human IT Resources

The IT department of a firm or IT consultants that come in for special tasks are a precious resource at most firms. Maintaining an internal department is very expensive but outsourcing to consultants may be even more costly. An external consultant may have greater knowledge about the system and its alternatives but an internal expert will understand the firm's processes, mission, and customers better. The tradeoff between these capabilities will vary from firm to firm, but most firms support an IT department only if they can afford it and then access external consultants only for short-term projects. Even so, many firms frequently have consultants that go from one short-term job to the next (and sometimes back when the previous job experiences problems) and almost seem to be permanent employees.

For many firms, if an IT department exists, it is almost certainly understaffed. The understaffing comes from a poor understanding of system needs and the benefits of a fully functional, well-maintained system. Management frequently has difficulty figuring out exactly how large the firm's IT support would have to be to eliminate suboptimal performance. ERP system benefits are still not well documented and vary tremendously from one firm to the next.[3] This complicates deciding on whether to adopt an ERP system but is even more significant in determining how much should be spent on IT support. Many firms experience so much difficulty in ERP selection and implementation that they become very conservative after the system goes live. In this environment, every IT project that goes beyond basic system maintenance is scrutinized. Many projects dating back to improper implementation are still awaiting the resources to properly activate them at many firms.

A large manufacturer/distributor had selected its ERP system based on manufacturing's need for a material requirements planning (MRP) program. The selected system was largely determined based on its MRP capability. Distribution was implemented first since the customer interface was necessary to drive all other processes. When the implementation got difficult, manufacturing decided not to use the system for its MRP scheduling for fear of experiencing the same problems of distribution. The program that played the largest hand in system selection was still not implemented seven years after the system had been bought.

IT specialists often see their efforts wasted by poorly considered projects. One firm was trying to measure fill rates and made it clear that each division would be responsible for its contribution to the fill rate. The fill rate itself was never really defined as being based on out-the-door shipments, items on the shelf when the customer called, whether before or after negotiation with the customer, or even whether the customer's request was reasonable. Staff did not know what would be expected of them, so multiple individuals requested fill rate reports, taking different measurements at different times to create reports that gave them different views of the firm.

Each department wanted different measures and used different formats and data. Management did not feel it could refuse to approve the IT requests since it had set the expectations and had to provide the tools necessary to measure, report, and respond to changes in company performance. By the time the issue had died down, the firm had more than 20 different reports measuring fill rates. In the final analysis, the firm decided it could not set a target fill rate since customer markets and product categories differed so greatly. The firm came to understand it needed multiple fill rates for each different class of customer and product category. It realized virtually all of the reports measured the wrong things. The IT expenditures to create and write all those reports had been a waste of time.

The cost of poorly used IT resources is even higher than many understand. If the IT specialists are internal to a firm, the firm suffers lost opportunity cost equal to the benefits that could have been achieved by a more successful use of their time. If the IT specialist is a consultant, the loss will be directly related to billable hours and, therefore, easier to quantify. For this reason, external consultants are less likely to have their time abused than internal resources, but even investments in hourly consultants are often not properly utilized.

Management has to carefully consider which projects will be carried out and ensure those projects are integrated with any related, supporting, or dependent projects. IT specialists then have to be integrated into projects with domain specialists and process specialists in the firm (to include management). The first step in planning such projects is for management to understand what IT specialists can and cannot do. Management, after thorough investigation, must decide how a project will proceed and not delegate the responsibility solely to IT specialists or business process experts without defining an enterprise view.

Most IT projects dealing with business process redesign or the creation of new processes will require cross-functional teams of specialists from different disciplines. If the project is left entirely to IT specialists, they may be tempted take the project in directions related to their perspective of efficiency, which may or may not match firm objectives for that process. Business process experts, on the other hand, may take the project in directions that make their jobs easier rather than making the process more supportive of firm objectives and efficient in its use of IT resources. In response to this IT/business process specialist gap, most firms end up developing an individual with expertise in system capabilities, firm objectives, and business processes. Commonly called domain experts, these individuals are frequently self-taught or took classes in their spare time to better understand the system and its capabilities.

Domain Experts

Domain experts often carry expertise in business processes such as best practices or common pitfalls in data handling or other process design issues. Domain experts are a valuable resource and should be developed to the greatest extent possible. One firm had activated its ERP system but found that most departments were working offline on many key processes, then keying the results of their activities into the system after the actions were complete. The system had been reduced to a historian, a role for file cabinets, and was not realizing the benefits the firm had originally planned in adopting ERP.

One department was different, however. The department was running off the system and using functionality from the system that management did not know existed. The IT department referred to this department as a model for the rest of the firm. When management investigated the success, the department manager said one of his employees had gone to the initial training and then, on his own time, had taken home the manuals to study further. While the implementation was underway, this employee had explored the system at night to determine what functionality was available. When implementation was complete, the department had suffered the same problems as others in the firm with not understanding the system and an inability to carry out basic tasks as well. Instead of finding work-arounds, however, the department found itself turning to this employee on a regular basis.

At first, this self-taught domain expert would advise others on the basic ERP functions, but eventually the harder questions arose. The domain expert would then hit the books and when he could not answer the question, he turned to IT for assistance. Usually by this time, the research had extended beyond the IT specialist's ability to do more than add a few more clues. Together, the domain specialist and

IT specialist would call on the support services of the ERP provider and resolve the issue. Management was impressed and asked why the department manager had not called their attention to the domain expert. He replied, ashamedly, that he was afraid he would lose the domain expert if everyone knew about him. He also pointed out, in his defense, that this expert was an expert only in his functional discipline and that every department needed such an expert.

The term *domain expert* indicates an individual with an understanding of IT capability who also understands a business functional area, or domain. ERP companies make a point of hiring and continually training domain experts to use in implementation projects. Consultants built successful divisions in the 1990s around this role. The consulting firm would combine business process reengineering (BPR) with basic domain expertise to enable firms to use their ERP systems properly. The strength of using a consultant or ERP expert in this role is this person's understanding of best practices, which they will apply with BPR to strengthen the goal of making the firm more successful. Most firm activities occur on a daily basis, however, and there is not enough time or money for the firm to call in consultants when these daily crises arise. Where no domain expert is available, it may be necessary to make judicious use of consultants, but firms should seek to integrate that expertise into their own domain experts.

Domain experts are the grease that keeps the ERP system's wheels turning. If well trained, they become a key resource to whom employees can turn for quick help from someone who understands how the firm works along with its strategic goals and objectives. If domain experts are not well trained, they can help in some cases, but in many others they may lead the firm astray. A poorly trained domain expert may only partially understand a process and access the wrong solution or may help IT to design solutions that are not useful and, therefore, waste resources. Domain experts will exist whether planned or not. The firm should seek to select and support them as well as expanding their knowledge to other employees and especially among all divisions.

The ideal project team would consist of domain and IT expertise. The level of the experts (internal versus external) depends on the nature and importance of the project. After the project is designed and the appropriate team assembled, the project design must then follow a step-by-step process with clear responsibility for each resource: domain expert, consultant, business process expert, management, and internal IT resource.

The Physical and the Information Networks

After the ERP system is activated, the ongoing process of running and upgrading business processes will continue indefinitely. The information mirror (the ERP system) will now offer many opportunities to redesign the physical network. Physical networks were created in response to changing customer demands. Many firms will stop from time to time and evaluate their physical network to see whether it is still efficient and make corrections, but many other firms just continue evolving without this periodic reassessment.

Physical networks, therefore, can become inefficient in terms of asset management. An information mirror of this system could also become inefficient if allowed to follow and copy the same evolutionary process. If properly managed, however, the very nature of ERP (connecting all information flows) may illuminate problems in the physical network. In particular, as examined elsewhere in this text (Chapters 4, 5, 8–10, and 14), much of the physical network may have come about in response to inefficient information flows. The ERP system will create many obvious opportunities to improve the physical network as it is activated.[4] Some of these opportunities will have been envisioned before the go-live stage and will be part of the plan for system payback. Others may be unexpected opportunities that employees identify after the fact. The ability to recognize and capitalize on these opportunities will be a function of planning and training.

Capitalizing on opportunities with limited IT resources requires effective management of them. To effectively manage IT resources, the firm must develop those resources (acquire IT specialists or consultants and train domain specialists) and then ensure they are deployed in an efficient fashion. Management must have a complete firm redesign plan in the greatest detail possible—or at least a well-defined set of goals that guide the utilization of these resources.

The redesign opportunities require an enterprise and possibly even a supply chain approach. Any plan requires a forecast of what is likely to be necessary in the near term, and a long-term forecast, of course, improves its potential success. This is no more true than when deploying large, somewhat inflexible resources like ERP. Supply chain management (SCM) is a highly dynamic movement, driven by the customer. When designing and managing IT projects, the customer should be considered first and major market shifts taken into account before designing IT processes. SCM gives us some insight into what the customer will be demanding next and can be used to determine the long-term need for changes in our IT systems and the effectiveness of those changes in meeting changing customer expectations: Will the process actually achieve what is intended?

One small distributor expended a great deal of effort to create a purchasing system that automated its inventory planning process. The system set safety stock levels, forecasted demand, and made order size recommendations. The system performed well for a while, but customer expectations continued to grow, and the distributor soon found its safety stocks expanding too fast. The distributor examined the causes of the safety stock problem and found large supplier lead-time variability to be the root of the problem (see Figure 11.3).

The highlighted text represents a product and its supplier performance. The distributor was using a mathematical model to calculate the safety stock (SS) and the average lead time multiplied by the forecast to get the inventory needed during the supplier's lead time (demand during lead time, or DDLT). The reorder point (ROP) was, therefore, SS + DDLT plus any outstanding backorders. The distributor became concerned when inventories became too large. Forecasting was investigated first and found to be adequate. Next, the supplier performance was examined and found to be the culprit. The long lead times associated with many suppliers (five

fig. 11.3 *A Small Distributor's Lead Time Issue*

SS	DDLT	ROP	Lead Times							
174	102	520	185	185	127	167	134	127	49	36
197	200	447	58	58	81	27	15	56	56	42
107	107	261	39	52	28	44	53	32	56	78

instances over 50 days and one over 80 in our highlighted example) were blowing up both the safety stock and the DDLT. When multiplied over 10,000 SKUs, the problem was overwhelming the distributor's ability to meet its financial goals.

The distributor examined the supplier relationship and found that the long lead times were a function of two problems. First, the supplier frequently lost orders and upon relocating them, shipped late. The distributor would often have reordered these same items in the intervening time. The distributor decided to implement a policy of canceling orders that were outside the supplier's stated lead time. The second problem was simply one of inquiring about order status. The distributor began routinely asking whether the product was in stock or production. If not, the distributor would use other sources more often.

In the final analysis, the distributor decided to set the system for an upper limit lead time based on some multiple of the supplier's stated lead time. If the supplier had a stated lead time of 20 days (as in the case above), the distributor would not allow its system to calculate off lead times exceeding 30 days (1.5 times the stated lead time). The distributor's need for safety stock and demand during lead-time inventory took a major drop (see Figure 11.4).

Cases that exceeded the new lead-time limit would be dealt with through more-aggressive purchasing procedures like those described above, or the supplier's product would be allowed to stock out. Suppliers willing to work with the distributor were informed of the new policy to give them an opportunity to find ways for controlling lead times. Since smaller manufacturers constituted a large portion of the distributor's business, many manufacturer salespeople started taking an interest in watching and improving their firm's performance for this distributor. The result was an improvement in lead times and a reduction in inventory. The system, however, had

fig. 11.4 *Lead Times Truncated and Inventory Levels Improve*

SS	DDLT	ROP	Lead Times							
174	102	520	185	185	127	167	134	127	49	36
53	113	216	30	30	30	27	15	30	30	30
107	107	261	39	52	28	44	53	32	56	78

to be reconfigured to perform the new calculation. SCM theory would have predicted the need to work with suppliers as customer expectations increased, and this exercise could have been avoided by anticipating the need in the original system design.

Redesign implies asset optimization, which in turn should lead to an improved ROI (return on investment). The ROI opportunity will frequently in turn lead to opportunities to invest more in IT projects. IT process improvement should be self-liquidating. Each project should pay for itself and provide resources for those that follow.

Matching Information Flows

The ongoing management of IT resources is merely an extension of the process begun when the ERP system was first adopted. In fact, the process is an extension of all firm efforts at information automation going back to whenever spreadsheets or any kind of computer data collection and analysis were first introduced to the firm. This process of matching information-automated flows to distribution processes means integrating all activities to the ERP system to include

- Customer Input—Sales order processing, contact management, quoting, and so on.

- Forecasting—Integration of customer input with internal experts for mathematical predictions of capacity needs to meet customer expectations.

- DRP/MRP Relationships—Controlling the forward flow of materials through the supplier/manufacturing operations (MRP) to the distribution network (DRP).

- Transfers Between Operations—Balancing capacity between branch and regional distribution center inventories.

- Work Orders—Controlling the final value-add processes provided by distributors before product goes out the door.

- Supplier Connectivity—Integrating the supplier's operations into the distributor's information processes (see Figure 11.5).

These key ERP activities have a natural match to physical processes and the rules that govern the physical network will also impact the information one. Once integrated, however, the information network will likely change our approach to the physical network. In addition to the ongoing material process flows in the figure, the IT department will be dealing with financial reporting mechanisms, human resource processes (payroll and so on). To capture the value of the information mirror, IT resources (consultants, internal IT specialists, and domain experts) must be managed well. Otherwise, opportunity to optimize the physical network will be lost to daily system maintenance and poor project choices.

Managing these resources requires a plan governed by return on investment. Each time an IT resource is consumed, the firm should have a well-defined objective in

| fig. 11.5 | **Matching the Information/ Physical Flows** |

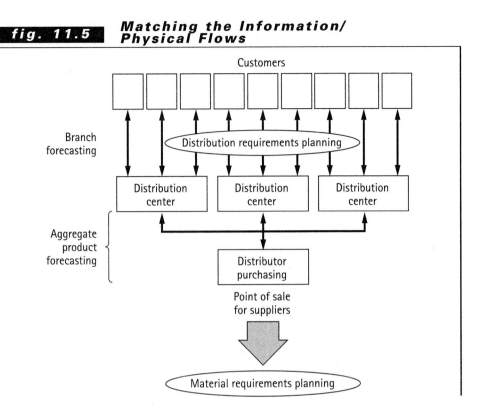

mind based on the firm's competitive strategies. IT resources should not be expended for convenience of a few employees or to satisfy one manager's curiosity. A holistic strategy should be in place, and IT resources should be managed to achieve that goal no differently than how firms manage other resources.

Conclusion

As described in Chapter 10, the information network must not only reorganize the physical one but must then measure the success of the new processes. The metrics will point to issues that must be addressed. As the firm makes the necessary adjustments, its IT and business process experts should alter performance that, in turn, should be reflected in the metrics. The firm can use these metrics to determine where best to direct its IT resources.

Understanding the relationship between the metrics and the improvements they can help us identify is an important human/IT interface issue. As noted throughout this chapter, improvement efforts require the right tools and IT will be called upon to provide those tools. At best, this can lead to an overwhelming number of requests to IT. At worst, it will lead to projects that should not have been undertaken and only waste IT resources that could have been engaged in real improvement efforts.

Distribution Retrospective

Bill asked Phil to review the priority list and recommend an alternative approach to the listing of projects and voting on which ones should be carried out first. Phil separated the list into the departments that had requested them. He then tried to align the requests according to his understanding of which processes were related across departments and would likely interact. He called separate meetings of groups of departments affected by related project requests and attempted to identify potential domain experts who understood the nature of the requests.

Phil was able to identify a few domain specialists in the firm and to get a relatively good handle on some interconnected job requests. Out of the 30-some-odd projects, he was able to cluster about 18 into related groups totaling three. He was then able to rank these three megaprojects by examining the original rankings. Two emerged as clear favorites with eight of the top ten requests related to one or the other or both. He decided to recommend these sets of projects be worked on this year.

He had a further problem. The total related projects numbered 13, an amount beyond the IT group's capability to complete. He called the domain experts together for a meeting with the IT department to see whether there was anything he was overlooking. He hoped that some of the projects might not be necessary, in spite of what he thought.

The meeting proved valuable. He found out that all of the projects were necessary by asking many questions and forcing the domain experts to reconcile their understanding of their business processes with IT's understanding of system capabilities. He also found out that a few other things would be necessary. He was becoming concerned about resources when the conversation took another turn. As the IT specialists began to explain how difficult a couple of activities would be, the domain experts starting asking why things had to be performed in the fashion *described. It became clear that, left to their own devices, the IT folks were going to take a far more complicated approach than necessary. Once each side came to understand the other, they began to take up the common cause of simplifying the projects.*

When the meeting had ended, Phil felt he understood several things he had not anticipated. First, he found that IT specialists often made the projects more difficult through their lack of understanding of true business needs. Second, he could see that, in spite of their obvious value, the domain experts needed more training to be effective. Many times the IT specialists would start asking questions and the domain experts would shut down and shrug. Phil did his best to keep things going but he felt some critical factors were not being considered due to domain experts' lack of understanding of the IT system's basic lingo. Finally, Phil felt there were many gaps among the different domain experts where no one understood the system or the business process.

Phil put his list together for Bill. Next he recommended that Bill institute a well-planned training program for existing domain experts to better complete their understanding of the system's basic functionality. After that, he felt the firm needed to start creating domain expertise in many employees, making sure that all functional areas were covered and supported both by IT and domain expertise. Phil justified his suggestions with the evidence of reduced IT workload caused by the interaction among the IT and domain specialists in his meetings. Bill accepted Phil's recommendations over some minor IT department objections, the new list was accepted, and Phil was asked to document the procedure he used to prepare the list. Bill then asked the ERP provider to deliver some classes that could assist in growing domain expertise. Managers nominated employees for the training and candidates were chosen based on the need for expertise in their area. Bill felt they were on the right track.

Issues to Consider

1. What problems arise from allowing the IT department to determine how business processes should work in the system?

2. What problems arise from top management prioritizing IT projects?

3. How do systems assist the sales force in the information-enabled model?

4. How do systems assist operations in the information-enabled model?

References

1. William J. Latzko and David M. Saunders, *Four Days With Dr. Deming: A Strategy for Modern Methods of Management* (Engineering Process Improvement Series) (Upper Saddle River, NJ: Prentice Hall, 1995).

2. Carol A. Ptak and Eli Schragenheim, *ERP: Tools, Techniques, and Applications for Integrating the Supply Chain* (Boca Raton, FL: Saint Lucie Press, 1999).

3. *ERP benefits are many, far and wide,'* Enterprise Resource Planning Newsletter, Information Technology Department, State of Iowa, http://www.infoweb.state.ia.us/newsletter/erp/erp_apr.pdf.

4. Grant Norris, James R. Hurley, Kenneth M. Hartley, John R. Dunleavy, and John D. Balls, *E-Business and ERP: Transforming the Enterprise* (Hoboken, NJ: John Wiley & Sons, 2000).

Putting the Tools to Work

Standardization and Putting the System to Work

Distribution Perspective

Samson Lawn and Garden Supply (SLGS) specialized in supplying small motors and their parts to lawn and garden retailers. These retailers had a variety of needs from motors for lawn mowers to spare parts and assorted items like sprinkler equipment, hoses, and such. The business cut across very different types of manufacturers. Small motor manufacturers might deal with anything from digging equipment to recreational vehicles whereas manufacturers of garden ornaments served retailers and distributors focused on professional gardeners and landscaping firms. The result was a set of suppliers for SLGS that had grown up within different customer market segments.

Customers tended to drive product identification in these industries. In the motor industry, for example, the customer expected the supplier to use a numbering system that identified the product in terms of its model (when it was produced and to what specifications) so that spare parts could be easily tracked for the item. In the garden ornaments business, the product had to meet the retailer's numbering system so that the retailer did not have to redo the bar code when the item was received. Smaller retailers did not use bar coding but the large ones did and were very insistent on a consistency between the distributor and themselves. They were not insistent on consistency between themselves and their competitors, however.

Ben Gonzales was in charge of the ERP system for SLGS. The company had been trying to unify its processes and centralize invoicing and fulfillment. Ben had been challenged by the wide variety of bar coding numbering systems suppliers used and the variability in customer requirements for bar codes when product was shipped. The company had grown through acquisition and many different branches used different numbering systems to meet different customer demands. Until he could come up with a solution, centralized invoicing and purchasing was going to be extremely difficult.

Introduction

The field of standardization has undergone great change in recent years. Standardization, in a general sense, is the process of making activities that accomplish the same essential task do so in the same fashion. There are many examples of standardization and the failure to standardize all around us. Two basic examples are language and currency.

Business is difficult to carry out without a common language and currency. Major trading blocs are formed specifically to deal with the standardization issue. The United States was a successful trading bloc that eventually adopted a standard language (English as opposed to Spanish and French spoken early on in many territories) and a standard currency. In recent years, the European Union (EU) has established a common currency. These standardization efforts typically reap tremendous rewards for the organizations that implement them—but those entities may run into considerable difficulties in establishing the standard.

Take language for example. The European Union has been successful in adopting a single currency but has not attempted a single language. While many non-English-speaking nations have accepted English as the language of business, many contracts and agreements between individuals and firms are made in their native language. This requires all documentation that connects to or affects nonnatives be translated into the other party's native language as well. The result is a great deal of redundant efforts in translation.

For ERP, standardization is critical to success. Firms need to capture ERP value quickly in today's climate. Many firms now require a two-year minimum payback on IT investments. This means that IT projects no longer have the luxury of time to figure out all the environmental issues before achieving gains. The standardization issue is a "brick wall" for ERP implementation since the inability for programs to exchange information will derail any attempt at successful system integration.

Standardization Issues

The reasons for continued resistance to the complete standardization of language are cultural. People and nations connect their language to their most cherished beliefs and principles. They also become attached to the language due to ease of use—they learned it as children. These two issues can be observed in companies when it comes to their communication standards for dealing with other firms. The currency issue is similar to those processes that do not affect cherished relationships and are, therefore, frequently easy to transition to IT systems. The language, on the other hand, is the communication between supply chain partners that has often been built upon relationships that took years to establish. For this reason, standardizing relationships between firms has proven much more difficult than within the firm. The connections to the customer and supplier, however, are part of our internal processes, and those internal processes often cannot be brought onto the ERP system if changes are not made in relationships (as we see in the Distribution Perspective on pages 256–257).

Corporations establish cultural beliefs in the same fashion as nations or other organized groups. Companies establish relationships with their customers that lead to success among firms and establish a pattern of behavior: who does what and how. The interchange becomes a standard for those supply chain partners. Before information automation made standardization an imperative, the firm would have differing modes of operation with individual customers or with groups of customers. As the different modes became more numerous, the firm would attempt to standardize some of the less significant activities with their customers to achieve efficiency in their operations. The standardized processes often only provided a small efficiency in human effort and were not treated with the same urgency needed for information automation.

The customer relationship was not the only variable, however. Relationships among departments and individuals within the firm would also arise. These differences were handled offline and might go unnoticed in the day-to-day activities of the firm. The patterns established with customers, suppliers, departments, and individuals all comprised the communication—language and its exchange between parties—of the firm. Some firms, for example, rely on their outside sales force for large or special orders, inside sales for replenishment decisions, operations for service or repair, and so on. Each of these functions has its own combination of human and IT service support. The variation between departments and firms can be quite complex.

Information Systems and Standardization Challenges

When information technology first appeared on the scene, it was disjointed and did not challenge our most cherished communication channels. Spreadsheet packages required we all keep financial figures in a somewhat consistent format but did not connect our communications with our peers to any great degree. Information technology tended to focus on individual tasks that occurred within a single department

fig. 12.1   *Disconnected Departments*

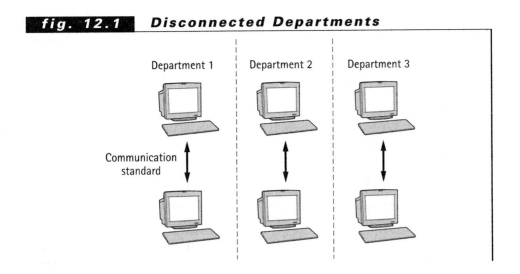

and did not require major change in the broader communication among individuals across the firm (see Figure 12.1).

In time, however, the systems grew in their functionality and many corporations began to understand and appreciate the cost and difficulty of having to take the data from one place, then reformat it for another program, run the analysis program, then reformat the outcome to the former program's format, and finally return it to its source (database) where it could be accessed in the future for further processing. The process would be repeated so many times it quickly became obvious that a standard process would add tremendous value to the firm through decreased human effort and a reduction in the errors associated with handling data again and again.

The obvious solution was to connect the systems and use a common format so that data could be exchanged, analyzed, and stored for future use without all the handoffs. Software firms began offering suites of programs that interacted with one another and firms began building systems that could communicate. These software suites and what would become corporate legacy systems served as a beginning to establishing a common communication standard within firms that had actually begun long ago with standards for data and programming languages.

Interconnecting the Functional Departments of the Firm

These early-connected packages still remained largely contained within the individual functional areas of the firm, however. Crossing functional boundaries was already proving difficult for noninformation-specific efforts like total quality management (TQM). TQM was seeking to break down the walls between the functional silos.[1] In the 1980s, however, the silos were proving extremely hard to overcome. ISO 9000, a program launched by a European standards-setting organization, and others like it were making efforts to standardize processes, but the process moved slowly in the United States and other non-European markets.[2] The success of these programs would eventually hold great importance to the information technology community of users and providers. ERP providers and their consulting partners came to rely on the documentation generated by such programs to implement systems in a consistent fashion.

Eventually these efforts at standardization began to take root as did parallel efforts in the IT arena. The large technology providers had a vested interest in standardization since they would like to take any software they created and apply it in many different environments. To do so, they needed standards for data exchange between firms and within firms and processes that would support the standards and allow for interconnection of departments (see Figure 12.2) and even supply chain partners. The IT providers worked closely with standards-setting organizations and encouraged new ones to develop through distributor and manufacturer associations.

Many firms and channels, however, had already spent many years developing processes and basic languages into both legacy IT systems and nonautomated processes that were becoming key components of their corporate and supply chain cultures. The interconnectivity issue concerned a great deal more than just the connection between systems, something the IT firms easily understood. The bottom line was a cultural issue. The firm would have to speak a single language and follow a standard protocol for when, how, and in what order its communication would take place. Companies and individuals from all functional areas—sales, operations, transportation, human resources, finance, and so on—would be affected.

Creating Standards

Numerous organizations have since taken on the difficulties created by nonstandard processes and data to varying degrees of success. The group with the most to gain or lose in the short term was the IT firms. IT providers routinely seek to eliminate nonstandard processes and data to allow for better system performance and increased

fig. 12.2   ***Connecting the Firm***

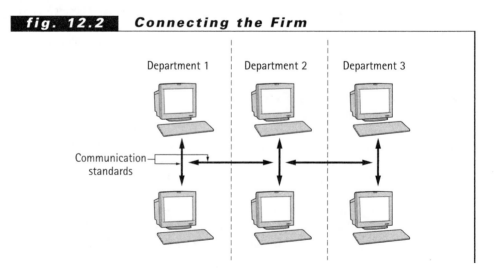

communication capabilities. The IT firms saw the potential to connect systems as a major opportunity to offer new products and services to a larger group of customers. In Chapter 1, we discussed how IT providers first connected a series of activities inside the firm with programs like material requirements planning (MRP), which evolved into cross-departmental efforts like manufacturing resources planning (MRP II) and ultimately to ambitious programs to connect the entire firm like ERP.

For these programs to live up to their promise, however, it would be necessary for the firm to seek higher performance through information automation. Better system performance, as we saw in Chapter 3 and throughout this book, is highly reliant upon the elimination of offline activity. Offline activity, however, is often driven by a belief that closely held principles (cultural standards) will be violated if the traditional method is abandoned in favor of the new automated system. Customer service or some other undisputed value is held up as the reason for not using the system. These departures from the system lead to data integrity problems and various other ills explored throughout this text.

To eliminate offline activity, all processes must be on the system. To put all processes on the system, however, processes must be consistent with system capabilities to the greatest extent possible. The clash between efficiency and cultural beliefs is similar to most countries' determination to hold onto their native language in the face of high costs of doing business. While nations may be able to afford resisting efficiency, few firms can afford to be caught with disconnected, inefficient processes.

Unlike the differences in languages, communication issues also stem from the lack of interconnectivity within the firm and its supply chain. The firm requires not only a common language to speak but also a consistent medium through which to communicate or share data. The system may have the hardware and software for analysis but it must also have specific times and a channel through which to carry out that communication. The issue is similar to using a telephone. The hardware is present (the phone) and communication is possible but if we do not have the correct phone number or know when the other party will be home or what language will be used on the phone call, no communication can take place. Systems have to be connected and protocols established as to when and what information is to be exchanged and in what format.

One large electrical distributor had a customer who wanted to order online. The customer insisted the distributor make its system capable of receiving automatic purchase orders through EDI. The distributor went to considerable trouble to establish an EDI connection that could read incoming orders for the customer. Two years later, the customer still did not have the EDI capability to transmit the orders.

While the problems associated with connecting supply chain partners have received a great deal of press, most firms struggle with connecting information technology within their own firms. Acquisitions, for instance, often lead to disparate systems. The acquired firm may be on a different system from the acquirer or have different formats or numbering systems for data or all of the above. The acquiring firm will be faced with standardizing all information between the acquisition's system and the existing system. The task can become more complex when the acquired firm can demonstrate that important customers will be adversely affected by changes in the formatting or alphanumeric systems.

One large HVAC (heating, ventilation, and air-conditioning) distributor built most of its market reach through acquisition. The firm would not allow its acquisitions to remain offline since managing new operations was difficult enough without losing visibility. Acquired firms were converted within months often at great expense—and equally great employee and customer discontent—when some capabilities were not able to transition to the new system.

Modifications and Other Special Issues

Modifications to the system also contribute to standardization problems. A mod will generate new data that may or may not be usable by other programs within the system. If the firm comes to depend on the output of the mod, it may not have proper data to carry out other tasks or will find it difficult to transition from one system to another. For example, suppose a firm sets up a mod that calculates weeks of supply as its key inventory measure but the ERP system relies on ABC classification schemes and uses those to determine inventory levels. The firm may have to make inventory determinations based on planner opinions of how many weeks' supply are appropriate rather than from a system estimate based on the automatically determined classification. The offline activity reduces the level of connectivity, thereby increasing the data integrity problems within the firm.

Specialized numbering systems present another problem. Special orders or work orders are often assigned temporary stock numbers. When the inventory hangs around too long, the numbers may get used again on different items leading to multiple types of items being listed under the same stock number. Confusion as to what exactly is in stock and what is not often then leads to obsolescence problems when items sit unnoticed for too long. One firm had a group of SKUs reserved for use on special orders. Since the number of potential products possible with special orders was numerous, branches gave up trying to keep such SKUs unique and just kept using the same ones over and over. The system could not identify which of these special products were saleable or even show the sales force the actual products. As a result, specials generated a great deal of obsolete inventory since they went into stock and might never been seen again.

When attempting to communicate with supply chain business partners, these problems are magnified. When one supply chain member cannot communicate with a standardized numbering system or format, the next member of the supply chain must set up special conditions like specialized stock numbers or other processes that specifically deal with that supplier/customer. The result is a plethora of numbering or formatting processes at the data-receiving firm that have to be translated to deal with the inconsistency of its supply chain partner. The problems associated with this data cleansing go beyond the scope of this text (see textbooks on management information systems,[3] XML[4] (Extensible Markup Language), or your system's documentation for specifics on data standards and conversion) but these problems are more about relationship failures than technology. If the relationship is set up to eliminate data integrity and standardization issues before they start, the information automation process is much easier.

Channel power often becomes a deciding issue. A more powerful supplier or customer will be able to force its customers or suppliers to either adhere to its data communication standard or bear the expense of building a translator. Many firms find it necessary to bar code products as they come in to be consistent with their numbering and formatting system and then redo the bar code as the product goes out to be consistent with their customers' needs. The redundancy is expensive and is repeated throughout the supply chain. The most powerful customer or supplier may benefit in the short term but the entire supply chain is made less successful in the long run.

The communication issues are driven more by data and formatting issues at individual firms than differences between disparate systems. Most systems adhere to data exchange standards but are thwarted by forms, reports, and other data extraction techniques that place data in different places, and by data fields that vary in length or mix alphanumeric patterns in varying configurations.

Standards Organizations

The significance of the problem has captured the attention of IT providers and the business community. While the IT firms seek faster and simpler data exchange methods and translators, industry organizations have gotten involved to varying degrees of success in the standardization process. Some have attacked the formatting and process of information exchange. Organizations like Rossetta.net have addressed the variations between processes for exchanging data. They have developed standard forms and processes for the exchange of data between entities.[5] Others have worked on the data formatting (length of fields, alphanumeric codes). Data standardization has been used in many industries for a long time and includes the universal product code (UPC), among many other efforts.

Other organizations have tackled the data standardization issue for each channel by establishing a standard format for the data specific to that industry. Organizations like the Industry Data Warehouse (IDW) in the electrical channel have compiled a standard numbering system for products within an industry. Different manufacturers are encouraged to put their products into this standard form. Sometimes referred to as a "dictionary" that demonstrates how to "spell" the description of different parts, the IDW can give the distributor and retailer a common numbering system on which to base their information handling.

While organizations like Rossetta.net and the IDW have enjoyed considerable support in some industries, others have been less willing to cooperate. Powerful customers frequently do not wish to change their processes for the convenience of their suppliers. They would prefer the world adjust to their way of doing things since that spares them expense and forces the competition to adopt their way of doing business. By the time competitors have adopted the dominant customer's processes, the dominant player has moved on, leaving the competition in a constant chase mode. This strategy has been employed many times before with varying levels of success. IBM held off the competition for some time by refusing to standardize its first personal computers. The IBM PC operating system became the standard when other competitors like Dell and Compaq mimicked IBM rather than Apple Computer. Standards are inevitable and in times of rapid technological change, it can be difficult to make a choice as to which will become the industry standard. A popular business saying at the end of the twentieth century was, "The great thing about standards is that there are so many to choose from."

Commoditization and Standardization

Customers are not the only obstacles to standardization. Suppliers often resist standardization as well. Many suppliers will resist standardization to prevent their customers from doing business with a rival. One major manufacturer consistently comes up with value-add programs that tie together its customers' systems with its own. It offers its distributors faster deliveries, leads on customers, guaranteed territories (franchises), special rebates, and so on. In return, its distributors are required to share market intelligence with it that would be difficult to exchange without system-to-system connectivity. That connectivity is, of course, capitalized upon for the distributor to take advantage of the supplier's other value-adds. The result is a relationship that is wired for real time and eases the process for the distributor. Since the system is based on this largest supplier for the distributor, establishing a similar relationship would require a prohibitively expensive process on the part of other suppliers unless those suppliers adopted the incumbent's technology, only some of which is transparent. In other words, the supplier has enticed the distributor into using the former's standard of communication.

Manufacturers are often resistant to standardization because they fear commoditization of their products. "Commoditization" is the tendency over time for all products to become commodities. Manufacturers attempt to combat this process with more highly engineered products, but the speed of technology advancement has shortened life cycles so much that the time window for profitability is very brief, and any action that can slow the process must be accessed to maintain margins above commodity levels.

Maintaining one-to-one relationships with distributors is key to fighting the commoditization problem since the distributor can wrap the supplier's products in services that are more flexible (changeable) in the short term and may more tightly tie the customer to the manufacturer's products. A high service level can hold off price wars (a common affliction for commodities) indefinitely. These exclusive relationships tend to lock the distributor and its services to the supplier. Manufacturers, like the one mentioned above, will cloak their products in distribution services and then lock the distributor in with exclusive information exchange methods to protect their products (see Figure 12.3).

The distributor gives up ability to negotiate prices (price flexibility) with the supplier when an exclusive relationship is in place. The distributor will also need to carry more of the supplier's products on a per-unit basis since switching to competitor's products will be limited under the relationship. The value of using standards in communication is that the distributor is better able to source from multiple suppliers. Therefore, distributors often favor standards but will face powerful suppliers who will oppose them in order to maintain their control over their distribution channels and partners.

Many distributors, especially the larger ones, will use the commoditization problem to squeeze their suppliers and ease their inventory problems. If a manufacturer's

| fig. 12.3 | *Standardization and Commoditization* |

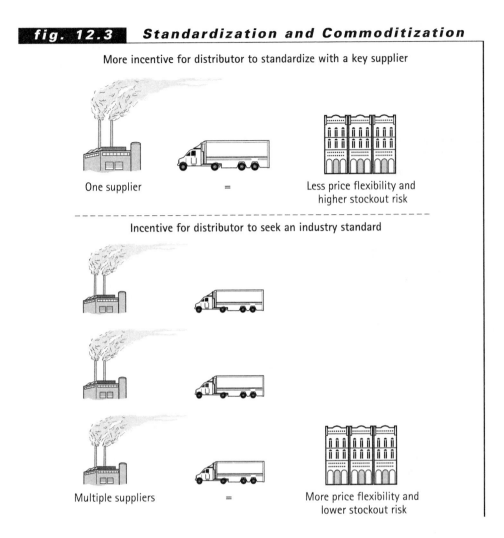

More incentive for distributor to standardize with a key supplier

One supplier = Less price flexibility and higher stockout risk

Incentive for distributor to seek an industry standard

Multiple suppliers = More price flexibility and lower stockout risk

product is perceived as a commodity, other products will be perceived as interchangeable with it. The distributor reaps two benefits from this situation. First, if a customer calls and the distributor is out of one manufacturer's supply of the commodity, the distributor can switch to another manufacturer and reduce the risk of losing the sale. In the event all items from all manufacturers are gone, the distributor can call all the suppliers and see who will direct-ship the product at the lowest cost. The second benefit comes in negotiating prices from the supplier: A commodity by definition has multiple reliable suppliers who can be pitted against one another to achieve price reductions. These benefits cause some distributors to encourage the commoditization process to the dismay and even anger of their suppliers. The lack of cooperation among the supply chain members makes each less likely to cooperate with any attempt to work together on standards.

Many manufacturers, therefore, believe that any attempt to make any portion of their offering standard will only increase the risk of commoditization. They will actually seek the opposite and prefer to have exclusive communication channels. The drive toward exclusivity may be only a short-term problem for IT firms, as we shall see, and may actually prove to be a long-run opportunity for supply chain partners and especially for the IT providers.

Data Standardization

From an information technology perspective, this may be the easiest problem to solve but its prevalence virtually guarantees the problem will be with us for a long time. Data can vary in terms of its length, alphanumeric configuration, and formatting. The length of a data field refers to the number of digits in the field. This problem is and has always been very common, but many system solutions have been developed for dealing with it. In older systems, however, the problem still remains.

The alphanumeric configuration refers to the use of letters and numbers together as well as case (capitalization) and the like. These various configurations can lead to an infinite number of possible combinations. Infinite combinations make translators very expensive to build since every possible combination has to be considered by a standard program or special programs have to be built for every environment.

Data can also vary in terms of its positioning in a document or placement in a database. The process of reformatting data for exchanges between systems is the key to interconnectivity of various information system components. ERP systems are interconnected through integration of all programs in the system. Integrating other software into the ERP system requires integration that is either programmed directly or through the use of enterprise application integration (EAI) software (see Figure 12.4). This software builds a link between other systems like bolt-ons or other channel partners' ERP systems.

fig. 12.4   *Translation Programs (EAI)*

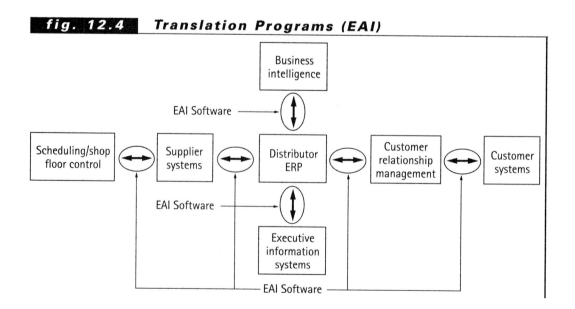

The arrows in the drawing indicate the two-way exchange of information between the systems enabled by the software. Without this exchange, the attached programs cannot access data and cannot return their analysis to the ERP system. While many bolt-on packages will allow the ERP system to drop information into simple database or spreadsheet programs that can be read into their system for analysis, the analysis can be read only on the bolt-on. This may be acceptable for report generation that management may access for decision making but will not be sufficient if the system is to use the analysis for further activities. Take forecasting, for example: If historical data is taken from the ERP system into a spreadsheet for analysis with a bolt-on forecasting program, the forecast may be the end of the process with no need to take data back into the ERP system.

On the other hand, if the forecasting process includes error metrics that might be used by the ERP system to determine safety stock needs, then the bolt-on would need to be able to issue the error metrics back to the ERP system. The error metrics could be downloaded into a database or spreadsheet that could be uploaded to the ERP system, but the process would be largely manual. Even if the manual exchange were not a problem, the firm would have to match both the formatting of the data from the ERP system to the bolt-on's needs and the format of the bolt-on's output to the ERP system's needs for reentry into the inventory program.

Multiple software providers are now developing and offering EAI programs. Others are developing specialized applications that exactly fit the environments of the host firm. These application providers are building a set of tools that will continue to improve the connectivity within the firm and ultimately will assist in connecting members of the supply chain. Standardization also involves the processes that generate the data. How these processes interact with the ERP system will be the most complex issue for many firms.

Process Standardization

Long after the data standardization problems have been solved with dictionaries and translators, the process standardization movement will continue. In Chapter 3, we examined process mapping and demonstrated its use in process standardization. As we discussed, the process mapping exercise is an opportunity for the firm to aggressively take noncore processes into the ERP system. We defined noncore processes as those the customer does not see or care about and can therefore be changed without harming the firm's competitive posture. The problems discussed above suggest, however, that even noncore processes may have cultural issues associated with them. Firms that reduce variability of processes within and outside of the ERP system are well on their way to successful information management.

As difficult as the internal issues may sound, the problem becomes even more significant when we introduce the customer and supplier into our standardization efforts. These external facing processes are very resistant to standardization due to competitive issues. Suppliers, as we discussed, fear standardization as part of the broader commoditization movement, and customers may not wish to change their patterns of behavior. While most firms continue with internal standardization, the supply chain movement has slowed considerably on the standardization effort.

Organizations like Rosetta.net have had some impact, but progress has been slow and new organizations that support like efforts in other channels (Rosetta.net was born out of the electronics channel) have either failed or found progress even more difficult.

Ultimately cultural issues will bring about a limit on how much standardization will take place, how much suppliers and customers will push back from further efforts for competitive reasons, and how much the movement will continue to slow until the next major impetus increases the need to go forward. The previous need was established during the hysteria surrounding the dot.coms, but once that craze faded, many firms fell back into their former patterns. The recession following the 2001 market crash also caused many firms to tighten up all efforts on advancing technology, and new investment in processes and equipment slowed considerably.

Process standardization is not dead, however, and will continue wherever the need can be proven or the threat of not changing can be demonstrated beyond any doubt. That was the case throughout the early stages of the information technology movement and will continue. It is possible we will see another ramp-up like the one associated with the dot.coms, however. The expectations associated with supply chain management (SCM) will continue to rise and will put increasing pressure on information handling. A breakthrough technology (increased bandwidth, for instance) could cause another race to be the first with a fully connected supply chain. The benefits of an integrated information supply chain have been demonstrated many times[6] and are still pursued aggressively by many influential supply chain leaders.

So standardization will likely continue at some rate. Does this mean that eventually all standardization problems will be solved? Actually they will never be fully solved, and that will be good news for information technology providers, distributors, and manufacturers. Distributors introduce new processes continuously to respond to customer and supplier needs. Since the early 1980s, the distribution community has introduced just-in-time support processes,[7] total quality management programs for distribution,[8] distributor managed inventory,[9] auto-replenishment, and integrated supply.[10] Each new program was more complex than its predecessor and most have still not been fully integrated into ERP, bolt-ons, or any other type of information automation. Increasing customer expectations and distributor creativity will continue to bring about ever more challenging environments for information management tools.

In the near term, the process diversity issue will be troubling to IT providers and their customers. IT providers will continue to have difficulty providing systems flexible enough to handle the multitude of services distributors create. Systems will lack functionality and distributors will continue to operate offline with all of the associated problems. The need to connect systems will continue to be problematic in the short term due to bandwidth problems. In other words, our current situation will be with us for some time.

In the long term, however, the process diversity issue will give IT providers and their customers niche markets and competitive advantage. Manufacturers are correct to believe that complete standardization of any kind removes competitive advantage. If distributors are to remain competitive, they must be able to offer services no one else does and not be constrained by their IT system. IT providers currently focus on creating functionality and then rolling it out to many customers.

In the long term, they will have the most common functionality fully enabled and will follow the business community closely to find new services they can adopt. IT providers will become more diverse and develop strong niche markets that protect their profitability and as well as that of their customers.

Standardization Rollout

The need for diversity to maintain competitive advantage does not, however, mean that firms should not strive to make as many processes standard as possible. Information automation makes standardization imperative and if a competitor automates a process first, the nonautomated firm will be placed at a disadvantage. To be successful, the firm must create new competitive advantage even as it standardizes much of what it depended on in the past.

Standardization requires a consistent process that first identifies variances among processes within and external to the IT system. Process mapping is the first step followed by comparison to best practices (BP). Next the process map should be compared to the capability of the ERP system. The processes within the ERP system are preferable, but improvements may be possible through first reorganizing the process according to BP and then examining how the improved process compares to the ERP process.[11] The information automation process then must develop alternative methods to bring the two processes (the nonstandard and the system process) as close to each other as possible.

The next step will be to develop a trust in the selected process that replaces one or both of the existent processes (ERP and the legacy process). If the ERP process differs from the newly developed one and sufficient cause can be demonstrated for changing the system, a modification will have to be written. If sufficient cause cannot be proven, the system process should be adopted. Finally, the new process will have to be implemented. IT resources will have to be properly deployed (see Chapter 11). Business process owners will have to adhere to the new process (see Chapter 3). Measurement and control will have to track the new process (see Chapter 10). Improvements in the process will need to be implemented (Chapter 11). The cycle will repeat until the process stabilizes in a final form that supports the firm's mission (Chapter 2). The final process will need metrics that control its performance and people's conformance to the new standard (Chapter 10).

Conclusion

Standardization is essential to information technology since variable processes create variable results making any analysis suspect. The standardization process has been slowed in recent years by a number of factors, but a key issue that will likely continue into the future is the changing nature of competitive distribution markets. While this problem will be very difficult to solve in the short term, it will prove useful to channel members and their IT providers in the future as they seek new niches and opportunities to create and add value to the supply chain.

Distribution Retrospective

SLGS faced a common dilemma: customers with varying bar code requests and suppliers with varying bar coding capability. Ben investigated how other distributors in noncompeting channels dealt with the problem and found that the most successful ones used a bar code that optimized their operations and set up a translator to match the supplier's bar code information with their own. When a shipment was received, the supplier's product was entered into the system and a new bar code was printed for SLGS inventory purposes.

The product was then tracked by the distributor's system until the customer's order was shipped. When the pick ticket dropped, the system would print the customer's bar code label for the warehouse to apply before shipping. Ben could see that the system would work but was not satisfied with all the redundant efforts associated with applying a bar code label and then relabeling. He did an analysis of who used which bar code standard and found that 30 percent of SLGS customers and 40 percent of their suppliers adhered to a UPC (Universal Product Code) standard for the industry. Another 20 percent of customers did not care and 10 percent of suppliers did not bar code at all. In all, he could see that using the UPC standards for each product line would lead to relabeling affecting only about 50 percent of their products either on receipt or at shipping.

Ben decided that SLGS would adopt the UPC standard so that a large percentage of its merchandise would not have to be relabeled upon receipt and shipping. He then asked the sales force to work closely with their customers to suggest they adopt the UPC standard. He also asked purchasing to do the same with suppliers or to switch, where possible, to ones who were using the standard in order to reduce the handling costs for SLGS. Finally he asked the owner, who worked closely with industry associations, to join standardization committees with various associations and push for adoption of the UPC standard for the entire industry.

Issues to Consider

1. Explain how commoditization affects standardization.

2. What impact did ISO 9000 and other international programs have on standards?

3. What major approaches have standards organizations undertaken?

References

1. Marshall Sashkin and Kenneth J. Kiser, *Putting Total Quality Management to Work: What TQM Means, How to Use It and How to Sustain It Over the Long Run* (New York: Prima Publishing, 1993).

2. Stanley A. Marash, Paul Berman, and Michael Flynn, *Fusion Management: Harnessing the Power of Six Sigma, Lean, ISO 9001:2000, Malcolm Baldrige, TQM and Other Quality Breakthroughs of the Past Century* (Fairfax, VA: QSU Publishing Company, 2003).

3. Efraim Turban, Ephraim McLean, and James Wetherbe, *Information Technology for Management: Transforming Business in the Digital Economy,* 3rd ed. (Hoboken, NJ: John Wiley & Sons, 2001).

4. Elliotte Rusty Harold and W. Scott Means, *XML in a Nutshell,* 2nd ed. (O'Reilly & Associates, 2002).

5. Rosetta.net Standards, http://www.rosettanet.org/standards.

6. Robert B. Handfield; Ernest Nichols, Jr.; and Ernest L. Nichols, "Supply Chain Redesign: Transforming Supply Chains into Integrated Value Systems," *Financial Times Management* 1 (August 2002).

7. André J. Martin, *DRP: Distribution Resource Planning: The Gateway to True Quick Response and Continuous Replenishment* (John Wiley & Sons, 1995).

8. Ibid.

9. F. Barry Lawrence, Daniel F. Jennings, and Brian. E Reynolds, *e-Distribution* (Mason, OH: South-Western Publishing, 2003).

10. Ibid.

11. "Matching Distribution Processes to ERP Functionality: A Study by Information Systems Consortium for Supply Chain Integration (Texas A&M University, 2002–2003).

Customer Relationship Management Modules

Distribution Perspective

Quigley Distribution specialized in Pipe/Valve/Fitting (PVF), a highly technical field of Maintenance Repair and Operations (MRO) distribution. Victor Beatty was the VP of sales and had recently come up against many complex customer requests. One of the most significant customers was among the world's largest chemical companies with worldwide operations. Quigley, on the other hand, was only a regional distributor covering Louisiana and the Texas Gulf Coast regions. The Houston and Coastal Louisiana markets, however, had many large petrochemical complexes due to the enormous amount of oil drilling and refining facilities in the area. The chemical firm had two plants in the area and was in the process of building a third.

Victor was having problems with this customer, however. The customer was always building new production lines and needed pipes, fittings, and, most expensively, the valves delivered from Quigley. The problem Victor faced was that quotes on new products were frequently inaccurate because salespeople would forget to add items to the quote—resulting in financial losses—or his sales force or the customer specified the wrong parts. In this environment, a product failure could result in a loss of life, and valves could be very expensive so an inaccurate quote could cost the firm a great deal of money. Victor, therefore, had to invest many resources in double-checking quotes. In spite of his best efforts, however, many quotes managed to get through the process with inaccurate information still included. The result was higher costs to fix the misspecified materials or lost profitability when products and services were required but not included in the quote.

The quoting process was very work intensive. The sales force had to gather all relevant information from the customer and prepare the quote in spreadsheets. The salesperson would next have to access the ERP system for pricing and availability. Finally, any products that were not part of Quigley's inventory would require the salesperson to go to the manufacturer's catalogs, Internet site, and/or call directly to get information on the part and the Material Safety Data Sheet (MSDS) from the supplier. The complexity of the systems and the quoting task were giving the company fits.

A further problem stemmed from the lack of follow-up. The initial sale consisted of a quote and usually a sizable transaction as the production system was built. This was especially true of the facility currently under construction. The long-run opportunity, however, resided with the maintenance and replacement parts, the MRO business. The handoff of what had taken place during the sale between the outside sales force, who were principally engineers, and the inside sales force, who were principally sales specialists, was not smooth and a great deal of MRO business was lost when histories on how the facility was built were not thoroughly documented. Customers would not tolerate many mistakes before they would take MRO business elsewhere. Eventually, the loss would extend to the original construction business as well. Victor was having a hard time impressing his outside sales team on the importance of proper tracking and controlling of quotes and working closely with the inside sales force. He felt the answer lay in better information management but was unsure what the ERP system could and should support and how much Quigley should depend on external bolt-on CRM technology.

Introduction

Customer relationship management (CRM) modules are present in virtually all ERP systems, in some form or fashion, as well as in many specialized bolt-ons. CRM, as a discipline, is as old as business itself. Since the first Arabian distributors began trading on the Silk Road to China throughout history to when the British and Dutch trading companies sailed around the world collecting tea and spices up until the time of the modern distributor, understanding the customer has been job number one for distributors. The collection and control of customer information has always been a challenge for a number of reasons. One problem has been the lack of information collection technology, which has forced firms to depend on human databases (salespeople's memories and handwritten files). Another problem stems from the large number of customers, as distributors must handle hundreds or thousands more customers than a typical manufacturer.

Even if powerful-enough systems for customer information handling were built (as has been the mission of many IT firms since the invention of the computer), one final problem will always remain: The distributor's relationship with the customer will always be changing, constantly leading to new functionality needs. This last problem is in fact an opportunity, however, since it offers distributors and their information technology providers the opportunity to offer new IT functionality and distributor services, thereby avoiding having their service offerings become mere commodities. CRM is important because it addresses that area where change is most rapid and, therefore, most likely to offer competitive advantage to the agile distributor. CRM has suffered its setbacks, with some reporting CRM failure rates in excess of 50%.[1] The high failure rate is not just a new-software issue nor is it a condemnation of CRM systems. The complexity of customer relationships and their relative inflexibility (customers will participate with the distributor's CRM initiative only if they choose) is more to blame than the systems themselves. The problem is shared by technology—IT firms making CRM more flexible to distributor customer needs—and by the supply chain: distributors developing solid reasons for their supply chain partners to work together with them.

In previous chapters, we have focused on the basics of ERP. Now we focus on emerging tools that are rapidly being introduced into ERP systems. These tools were first developed by bolt-on providers, so in this chapter we will discuss CRM in the context of both bolt-on and an integrated part of ERP. The chapter begins with defining the CRM components, proceeds to ways CRM tools can be used to make the firm more successful, and closes with action options when the ERP system does not have the functionality needed to serve critical customer service needs.

CRM Components

CRM is still being defined from an IT perspective. While CRM is easy to understand in a business process sense—all processes that connect the customer to the distributor—many ERP and bolt-on systems have different approaches to CRM. The principal difference between ERP systems and bolt-ons is the degree of functionality offered. ERP systems started with a simplistic approach to CRM by offering a sales order processing (SOP) module that could be used by the sales force to record sales. In time, the SOP module became more capable of offering information about the distributor's operation like inventory status or production scheduling. In addition, the ERP systems typically offered sales order processing tools for the inside sales force but often still did not have much connectivity to the outside sales force, causing them to work offline.

The Roots of CRM: Order Processing

These SOP tools were designed and used for customer service purposes but did not really constitute a full customer relationship management capability (see Figure 13.1). This meant the ERP capability would only partially cover the needs of the

fig. 13.1 *Early ERP Applications Capture Only a Small Portion of CRM*

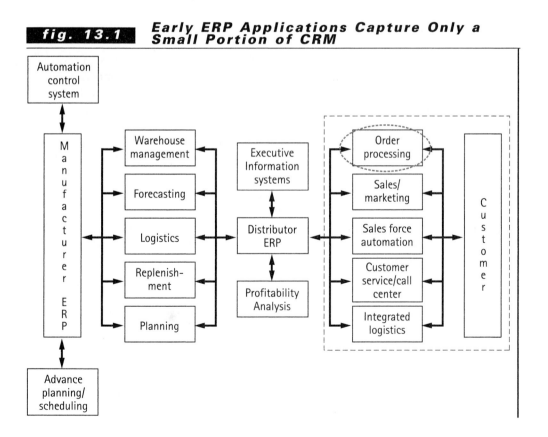

sales force and could not capitalize on more-complex analysis for marketing or outside sales purposes. Inside sales could see operations information but the outside sales force would not be able to directly access the system. During the 1990s, this approach was entirely appropriate since the lack of wireless capability would have made outside sales access to the system impractical anyway. As a result, the CRM systems grew up as standalone software present on the outside salesperson's laptop that could be downloaded to the ERP system.

The growth of wireless capability coincided with the capability of extensive modules like Siebel's CRM systems.[2] These large CRM systems could provide CRM capability to large firms that had high-speed connections to customers' and/or other remote facilities. During the 1990s software capability would become more widely available as wireless technology became both more pervasive and available at higher capacity levels. The Europeans were experimenting with high bandwidth technology in the early 2000s that held promise for the kind of high-speed wireless capacity that would enable CRM for remote salespeople and customer locations.[3] CRM could provide an understanding of the customer that could be used for capacity planning at the distributor's operation, opportunity generation for the sales force, connectivity for field sales, and the convenience of having a supplier that maintained up-to-date information for the customer. The amount of data that will support such applications requires high-capacity data transmission and the ability to access it at any convenient time or place.

Sales/Marketing Tools

The sales/marketing components of a CRM system consist of a variety of tools (see Figure 13.2). For capacity planning, CRM held great promise to improve forecasting due to its close connection to the customer. Forecasting is offered in ERP systems but collaborative models tend to be offered in CRM systems. As described in Chapter 8, collaborative forecasting is most valuable with large-volume customers that have stable forecasting processes and a willingness to share that information. The potential can be significant under the right conditions but the IT and supply chain processes to support them are still evolving.

Data mining is the process of finding relationships within customer data that can further focus the firm's marketing efforts. Amazon.com develops a profile on its customers that is then used to recommend other books the customer might be interested in when the customer logs on. Customers can also be directed to other complementary products to a transaction. One plumbing distributor's system recommends products that the customer will likely need for the job when parts are purchased (tools, attachments, etc.). The system can also recommend substitute products if the customer's first choice is out of stock or if a special is running on a product that can be used instead of the original selection.

Sales Force Automation

Contact management capability is more often associated with CRM than with ERP. Contact management is the process of tracking customer requests, sales force

fig. 13.2   *Sales/Marketing Tools*

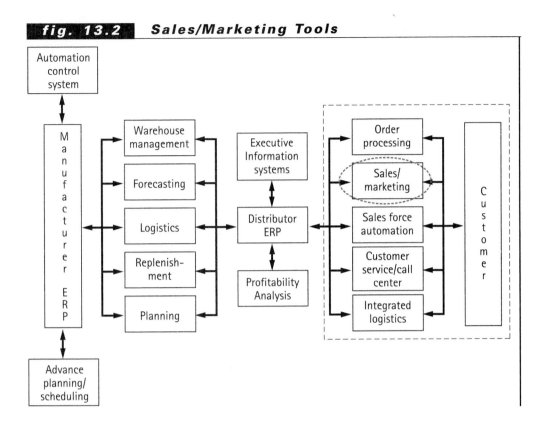

actions to support or otherwise interact with the customer, communication with other support personnel about customer requests, and so forth. Contact management offers the firm the opportunity to ensure proper follow-up and, with sufficient information, possibly predict future needs. Task management remains principally a CRM activity but has a long history in personal scheduling software. To be effective as a team tool (where the software manages all support personnel as well as the salesperson's efforts) task management software has to be connected through a network (the ERP system, for instance) to others in the firm the customer routinely relies on. Contact and task management are often referred to as sales force automation tools (see Figure 13.3).

Many firms embark on contact management in order to track customers and prevent lost information due to sales force omission or personnel changes. Salespeople frequently view contact management efforts as an attempt by the firm to track their activity and thereby measure their performance or get between them and their customers. As a result, many believe the principal problem driving CRM failure can be attributed to contact management being stressed before other CRM benefits. Contact management software has been around for a long time and is well understood but is most often found in a salesperson's private files (personal software) and not yet enabled on or connected to the ERP system, limiting the firm's ability to plan customer needs and internal collaboration to serve those needs.

fig. 13.3 **Sales Force Automation and CRM**

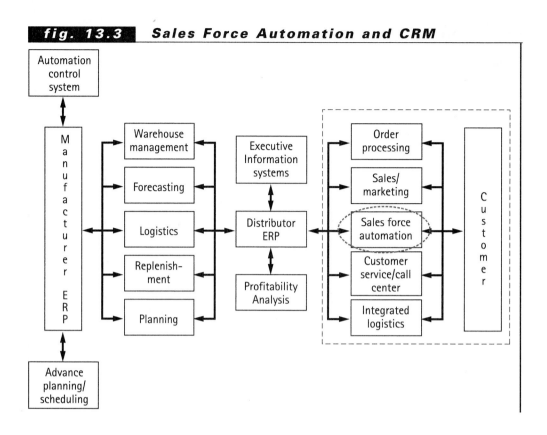

Quoting systems, another sales force automation tool, are also most often resident in CRM but typically require a great deal of connectivity with ERP. The quoting system will need pricing information, availability, supplier lead times, material specifications, and the like that are most likely contained within the ERP system or through supplier connectivity more likely established with distributor ERP. The complexity of quoting requires solid information planning. Quoting has not been as common on ERP systems for complex quotes but it has existed in the form of inquiries that inside sales carries out routinely in answering customer questions. Quoting has been associated with bolt-ons or other software more often because of its complexity than its natural relationship with other CRM tools. Still, complex quotes are often the responsibility of outside sales or other technical personnel who have to directly visit customer locations. Therefore, many CRM packages have developed or integrated quoting processes into their software applications.

Customer Service/Call Centers

During the 1990s, the burden on the inside sales force grew to such an extent that many firms opened up centralized call centers and/or customer support service centers. These centers handled calls that required less technical product expertise or constituted warranty claims or other customer complaints. Since the centers handled all calls for much larger geographic areas and had less need for product technical support, the software was more focused on fast retrieval of specific information and efficient call turnaround: Too short could mean poor customer service; too long could be a sign of inefficient information handling.

Integrated Logistics

These modules track customer orders through logistics providers' systems or, in the case of a private fleet, global positioning systems. They can also be used to interconnect with customer ERP systems allowing for real-time visibility of vendor managed inventories or other assets at the customer's location. Insufficient bandwidth has limited the number of applications in place to date, however.

The reader may be wondering why so many typically bolt-on offerings are included in a book on ERP. These last three chapters focus on key bolt-ons because CRM and other bolt-on capability are rapidly being absorbed by ERP either through direct development of the functionality or through integration of a bolt-on package. The significance of managing customer relationships makes CRM an almost irresistible offering to ERP providers. Indeed, many ERP companies have begun to refer to themselves as distribution information solution providers to avoid being pigeonholed into back-office (ERP) systems. It seems likely that this trend will continue and that CRM will continue to be one of the most sought-after areas in the development of these solution providers. Since virtually every ERP provider seems to be involved in providing CRM capabilities, it seems appropriate to address CRM as both a current and future offering of ERP systems—however one thinks of them.

SFA and Firm Productivity

Sales force automation (SFA) is an effective tool for solving the timeliness issue so critical to real-time operations. Real time requires connection of the customer to the supply chain, but most customers are either unwilling or unable to establish electronic connections. Even where electronic connections are possible, they may not work as planned. Many distributors receive EDI (Electronic Data Interchange) orders from customers but have to manually intercept and review those orders to prevent the customer from making errors that will cost both the distributor and the customer money. Customers do not place as many orders as distributors receive and, therefore, are more apt to make a mistake and less likely to catch it before the order is completed than an inside salesperson at the distributor's operation.

Contact Management

The inability of many vertical distribution channels to do away with sales force oversight of even the simplest of transactions has made SFA that much more critical. The salesperson must be able to pass timely, accurate information through the supply chain in real time. That means the software needs to be accessible and automated to the greatest extent possible to prevent errors. The principal responsibilities of a salesperson include understanding the customer, identifying and following up on

fig. 13.4 *Contact Management*

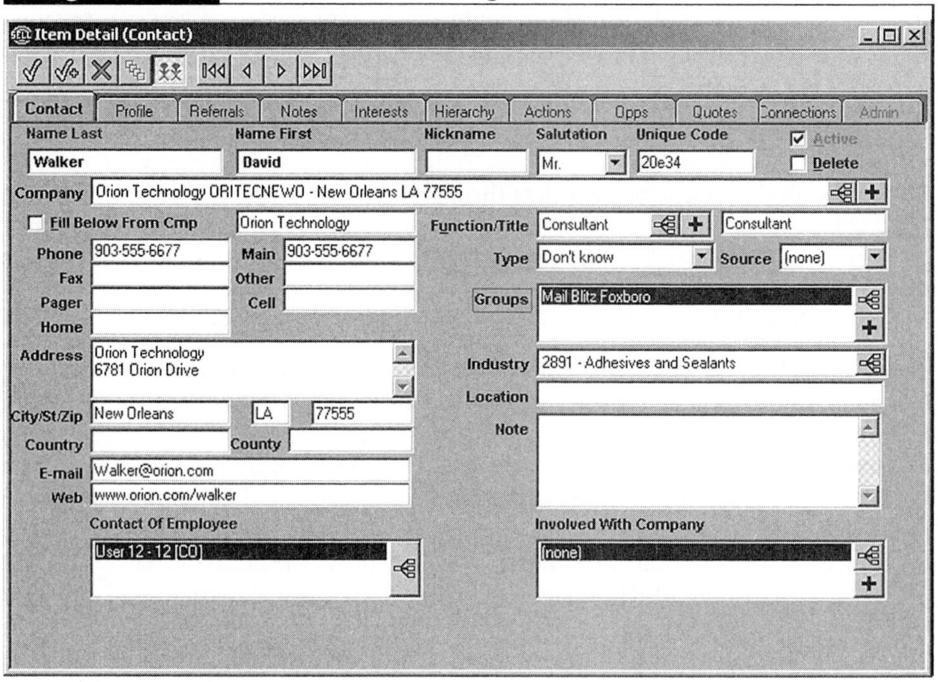

Source: Selltis L.L.C.

opportunities, and in many cases, completing the transaction. Transactions are carried out in the sales order processing module. Understanding the customer and managing opportunities falls under the contact and task management parts of the CRM system. Finally, closing the sale frequently requires a quoting process.

Contact management refers to the set of tools that manage the touch points between the customer and the sales force. Tracking these points allows for faster reaction to customer requests when the salesperson is not available and for the firm to retain a documentation trail on the customer if the salesperson leaves the firm. The tracking also serves as a reminder system for the salesperson or other responsible parties for service promises made or in process (see Figure 13.4).

Quotes

Quoting in many applications is a slow and complex process. Salespeople and engineers are often dependent on multiple data sources and customer information to provide a quote. Even when these sources are available, the sales engineer may not make the best use of company resources. Manufacturers of highly engineered products, for instance, often have problems with engineers specifying parts that are at "end of life" or are otherwise hard to procure through their supply chain. In other cases, the engineer may be unaware that a substitutable part is already available

fig. 13.5 *Quoting Systems*

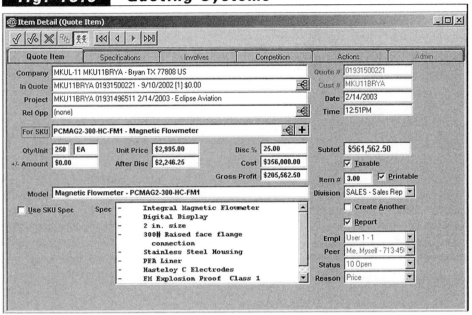

Source: Selltis L.L.C.

through existing inventory. If the part could be taken from existing inventory, the customer could save money not only through using a part that may already be on the shelf but also through reducing the number of parts they carry. Since every part number carries a safety stock, the fewer parts the customer carries, the better.

Some electronics distributors have offered CRM-type solutions by building web-sites that contain information on product status. The site will list whether a part is nearing end of life (an electronics term for a part on which suppliers will soon discontinue production) as well as how many suppliers are producing the part. Multiple suppliers may be an indication that the part is going to be easy to access, at lower cost, with shortened lead times. The process allows engineers or salespeople supporting those engineers to research parts before including them in finished goods they plan to manufacture (see Figure 13.5).

Putting real-time information in the salesperson's or other quote specialist's hands reduces complexity and increases quote accuracy. Reduction in quote processing times leads to a reduction in customer service cycle times. Automation of quotes also leads to better information capture from the quoting process. Another benefit of the quoting process becoming more rapid is that the firm can process more quotes since salespeople will have more time to pursue other projects. More quotes will mean more sales. Further, the information-automated process improves agility to market since the additional information capture allows for better analysis that in turn will create more opportunities. More information allows for earlier identification of new product or service offerings the market will need.

fig. 13.6   *Task Management*

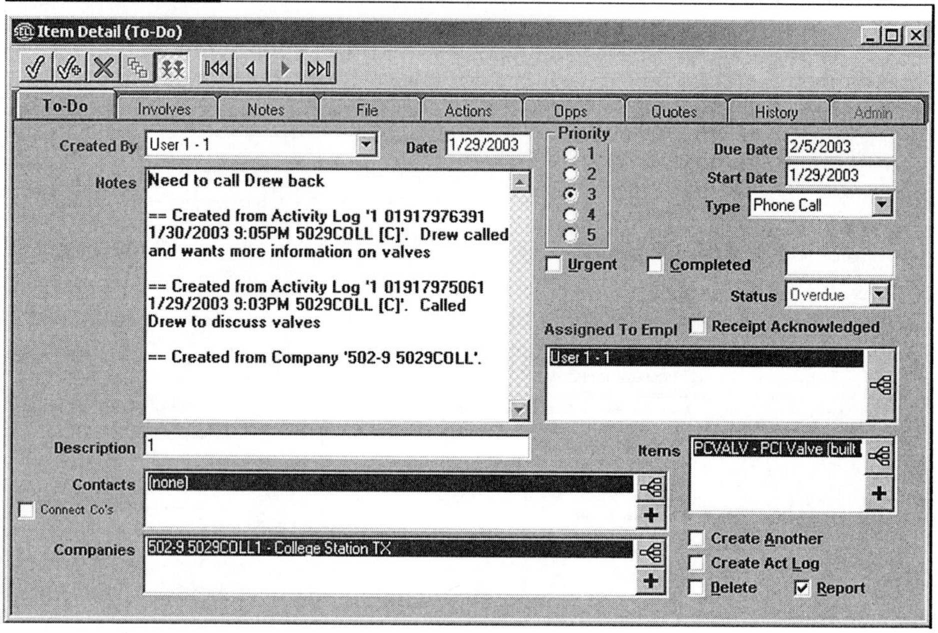

Source: Selltis L.L.C.

The firm will also experience increased sales opportunities due to responsiveness. Faster quote processing times not only frees up the sales force, it makes it possible for the firm to respond to requests for quotation (RFQ) with short time fuses on them. Many times a firm will submit an RFQ to which only a select group of suppliers is allowed to respond. If a few competitors drop out, the firm may ask a few others to come in with the requirement that they still meet the originally stated deadline for quote. An automated quote process makes it possible to capitalize on such opportunities and establish long-term relationships with new customers.

Task Management

Task management, often tied to the contact management process, allows each player in the customer service process to track activity and meet obligations on time. Salespeople frequently set several processes in motion when they initiate a transaction or develop a new customer relationship. The customer may require assistance from finance (setting up an account), logistics (placing them in a delivery route), the warehouse (implementing quality standards on their deliveries), technical support (installation of purchased goods), repair (scheduled maintenance), and many other services. When the salesperson makes contact, many promises are likely to be exchanged and the reliability of the rest of the firm will determine whether the salesperson's efforts will stick or the customer will ultimately cancel the relationship. Task management allows the salespeople to not only follow up on their own activities but to initiate the supporting divisions' actions as well by assigning tasks to them through the CRM system (see Figure 13.6).

Web Order Processing

Web order processing was perhaps the most oversold concept from the 1990s and caused many to overlook the more effective tools like instant data capture (radio frequency identification) that had a better chance of improving a firm's operations in the near term. The problem with web order processing was that the technology was not ready for the vast majority of channels and would not be ready for many channels for many years to come.[4] The process was sold, however, as happening immediately and that those not onboard would find themselves "Amazoned," a phrase referring to Amazon.com's surprise entry into the bookselling market. This market, however, was one of a very few perfectly suited to web order processing (Dell Computer is another example) and, as has been well documented, did not go as well as most analysts had predicted.[5]

Web orders have been most effective in commodities or products that heavy web users can buy with little fear of receiving the wrong product. Even though companies like Dell and Amazon go to great lengths to ease the return or product repair process, the fact that a product is ordered through the Internet often means little or no local support for customer service failures. In the book market, this problem is minimal as long as the ordering process is stable enough to ensure the buyer gets the correct book. In the computer market, the problem is more complex but the heavy use of the Internet by Dell and their competitors' customers has acted as a strong marketing tool. If we extend this process out to other product offerings, the problems become even more difficult.

Many industrial customers still have difficulty accessing web order processing tools.[6] Industrial replenishment still takes place in locations without Internet access (construction or maintenance, repair, and operations plant sites), with personnel uncomfortable with computers (low-tech firms), and/or with firms that have to use a paper-processing trail for quotes and transactions (government projects). Still, as the software and hardware tools progress, it seems likely that this method of ordering will grow in popularity.

Internet access, at the beginning of the twenty-first century, was still dealing with bandwidth issues.[7] Software applications that allowed for creative use of the web in managing industrial relationships still were not available. The experimentation with high bandwidth capability in Europe[8] seemed likely to solve the bandwidth problem, however, and many believed the software would follow bandwidth. As "killer apps" (software applications that overwhelm hardware capability) were developed, more powerful hardware would follow the software, leading to a continuous improvement process that would ultimately offer connectivity to most channels. The connectivity would bring the CRM tools into everyone's hands, making it appear that CRM was to be a major growth industry.

Forecasting Modules

Forecasting is a key component of communicating with the customer and CRM, as a customer contact tool, has an important role to play in forecasting. The forecasting hierarchy, as described in Chapter 8, begins with a proper data extract, activates the analysis, and then offers the results to the planner for evaluation. If we view the process from the mathematical/ERP system side the process goes from history (data in the system) forward to the inventory planners. If we view the combination process after the mathematical model has presented its output, the process now rolls backward from the customer and can be greatly facilitated by CRM capability.

One distributor used CRM capability to determine when and where to anticipate large transactions. The distributor specialized in products used for manufacturing production lines. The final customer was a large manufacturer who would open up a bid process with a group of general contractors whenever they planned to build a new production line. The general contractor would then take bids from subcontractors that built the components for the facility. Finally the subcontractor would ask its distributors to quote prices and delivery on the final products that went into the subcontractor's assemblies. The process is depicted in Figure 13.7. The distributor does not have a sale until the subcontractor wins the bid, which will not be final until the general contractor wins his or her bid. The subcontractor and the general contractor, in turn, are dependent on the distributor's ability to meet the customer's timetable.

The distributor had some subcontractor relationships that were exclusive and some others that were sent out for multiple bids. The subcontractors, on the other hand, did not have an exclusive relationship with the general contractor but usually

fig. 13.7   *A Bid/Quote Hierarchy*

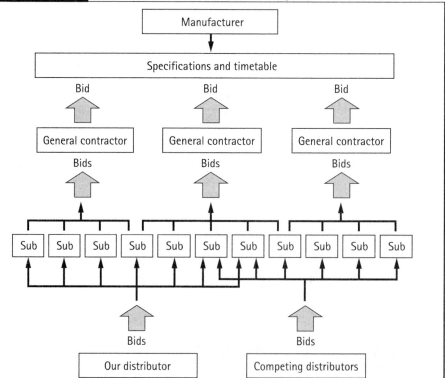

had a fairly good idea of which projects would come their way and which would not based on the type of job and the general contractor in question. The distributor gave subcontractors that interacted with it exclusively access to its extranet which, in turn, provided the subcontractor with quoting tools and access to the distributor's inventory schedules as well as supplier specification information. In return, the customer supplied the distributor with its customer's bid information as soon as possible.

The environment raises several issues for the distributor's capacity planning. If the distributor is unable to forecast accurately, proper materials will not be in place when the subcontractor needs them. Distributor stockouts could lead to schedule delays on the part of the subcontractor, which could, in turn, lead to delays for the general contractor. Since the end customer (the major manufacturer) will not tolerate any delays, failure by the subcontractor could eliminate the general contractor's opportunity to bid on future projects with that customer.

The customer is one of only a few that these general contractors support, and loss of a customer would be catastrophic, costing the general contractor hundreds of millions dollars and the subcontractor and distributor tens of millions each. If the general contractor loses a customer or is put at risk of missing deadlines, the subcontractor would likely not be given a second chance. In addition to the initial construction job, the distributor could also lose the replacement parts business (MRO).

An important key to success for this distributor, therefore, is to make sure that the right parts are available when the subcontractor needs them. The problem is the timetable and specifications from the general contractor's customer. If the customer specifies a nonstock product with long lead times (longer than the supplier's lead time), the distributor may be caught flat-footed. If the distributor can get information about the bid faster and if the customer's needs can be anticipated, it has a better chance of ensuring the products will be in place. The process requires a strong collaboration between the subcontractor, the general contractor, and the distributor. In fact, the distributor has to know not only what the customer specified once the bid has been won, but also what the customer has specified before the general contractor wins the bid as well as the probability that the contractor's bid will succeed and the probability that the general contractor will choose a subcontractor that will use the distributor to supply the parts.

Collaborative forecasting brings together existing knowledge on the general and subcontractors' behavior in winning a particular type of bid and information the customer shares on the details and status of the bid's progress. This information can then be matched with lead times from suppliers to determine which items can be delayed until the forecast becomes more certain and which items have to be procured before the bid process is complete. The accuracy of the forecast will determine the distributor's success or failure to meet the customer's needs with minimal resources (excess inventory, for instance). This capacity planning process was described in Chapter 11 as part of the information-enabled enterprise in the operations customer service processes (see Figure 13.8).

Forecasting is critical to the capacity planning process since appropriate capacity (inventory, people, equipment, facilities, etc.) cannot be staged until the firm knows what it needs. The forecasting process is a 100% customer-focused information activity to which CRM functionality can add a great deal. Figure 13.8 shows data collection and exchanges between the system's databases and analysis programs that drive capacity planning.

Multiple CRM tools can interact with the forecasting process. Sales force automation (SFA) provides customer information collected by salespeople on the contractors' bid processes and other progress achieved with their customers during the bid process. The order processing module collects and provides the data for customer history that can be used by mathematical models to determine what would happen if sales volumes were to follow last year's pattern. The sales/marketing modules analyze the bid and historical data to assist the projection (forecasting) process by including information not available to traditional mathematical forecasting environments like bid and quote status (see Figure 13.9).

Some mathematical forecasting methods are capable of working with CRM. CRM processes provide additional information that specialized models can capitalize on in developing a mathematical forecast. Regression allows the user to introduce influencing variables into the equation: Variables like city growth patterns, building permits issued, and others can be entered into the model and used in the final fore-

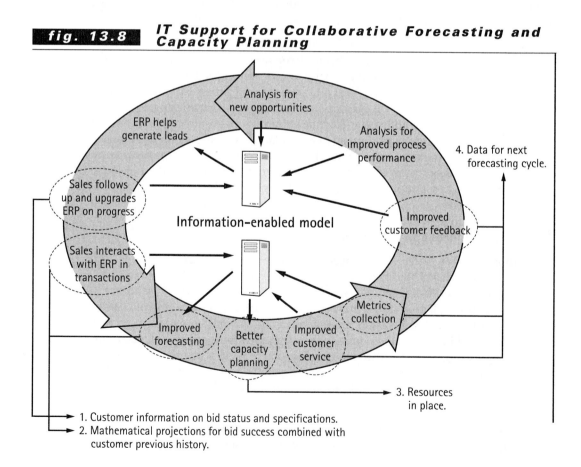

fig. 13.8 *IT Support for Collaborative Forecasting and Capacity Planning*

fig. 13.9   *CRM and Collaborative Forecasting*

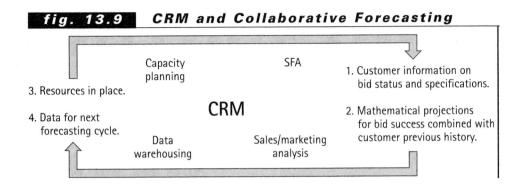

cast. The technique requires numerical input but most activities can be reduced to some form of mathematical expression. The regression techniques, however, may have difficulty adjusting to the changes in the market and do require some expertise to set up and interpret.

Simulation allows the user to include a broad array of variables as long as the connection of those variables to the model's results is established. The model is a representation of the real world and, therefore, can require considerable effort to construct. All variables believed to have a significant impact on the forecast have to be included and their effect has to be calibrated. While models like regression and simulation may have their place in some environments, the cost of building such models is often prohibitive and their accuracy is dependent on expertise of the user. To date, most firms and ERP/CRM providers have not introduced simplified methods to use these techniques. A more successful approach to forecasting is to make sure that the combination/collaborative forecasting processes are properly implemented.

Proper collection of CRM data becomes critical to the use of these models. Data must be timely. In our example, the specification information must be in the distributor's hands immediately in order to begin preparing supply sources. Data must also be relevant for forecasting purposes and formatted for use. Relevant data is actually used by the forecasting technique and does not include information that cannot be quantified or does not affect the product or service. Formatting refers to putting the data into the same time period length (days, weeks, months, etc.), unit of measure (pieces, bags, boxes, etc.), and typically in a numerical form that the forecasting model can use and that fits the conventions the company operates under.

Collaborative forecasting is merely another level in the forecasting hierarchy described in Chapter 8 (see Figure 13.10). As described earlier, measures of forecast accuracy will have to be collected on the new forecasting techniques. The user may even choose to do a more detailed analysis:

1. Mean absolute deviation (MAD) and mean forecast error (bias) are still appropriate.

2. Other measures that demonstrate error magnitude like mean squared error (MSE) may also be appropriate.

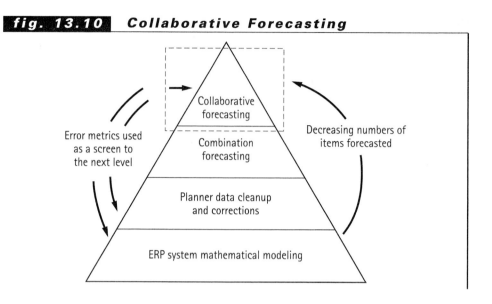

fig. 13.10 *Collaborative Forecasting*

The collaborative forecast should only be created with the assistance of the firm's largest customers who have the greatest ability to add value to the process. The reason for limiting the number of customers involved has to do with the complexity of the task. Setting up and maintaining communication with many customers may actually consume more resources than it ultimately saves both in technology and sales force effort. In addition, the many small customers when added together will likely have a smoothing affect on their activity that typically cancels out the many spikes associated with their businesses.

Tools that allow the customer to share information in real time are numerous. E-mail is the most pervasive but still requires a great deal of human touch. E-mail may not be able to directly transfer data or other information from the customer's to the distributor's system without people downloading and uploading the data. These processes may not be as error ridden as those where the data is collected on paper and keyed in but are still work intensive and less accurate than automatic data collection and exchange methods.

As we discussed in previous chapters, automated collection tools can be connected to CRM capability to deliver forecasting information like POS data. Rule-based procedures can be matched with automated data collection and quoting systems to increase the richness of forecasting information. If the customer is willing to exchange data with the distributor, forecasting can be improved.

In the most extreme form, the customer can be encouraged to cooperate with lead times to all but eliminate the need for forecasting (a 100 percent accurate forecast). Customer manufacturing firms, for example, that share material requirements planning (MRP) schedules can allow the distributor to use their time fences for more accurate forecasting if the customers practice scheduling discipline. A "time fence" is the number of time periods a manufacturing firm will freeze production schedules.

fig. 13.11   *Forecasting and MRP Time Fences*

Time period	1	2	3	4	5	6	7	8	9	10	11	12	13
Sales and transfers		750	560	520	660	675	655	715	705	755	820	810	703
Inventory	4200	3450	2890	2370	1710								
ROP		2000	2000	2000	2000	2000	2000	2000	2000	2000	2000	2000	2000
Schedule						1000	1000		1000		1000	1000	

Reorder point triggers ——

Time fence

Certain production amounts ——

MRP time fences are used so that the manufacturing firm can plan its raw material acquisition and set up production lines efficiently. If the firm shares these time fences with its suppliers, the suppliers will be able to plan for those periods with absolute certainty. If the distributor's suppliers deliver in less time than the customer's time fence, there is actually no need for the distributor to carry inventory (see Figure 13.11).

Figure 13.11 depicts a master production schedule from a manufacturer using MRP. The Sales and transfers row shows product that manufacturing has produced that was either sold or transferred elsewhere in the firm's operations (distribution warehouses, for instance). Once the reorder point triggers, this line is represented by forecasted demand. The next row is current inventory status followed by the reorder point (ROP). The last line is the schedule.

Real sales and transfers have triggered the reorder point (inventory has slipped below 2000 units) and the firm has planned production for the coming periods represented by its standard production-lot size of 1000 units. The time fence is set at four periods, which means the firm will definitely make anything planned within the fence. The firm has scheduled 1000 units each for the next two periods and 1000 for the fourth period that will definitely be made. Raw-materials suppliers can treat that demand as certain (100 percent accurate forecast) and forecasts for coming periods as less reliable but more accurate than projections made without the customer's input.

If the customer can be flexible on delivery lead-time requirements, forecasting becomes unnecessary for short-term scheduling but still cannot be avoided for long-term capacity planning. The distributor can even drop-ship (ship directly from manufacturer to customer) the customer's order, thereby eliminating the extra handling and inventory. Longer-term forecasts (beyond any time fence) will still require inventory planning, but if the customer shares its forecast, the distributor may have a better chance of correctly anticipating the customer's needs.

Combination forecasting can also be greatly facilitated by CRM. Since expert (inventory planner or other expert) reviews are a routine part of combination forecasting, the additional information that CRM systems provide can offer many opportunities. The additional information must be timely and well understood by planners.

Data Mining and Customer Profiling

Data mining and customer profiling are useful tools for managing the customer relationship. Data mining allows the firm to discover things about the customer that may not be apparent from normal analysis. The process is a statistical analysis based tool that offers the firm the ability to identify opportunities not immediately obvious to the firm. For example, buying patterns for a particular customer segment may indicate an unmet need that offers opportunities for new product introduction. Some customer segments may buy in a fashion that indicates a potential to target that market more aggressively. As suggested earlier, a customer segment may have an exceptional payment record, indicating financial health, or may start purchasing a group of products that do not normally sell together, indicating a need for a product or service offering not currently available.

Customer profiling allows for customer convenience and follow-up on sales opportunities without the customer having to notify the supplier (see Figure 13.12 for an example customer profiling screen). Customers can be pulled up with complete information that prevents the supplier from subjecting the customer to repetitive processes. Additional products can be suggested for the customer based on identified buying patterns.

fig. 13.12   *Customer Profile Screen*

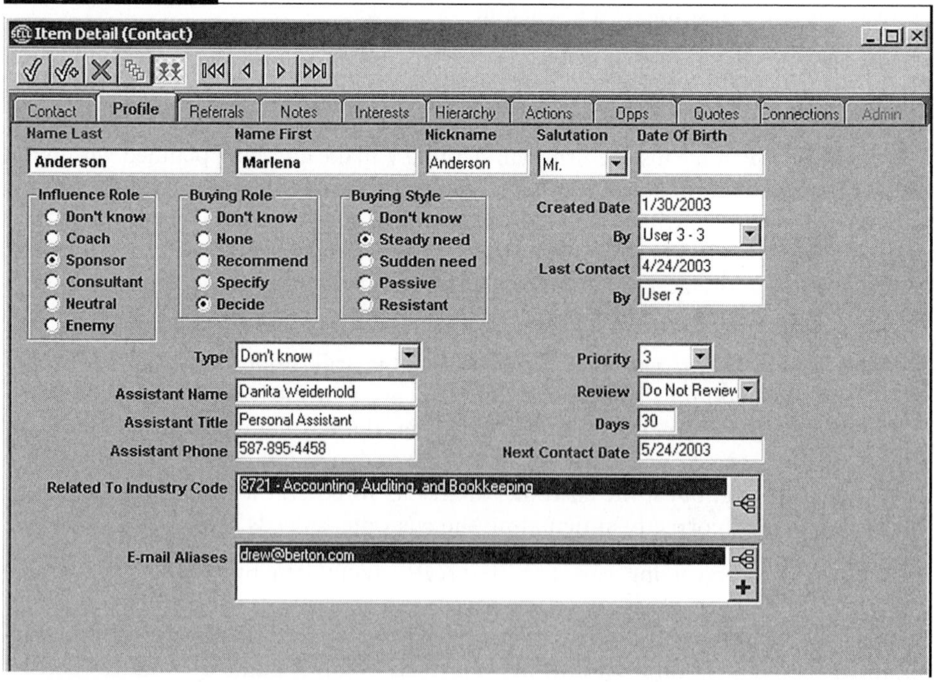

Source: Selltis, L.L.C.

One distributor planned to use global positioning systems to notify the sales force when they are in a customer's area that had not been visited recently or had an otherwise demonstrated potential benefit for a sales call. The process has been used extensively by Amazon.com and other firms for suggestive selling or customer follow-up.[9] One computer firm raised the credit limit on a customer that had examined a product a few days before that was then considered out of its credit range without the customer requesting the increase, thereby increasing the likelihood of a purchase.

The customer had not completed the transaction for a different reason but the manufacturer's system identified the incomplete transaction and the unused credit application and assumed credit was the problem. As it turned out, the customer had planned to go to a competitor's site but the e-mail on the raised credit limit changed the customer's mind because it was impressed with the effectiveness of the manufacturer's system. The data analysis might have properly identified the reason but even if it had not, the additional contact and thought placed onto the customer's needs was sufficient to win the sale.

System Capabilities

ERP systems will typically not have the functionality of a bolt-on or the specificity of a mod. The purpose of a bolt-on is to offer functionality beyond the capability of the customer's base system. Bolt-ons will examine these unmet needs and integrate them into their offering while at the same time seeking to create connectivity to as many systems as possible. The ERP provider will be seeking to add the same degree of functionality but may not be able to focus on all areas at once. The bolt-on is, therefore, a niche market and, like all such markets, either grows, remains too small to be worth much notice, or grows large enough to cause the ERP provider to add that functionality. The bolt-on provider will then need to be both well regarded (many customers use or would like to use the system) and easily connectable to the ERP system.

What to Do When the System Will Not Support Your Needs

If the ERP system does not have sufficient or properly configured capability to support your market, the firm may need to use bolt-ons or develop mods. Bolt-ons serve the market niches that ERP has not yet gotten to but require sufficient volume to justify their existence. In some cases, the firm may have a very specialized need that is not supported by bolt-on applications. In other cases, the firm's need may be supported through an available bolt-on, but the rest of the bolt-on's functionality is not necessary and too expensive to justify.

In these cases, many firms resort to mods, special programs written by the firm or consultants to carry out a specific activity that adds value but not sufficient value to buy bolt-on or ERP capability. Mods have their problems, as we have discussed throughout this text, in that they may be hard to migrate to upgrades in the ERP system and become the sole responsibility of the firm. Many mods are picked up by ERP and bolt-on firms if there is a large enough demand for their use. Therefore, some mods are created but no longer necessary after a system upgrade. The key to determining when to add a bolt-on or a mod is to determine what the probability is that the functionality will soon be offered elsewhere and how much value can be added in the meantime.

Valuing Functionalities

Differing functionalities have different values depending on the firm, its market, and its customer expectations. The firm has to determine the cost of not having the process in place and, therefore, having to operate offline, and compare that cost to the cost of purchasing the bolt-on or building and maintaining the mod. Firms that custom-build solutions, for instance, derive greater value from quoting capability and may need to give greater consideration to CRM bolt-ons than those that have a very routine quoting process that can be easily handled or modified within their ERP system.

Firms that sell commodities to technologically advanced customers will gain greater value from web order processing than those that sell custom solutions to lower-tech firms. High-technology customers are more likely to use the Internet as a purchasing tool and will likely come to expect suppliers of commodities to simplify and automate the ordering process. CRM is likely to gain a foothold quickly in such markets, and those that cannot connect may be eliminated from the supply chain.

Contact and task management will be useful to many firms but requires a disciplined approach as discussed above. An overly powerful and resistant sales force will kill any contact management program. Before investing in technology, the firm should invest in change management and making the case for the sales force to be CRM advocates rather than critics.

Forecasting and data-mining techniques can be extremely valuable if the firm has the human capability to manipulate them. If not, the techniques can still be useful if the firm has the discipline to limit interference with the process. The best option is to train all personnel involved with forecasting on the system's capabilities and where they can and should add value. Combination and collaborative forecasting are useful only in environments where inventory planners and all other contributors to the forecast understand their role.

Choosing Bolt-Ons

The evaluation process for bolt-ons is the same as for ERP in general, with a few exceptions:

○ Bolt-ons may offer capability that the firm and/or its customers cannot use.

○ Bolt-ons may require internal expertise that does not exist in the firm.

    ○ *These internal experts will be the audience for bolt-on selection.*

    ○ *The involvement of these experts will also be key to system implementation.*

Conclusion

Customer relationship management software will continue to grow in significance as customer expectations grow and supply chain management advances in years to come. The increased significance of CRM will continue to attract the interest of ERP providers and the consolidation of distribution software providers will likely continue as a result. Distributors will follow a process of determining where new functionality is needed based on customer relationships, adding that functionality through the use of bolt-ons or mods, and eventually seeing that functionality absorbed by their enterprise system.

The early years of CRM experienced many of the same difficulties as ERP with many systems only partially implemented and many firms failing to achieve the value they first envisioned. As with ERP, however, CRM will eventually become stable and firms will derive many expected benefits. The connection to the customer means that, unlike ERP, CRM will continue to offer new processes and successful firms will need to make the implementation process a standard business process since CRM will never stop changing. The constant changing nature of CRM is one of its great strengths, however, since it will act as an endless field of opportunity for companies that both distributors and IT providers look to for creating competitive advantage.

Distribution Retrospective

Victor had heard of CRM software and had been told that it could handle all of his problems. He was somewhat skeptical, however, since Quigley had examined the bolt-on CRM software that came with its ERP system and had deemed it not capable of handling its quoting process. In particular, it was unable to collect data off manufacturers' websites for product information needed in the quoting process. In addition, the sales force had found the CRM contact and task management modules to be inflexible, forcing them to adjust their customer filing methods to the system's processes.

Victor put together a team of salespeople and IT specialists to evaluate and find a bolt-on CRM package that could meet as many of the firm's needs as possible. One CRM provider had been developed at a PVF firm and then spun off as CRM package that specialized on PVF and other MRO channels. The system came with a CD that carried the most up-to-date product specifications (available through a firm that specialized in electronic catalogs) and could access manufacturers' websites for downloads. The selection team compared the quoting system and found it to be comparable to what many salespeople used in spreadsheets or other packages. The CRM firm also promised it could establish a connection to the Quigley's ERP system.

Victor knew the real test would come in winning the confidence of the sales force. He set up training sessions for all salespeople and developed the selection team members' skills to the level that they could act as domain experts for implementation, identifying and adding functionality as necessary, and supporting their peers' inquiries. The new system implementation plan was set, and the process began.

Issues to Consider

1. What functionalities should a distributor look for in a CRM system?

2. How do you quantify the value (ROI) of a CRM system?

3. How do you effectively use CRM for internal operations such as forecasting, warehousing, and so on?

4. What can we expect to see in the CRM of the future?

Case Study: What to Do About CRM

Note to the reader: The following case is based on an actual distributor. The name of the firm has been changed for confidentiality reasons.

High Voltage Inc. (HVI) specialized in electrical panels for manufacturers of high-technology equipment. These manufacturers would introduce new product models virtually every year and would have to build a new manufacturing line every time a new product was introduced. A general contractor who then selected subcontractors to build the components of the production line built the new manufacturing line. The general contractors went through a bid process with the customer and the winning bidder would then select the subcontractor based on its input to the bid process. The distributor would get business based on which subcontractor was selected and what inclination that subcontractor had toward the distributor.

The process was already complex but adding to the mix were HVI's principal supplier and its competitors trying to influence the decision-making process at the end customer's site. The specifications for the manufacturing lines were drawn up by the high-tech firm's engineers with assistance from HVI's supplier's and competitors' suppliers' sales engineers. The customer's design engineer worked on a basic concept and then turned to these product specialists (sales engineers) for their input in preparing an optimal production line capability. The supplier's sales engineers had both a responsibility to demonstrate efficiency using their parts and an opportunity to influence the specifications—which, they hoped, would lead to a sale when the final specs went to the distributor (see Figure 13.13). It was a long journey from the initial specs to the distributor's services, however.

The initial specs came out after this process and were presented as part of a request for quotation (RFQ) to a few approved general contractors. The general contractors would divide the quote up among themselves and their potential sub-contractors. The subcontractors might be asked to quote on their portion of the job to be placed in the general contractor's bid for the high-tech manufacturer. The sub-contractor would turn to the distributor's sales engineers for advice on their components and the connection between the distributor and the general and sub-contractors was established. Since the customer left some items up to the general contractor to specify, the subcontractor and distributor could affect the final specs. If the final specs had more products from HVI's supplier, it would mean more business for both the supplier and HVI (see Figure 13.14).

HVI's suppliers' sales engineers would have intelligence that could increase their distributors' chances of not only getting the nonspecified (general and subcontractor choice) items but possibly to alter some of the specs from their competition over to HVI's suppliers' products. HVI's suppliers realized there was considerable opportunity for collaboration between the supplier and the distributor to control the influencing of the specs as they move from the customer to final specs. The benefit for the supplier would be higher sales. HVI might realize some gains by selling its

fig. 13.13   *Suppliers Affect Final Specs*

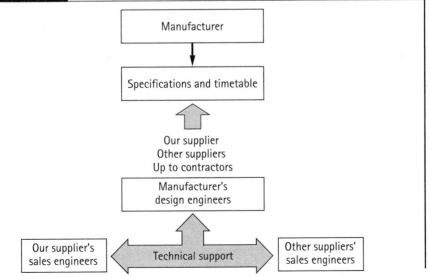

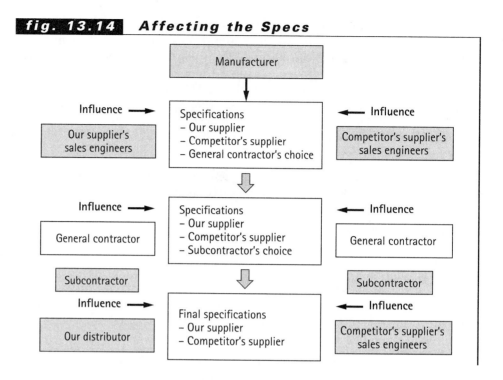

fig. 13.14 *Affecting the Specs*

core products—which carry higher margins and have better inventory management status—from its key supplier. HVI also likes its manufacturer's products "spec'd in" since it has an exclusive arrangement with the supplier. More product from its key supplier means more sales for HVI since it is the only distributor for the customer's region.

HVI's key supplier was concerned, however, about sharing too much information because HVI feared it could backfire: The customer might take a suspicious view of itsr sales engineers if it saw too great a team effort with the distributor and contractors. HVI did, on the other hand, want all of the distributor's information since that would improve its scheduling and market knowledge. It implemented a CRM system and asked all its distributors to allow it to envelope their information systems and share all point of sale data.

The distributors were skeptical since the key supplier represented only 40 percent of their business at most and the CRM system would require some process redesign, training, and licensing fees. Most of these distributors were already in the process of implementing their own CRM systems and did not see the value in trying to maintain or integrate two systems. Many others did not have the resources to set up a CRM solution, and others that did have the financial ability were unsure how well it would work. Some of these distributors thought it might be better to work with the supplier's system first since most of the investment had already been made by the supplier (see Figure 13.15).

HVI had an ERP system with CRM capability and was, therefore, one of the distributors that questioned using the supplier's system. The supplier had suggested

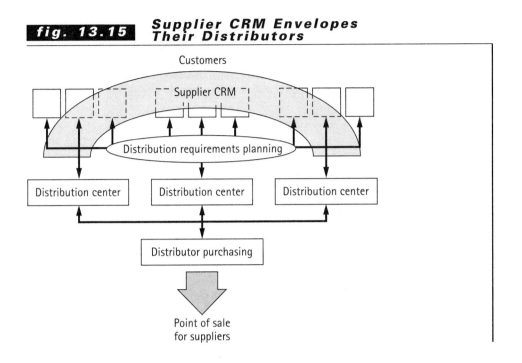

fig. 13.15 *Supplier CRM Envelopes Their Distributors*

connecting the two CRM systems (HVI's and the supplier's) but HVI was not comfortable with its in-house implementation challenges and thought it wiser to wait until its own system was complete before integrating with the supplier. In addition, several HVI sales specialists felt that while point of sale data was useful to the supplier, it did not help HVI much, if at all. They wanted the supplier to tell them how the initial specification process had unfolded, who supported their brand, how they felt about the various contractors, who supported the opposing brand and why, and so forth. The supplier saw sharing this proprietary information with the distributor as a violation of trust that would be vigorously resisted by the supplier's sales force.

HVI and its supplier seemed to be at a standstill. Until the supplier offered greater benefits to HVI for CRM collaboration, HVI was not interested in all the effort and expense. The supplier was struggling with how to improve the value for HVI and HVI was struggling with what direction to take on CRM in general. HVI knew that eventually the supplier would improve the value of its CRM program and that it was inevitable they would work together. If HVI were late to implement the CRM connection, it could find itself behind the curve with the supplier's customers who were dealing with other distributors selling this supplier's parts in other parts of the country. If HVI were an early adopter, it would face higher implementation costs as the supplier, CRM provider, and distributors worked out kinks in the process.

Case Challenges

1. How can the manufacturer make the CRM system connection more attractive? Are there benefits neither side has considered?

2. What information should the supplier and HVI share? To what benefit?

3. Should HVI adopt the supplier's system alone? Should it adopt its own CRM and not the supplier's? Or both? Why?

References

1. Pankaj Sehgal, and Jay Mitchell, "Managing the Demand Chain to Overcome CRM Challenges," Montgomery Research, Inc., http://www.crmproject.com/documents.asp?grID=183&d_ID=1439.

2. Jack McCarthy, "Un-wired to the customer," *Info World* (April 26, 2002), www.infoworld.com/articles/ct/xml/02/04/29/020429ctwireless.xml.

3. Andrew Craig, "Europe Set To Wallow In Bandwidth," *TechWeb News* (July 21, 1998), http://www.techweb.com/wire/story/TWB19980720S0010; Steve Broadhead, "High-bandwidth functions move closer to reality for wide area corporate networks," *Computer Weekly* (September 30, 2003), http://www.computerweekly.com/Article125224.htm.

4. Martin Piszczalski, "The Promise of eProcurement," *Automotive Design and Production* (n.d.), http://www.autofieldguide.com/columns/martin/0601it.html.

5. Dell Direct, Stanford Business School, Case Number EC 17 (November 2000), http://www.gsb.stanford.edu/CEBC/cases.htm.

6. Michael Pastore, "Electronic Procurement Not Catching on with Fortune 500," *Markets b-to-b* (December 1, 2000), http://cyberatlas.internet.com/markets/b2b/article/0,1323,10091_524631,00.html.

7. K. G. Coffman and Andrew M. Odlyzko, "Internet growth: Is there a 'Moore's Law' for data traffic?" AT&T Labs–Research (June 4, 2001), http://www.research.att.com/areas/transport_evolution/internet.moore.pdf.

8. Andrew Craig, "Europe Set to Wallow in Bandwidth," *TechWeb News* (July 21, 1998), http://www.techweb.com/wire/story/TWB19980720S0010.

9. Paco Underhill, *Why We Buy: The Science of Shopping* (New York: Simon & Schuster, 2000).

Logistics and Procurement Systems

Distribution Perspective

Anderson Roofing Supply (ARS) distributed all manner of products to contractors specializing in putting roofs on public and private buildings. The company had found that customer relationship management (CRM) held little value due to its customers' lack of technology adoption beyond the cell phone. Instead, ARS had focused its attention first on ERP adoption to control the sales order process and financials. The ERP implementation had been difficult but successful and the firm was now looking to achieve greater value through better control of its logistics processes.

The firm managed a large transportation fleet across multiple warehouses that delivered to customers at their job sites next day. The company had a policy that customers could call in orders until noon the day before required delivery. The time limit was required because the firm needed at least six hours to drop the pick slip, pull inventory off the shelf, and stage it in the yard for loading the truck that evening.

ARS had been experiencing problems, however, with customers wanting to change orders after noon or to place orders after the deadline in general. The change orders were often allowed due to pressure from the sales force, and the process was creating chaos in the warehouse. Customers who wanted to order late were also allowed to do so in certain cases. Large, powerful customers were often given exceptions, for instance. The firm was certain that the changes were hurting profitability since they frequently required the unloading and reloading of trucks, resulting in lost loading efficiencies, mistakes, damaged products, loader overtime, and traffic delays. The large customer exceptions also frequently led to trucks being unloaded and reloaded as routes were readjusted.

The entire process was made worse by being so labor intensive. The ERP system dropped the pick ticket, which was then hand-carried to the in-basket in the warehouse. A picker would collect the pick ticket, pull the order, check the truck routes to find available capacity, establish with the dispatcher which truck to put the load on, and stage the order for loading on the correct truck. After all orders had been processed, the loading process would commence with the evening shift of loaders after 6 p.m. The dispatcher had already estimated the loads and the staging process had been set up for each truck. Even so, the loading process was so complex due to odd shapes and sizes of products that it was considered an art in itself and the loader had a great deal of discretion in determining how loads went on the truck and could even shift loads and routes if necessary.

The loaders could expect changes or new orders made in the afternoon to find their way to the yard as late as eight or nine o'clock at night. However, the loading process being so labor-intensive meant they could not afford to wait for late loads before beginning the process. The trucks needed to leave by 4 a.m. and any delays could result in lost driver time—very expensive—or, worse yet, missed customer delivery windows. They would proceed, therefore, and deal with problems as they arose. Sometimes an add-on was easy because the truck was not full; other times the entire truck had to be reloaded and some items taken over to other trucks and their routes adjusted.

ARS wanted to find a way to ease the burden on its loaders and at the same time actually push back the deadline before which customers could place orders. Competitors with less business were eating into ARS's market by allowing later orders, and smaller customers were beginning to treat this later order limit as their standard for doing business. It was only a matter of time before larger customers followed suit or these smaller customers became the future large customers. ARS wanted to remain the market leader and knew a proactive approach was crucial. It began considering how to reduce cycle times associated with the entire picking and loading processes. It wondered how it could leverage its ERP investment to achieve its goals.

Introduction

Logistics and procurement systems are critical to all firms' operations and are, therefore, standard in many ERP and bolt-on applications. The logistics process begins with the initial pick-slip drop and proceeds all the way to final delivery to the customer. The term *pick-slip drop* is a throwback to the old paper-based systems that are still in existence at many firms and refers to the act of dropping the pick slip in an in-basket in the warehouse for the pickers to collect on their rounds. There are many touch points along the pick slip's route to the customer for the ERP system and its associated programs to make an impact on the firm's efficiency. The pick slip is generally created by the system but most distributors stop the automation at that point. The processes that follow can be automated (as described in Chapter 9) through the use of hardware like scanners and software designed to route pickers, interact with transportation providers, load vehicles, route trucks, and/or select carriers. These touch points can have a considerable impact on resource utilization. The system is accessed in carrying out the firm's activities and for storing the results from operations.

As was the case in CRM, the principal difference between ERP systems and bolt-ons is the degree of functionality offered. The opportunities for automation within the procurement and logistics processes are considerable such that there are many different areas to be pursued by IT providers seeking to differentiate their products. Many algorithms for optimizing operations have been designed over the years. Most were developed at a time when information technology could not be used to solve real-world logistical problems. The tremendous variation faced in recreating the real world tended to create models that could not be solved by even the fastest of computers, a trait called NP Complete.[1]

"NP Complete" means that not all cases of a problem type (business decision) could be solved in polynomial time. "Nonpolynomial time" means exponential (increasing at an increasing rate) solution times, which simply means that many decisions could not be solved no matter how fast computers may become. Therefore, any IT solution would get stymied on a regular basis with a problem (decision) it could not solve. The issue applies to all kinds of problems, from purchasing decisions to transportation routing.

This chapter explores more-advanced topics in logistics software implementation. It begins with an explanation of where theory has been and is likely to go, and then pinpoints where ERP and bolt-on software are in terms of implementation of these processes. The chapter ends with a discussion on how to integrate these tools into a real-time environment.

Logistics Optimization

The researchers attempting to optimize operations planning decided to simplify the problem environments to get as close to optimal solutions as possible with reasonable solution times. The most common technique used was to eliminate, through assuming they did not exist, the problem characteristics that caused the most difficulty. Capacity limitations, for example, would be assumed away by using formulations with no capacity constraints. This technique would often create solutions that were not feasible and would have to be altered to fit the reality of the business environment. Since the solution boiled down to a simple adjustment to an infeasible solution, the firm could not be certain it was optimal. Another technique that became popular in later years was to use heuristics—simple rules of thumb that allowed for an almost optimal solution to be achieved with most of the real-world characteristics taken into account.

One of earliest and most successful algorithms developed for purchasing decisions was the economic order quantity (EOQ), created in 1914.[2] The EOQ made some basic assumptions that would simplify calculations. The model assumed that demand (customer orders) came at a steady and continuous rate. In other words, forecasting was not only certain but demand never differed from one period to the next. The model assumed no quantity discounts (later models were created that offered corrections for this assumption) and no capacity restrictions (capacity constraints are among the most difficult for computer solution). The EOQ was not intended for computer solution—business computers had not been invented yet—but for hand calculations. Since human calculation is so slow, the model was designed for the very issues that would later plague computers as well: slow processing of complex environments.

Through these means, the real-world problems could be reduced to simple mathematical equations that could be solved. Later computer models would require multiple steps before solution and many of the individual steps of these algorithms would prove difficult to solve. The purchasing/scheduling research stepped into high gear in the late 1950s with the creation of the Wagner Whitin model.[3] This model allowed demand to vary from one time period to the next. The algorithm could be used by hand but, for real-world-sized problems, computer technology that did not even exist at the time would be required to reach a solution. Many more algorithms followed, and eventually during the 1970s and '80s, algorithms to solve complex capacity-constrained problems were developed.[4] The problem with these algorithms was that they all required computer capability that was not practical for standard business use.

The researchers still were aware that the current rate of development for computer technology would make their algorithms usable in the future, so they forged ahead. In the 1990s the explosion of desktop computing and increases in computing speed made it possible for many of the algorithms to be used. The problem now lay with human understanding since use of the algorithms required a command of their basic functions. Many IT providers opted instead to use simpler algorithms in their software, like the EOQ and others created by consultants that were easier for practitioners to understand. By 2000, more-complex algorithms were being introduced into ERP and other bolt-on software. The industry was finally beginning to catch up with the research. Many advanced algorithms have yet to be absorbed, and even the most advanced systems frequently operate on algorithmic logic created 20 years ago or more.

The many opportunities for more advancement in both research and its application mean a wider choice of approaches for ERP and bolt-ons to use and more firms claiming theirs is better than their competition's. A company must investigate what its needs really are, what input the new functionality will require, and what the benefits of implementing that capability will be.

The procurement algorithms like EOQ are not unique in their development, and the problems faced in placing them into practical application have been faced elsewhere. Transportation and picker routing algorithms were also being developed throughout the same period. The traveling salesman problem (TSP) was solved in the late 1960s and early '70s by several researchers and those algorithms serve as the basis for many of today's transportation computer solutions for truck and picker routing.[5] Like the EOQ, the TSP limits the number of variables and constraints that can be considered in any particular decision. New algorithms are being developed by researchers to offer a more inclusive approach to the problem environment. Different customers have different needs, and the routing system can map the truck's route with each site's specific needs in mind: what kind of truck should be used (flatbed or van), what equipment will be available for unloading (forklift, hand truck, people, etc.), delivery time windows (restaurants and retailers frequently take delivery only before opening, for instance), and so on.

CRM serves as the front end of the logistics and procurement processes and has to be integrated for optimal firm performance. The CRM system must supply information for the outbound transportation function and for any internal customer inventory management activities and then format, collect, and transfer that information back to the procurement and logistics functions of the distributor. The information feed to the logistics modules through CRM and ERP governs the customer-support processes.

The procurement processes connect and interact with suppliers. The connection for most firms, however, is usually only a delivered purchase order. As described in the IBM Roadmap for e-Distributors,[6] the set of information most often exchanged

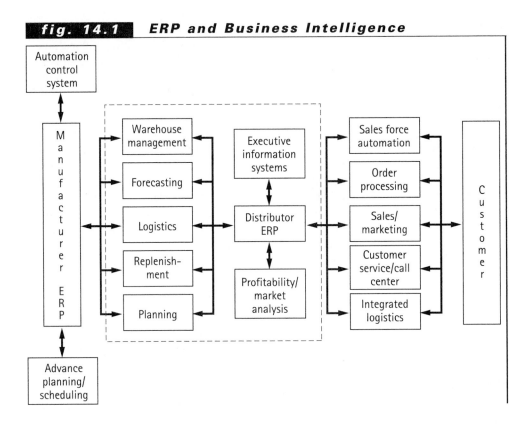

fig. 14.1 **ERP and Business Intelligence**

between the manufacturer and distributor consists of purchase orders, changes to those orders, and payment (possibly as an electronic funds transfer, or EFT). The supplier also gives the distributor limited information in return: advanced shipping notices (ASN), basic product information, and invoicing.

The combining of internal processes and supplier interaction constitutes the next phase of the firm's supply chain planning, and many firms have begun pursuing tools to support these efforts. Commonly considered the domain of ERP and business intelligence, the logistics and procurement functions link the distributor back to its suppliers and forward to its customers (see Figure 14.1). In so doing, the supply chain management (SCM) process reaches beyond the four walls of any individual firm.

Is Your Firm Ready?

Many firms enter into logistics/procurement information automation without a clear understanding of the potential value and/or no clear path to achieve that value. The value is not only achieved through individual software programs but through the integration of multiple solutions. Each logistics and procurement activity ultimately ties to the others and becomes more valuable as the interconnectivity increases. Supply chain management logic dictates that all members of the chain must connect their processes; the same is true of all information technology tools employed in the process. If the information tools are not connected, the logistics processes will not be, either.

Significance of Automation

IT providers understand the significance of logistics and procurement information automation better than most other opportunity areas. In particular, considerable work has been done in development of purchasing procedures. The research discussed above is one example. APICS and the Institute for Supply Management (ISM)—formerly known as the National Association of Purchasing Managers (NAPM)—have also worked on creating documentation of best practices.[7] That documentation is often programmed into software solutions that become embedded in ERP or bolt-on technology. The interest in purchasing decisions has been largely driven by the value to be had through reducing inventory.

Many different tools have been created for routing procedures. The routing decision for transportation has been explored by common carriers and 3PLs in detail for many years. Researchers have also put considerable effort into creating routing algorithms that can be automated. The transportation routing problem requires optimal usage of fleet resources. If a fleet is optimally managed, it requires fewer resources. The airlines studied the problem extensively in the 1970s and '80s and other transportation providers have adopted much of what they learned. The key issue is that capacity in an inventory setting can be stored. The transportation capacity, however, becomes obsolete the moment we are no longer able to use it. If a plane takes off with empty seats, the inventory (seats) unused on that flight becomes immediately and completely obsolete. The models developed for the airlines have been adapted to other scenarios and are becoming available for fleet management.[8]

Warehouse layout, routing, physical automation tools, and bar coding have come a long way in the past few years of application. The routing of pickers is similar to the truck routing problem but other factors have to be considered, such as task interleaving (put-away and picking simultaneously) and capacity constraints on the picker. While capacity constraints do exist in transportation models, their nature is somewhat different. The warehouse management process is further assisted and complicated by physical automation tools, automatic data collection, and layouts. The distributor has more control over its internal operations than it does its customers. Internal operations, therefore, can be more easily designed for optimal performance. The interaction among these tools, however, leads to different models for the information systems to control. The warehouse automation tools and warehouse management systems, therefore, are linked and must be planned together to support one another.

When all the potential automation (information and physical) tools are interlinked, the potential savings becomes quite significant. Many private fleets operate at well below 50 percent utilization.[9] Warehouses frequently operate at the same rates: Pickers spend the majority of their time in transit, inventories are often as much as 40 to 50 percent higher than necessary, and capacity is wasted due to poor planning processes. Lost sales are also a result of poor planning when inventory is too high for the wrong products and the company's financial constraints prevent the firm from carrying enough inventory in its fastest-moving products. Earlier chapters have demonstrated the costs and value of better planning under information automation. When added together, the potential savings can easily outweigh the cost of software and implementation. Most firms, however, have not fully captured the potential savings and thus either do not attempt improvement or do not properly design their implementation to capture the fullest of benefits.

Automation Challenges

Automation challenges have been described in detail throughout this book and will continue to make information technology adoption difficult. These challenges have slowed the information automation process by either making it impossible or by causing so much confusion that the company gives up and settles for no system or a less effective one than it could have had. The challenges that hold up information automation, however, are primarily short term and, for the most part, made worse than they need be by poor implementations or relationship problems in the supply chain.

Data integrity remains the biggest challenge to information technology adoption. If the system does not get good data, it cannot perform well. With data integrity as the base for all information automation, a key to successful automation is achieving accuracy in data collection. This accuracy is sometimes improved by automated data collection, as described in earlier chapters, but design of the data collection process and a willingness of people to work with the system are key.

Standardization has improved but continues as a leading information automation problem. The efforts on the part of IT firms and industry organizations were having an impact by the early 2000s but many challenges still remained. Some groups began to consolidate their efforts through the Uniform Commercial Code (UCC) while others continued to explore vertical channel-specific solutions.[10] Distributors who began to adopt the UCC standards put pressure on suppliers to adopt the same standards. The pressure added to standardization momentum but in the early 2000s it still was not clear which standards would eventually win out.

Hardware and software shortcomings will continue to arise, be solved, and be replaced by new problems as distributors and their customers continue to evolve their environment. The distribution community continues to develop new processes to differentiate each from its competition by new service offerings. These will challenge the IT providers and assist them in their own product differentiation as they automate these new processes.

Lack of managerial understanding of automation's true value continues to cause failures and erode confidence. Automation often carries a focus on headcount (reduction in personnel) that is driven by the ability to capture short-term financial gains by letting people go. This focus, however, leads employees to distrust information technology as they come to view it as merely a program to eliminate jobs. The best gains, as described throughout this text, come from other sources but require the assistance and support of employees. The headcount issue often derails the best benefits of IT implementation before it can even be completed.

After a decade of massive IT growth in the 1990s, many firms were left with only partially implemented systems. Some had given up when they were unable to make it work and others had not fully implemented because the value of some modules was not understood. In many cases, the modules not activated were necessary to make activated ones achieve their potential or even work as intended, which exacerbated implementation of complete systems.

Lack of Training

Finally, insufficient training is another significant problem with IT implementation. As technology continues to advance, most firms have been experiencing a training crisis they may not fully realize. Most implementations assume that simply training employees on how the software works will be sufficient—which assumes that once the new process (the one on the ERP or bolt-on system) is learned, it will be understood. IT systems tend to be set up for Best Practice wherever possible, with an underlying logic that may or may not reflect the firm's needs. Even if it does, the logic may not be clearly understood by employees who may then fall back on tried-and-true offline procedures simply because they do not see a good reason for doing things according to the system's procedures. The offline activities cause data integrity problems. Many managers see this problem as a lack of discipline and believe they must enforce blind obedience to system procedures. A more useful approach is to educate the employees not only on how but on why the system procedures are designed to function as they do.

Procurement

Procurement is one of the most competitive fields for IT providers. The success of procurement automation, both real and perceived, has spawned a high level of expectations for inventory reduction. Journals and other publications are filled with articles on the almost unbelievable savings that can be achieved through even the slightest improvement in procurement procedures.[11] Virtually all ERP systems have a procurement module, but few can claim to have included all potential environmental variables in their models. Bolt-on technology, therefore, has made considerable strides in developing solutions for procurement specialists. The promised benefits for improved procurement coupled with the large number of providers attempting to develop new solutions have led to an often confusing proliferation of procurement solutions.

ERP versus Best of Breed

Many applications have been developed to work in ERP but the bolt-ons are continually offering new capabilities in what is known as the "best of breed." The concept refers to use of the best solution for your application being used as part of your overall technology network. Many firms, with some developing their own suite of processes, have used this modular approach to great success. The principal issue is integration. If the modular systems cannot be integrated with the rest of the firm's operations, the overall system may underperform versus an integrated system with less functionality. The need for functionality not offered by existing systems, however, has caused many to go this route. The following sections describe functionality areas not always offered by ERP systems in the form necessary for certain firms, which are therefore likely candidates for a modular (bolt-on) approach.

Dynamic Reorder Points

Reorder-point techniques vary widely across different methodologies. Most systems make min/max procedures available. Min/max procedures are very popular but tend to be too rigid to capture business realities. The typical min/max model sets a min that operates as the reorder point. The reorder point, as we described in Chapter 8, is the inventory level at which the firm will replenish its inventory. The process requires the firm to notice that the current inventory level has fallen below the min. If the ERP system immediately notifies and initiates the replenishment process, the system will generate an order at that point.

How much to order can be handled in multiple ways as well. For the simplest case, firm experts can set the min for each SKU along with a standard order quantity as a static number in the system. This standard order quantity (SOQ) is usually a convenient order amount (a case pack, for instance). The min is an estimate of the amount of inventory needed during the supplier's lead time plus extra inventory (a fudge factor) for unexpected contingencies—also known as safety stock. The min is not based upon current forecasts, their accuracy, current supplier performance, and the like, but only an inventory planner's best guess. The min/max system is depicted in Figure 14.2.

Under this model, the order comes in and inventory hits a high point but begins depleting at a steady rate. Sales deplete inventory until the min (ROP) is penetrated, at which point an order is entered for the SOQ. When the order arrives, inventory will go up to its typical high point or max. The max, in most cases, will vary over time, as seen in Figure 14.2, due to unexpected demand during the supplier's lead time or the supplier extending that lead time when demand exceeds supply. The safety stock is used and the incoming order does not push the max as high as expected.

This min/max procedure is very common and can be found on virtually all ERP or bolt-on systems. Another min/max procedure is to set the min and, when the min is penetrated, the firm will order up to the max. Under this model, the order amount will vary since the firm will add to the SOQ any missing safety stock. While many systems offer this method, few firms actually use it since it can increase inventory and has little effect on customer service. In addition, this method increases logistics costs since the varying order amount will often force the company to buy in broken lot sizes.

Statistical calculation captures environmental conditions that are not directly considered under most min/max procedures. The min is broken up into two forms of inventory: demand during lead time (DDLT) and safety stock (SS). DDLT is calculated as the average supplier lead time for the product in question times the period forecasted demand. If a supplier ships in two weeks on average, for example, and

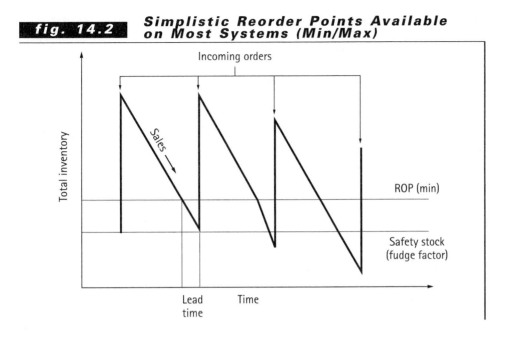

fig. 14.2 *Simplistic Reorder Points Available on Most Systems (Min/Max)*

forecasted demand is 100 units per week, then the DDLT will be equal to 200 units and added together with the safety stock to get the reorder point or min. This amount will vary with the supplier's performance. Most suppliers ship quickly during slow periods and tend to stretch out their lead times during the busy season due to increased demand straining production resources.

Safety stock calculation is far more detailed under statistical calculation. A statistical model will consider the supplier's lead time (its length), the variability of that lead time, and the level of forecast error. The average length of the lead time is important to safety stock calculation as well as to DDLT because longer lead times mean longer forecasting time periods. Longer-term forecasts are inherently less accurate[12] and, therefore, require additional safety stock. Supplier lead-time variability is another cause of uncertainty and poor supplier performance requires higher safety stock levels as well (see Figure 14.3). The system generates forecasts into the future when the reorder point is triggered, and the farther out it must reach, the less reliable the forecasts become.

Software solutions for reorder point calculation consider some or all of the causes of variation. Lead-time variability-driven models use only supplier performance to establish safety stocks. These techniques assume that the supplier is the principal driver of safety stock needs. They will typically take the standard deviation of the supplier's lead time (σ_L) in an equation that provides more inventory as the variability of supply increases.

Forecast-error-driven models use only forecast accuracy to establish safety stocks. These models assume that forecast error is the principal driver for safety stock. The models will typically use a measure of forecast deviation from actual demand to determine the need for inventory. Seasonal or trend environments can carry a great

fig. 14.3   Longer-Term Forecasts and Safety Stock Needs

Date		Jan	Feb	Mar	Apr	May	Jun	Jul	Aug	Sep	Oct	Nov	Dec
Sales and transfers		750	560	520	660								
Inventory	4200	3450	2890	2370	1710								
ROP		2000	2000	2000	2000	2000	2000	2000	2000	2000	2000	2000	2000
Forecast		680	600	550	610	675	655	(715)	(705)	(755)	820	810	703
Error (MAD)		42	38	47	40								

Less reliable forecasts ⎯⎯⎯⎯⎯⎯⎯⎯⎯⎯

Source: Silvon Software Inc.

deal of variation that could be predicted by the forecasting system. The mean absolute deviation (MAD) is included in many software offerings' calculation of safety stock.

Dynamic reorder points are created when these variability conditions are used to calculate the safety stock and demand during lead time and an inventory level is set to meet a prespecified fill rate. A dynamic reorder point will vary with total demand, supplier performance, and forecast accuracy (see Figure 14.4). In fact, the reorder point will move considerably, since slower time periods will lead to faster supplier deliveries, which, in turn, lead to shorter forecasting periods (reduced forecast error).

fig. 14.4   A Dynamic Reorder Point

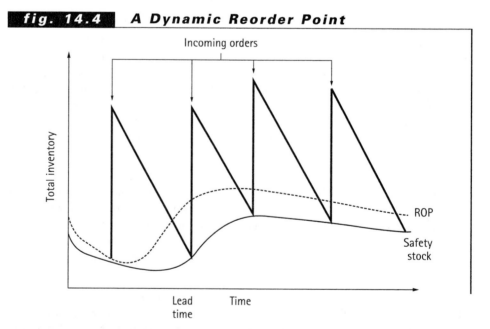

Source: Master Halco Logistics Report, Texas A&M University, 2001.

If the firm's products have a high degree of seasonality, the dynamic reorder point can make a considerable impact on the min and, therefore, the total inventory levels (see Figure 14.5). Virtually all firms, however, experience variation in supplier performance and forecast errors, so a dynamic reorder point is usually preferable to a fixed (static) system. The inventory realignment can be used to reduce inventory or increase customer service as described in Chapter 8. The dynamic reorder point has to be thoroughly understood when selecting among various methodologies contained within different ERP or bolt-on offerings.

Some procedures tie the ROP to ABC classification techniques. The ROP is set higher for A items by increasing the fill rate expectation. The fill rate is typically included in some fashion in the safety stock calculation since the firm must have a target to hit before it can determine what inventory it needs. This customer service target is most commonly expressed as a desired fill rate either set by the firm or its customers. Most firms still do not directly calculate their fill rate even though virtually all ERP and related bolt-on software will give them the capability to do so. The desired fill rate is essential to setting the safety stock level. Without it, the firm can only guess at what inventory levels will best serve the customer and keep the company profitable.

Functionalities associated with optimizing safety stock therefore can include supplier lead times, lead-time variability, forecast accuracy, and desired fill rates. At a minimum the system must be able to collect the data needed for whichever techniques it uses in setting the safety stock. The firm should address how much functionality it would like to receive, how it plans to use that functionality, and what the projected benefits are before selecting the bolt-on or ERP technology appropriate for its needs.

fig. 14.5 **Inventory Savings Under Dynamic Reorder Points**

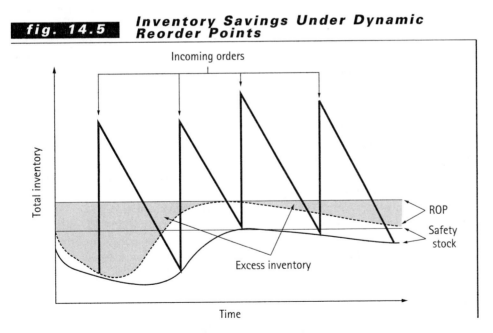

Source: Master Halco Logistics Report, Texas A&M University, 2001.

E-Procurement

E-procurement has been gaining momentum as an integration of the foregoing principles. Essentially, e-procurement is the interconnecting of all processes associated with replenishment processes. Since the principal aim of logistics processes is the replenishment of goods to the supply chain, the e-procurement process is an important component of logistics management. Inventory visibility is the key and will be the methodology to bring reorder point and purchasing automation to fruition. The e-procurement tools of inventory tracking and automated purchasing are designed to interact seamlessly with the transportation and warehouse functions. These tools have been developed by automating much of the research discussed at the beginning of this chapter, and the development of e-procurement will continue for the foreseeable future. Ultimately, e-procurement will be the only method used, and that "e" at the front of the term will simply go away.

Transportation

Transportation is a highly significant cost area for most distributors. While the function is extremely important to all distributors, it carries greater significance where the fleet is owned by the firm. Transportation, therefore, splits into two areas: private fleets and outsourced transportation. The necessary IT solutions, whether bolt-on or ERP, are also different. Private fleets are more expensive but usually critical for customer service.

Private-fleet management requires the firm to optimize utilization. A low utilization rate indicates wasted resources. If the fleet is optimized, a smaller fleet will be able to meet customer service objectives or a previously underutilized fleet can exceed customer objectives. The fleet management process involves optimizing the routing as described in this chapter in the discussion on the traveling salesman problem (page 303) and other routing algorithms. The process also requires effective loading of the trucks so that optimal routes can be achieved from fully loaded trucks.

Researchers have also studied the loading problem. The solution requires the cubic dimensions of all parts and truck capacities be available to determine the optimal load. The problem is further complicated by the routing decision since the load for an optimal route may not be feasible for loading purposes. Most transportation algorithms use weight as a limiting factor since trucks are usually operating under legal restrictions for weight. The cubic space of the truck can also be a limiting factor, however (see Figure 14.6). Loading algorithms generally will work interactively with the routing ones, with the routing algorithm setting the routes and the loading algorithm checking the feasibility of the loads associated with those routes. If a truck cannot carry the load associated with the route, the routing algorithm will be prevented from setting that same load. The process goes back and forth between the two algorithms until it finds a feasible set of routes.

Transportation software is highly specialized due to the complexity of the routing and loading processes. Bolt-on technology is still more likely to carry transportation

fig. 14.6   *Loading and Cubic Space Algorithms*

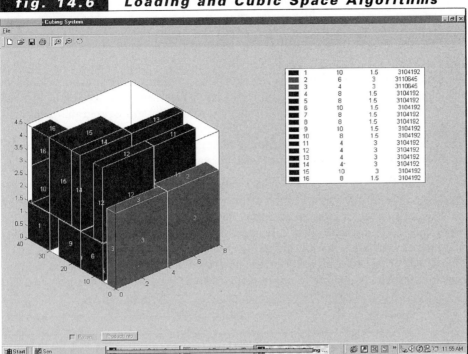

Source: Master Halco Logistics Report, Texas A&M University, 2001.

algorithms, but some ERP systems have purchased bolt-on capability and are starting to integrate the functionality into the ERP processes. Even most bolt-ons have their limitations, with some able to solve only routing problems with weight restrictions and others that can integrate cubic dimensions but are limited to fairly simple product dimensions (such as square boxes with no stacking restrictions).

Outsourced transportation can be further subdivided between common carrier and third-party logistics (3PL) management. The use of common carriers is frequently an in-house management activity. The warehouse usually handles scheduling after contracts have been negotiated with approved carriers. The contract negotiation and freight bill auditing functions are tied together and usually carried out by the accounting department. Transportation providers have facilitated the scheduling process with specialized software like United Parcel Service's World Ship. These programs make scheduling easier and print labels for shipping. Many ERP systems do not have a direct interface into these programs, however; shipments have to be picked and then reentered into the transportation provider's software.

Third-party logistics firms (3PLs) frequently take over the entire transportation (private fleet and common carriers) management process. The providers will schedule deliveries and sometimes hire drivers and dispatchers from the firm to continue running the operation. The 3PL will likely have greater information technology capabilities and may tie those to its customer (the distributor). The interconnectivity is established by drawing information necessary for the 3PL's routing and loading programs from the distributor's ERP system.

The issue becomes more complex when private fleets are blended together with common carriers. The firm or 3PL can use common carriers where the private fleet would be less than effective, such as when customer or supplier deliveries are in remote territories outside the typical delivery zone. The principal challenge lies in collecting information on the cost and availability of common carriers. Some 3PLs maintain programs that track this information, but few programs have been developed to fully integrate decision making on integrating private fleets with common carriers. Most firms continue to carry out the function offline, but more programs to directly address the issue are likely to develop. The Internet will play a major role as more and more transportation providers make their capacity and pricing available online or through prearranged connections with customers.

The complexity of managing transportation in its various contractual forms has challenged IT solutions and impacted contract negotiations at many firms due to a poor understanding of costs and capacity needs. Transportation providers frequently are unable to understand their customers' needs and, therefore, may find capacity planning challenging. Distributors frequently do not properly track and understand their transportation costs, routes, demand patterns, and so on. As a result, transportation providers operate in an on-demand environment where alliances to assist in capacity planning are difficult to achieve.

Getting to Real Time

Getting to real time is difficult since so many of the software solutions are missing or still cannot be connected. ERP has developed relationships among many programs like WMS, procurement, inventory classification, and reorder points. Others in transportation and connectivity external to the firm still need to be established. ERP systems either need to incorporate hooks to these bolt-ons or develop the functionality within the systems themselves.

The functionality in many of these programs was still not completely adequate in the early 2000s, but the vision was clear: New technologies will make complete interconnectivity of logistical processes possible in the near future. The principal issues to iron out will be relationship-based as firms try to determine who should get and/or control which information and for which purpose. Connectivity to supplier and customer systems, which hampers the extension to real time of many processes, still needs resolution. These issues take ERP into the supply chain. Given the difficulty experienced in building reliable ERP systems, the concept of connecting the supply chain is considered by many a long-range challenge.

Conclusion

Evaluating systems has come to depend more and more on their ability to connect to or automate existing processes. The value that systems add can be measured only by their ability to improve customer service or decrease costs. Both of these objectives depend on the firm's ability to automate processes and connect systems. Optimization of these processes requires real-time information from many activities and the ability to conduct analysis, take action, and share results of those actions in real time.

Systems will have to be even more flexible, capable of readily absorbing and integrating new functionality. Firms will need to include interconnectivity capability in their system selection to assure their future improvement processes are not limited by technology purchased in the past.

Distribution Retrospective

ARS decided that the increasing customer demand for late and/or change orders was an inevitable process that would continue into the future. Rather than fighting this process, ARS decided to enable it. The firm decided to look at a best-case scenario for the customer and work toward fulfilling that goal. Since customers worked until 5 p.m., ARS appointed that time as the latest orders could be received in the sales department. Working backwards from there, it decided to determine what was preventing it from pushing back the order deadline to five o'clock.

Picking was one problem; from the time the order was called in until it was picked could be anywhere up to two hours. If an order arrived at 5 p.m. it could be 7 p.m. before it reached the yard—one hour after loading began. A further problem was the dispatching process: The dispatcher spent two to three hours determining what was to be loaded on which truck for which route before staging could begin.

ARS decided to purchase a transportation software package that included both routing and loading software. The ERP system currently had Warehouse management capability but it had not been activated. The firm purchased radio frequency bar-coding capability and engaged the WMS. The resulting process speeded picking, and the routing and loading software eliminated the need for manual dispatching. The dispatching process went from two to three hours to just five to ten minutes and produced a loading map for loaders, reducing their workload that evening. The automated picking process decreased average picking times to less than 15 minutes. The result was a worst-case scenario of a customer calling at exactly 5 p.m., the sales transaction taking 15 minutes, picking taking an average of 15 minutes, and the routing and loading software determining loads in 5 to 10 minutes, leaving 20 to 25 minutes for staging the orders before the loaders arrived.

The firm could also prestage materials by identifying loads that were unlikely to change (due to high volumes on those routes) and staging those first. The routing/loading software could be run repeatedly throughout the day and when such loads were identified, they were frozen in the system. Loaders could take these prestaged loads first while the pickers proceeded to stage the later-arriving orders. The firm enforced its order deadline and made the announcement well ahead of its competition's capability to respond.

Issues to Consider

1. Why is it important and necessary to automate the logistics processes?

2. What are the opportunities associated with transportation optimization?

3. What are the challenges and complexities associated with purchasing?

4. Why are the procurement processes more important than the technology?

5. How can an automated and synchronized ERP system be a competitive advantage to distributors?

Case Study: Operations Automation

Dunston Supply, an HVAC (heating, air conditioning, and ventilation) distributor, supplied small and mid-sized contractors in a small Texas town. The firm was 30 years old and had served the local community and other small towns in the area. Contractors would come into Dunston's counter (a retail store) and buy construction equipment for ongoing jobs and plan for larger orders that would be needed but not carried in stock.

The counter was manned by an inside sales force that handled all sales transactions for the firm, but an outside sales force would also work with customers in planning large jobs that needed materials ordered in advance. The warehouse was located behind the retail operation and had both a small-parts area and a bulk storage one. Although 60 percent of all merchandise came in bar coded according to UCC standards, the firm had not yet enacted a bar coding system and had not activated a warehouse management system (WMS) that was available within its ERP system. The lack of an effective WMS also prevented the firm from connecting its systems to its shipping software: UPS World Ship. The packaging process required a rekeying at the shipping area for any products being shipped to other branches.

When new merchandise came in, it was put away according to established fixed locations based upon the size of the products and shelving capacity. Pickers, therefore, were the only ones who knew with any certainty where parts were located. When the store needed products to fill its shelves or customers ordered products that were stored in the warehouse, a handwritten order (pick ticket) was passed to the pickers for pulling the customer's order.

Cycle counting was carried out periodically by SKU number, but only the most experienced pickers could do an effective job, and even they would reduce inventory status when product could not be found only to increase it on the next cycle count. The firm suspected that its inventory counts were quite inaccurate and were usually proven right when the full inventory count took place at year's end.

Dunston's management team was certain that picking and putaway was consuming more human resources than necessary and that its data integrity problems were causing customer service failures as well as generating inventory problems. The firm decided to implement the WMS concurrent with an RF bar coding initiative. The system would be set up to determine where merchandise should be stored and how pickers should be routed while pulling orders. The system would send electronic pick slips to the RF guns the pickers carried and direct them along the shortest route. The resulting decrease in picker travel time was expected to reduce the number of pickers from five to four and decrease picking cycle time (customer wait time) by 25 percent.

The firm did not know how increased data integrity would influence its inventory needs and customer service levels but figured any improvement would be terrific. Finally, the WMS would be connected to the shipping software if possible, so that the packaging process would be smoother and quicker. The firm expected the systems upgrade to be completed within six months with a two-year payback period.

Case Challenges

1. What problems will prove the most daunting for Dunston and why?

2. Do the savings in picker headcount and cycle time seem reasonable? Why or why not?

3. Will the firm achieve its objectives in the specified time period? Which processes might take longer? Which ones will be easier?

References

1. Ronald L. Rardin, *Optimization in Operations Research* (Upper Saddle River, NJ: Prentice Hall, 1997).

2. "History of Operations Research, 50 year Anniversary," *Operations Research Journal* (n.d.), http://fens .sabanciuniv.edu/msie/operations_research_50_years/anniversary/timeline.pdf (accessed July 9, 2003).

3. Steven Nahmias, *Production and Operations Analysis,* 3rd ed. (New York: McGraw-Hill, 1997).

4. Philip S. Eisenhut, "A dynamic lot-sizing algorithm with capacity constraints," *AIIE Transactions* 7, vol. 2 (1975), pp. 170–176; S.Selcuk Erenguc and Yasmin Aksoy, "A branch and bound algorithm for a single item nonconvex dynamic lot-sizing problem with capacity constraints," *Computers Operations Research*

17, vol. 2 (1990), pp. 199–210; James R.Evans, "Network-based optimization algorithms for the capacitated multi-item lot-sizing problem," *Computers and Industrial Engineering 9,* vol. 3 (1985b), pp. 297–305.

5. Stefan Voss and David L. Woodruff, *Introduction to Computational Optimization Models for Production Planning in a Supply Chain* (New York: Springer, 2003).

6. "Technology roadmap for e-distributors" (IBM white paper), http://www-1.ibm.com/mediumbusiness/resources/whitepapers/whitepaper.jsp?contentId=4342.

7. Institute for Supply Management, "ISM Supply Management Series: Purchasing and Supply Management Policy and Business Management Guide" (2002), http://www.ism.ws/shopping/product.cfm?ID=193.

8. Andrew Boyd, "Yield Management," *OR-MS Today* (INFORMS Publication, October 1998).

9. James A. Cooke, "What's It Worth to You?" *Logistics Management* (April 2002).

10. Industry Data Exchange Association (IDEA), "Our Solutions," http://www.idea-inc.org/solutions/index.php3.

11. Paul Korzeniowski, "Automated Procurement Offers Dramatic Savings, Fast Payback," *Global Logistics and Supply Chain Strategies* (April 2000).

12. F. Barry Lawrence, Daniel F. Jennings, Brian E. Reynolds, *e-Distribution* (Mason, OH: South-Western Publishing, 2003).

15

Building a Best-in-Class ERP

Distribution Perspective

Keith Rainwater made a critical decision in the fall of 2002. He had bought Ray Distributing, a small fishing distributor, in the early 1990s and built it into a thriving business by the end of the decade. The company sold fishing gear to bait shops along the Texas coast and to a few larger retailers. Keith set to work increasing his business with the larger retailers and was successful in growing sales by over 50 percent in the first ten years.

An interesting aspect of Ray Distributing was Ray Manufacturing (Chapter 9 case study). When Keith bought the firm, manufacturing consisted of retirees who picked up a product's components at the warehouse, assembled a finished product, and returned it to Ray Distributing for packaging and sale under the firm's private label. The products sold extremely well due to the fishing community's interest in new products and their loyalty to those products that catch fish. Keith, a fisherman himself, turned out to be a good designer of new lures and other products for Ray Manufacturing to produce.

Perhaps the best thing about Ray Manufacturing was its profitability. With margins running as much as twice those of other manufacturers' products distributed by Ray Distributing, Keith quickly realized he should focus his sales resources on the very profitable Ray Manufacturing. In time, Keith decided he needed a catchy name not related to previous ownership and renamed Ray Manufacturing: Texas Tackle Factory.

Texas Tackle Factory continued to grow as a portion of Ray Distributing's business when, in 2001, a small manufacturer called Team Nu Mark came up for sale. Team Nu Mark's products were complementary to Texas Tackle Factory (TTF) with no overlapping products. Keith bought Team Nu Mark and now had two manufacturing operations under his control. Meanwhile, he had established a relationship with a Houston importer that represented contract manufacturing plants in China. This importer could outsource both Team Nu Mark and Texas Tackle Factory products to Chinese manufacturers at a lower cost than Keith was facing with his U.S. production.

Keith had already established relationships with firms that produced product in Haiti and the Dominican Republic (as described in Chapter 9's case) and was comfortable with outsourcing more. He eventually decided to outsource all but a small proportion of his production to China. He wanted to keep a few retirees working on product in case of shipping delays, a big problem with shipping from China.

Suddenly Keith was faced with a dilemma: TTF and Team Nu Mark were accounting for over half of Ray Distributing's sales. What could he do if he stopped trying to maintain his low margin distribution and focused on the two main brands? He decided to shut down Ray Distributing and pursue not only large retailers but also distributors who would be more likely to buy his products if he stopped competing with them. In October 2002, he took the plunge and became a distributor of just his two brands outsourced to China and other locales. To the rest of the world, Keith's firm was a manufacturer but internally he still ran a distribution firm. His former competitors came around faster than he expected and he recovered his sales volume well ahead of his target schedule.

Now Keith had another problem: The move had disrupted his information system processes. Even before the transition, his ERP system had inadequate support for customer relationship management as well as for forecasting and replenishment. Now he had to manage far-flung manufacturing processes. He was having difficulty controlling the simple bill of materials associated with the retired workers; now he had inventory all over the world and had to schedule for long lead times and movement among different manufacturing operations. He had heard that large firms with hugely expensive systems struggled with this process. How could a small firm hope to control it?

Introduction

This chapter addresses ERP and its associated bolt-on technologies with a step-by-step approach to laying out a firm's information management processes. We begin with an examination of what value other technology providers like bolt-ons and ASPs can bring and then proceed to integrate each of the information tools adopted whether ERP-based or not. The material challenges the concept that ERP is an all-or-nothing issue. Many ERP providers have, in fact, begun moving in a modular direction and are beginning to refer to themselves as distribution information systems providers rather than as ERP firms.

When the Bolt-Ons Make Sense

Bolt-ons make sense when either ERP functionality is not there for a critical function or the firm is capable of capitalizing on highly personalized technology. The ability to capitalize on specialized technology is more complex than it may seem. The issue is about more than having smart people, powerful computers, or environmental issues that could be eased by improved information handling. The firm must address the fundamental problems associated with corporate culture along with the complexity of the environment. Before deciding the problems are insurmountable, however, the firm should remember that complexity means opportunity. Distribution firms are very complex due to their proximity to the customer and the constant changes in expectations that proximity generates.

Specialized technology can consist of more powerful algorithms, better data-handling capability, or the interconnectivity among multiple systems. Bolt-ons can be evidence that user firms have invested more in more specialized technology or the ability to adapt to variations in the environment, but traditional ERP providers are now working toward achieving the same specialized capability and adaptability. The tradeoff between built-in functionality and adaptable systems goes to the heart of the best-of-breed argument. ERP providers who offer all functionality as part of their basic offering will sell many customers processes they may not need. The other option is to become more modular and allow the customer to pick and choose the functionality it requires. This latter strategy leaves the customer with a base system that can easily integrate to other functionality. This model we refer to as "build your own ERP" since the customer is able to configure its ERP system to its business needs. The build your own model does leave the door open to competition for ERP providers from bolt-ons that have developed a more focused functionality and integration capability.

As more and more customers come to require specialized technology, the movement to modular ERP seems inevitable. Firms will be offered more-powerful systems but will face more challenges to put that technology to work. The challenges will be less and less about integration and more and more about the firm's own ability to make appropriate use of the functionality. Before worrying about whether the firm can absorb the functionality, the processes adopted should first pass a needs assessment. A cost analysis should be conducted, as discussed in Chapter 14, that demonstrates the value of not having any information automation for the processes in question and for each potential technology offering (ERP module and bolt-ons). The potential improvement in significant processes can then be measured against the system and its implementation costs.

One key component of new information automation is technology-friendly corporate culture. Many management teams conduct studies and identify solid savings with new technology but do not prepare their firms for technology adoption. One firm adopted bolt-on technology for purchasing decisions. The firm had conducted a study that demonstrated the new software would pay for itself inside six months. The firm did not invest in analyzing its organization's approach to information handling. Soon after the new system went live, the firm found that most purchasing people were not using the system as envisioned. Instead of allowing the system to make forecasting and inventory level decisions, the purchasing people had adapted the system to give them inventory status and to fix reorder points rather than have them determined dynamically. When management tried to discover why the new system was not being used, they found several reasons that are common to many such failures:

1. The new system would instruct purchasing people to buy in smaller amounts to decrease inventory. Management, however, rewarded purchasing people on PPV (purchase parts variance), a methodology that gives incentive to buy at the lowest possible price by measuring variance from a standard price set by the firm for individual products. If the purchase price is below the standard, the buy is deemed a good one. If the system recommended buying 500 units, on average, and the supplier offered a 5 percent discount at 1000 units, the purchasing people could not understand why the system did not capitalize on the discount and would override the decision. After a few such episodes, the purchasing people assumed the system did not calculate discounts correctly and stopped paying any attention to the recommended buy signals. The system's decision would have reduced regular inventory by 50 percent (see Chapter 14 for an explanation of how inventory is reduced through smaller order sizes) as well as having a positive impact on safety stock as forecasting cycles shortened. Management's emphasis on PPV, however, seemed to indicate that the firm did not believe in smaller purchase sizes. In the end, "what gets rewarded gets done" held sway and the recommended order amount was shelved.

2. The system also set a dynamic reorder point based on forecast accuracy and supplier performance. The sales force quickly overrode the reorder point, however, by forcing purchasing to raise the safety stock every time a stockout occurred. The system was attempting to maintain a 95 percent fill rate (higher than the firm's former average), which meant that one in 20 times, a stockout would occur. With a new system in place that was reducing overall inventory, sales was on watch for customer service failures. When they occurred, sales assumed the system had miscalculated rather than realizing this was a natural event, in fact less common than before. Management actually viewed the system as being in startup mode and had encouraged purchasing and sales to watch for customer service problems. Management had again showed a lack of confidence in the system that emboldened people to set it aside in favor of their former methods.

3. With the reorder point and recommended order sizes disabled or ignored, the only thing left was forecasting. Most purchasing and sales staff had already lost confidence in the system by this time anyway and when forecasting problems arose due to data integrity issues caused elsewhere, it was a only a matter of time before forecasting was jettisoned as well.

The system was retuned to provide the same reports the old system did and to let the purchasing people make all the reorder, forecasting, and buying decisions. People spoke wistfully about the old system that had been even further tooled to the purchasing department's specifications. All deemed the new system a mistake and many believed the firm had yet to achieve its efficiency level from before adoption of the new software. The firm was not prepared for new software adoption. The firm's culture was not technology friendly and exhibited some key characteristics that lead to new technology failures. These traits are important for all system adoptions and will hinder ERP implementation as well as other new technologies. They are especially troubling for specialized technology, however, since such technology is even more likely to be feared or distrusted by key players in the firm. The cultural traits driving this firm's (and many others') problems along with potential solutions are as follows:

1. A management approach that treats information technology as a tactical rather than strategic tool that does not require them to align performance metrics and other strategic planning tools with the new technology. *Solution*: Management must understand that the new technology will likely follow many new best practices. Key performance indicators (KPIs) must do the same or the firm will pull the system apart with conflicting objectives.

2. A belief that most information technology systems are problematic and have to be modified before they work right. This belief is often driven by a history of poor implementations that forced the firm to endlessly modify software and settle for less than originally hoped-for results. *Solution*: This problem is particularly difficult to solve. The firm must seek small successes to overcome biases against new technology. Processes that capture "low-hanging fruit" (objectives with low risk of failure and high rate of return) should be enacted first, with the positive results captured and reported to all.

3. An unwillingness to "throw good money after bad" that causes the firm to constantly economize on IT support by understaffing its IT department or hire consultants only in an emergency. *Solution*: Management must recognize and capture value in a step-by-step fashion that allows justification for further investment in the system. The low-hanging fruit in solution 2 is particularly useful for justifying investment in these resources.

4. A general fear of the system brought on by many admonishing remarks about making mistakes on the system from management and the IT provider. *Solution*: Management must be the first to lose its fear of the system and then encourage others. Do not choose an IT partner who engenders a fear of the system in order to increase its consulting opportunities.

5. A lack of training and support for domain experts in particular and regular employees in general. *Solution*: Train, train, and then train some more.

6. A feeling of distrust coupled with a fear of customer service failures that lead to shutting down programs before they are given the chance to succeed. *Solution*: Customer service levels must be accurately measured both before and after system go-live. System processes should be shut down only after all other options have been exhausted, especially if the system is performing as well as or better than its predecessor. Collect accurate measures; do not allow hearsay or opinions to determine which actions to take.

7. A not-invented-here approach to new processes that may be best practice but are not the way "we've always done it." *Solution*: Educate all parties as to what the best practices are, how the system supports best practice, and how best practice or the system's approach will benefit the firm and its customers.

Creating a technology-friendly firm is critical to successful adoption of any information automation. The process will lead to easier ERP adoption but will have the greatest effect when firms engage in specialized technology like bolt-ons or modularized ERP. As basic ERP becomes more common in the form of back-office systems, the modular ERP components and bolt-ons will become the differentiating factors among firms (see Figure 15.1). The savings discussed in these last three chapters indicate that failure to capitalize on specialized technology (transportation, WMS, purchasing tools, CRM, etc.) could result in an inability to compete with more technologically adept firms. Many of these modules are now available and many more advancements are expected in the near future. ERP was a basic first step for many firms in the information automation movement. The modular approach will be next with the firm continually improving and developing new capabilities in a plug-and-play technology environment that both supports and encourages innovation in customer service and cost reduction.

fig. 15.1 **Build Your Own ERP**

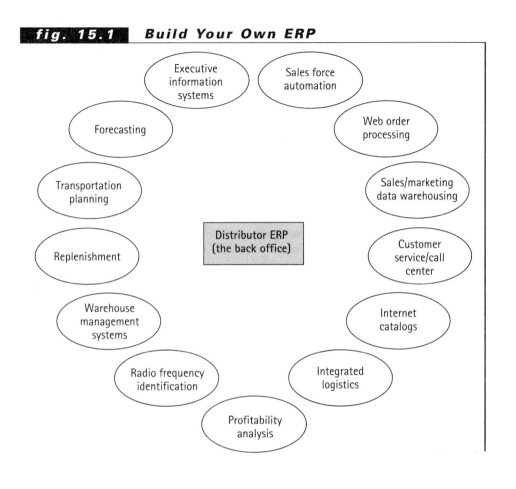

Are ASPs a Good Idea?

ASP technology at the beginning of the 2000s was a hotly debated topic. Application service providers were created in the 1990s to offer ERP and other software to smaller firms that could not afford to buy such expensive systems. The pay-as-you-go plan was viewed as more affordable and upgrades to the technology could be capitalized on as soon as the technology provider made them available. Unfortunately, the first generation of ASPs got caught up in the dot-com debacle. When Wall Street and other venture capitalists ran from tech stocks, the ASPs got caught in the downturn. To make matters worse, customers had a difficult time differentiating between ASPs and dot-coms in general. Fear of technology is more rampant in smaller firms than large ones and the dot-com problems caused the ASP target market (small companies) to stay away in droves. The result was slower-than-expected demand growth while the sources of startup funds were disappearing rapidly.

Some of the blame lay with the ASPs themselves: The cost of implementation was much higher than originally anticipated (see Chapter 1 for a discussion on the 1990s' underestimation of implementation costs). Since implementation occurred regardless of whether the software was purchased or not, the purported benefits of someone else owning the software was less than expected. ASPs also tended to offer noncustomized solutions that forced the adopting firm to do things the software's way. This rigidity proved very unappealing to many firms. Finally, the cost of ERP software came down quickly with many providers offering scaled-down packages for smaller firms.

Was the ASP merely an idea ahead of its time? One could argue that, in the case of modular technology, the ASPs could offer value by hosting software that is highly specialized and goes through rapid upgrades. The ASP would need a simple, stable, and secure method to exchange data with the ERP database. Likely candidates for ASP technology are highly technical purchasing decisions since the software may go through frequent upgrades as new algorithms or functionality are developed, or sales force automation tools become accessible through the Internet. In purchasing, for example, new, more-powerful algorithms are being offered for line buying (coordinated replenishment) and improvements in forecasting are constantly being introduced. New data exchange methods and connectivity to other software providers could also drive the need for upgrades.

ASPs might make the most sense for low-utilization but occasional high-value analysis. If a firm should decide that hosted software makes sense, selecting an ASP will be a function of

1. The potential improvement (savings or customer service) offered by occasionally significant technology.

2. Whether rapidly changing technology requires frequent upgrades.

3. The ASP qualifying as a financially stable, technologically proficient provider.

Designing Your Modular System

Contrary to popular belief, it is possible for even small firms to build a modular ERP that captures best-in-class traits. Many small ERP providers offer the basics for back-office needs. The shortcomings of these systems are typically their relative weakness in exchanging information with other programs and a lack of functionality for more-complex programs like CRM, transportation, and purchasing decision support systems. The small firm can buy the basic back-office package that will likely contain financial management tools and sales order processing at a minimum. The firm can then examine its entire supply chain from how it serves customers to how it accesses and relies upon suppliers.

Customer Relationship Management

Customer relationship management can be handled from the most simplistic to the most complex scenarios. The CRM tools can be taken as an entire package (some ASPs specialize in hosting CRM for small firms) or added component by component, slowly building a firm's CRM capability. The component-by-component method will challenge the firm to achieve real-time information exchange since integrating the various tools will be difficult if not impossible. Any connectivity gaps will result in lost information or reduce the firm's ability to react to customer needs in a timely fashion.

Contact management implementation will require an understanding of how the customer interacts with the firm and how its internal functions interact (see Figure 15.2). *For Ray Distributing (see the Distribution Perspective for Chapter 9 for more), the contact management function was carried out by the use of PDA software. Keith and his sales force would capture as much information as possible in their interaction with customers on the PDA software. The software could download to a personal computer but the ERP system was not able to interact with it. This inability to store and share the contact management information between inside and outside sales conceivably meant that customers could tell an outside salesperson something and then try to follow up with an inside salesperson or management for credit decisions or other orders and have to start from the beginning of the process.*

Keith wanted the system to give visibility to every customer transaction to anyone who needed it to support customers. He investigated using an ASP offering of CRM software or buying an inexpensive version of contact management software to manage the customer interaction process. After some consideration, he decided that

fig. 15.2 *Contact Management Software*

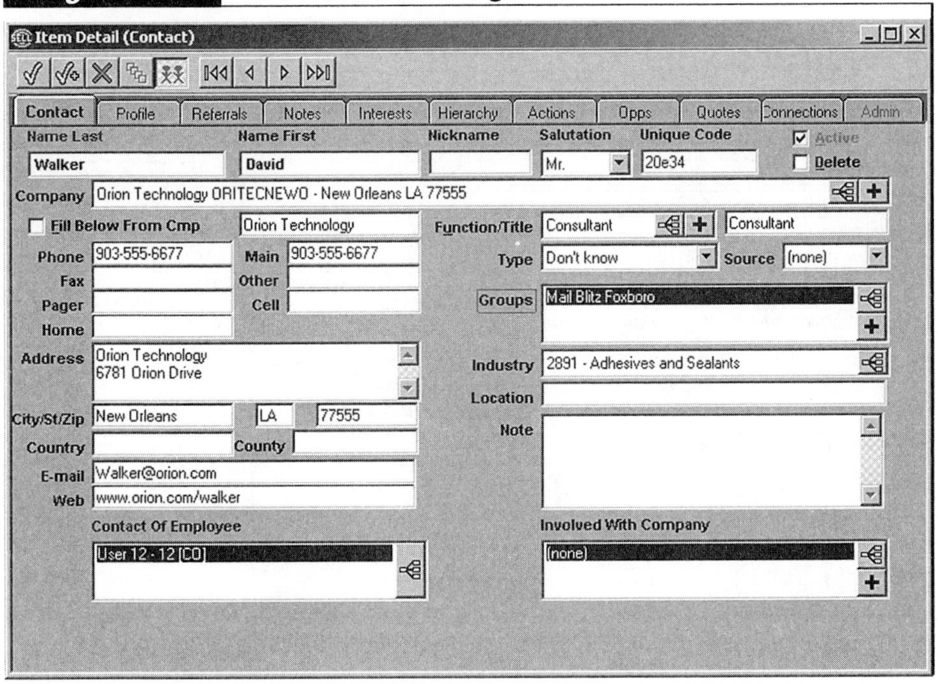

Source: Selltis CRM System

since he and his sales force spent so much time on the road, that the Internet might be the best way to go and began investigating using hosted software. He still felt, however, that this approach could be slow and cumbersome and might not be able to connect to his ERP system.

Quoting systems remain one of the more complicated processes for distributors (see Figure 15.3). Quoting options include the simple price quote to advanced, large, multiprocess ones. For Keith, his quoting process included an update to his catalog that had to be arranged well in advance of his yearly meetings with large customers. During these meetings, he would discuss his new product offerings, negotiate for shelf space, and establish agreements on rebates and pricing. The quote was very difficult to negotiate and once agreed upon, Keith would have to react quickly on all follow-up. The quote process was, therefore, a combination of contact management and quoting tools. He examined the process and decided he would need to establish templates in his CRM system for his agreements and align all actions through the system. Keith also wanted the system to keep basic intangible information such as who the decision makers are and what communication has taken place with them so that other support personnel in his firm could assist the sales force.

Connection to the ERP system was the next key step and required the CRM system to either have direct connection to ERP or a data transfer that can be made seamlessly. Keith's system was not easy to connect to and required uploading and downloading data. A common format used by the CRM providers was to drop information into spreadsheets or other forms like comma delimited (a format for data where data fields are separated by commas). Keith's system could exchange

fig. 15.3 Quoting Software

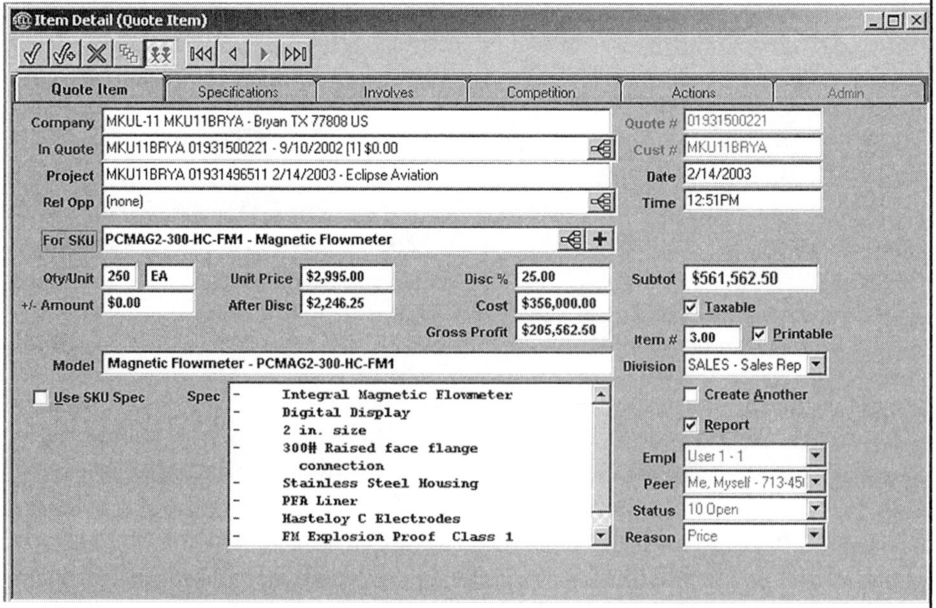

Source: Selltis CRM System

information through spreadsheets. He decided to hire a consultant specializing in his ERP software to establish a process for information exchange between his ERP system and the new CRM system.

Enterprise Resource Management

ERP systems differ in functionality but some firms choose to use a less comprehensive package and support it with bolt-ons. Keith had decided to stay with his system and support it with external packages. He wanted his sales order processing (SOP) module to be enabled to supply appropriate information to the sales force. He wanted an established procedure for receiving orders, order review and approval, customer setup, payment terms, freight policies, pricing policies, pick-ticket generation, and back-order management. The ERP system could directly support some of these activities but not all of them. Keith was satisfied with the system's order handling functions and its ability to keep and display terms and policies.

He was not satisfied, however, with the system's ability to pass pick tickets from the ERP system to the warehouse. He had established an RFID system that did connect to the ERP system, but the software provider for the connection and the RFID hardware provider had parted ways and now Keith had to find a new way to connect his ERP system to the warehouse activity. He decided to buy an inexpensive WMS and RFID system and to establish the connection again with a handoff of information. He would need the process to be as simple as possible so that pick slips could be passed at regular intervals during the day without much effort from his inside salesperson or warehouse manager. He set up the process so that pick slips could be downloaded on demand to the RF scanners at the warehouse manager's discretion and the ERP system would be updated either whenever the warehouse had time or at the end of the day. He realized this could lead to information gaps that could cause product to be sold twice but could not come up with another solution. He asked his sales force to be especially careful and double-check large orders or ones for which the inventory levels were running low.

Keith was aware that modifications, like these data-transfer bridges, built into the system may or may not be difficult to transfer to future versions of the ERP system but he planned to stay with his current ERP version until substantial change was necessary. He felt that a firm his size could be more agile than a larger one and would be able to make changes to processes and/or data exchanges with relative ease. He had no plans to introduce modifications to the base software of any ERP or bolt-on system he implemented and so he was not concerned about the need to transfer these modifications to a new software release.

Business Intelligence

Purchasing decisions were another matter, however, and Keith wanted better forecasting. His customers required any decisions on obsolete inventory or new products to be included in his catalog as much as a year in advance. This requirement meant Keith could be facing extremely long forecasting decisions. He wanted a system that would forecast as effectively as possible for the long term while managing his near-term replenishment cost effectively. His ERP system was totally inadequate for the task. The system would use a simple moving average together with static safety stock estimates provided by Keith himself to determine when and how much to buy. The system had no provision for eliminating an item from inventory unless someone within the firm intervened.

Business intelligence (see Figure 15.4) is a composite of many different capabilities that are often found in ERP or bolt-ons and can include

○ Purchasing tools.

○ Inventory management.

○ Executive information systems.

Keith decided that a simple bolt-on could handle his forecasting and inventory management processes more easily than building modifications. He would download the inventory status data to spreadsheets, again on a weekly basis, and upload it to the bolt-on. The bolt-on would immediately calculate the forecast for the near and long term and make recommendations as to safety stock, demand during lead time, and order purchase sizes (see Figure 15.5). He realized that doing this weekly rather than having the system warn him when reorder points triggered was another

---

fig. 15.4 **Business Intelligence**

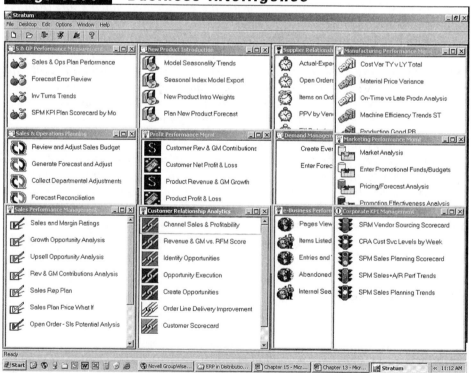

Source: Silvon Software Inc.

fig. 15.5 *Inventory Management in a Bolt-On*

SKU/Prod	Description	Count	ABC Estimate	Sales Amount Jan 03 to Sep 03	Sales Amount % of Total	Sales Units Jan 03 to Sep 03	Sales Units % of Total	GM Amt (Std) Jan 03 to Sep 03	GM Amt (Std) % of Total	GM Pct (Std) Jan 03 to Sep 03
954018	Frozen Lasagna Dinner	1	A	$9,568,419	6%	86,635	3%	$3,950,790	7%	41%
954019	Meatloaf, Frozen	2	A	$9,198,817	5%	86,738	3%	$4,610,554	8%	50%
954006	Pork Chops - Butterfly	3	A	$7,057,493	4%	92,690	3%	$4,214,753	7%	60%
954014	Asparagus	4	A	$6,881,585	4%	85,679	3%	$2,570,453	5%	37%
954024	Orange Juice Conc.	5	A	$6,406,325	4%	86,002	3%	$3,182,356	6%	50%
974003	Applesauce 106oz PL*	6	REVISE	$5,793,964	3%	91,505	3%	$552,686	1%	10%
954017	Cherries, Bing	7	A	$5,563,446	3%	68,150	2%	$2,137,078	4%	38%
954012	Sweet Onions, Chopped	8	A	$5,225,953	3%	85,151	3%	$2,845,628	5%	54%
954304	Peach Slcs LS 106oz BR*	9	A	$4,576,683	3%	58,050	2%	$1,215,437	2%	27%
914322	Peach 6oz LnchPk BR*	10	A	$4,448,812	3%	48,107	2%	$1,099,036	2%	25%
974404	FrtCktail LS 106oz PL*	11	REVISE	$4,117,930	2%	63,129	2%	$689,161	1%	17%
954020	Navel Oranges	12	A	$3,993,003	2%	86,391	3%	$2,309,125	4%	58%
954009	Apples Red Delicious	13	A	$3,946,976	2%	86,551	3%	$2,808,724	5%	71%
954021	Romaine Specialty Salad	14	A	$3,854,977	2%	50,193	2%	$1,929,444	3%	50%
914022	Pear 6oz LnchPk LS	15	A	$3,777,051	2%	40,848	1%	$932,731	2%	25%
914304	Peach Slcs LS 12oz BR*	16	A	$3,741,547	2%	81,749	3%	$1,106,851	2%	30%
954007	Ground Round 90% Lean	17	A	$3,713,136	2%	69,171	2%	$1,715,168	3%	46%
954404	FrtCktail LS 106 oz BR*	18	A	$3,626,841	2%	45,991	2%	$1,128,900	2%	31%
914401	Pnappl Slcs 12 oz BR*	19	A	$3,592,835	2%	76,881	3%	$933,452	2%	26%
914422	FrtCktail 6oz LnchPk BR*	20	A	$3,147,467	2%	34,035	1%	$777,549	1%	25%
924003	Applesauce 12oz PL*	21	B	$3,069,273	2%	76,873	3%	$364,635	1%	12%
974401	Pnappl Slcs 106oz PL*	22	B	$3,001,431	2%	44,678	2%	$365,135	1%	12%
914008	Pear Slcs LS 12 oz BR*	23	B	$2,773,445	2%	60,627	2%	$435,838	1%	16%
954000	Red Ripe Tomatoes	24	REVISE	$2,606,183	2%	59,111	2%	$1,071,366	2%	41%
924401	Pnappl Slcs 12oz PL*	25	B	$2,513,210	1%	64,520	2%	$281,405	0%	11%
914404	FrtCktail LS 12 oz BR*	26	REVISE	$2,303,154	1%	50,335	2%	$642,472	1%	28%

[103] Rows Found ...

Source: Silvon Software Inc.

time gap but the effectiveness of the tool was better than his current process by a considerable margin.

Another important feature was the presence in the business intelligence module of an executive information system (EIS) that could give Keith himself valuable information to track his daily operations. The EIS was designed to generate any reports Keith deemed necessary for his own decision making. Keith wanted reports on the following:

1. Incoming shipments—in-transit merchandise, arrival dates

2. Logistics status

    a. In the air

    b. Water

    c. Supply chain visibility

    d. Customs status

3. Capacity Management

    a. Negative availability—items with a negative on hand and purchased availability (on order) minus outstanding orders total availability *b. Current actual inventory levels*

    c. Open orders and trends in same—Were the open (unfilled) orders growing on a particular product?

4. *Transportation Costs*
    a. Inbound/outbound freight costs
    b. Total transportation cost status

5. *Cash-to-Cash Cycle Management*
    a. Accounts Receivable status reports
    b. Accounts Payable status reports
    c. Number of Days Sales Outstanding

6. *Customer Service*
    a. Fill rates
    b. Back order rates and status

7. *Profitability measures*
    a. Margins
    b. Cash flow

The system could easily collect such information and report it in a format usable to Keith. He intended to use these key performance indicators to run his business more profitably while still improving customer service. His current system had virtually no capability to meet these requirements.

Manufacturing Relationships

More and more distributors are being faced with a need to understand materials requirements planning (MRP). Kitting, for instance, requires a single level bill of material, something that Keith worked with on a regular basis. Keith would bring in materials from his suppliers and assemble kits. One example was the fishing belt described in the Chapter 9 case study (see Figure 15.6).

Distributors are outsourcing more and more production to contract manufacturers and Keith's operation not only was a perfect example of this trend but could even be described as an extreme case. He had outsourced all his production except for some final packaging. Like most such distributors, Keith branded his merchandise under private labels (Texas Tackle Factory and Team Nu Mark).

Keith, like many other distributors, was now managing multilevel BOMs across multiple locations with multiple facilities and supplier firms involved. Keith had to manage inventory and production that he may or may not own. The long distances (China to Haiti) and multiple suppliers coupled with his need for long-term forecasts for planning new products and rendering others obsolete meant that lead-time management was critical. Simply put, Keith needed an MRP system. If he used a business intelligence bolt-on for purchasing, the bolt-on would need to be based on DRP (Distribution requirements planning) logic and have business partners that could connect MRP functionality to it.

In the end, Keith needed to use a CRM ASP and configure his activities and reporting with standard tools, which required setup and monthly fees. He would

fig. 15.6 *A Fishing Belt Kit*

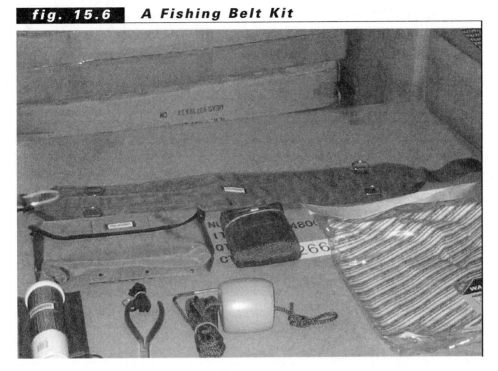

Source: Reprinted with permission by the authors.

also need an information connection between the ERP system and the CRM system that would no doubt require consulting assistance from either the ERP or CRM provider or both. Next the ERP system would have to be connected to a new WMS/RF system with software and information connectivity (consulting) costs. He would then need to buy a business intelligence system and configure its reports and tools for his environment. This system would also require connectivity with the ERP system. The costs would include consultants and software fees. Finally, he would need to do the same with his MRP system but establish the connection to the business intelligence DRP system.

The costs were bearable but not insignificant for a small firm. The modular approach, however, would allow Keith to take on the projects one at a time and allow the savings from one process to help pay for the next. Given his current environment, Keith believed the greatest impact could be had in the following order: business intelligence, WMS/RF, MRP, followed by CRM. He would begin with purchasing decisions and extend first backward to suppliers, then forward to customers.

The modular approach worked for Ray Distributing and was becoming more common by 2004. The ability to build your own ERP has provided flexibility to all firms but may be even more beneficial to small firms. For larger firms, this flexibility will offer opportunity to introduce new functionality virtually at will rather than waiting for the ERP provider's next revision and hoping the desired functionality will be in the new package. As ERP continues to become more common, this differentiation of processes will be how both distributors and IT providers differentiate their service and product lines from their competition. The race to be competitive either by offering functionality first or by concentrating on services for specific vertical channels will ultimately become the norm for IT providers and their customers.

Conclusion: The Next Generation of ERP

Although prediction is difficult, some future directions of ERP are starting to take shape. In 2003, ERP companies were beginning an industry consolidation that seemed likely to continue for some years into the future. The summer of 2003 saw PeopleSoft bid for JD Edwards only to have Oracle make a bid to purchase PeopleSoft.[1] While three of the largest ERP providers were wrangling, NxTrend (a specialist in construction and industrial channels) quietly bought Dimasys.[2] Many other such purchases were taking place across different vertical channels. The ERP market appeared to need more companies with more critical mass and consolidation seemed likely to continue for some time. New players also entered the market. Microsoft bought Great Plains, which provided software to very small firms, and then bought Navision, which competed in the mid-sized market.[3]

The greatest activity, however, were ERP firms purchasing bolt-ons as part of their modular strategy. The ERP firms may or may not evolve into distribution information providers without the ERP designation but one thing seemed clear: The modularization of their offering was going to continue. Distribution information technology will follow distributors into new service offerings and will mirror the channels in which they operate. The ERP providers and the various bolt-ons had taken on the task of information automation for distributors and, with the continual assistance of the distribution community, seemed likely to continue developing the information-driven distributor.

Distribution Retrospective

Keith decided to use a modular approach and develop his supply chain step by step. He found that the software could be found or developed for even a small distributor to be successful in information automation. The important thing was to develop an overall strategy and stick to the plan. He knew that costs were inevitable but he planned to capture the savings of one program before proceeding with the costs of the next. Keith's agility had been his greatest strength in the past (Texas Tackle Factory and Team Nu Mark served as perfect examples) and he intended to use it in developing his information management strategy.

Issues to Consider

1. How can best of breed be a cost-effective technology solution for some distributors?

2. What are the connectivity problems associated with integrating several best-of-breed applications?

3. What are the positive and negative factors that will shape the success of the emerging application service provider (ASP) model?

4. Will the ERP consolidation movement lead to fewer software choices?

References

1. Reuters, "PeopleSoft Completes JD Edwards Purchase," *Forbes.com* (July 18, 2003), http://www.forbes .com/newswire/2003/07/18/rtr1029713.html.

2. "NxTrend Technology Inc. Acquires Dimasys Software," *EE Times* (May 16, 2003), http://www.eetimes .com/pressreleases/prnewswire/76556.

3. "Microsoft Acquires Navision," *Microsoft.com* (July 11, 2002), http://www.microsoft.com/presspass/ press/2002/jul02/07-11NavisionAcquisitionPR.asp.

Index